# ADOPTING THE STRANGER
# AS KINDRED IN DEUTERONOMY

# ANCIENT ISRAEL AND ITS LITERATURE

Thomas C. Römer, General Editor

*Editorial Board:*
Susan Ackerman
Mark G. Brett
Marc Brettler
Tom Dozeman
Cynthia Edenburg
Konrad Schmid

Number 33

# ADOPTING THE STRANGER
# AS KINDRED IN DEUTERONOMY

Mark R. Glanville

**SBL PRESS**

**Atlanta**

Copyright © 2018 by Mark R. Glanville

Library of Congress Cataloging-in-Publication Data

Names: Glanville, Mark R., author.
Title: Adopting the stranger as kindred in Deuteronomy / by Mark R. Glanville.
Description: Atlanta : SBL Press, [2018] | Series: Ancient Israel and its literature ; number 33 | Includes bibliographical references and index.
Identifiers: LCCN 2018020286 (print) | LCCN 2018039721 (ebook) | ISBN 9780884143123 (ebk.) | ISBN 9780884143116 | ISBN 9780884143116 (hbk. alk. paper) | ISBN 9780884143109 (pbk. alk. paper)
Subjects: LCSH: Bible. Deuteronomy—Criticism, interpretation, etc. | Strangers in the Bible. | Emigration and immigration in the Bible. | Refugees. | Asylum, Right of—Religious aspects—Christianity. | Emigration and immigration—Religious aspects—Christianity.
Classification: LCC BS1275.6.S76 (ebook) | LCC BS1275.6.S76 G53 2018 (print) | DDC 222/.150830590691—dc23
LC record available at https://lccn.loc.gov/2018020286

Printed on acid-free paper.

This study is dedicated with gratitude and love to my wife, Erin Goheen Glanville, who advocates for displaced people through her scholarship and who has also embraced displacement for my sake and for the sake of our family.

This study is dedicated also to forced migrants around the world and to those who support them.

# Contents

# Acknowledgments

Thanks to friends, colleagues, and mentors for their willingness to dialogue within their areas of expertise in support of my research and to offer their comments on portions of this study, in particular Craig Bartholomew, Gordon Wenham, M. Daniel Carroll R., Peter Altmann, Bruce Wells, Reinhard Achenbach, Dick Averbeck, Markus Zehnder, Christopher Wright, Nathan MacDonald, Gary Knoppers, Daniel Fleming, Avi Faust, Shalom Holtz, Gordon McConville, Eckart Otto, Kurtis Peters, David Reimer, David Firth, Erin Goheen Glanville, and my brother, Luke Glanville.

Thanks to the Reid Trust for their generous financial support throughout the duration of this project.

Thanks to Kinbrace and Journey Home, two organizations providing support and housing for asylum seekers in Vancouver, for their self-giving, perseverance, collegiality and support.

Thanks to my parents, George and June Glanville, and to my parents-in-law, Michael and Marnie Goheen, for their love and for their encouragement of my scholarship. My parents' compassion in walking with vulnerable people, as well as their awareness of their own vulnerability, has also shaped this project. Thanks to Sarah, my sister, for "kin-keeping" our extended family, across the Pacific.

I also acknowledge with love our children Mahla and Lewin Glanville. Mahla was one year old when I first began to think about the *gēr* in Deuteronomy, and Lewin was born halfway through the project. Now aged four and seven, you guys are the delight of our lives and terrific bike riders.

# Abbreviations

| | |
|---|---|
| *AAnt* | *American Antiquity* |
| *AmA* | *American Anthropologist* |
| AASOR | Annual of the American Schools of Oriental Research |
| AB | Anchor Bible |
| ABAW | Abhandlungen der Bayerischen Akademie der Wissenshaften |
| ABS | Archaeology and Biblical Studies |
| *ACF* | *Annali di Ca'Foscari* |
| *AmE* | *American Ethnologist* |
| Akk. | Akkadian |
| AnOr | Anelecta Orientalia |
| ApOTC | Apollos Old Testament Commentary |
| ASOR | American Schools of Oriental Research |
| *BASOR* | *Bulletin of the American Schools of Oriental Research* |
| BBB | Bonner biblische Beiträge |
| BBRSup | Bulletin for Biblical Research, Supplements |
| BDB | Brown, Francis, S. R. Driver, and Charles A. Briggs. *A Hebrew and English Lexicon of the Old Testament.* |
| BETL | Bibliotheca Ephemeridum Theologicarum Lovaniensium |
| BibInt | Biblical Interpretation Series |
| BibSem | The Biblical Seminar |
| *BMB* | *Bulletin du Musée de Beyrouth* |
| BMes | Bibliotheca Mesopotamica |
| BWANT | Beiträge zur Wissenschaft vom Alten und Neuen Testament |
| BZABR | Beihefte zur Zeitschrift für altorientalische und biblische Rechtsgeschichte |
| BZAW | Beihefte zur Zeitschrift für die alttestamentliche Wissenschaft |

| | |
|---|---|
| *CAD* | Gelb, Ignace J., et al, eds. *The Assyrian Dictionary of the Oriental Institute of the University of Chicago.* Edited by 21 vols. Chicago: The Oriental Institute of the University of Chicago, 1956–2010. |
| CC | Covenant Code: The law corpus of the book of Exodus |
| *CIS* | *Corpus Inscriptionum Semiticarum.* Paris, 1881– |
| *CKLR* | *Chicago-Kent Law Review* |
| *COS* | *The Context of Scripture.* Edited by William W. Hallo. 3 vols. Leiden: Brill, 1997–2002. |
| DATD | Das Alte Testament Deutsch |
| DC | Deuteronomic Code |
| DH | Deuteronomic History |
| *DNWSI* | *Dictionary of the North-West Semitic Inscriptions.* Jacob Hoftijzer and Karen Jongeling. 2 vols. Leiden: Brill, 1995. |
| Dtn | Deuteronomic (History; writer) |
| Dtr | Deuteronomistic redaction (History; writer); Deuteronomist |
| EdF | Erträge der Forschung |
| *EFN* | *Estudios de filología neotestamentaria* |
| *ER* | *Encyclopaedia of Religion.* Edited by Lindsay Jones. 2nd ed. 15 vols. Detroit: Macmillan Reference USA, 2005 |
| ET | English Translation |
| FAT | Forschungen zum Alten Testament |
| FRLANT | Forschungen zur Religion und Literatur des Alten und Neuen Testaments |
| FThSt | Freiburger theologische Studien |
| *HALOT* | *The Hebrew and Aramaic Lexicon of the Old Testament.* Ludwig Koehler, Walter Baumgartner, and Johann J. Stamm. Translated and edited under the supervision of Mervyn E. J. Richardson. 4 vols. Leiden: Brill, 1994–1999. |
| *HBAI* | *Hebrew Bible and Ancient Israel* |
| HBM | Hebrew Bible Monographs |
| *HBT* | *Horizons in Biblical Theology* |
| HC | Holiness Code (the law corpus of the book of Leviticus) |
| HL | Hittite Laws |
| HOS | Handbook of Oriental Studies |
| *HPS* | *Hebraic Political Studies* |
| HSS | Harvard Semitic Studies |
| HThKAT | Herders Theologischer Kommentar zum Alten Testament |

| | |
|---|---|
| *HUCA* | *Hebrew Union College Annual* |
| IBC | Interpretation: A Biblical Commentary for Teaching and Preaching |
| ICC | International Critical Commentary |
| *IOS* | *Israel Oriental Studies* |
| *Int* | *Interpretation* |
| *JANESCU* | *Journal of the Ancient Near Eastern Society of Columbia University* |
| *JAOS* | *Journal of the American Oriental Society* |
| *JBL* | *Journal of Biblical Literature* |
| *JCS* | *Journal of Cuneiform Studies* |
| *JNES* | *Journal of Near Eastern Studies* |
| JPSTC | The Jewish Publication Society Torah Commentary |
| *JQR* | *Jewish Quarterly Review* |
| *JSOT* | *Journal for the Study of the Old Testament* |
| JSOTSup | Journal for the Study of the Old Testament Supplement Series |
| *KAI* | *Kanaanäische und aramäische Inschriften.* Herbert Donner and Wolfgang Röllig. 5th ed. Wiesbaden: Harrassowitz, 2002. |
| *KTU* | *Die keilalphabetischen Texte aus Ugarit.* Edited by Manfield Dietrich, O. Loretz, and Joaquín Sanmartin. Münster: Ugarit-Verlag, 2013. 3rd enl. ed. of *KTU: The Cuneiform Alphabetic Texts from Ugarit, Ras Ibn Hani and Other Places.* Edited by Manfield Dietrich, O. Loretz, and Joaquín Sanmartin. Münster: Ugarit-Verlag, 1995. |
| LAI | Library of Ancient Israel |
| LBS | Library of Biblical Studies |
| LHBOTS | The Library of the Hebrew Bible/Old Testament Studies |
| LSTS | Library of Second Temple Studies |
| LXX | Septuagint |
| MAssL | Middle Assyrian Laws |
| NCB | New Century Bible |
| *NEA* | *Near Eastern Archaeology* |
| NICOT | New International Commentary on the Old Testament |
| OBO | Orbis Biblicus et Orientalis |
| OBT | Overtures to Biblical Theology |
| OLA | Orientalia Lovaniensia Analecta |
| OTL | Old Testament Library |

| | |
|---|---|
| OtSt | Oudtestamentische Studiën |
| P | Priestly material |
| POS | Pretoria Oriental Series |
| *RB* | *Revue biblique* |
| *RO* | *Rocznik orientalistyczny* |
| RS | Ras Shamra |
| *RTR* | *Reformed Theological Review* |
| SAHL | Studies in the Archaeology and History of the Levant |
| SBAB | Stuttgarter biblische Aufsatzbände |
| SBLDS | Society of Biblical Literature Dissertation Series |
| SBS | Stuttgarter Bibelstudien |
| SBTS | Sources for Biblical and Theological Study |
| *SCE* | *Studies in Christian Ethics* |
| SemeiaSt | Semeia Studies |
| SP | Samaritan Pentateuch |
| StBibLit | Studies in Biblical Literature |
| StOr | Studia Orientalia |
| StudBib | Studia Biblica |
| SSN | Studia Semitica Neerlandica |
| TAPS | Transactions of the American Philosophical Society |
| TB | Theologische Bücherei: Neudrucke und Berichte aus dem 20. Jahrhundert |
| TDNT | *Theological Dictionary of the New Testament*. Edited by Gerhard Kittel and Gerhard Friedrich. Translated by Geoffrey W. Bromiley. 10 vols. Grand Rapids, MI: Eerdmans, 1964–1976. |
| TDOT | *Theological Dictionary of the Old Testament*. Edited by G. Johannes Botterweck and Helmer Ringgren. Translated by John T. Willis et al. 8 vols. Grand Rapids: Eerdmans, 1974–2006. |
| Tg. Neof. | Targum Neofiti |
| Tg. Onq. | Targum Onkelos |
| Tg. Ps.-J. | Targum Pseudo-Jonathan |
| *TLOT* | *Theological Lexicon of the Old Testament*. Edited by Ernst Jenni, with assistance from Claus Westermann. Translated by Mark E. Biddle. 3 vols. Peabody, MA: Hendrickson, 1997. |
| *TQ* | *Theologische Quartalschrift* |
| *TRu* | *Theologische Rundschau* |

| | |
|---|---|
| *UF* | *Ugarit-Forschungen* |
| *UT* | *Ugaritic Textbook.* Cyrus H. Gordon. AnOr 38. Rome: Pontifical Biblical Institute, 1965. |
| *VT* | *Vetus Testamentum* |
| WAW | Writings from the Ancient World |
| WBC | Word Biblical Commentary |
| WMANT | Wissenschaftliche Monographien zum Alten und Neuen Testament |
| YNER | Yale Near Eastern Researches |
| *ZABR* | *Zeitschrift für altorientalische und biblische Rechtgeschichte* |
| *ZAW* | *Zeitschrift für die alttestamentliche Wissenschaft* |

# Introduction

> I take it as fundamental that creativity is not only central to kinship conceived in its broadest sense, but that for most people kinship constitutes one of the most important arenas for their creative energy.
> It is, among other things, an area of life in which people invest their emotions, their creative energy, and their new imaginings.[1]

Since the inception of human sociality, humankind has associated via rich networks of kinship connection. And, contrary to Western Caucasian assumptions, kinship historically has not always consisted of a discrete and static set of blood relations. Rather, there are seemingly endless ways in which kinship has been forged, apart from blood descent. In fact, in some cultures genetics plays a very minimal role in determining kinship.[2]

Not surprisingly, the social matrix that forms the background to the Deuteronomic vision was conceived in terms of kinship. The ancient Israelite/Judahite was "at a point of intersection among many genealogical relationships, both to living relatives and dead ancestors…. An individual is the child of X, of the clan of Y, of the tribe of Z, of the people of Israel."[3] Not only kinship but also want of kinship is present in the biblical text. Behind the pages of Deuteronomy are social-historical phenomena of large numbers of people who had been separated from kin and from patrimony. These people sought out a living within a kinship grouping that was not their own. Deuteronomy uses the term *gēr to* refer to such people. The sheer number of occurrences of *gēr* in Deuteronomy (twenty-two) as well as the literary and theological prominence given to Deuteronomy's response to this figure points to the gravity of this social problem.

---

1. Janet Carsten, *After Kinship* (Cambridge: Cambridge University Press, 2004), 9.
2. See Marshall Sahlins, *What Kinship Is—and Is Not* (Chicago: University of Chicago Press, 2013), 74–86.
3. Ronald S. Hendel, *Remembering Abraham: Culture, Memory, and History in the Hebrew Bible* (Oxford: Oxford University Press, 2005), 34.

"The landless and their families needed to be integrated into the clans," Eckart Otto has stated.[4] This study explores how Deuteronomy may be responding to this basic need of displaced people, to be incorporated into a household, into a clan grouping, and even into the "national" group. As a laborer or servant, the *gēr* was extremely vulnerable to indebtedness and enslavement. Deuteronomy was transforming the relationship of the *gēr* with a landed master, nourishing a deeper association than mere master-laborer, in line with the ethical trajectory of Israel's own narrative history.

How does Deuteronomy achieve this? Central to Deuteronomy's legislative strategy for the *gēr* is the interplay within various subgroups of law, namely, social law, feasting texts, and law of judicial procedure. The framework of Deuteronomy introduces another later group of covenant texts that operate at the level of national Israel. This study probes these legal subgroupings in order to discern how each contributes distinctively to Deuteronomy's response to widespread displacement.

Within these various subgroupings, there is also historical development. For example, while earlier Deuteronomic texts address the *gēr* among other vulnerable populations, namely, the Levite, fatherless, and widow, in later texts other categories for vulnerability recede into the background and displacement becomes the dominant social concern. Also, various literary tropes concerning the *gēr* morph and develop through the redaction strata in order to address new contexts of displacement with new rituals and theological motifs (e.g., the Feast of Booths, 16:12–15, 31:9–13).

There is an apparent tension in Deuteronomy between the twin poles of election (and exclusivism) and an ethic of incorporating the stranger. We will explore how this tension discloses Deuteronomy's attempt, on the one hand, to preserve the religious and social identity of ancient Israel as a community whose identity and very existence is under threat, and, on the other hand, to foster an inclusivism that is central to this very identity. Regarding Deuteronomic identity, at the heart of Deuteronomy is being/becoming the people of Yahweh. In earlier Deuteronomic texts, the cohesiveness of the community is pursued through cultic feasting (16:1–17) and through law. Later texts pursue this vision though covenant assemblies and through the public reading of Torah (29:9–14, 31:9–13). Through these various tropes, Deuteronomy also sweeps up the displaced within

---

4. Eckart Otto, "שׁעַר," *TDOT* 15:380.

the divine invitation. Of course, there is an inherent vulnerability to such an incorporative invitation, and the *gēr* herself or himself contests and defines what it means to be/become Israel.

This study uses a wide variety of tools related to the study of the Hebrew Bible in order to investigate Deuteronomy's response to the *gēr*. Uniquely, cultural-anthropological research into adoptive kinship and the role of cultural symbols in signifying kinship will assist in discerning the social significance of the relevant texts.

The dialectic mentioned above between exclusivism and inclusivism may be related to tensions in contemporary Western discourse between, on the one hand, national identity and security and, on the other hand, granting admission to displaced people. In light of this association, the reader may ponder the ways in which this ancient book's response to widespread displacement could be evocative for reimagining conceptions of identity, statehood, and inclusivism today.

# 1

# Review of the Scholarship and Methodology

Deuteronomy's response to the *gēr* is the central investigation of this study. The noun *gēr* in Deuteronomy refers to a vulnerable person who sought sustenance within a new kinship group that was not the *gēr*'s own. Such people had been displaced from their former kinship group and patrimony and from the protection that kinship and land affords. The *gēr* in Deuteronomy is impoverished; the *gēr* is also free or semi-free. We might say, the *gēr* is a *dependent stranger*.[1] Deuteronomy is the key text within the Pentateuch, and even within the Hebrew Bible, in which an explicit ethic concerning this population may be discerned.[2] Understandably then, faith-based advocates for asylum seekers and refugees often turn to Deuteronomy for its ethical resources.

Displaced people were vulnerable to oppression and to forced bondage in ancient Israel and in the ancient Near East. This is visible in Israel's own story recorded in Gen 15:13:

> Then Yahweh said to Abram, "Know for certain that your offspring will be strangers in a land that is not theirs [כי גר יהיה זרעך בארץ לא להם] and will be slaves there, and they will be afflicted for four hundred years." (Gen 15:13)[3]

In Gen 15:13 Israel, as *gēr*, is a displaced stranger who is vulnerable to exploitation. The narrative of this single verse moves rapidly from Israel as *gēr* to Israel as exploited slave. This shift displays what must have been well

---

1. See §3.9.

2. The *gēr* in the Holiness Code is not the same vulnerable figure with which Deuteronomy is concerned. This difference is discussed in §2.2.

3. Throughout this study, a small number of English translations are taken from the ESV. All other translations are my own.

appreciated in Israel and in the ancient Near East that only a thin line exists between living as a *gēr* and enslavement. A lack of patrimony and of kinship connection rendered displaced people vulnerable in every way. This study investigates the ways in which Deuteronomy sought to intervene in the impoverishment and the oppression of displaced people. It inquires, especially, into how Deuteronomy may have been fostering the incorporation of those without kin and patrimony into the kinship groupings.

The noun *gēr* is used almost exclusively in legal texts. In the Pentateuch it appears four times in the Covenant Code (hereafter CC),[4] twenty-two times in Deuteronomy,[5] once in each version of the Decalogue,[6] twenty times in the Holiness Code (hereafter HC),[7] thirteen times in the so-called "holiness redaction,"[8] twice more in other Priestly material (hereafter P),[9] and four times in other places.[10] The sheer frequency of the word in Deuteronomy suggests an unusually high concern for the dependent stranger among the books in the Hebrew Bible. This peculiar focus of Deuteronomy invites a close investigation into Deuteronomy's distinctive ethics for the dependent stranger and into how Deuteronomy embeds these ethics in its own theology and narrative. It also invites inquiry into the social forces behind the massive population displacement that Deuteronomy addresses.

This present chapter will review the scholarship on the *gēr* in Deuteronomy, noting the emerging issues. It will then outline the aims of this investigation and the methodology and structure through which those aims will be pursued.

---

4. Exod 22:20; 23:9 (2x), 12.

5. All citations from the Hebrew Bible are from Deuteronomy, unless otherwise indicated. 1:16; 5:14; 10:18, 19 (2x); 14:21, 29; 16:11, 14; 23:8; 24:14, 17, 19, 20, 21; 26:11, 12, 13; 27:19; 28:43; 29:10; 31:12.

6. Exod 20:10, Deut 5:14.

7. Lev 17:8, 10, 12, 13, 15; 18:26; 19:10, 33, 34 (2x); 20:2; 22:28; 23:22; 24:16, 22; 25:23, 35, 47 (3x).

8. Exod 12:19, 48, 49; Lev 16:29; Num 9:14 (2x); 15:14, 15 (2x), 16, 26, 29, 30. See Christophe Nihan, *From Priestly Torah to Pentateuch: A Study in the Composition of the Book of Leviticus*, FAT 2/25 (Tübingen: Mohr Siebeck, 2007), 569–72.

9. Num 19:10, 35:15.

10. Gen 15:13, 23:4 (on these texts, see the discussion of the literary history of the term *gēr* in §4.9.1). Two possibly ancient non-P texts are Exod 2:22, 18:3.

## 1.1. Scholarship on the Gēr and the Emerging Issues

A number of monograph-length works have been produced on the *gēr* in the Hebrew Bible. Christiana Van Houten has produced a diachronic study of the *gēr* across the Hebrew Bible, concluding that the law codes envision increasing inclusivism for the *gēr* over time.[11] José E. Ramírez Kidd has traced the development of the noun *gēr* from its use in earlier texts regarding social ethics to its later use referring to Israel's own identity as *gēr* before Yahweh.[12] An achievement of Markus Zehnder's monograph is his detailed investigation of the stranger in Neo-Assyrian and Neo-Babylonian texts.[13] Three monographs that are particularly relevant to this present study are now described in more detail.

### 1.1.1. Christoph Bultmann

Bultmann's 1992 monograph length study, *Der Fremde im antiken Juda: Eine Untersuchung zum sozialen Typenbegriff "ger" und seinem Bedeutungswandel in der alttestamentlichen Gesetzgebung*, examines the term *gēr* in law and related texts within the Hebrew Bible.[14] His study explores the question "whether the term *gēr* in the Old Testament means a stranger who is of non-Israelite origin."[15]

Bultmann designates the *gēr* in the Deuteronomic tradition as an internally displaced Judahite, located sociohistorically in the late seventh century. The term *gēr* designates a social substratum of impoverished and landless people who are dependent upon those with property and the means to cultivate it. Due to rising social inequality, families did not have

---

11. Christiana Van Houten, *The Alien in Israelite Law: A Study of the Changing Legal Status of Strangers in Ancient Israel*, JSOTSup 107 (Sheffield: Sheffield University Press, 1991).

12. José E. Ramírez Kidd, *Alterity and Identity in Israel*, BZAW 283 (Berlin: de Gruyter, 1999).

13. Markus Zehnder, *Umgang mit Fremden in Israel und Assyrien: Ein Beitrag zur Anthropologie des Fremden im Licht antiker Quellen*, BWANT 168 (Stuttgart: Kohlhammer, 2005).

14. Christoph Bultmann, *Der Fremde im antiken Juda: Eine Untersuchung zum sozialen Typenbegriff "ger" und seinem Bedeutungswandel in der alttestamentlichen Gesetzgebung*, FRLANT 153 (Göttingen: Vandenhoeck & Ruprecht, 1992).

15. Bultmann, *Fremde*, 9: "ob die Bezeichnung ger im Alten Testament einen Fremden meint, der nicht-israelitischer Herkunft ist."

a binding force in late seventh-century Judahite society that could provide a safety net for impoverished people. This was the case in both rural
and urban society.[16] Bultmann distinguishes between the *gēr* in Deuteronomy and in the HC, including in this distinction other texts that are
related to each of these law corpora. In the HC, the *gēr* is a foreigner in
relation to Israel as defined by adherence to Yahwism, during the Persian
period, both in Yehud and in the diaspora.[17] Critical for understanding
Bultmann is to distinguish between his social-historical conclusions and
his definition of the term *gēr*. Bultmann defines the term *gēr* thus: "The
*gēr* is therefore alien in relation to where he is residing."[18] Beginning with
this definition of the term *gēr* as an outsider in relation to his or her
place of residence,[19] Bultmann then makes the further supposition that
the *gēr* in Deuteronomy is a displaced Judahite. Bultmann asserts this on
the basis of his reconstruction of Deuteronomy's dating and of the social
history of monarchic Judah and beyond.[20] Some scholarship has failed
to give due weight to Bultmann's argumentation by confounding Bultmann's social-historical reconstruction of the *gēr* as a displaced Judahite
with his definition of the term *gēr*.[21] Confusing these removes the possibility of granting Bultmann's definition of *gēr* while also disputing his
social-historical reconstruction.

### 1.1.2. Mark A. Awabdy

In 2014, Mark A. Awabdy and Ruth Ebach each produced a book-length
study of the stranger in Deuteronomy. Like the present study, Awabdy's monograph is focused on the *gēr*, whereas Ebach investigates the
stranger more broadly.[22] Awabdy thoroughly investigates each text in
Deuteronomy dealing with the *gēr*. He references four methodologies:
lexico-syntagmatic (Awabdy's most developed approach), sociological,

---

16. Bultmann, *Fremde*, 214.

17. Bultmann, *Fremde*, 216.

18. Bultmann, *Fremde*, 17: "Der *ger* ist von daher 'fremd' in der jeweiligen Relation zu seinem Aufenthaltsort."

19. See Bultmann, *Fremde*, 17–33.

20. See Bultmann, *Fremde*, 213, for an explanation of this logic.

21. E.g., Mark A. Awabdy, *Immigrants and Innovative Law: Deuteronomy's Theological and Social Vision for the* גר, FAT 2/67 (Tübingen: Mohr Siebeck, 2014), 18–19.

22. Awabdy, *Immigrants*.

"sociohistorical referential" (Awabdy rarely adopts this approach), and "theological and related approaches" (developed especially in chapter 6). His study is largely synchronic. Awabdy translates *gēr* as "immigrant," arguing that the *gēr* in Deuteronomy is a non-Judahite and non-Israelite who is residing within Israelite settlements.[23] Awabdy defends this in part on the basis of his definition of אח, which Awabdy translates as "fellow countryman."[24] Awabdy's interest in theology and in ethics connects with the present study. His study concludes that Deuteronomy casts a vision to integrate the *gēr* both socially and religiously. This ethic "was embedded in Israel's own identity, shaped by its diverse experience in Egypt and reoriented by the generous and redeeming nature of its deity, YHWH."[25]

Nonetheless, a number of Awabdy's major conclusions need further attention and will be pursued later in this study. Key to Awabdy's analysis is his observation that the prologue and the epilogue of Deuteronomy (Deut 1–11, 27–34) offer a deeper integration for the *gēr* than does the Deuteronomic Code (the law code of Deuteronomy, Deut 12–26; hereafter DC). While in the DC the *gēr* was integrated socially, in the prologue-epilogue the *gēr* was integrated both socially and religiously.[26] Awabdy suggests that the laws of admission (Deut 23:2–9) are an interpretative key explaining this difference. On the basis of this text, Awabdy suggests that those who demonstrated commitment to Yahweh and to his people for three generations were admitted into the assembly. Thus Deut 23:2–9 provides a "religious and social transition from the DC to the P-E [prologue-epilogue]."[27] Awabdy explains the enhanced inclusion of the *gēr* in the prologue-epilogue vis-à-vis the DC on the basis that the prologue-epilogue is referring to immigrants who have been admitted into the assembly by virtue of their satisfying the requirements of the laws of admission. This thesis, should it be valid, would entail a significant limitation to Deuteronomy's ethic of inclusivism.

---

23. Awabdy, *Immigrants*, 110–16.
24. See the discussion of אח in §4.2.3. of the present study.
25. Awabdy, *Immigrants*, 253.
26. Awabdy, *Immigrants*, 122–23.
27. Awabdy, *Immigrants*, 66–83, 123–25, 242.

### 1.1.3. Ruth Ebach

Ruth Ebach's German study examines the role of the stranger, "das Fremde," in Israel's own identity construction.[28] Ebach's subject is not only the *gēr* but also the נכרי and the foreign nations, both within and outside of the land. Thus Ebach's study relates less directly to the present study than does that of Awabdy. Throughout Deuteronomy, she argues, the *gēr* is a vulnerable foreigner who is associated with and dependent upon an Israelite household.[29] The monograph is structured according to composition layers in three sections: preexilic, exilic, and postexilic. Ebach's exegesis is closely related to a reconstruction of the composition history of Deuteronomy and to the proposed social-historical context of the text.

The goal of Deuteronomy's treatment of political relations with the "other" is collective Israelite identity formation. On the one hand, Israel's own boundaries are established in relation to the stranger, fostering cohesion. On the other hand, Deuteronomy's system of solidarity is expanded to include material protection for the poor foreigner.

Ebach's study does not include a close investigation of texts relating to the *gēr* as does Awabdy's monograph and the present study. However, her conclusion that through these texts Deuteronomy is negotiating Israel's identity in relation to the "other" is most significant. I will inquire into the ways in which the *gēr* contests and defines what it means to be/become Israel.

Other shorter studies of the *gēr* include a collection of essays recently edited by Reinhard Achenbach, Rainer Albertz, and Jakob Wöhrle,[30] and individual studies such as those by Reinhard Achenbach, Nadav Na'aman, G. Barbiero, and M. Daniel Carrol R.[31] Some less recent studies remain

---

28. Ruth Ebach, *Das Fremde und das Eigene: Die Fremdendarstellungen des Deuteronomiums im Kontext israelitischer Identitätskonstruktionen*, BZAW 471 (Berlin: de Gruyter, 2014).

29. See Ebach, *Das Fremde und das Eigene*, 311–21.

30. Reinhard Achenbach, Rainer Albertz, and Jakob Wöhrle, eds., *The Foreigner and the Law: Perspectives from the Hebrew Bible and the Ancient Near East*, BZAR 16 (Wiesbaden: Harrassowitz, 2011).

31. Reinhard Achenbach, "Der Eintritt der Schutzbürger in den Bund (Dtn 29, 10–12): Distinktion und Integration von Fremden im Deuteronomium," in *"Gerechtigkeit und Recht zu üben" (Gen 18,19): Studien zur altorientalischen und biblischen Rechtsgeschichte, zur Religionsgeschichte Israels und zur Religionssoziologie; Festschrift für Eckart Otto zum 65. Geburtstag*, ed. Reinhard Achenbach and Martin Arneth,

important, such as those by Rolf Rendtorff, Norbert Lohfink, Georg Braulik, P. E. Dion, and Frank Anthony Spina.[32]

## 1.1.4. The Provenance of the *Gēr*

A critical question in the scholarship concerns the provenance of the *gēr*. The observation that Deuteronomy has a distinctive and marked focus on displaced and vulnerable people within the law codes of the Pentateuch suggests that Deuteronomy originally addressed a unique context(s) where displaced people formed a significant part of the population. This observation in turn invites an inquiry into the social and historical phenomena that produced such a situation. There are three primary contending views in the scholarship for the origin of the *gēr*: a refugee in the wake of the Assyrian invasion of the Northern Kingdom, a foreigner from a kingdom other than either Judah or the Northern Kingdom, or a displaced Judahite. The second model is the dominant position in the most recent publications.

---

BZAR 13 (Wiesbaden: Harrassowitz, 2009), 240–55; Nadav Naʾaman, "Sojourners and Levites in the Kingdom of Judah in the Seventh Century BCE," *ZABR* 14 (2008): 237–79; Gianni Barbiero, "Der Fremde im Bundesbuch und im Heiligkeitsgesetz: Zwischen Absonderung und Annahme," in *Studien zu alttestamentlichen Texten*, ed. Gianni Barbiero, SBAB 34 (Stuttgart: Verlag Katholisches Bibelwerk, 2002), 220–54; M. Daniel Carroll R, "Welcoming the Stranger: Toward a Theology of Immigration in Deuteronomy," in *For Our Good Always Studies on the Message and Influence of Deuteronomy in Honor of Daniel I. Block*, ed. Jason S. DeRouchie, Jason Gile, and Kenneth J. Turner (Winona Lake, IN: Eisenbrauns, 2013), 441–62.

32. Rolf Rendtorff, "The Ger in the Priestly Laws of the Pentateuch," in *Ethnicity and the Bible*, ed. Mark G. Brett, BibInt (New York: Brill, 1996), 77–87; Norbert S. J. Lohfink, "Poverty in the Laws of the Ancient Near East and of the Bible," *TS* 52 (1991): 34–50; Georg Braulik, "Deuteronomy and Human Rights," in *Theology of Deuteronomy: Collected Essays of Georg Braulik, O. S. B.*, trans. U. Lindblad (N. Richland Hills, TX: Bibal, 1994), 131–50; trans. of "Das Deuteronomium und die Menschenrechte," *TQ* 166 (1986): 8–24; P. E. Dion, "Israël et l'Étranger dans le Deutéronome," in *L'Altérité: Vivre ensemble différents; Approches Pluridisciplinaires: Actes du Colloque pluridisciplinaire tenu à l'occasion du 75e anniversaire du Collège dominicain de philosophie et de théologie, Ottawa, 4, 5, 6 octobre 1984*, ed. M. Gourgues and G. D. Mailhiot, Recherches n.s. 7 (Montréal: Bellarmin, 1986), 221–33; Frank Anthony Spina, "Israelites as *Gērîm*: 'Sojourners,' in Social and Historical Context," in *The Word of the Lord Shall Go Forth: Essays in Honor of David Noel Freedman in Celebration of His Sixtieth Birthday*, ed. Carol L. Meyers and M. O'Connor (Philadelphia: American Schools of Oriental Research, 1983), 321–36.

### 1.1.4.1. Is the *Gēr* a Refugee in the Wake of the Destruction of Samaria?

Since Alfred Bertholet's seminal work on the *gēr* in the late nineteenth century, the theory that *gēr* refers to a northerner who had fled into Judah in the wake of the Assyrian conquest of Israel has received support.[33] In 1991, Lohfink wrote that this is "the fashionable guess among scholars,"[34] namely, the northerners who have fled into Judah who are mentioned in connection with Hezekiah's Passover festival (2 Chr 30:25). Also, archaeology confirms that Jerusalem expanded greatly in the seventh century, and while some scholars attribute this to Sennacherib's invasion in 701 BCE,[35] Lester L. Grabbe is among those who suggest that one reason for this growth was immigration following the conquest of Samaria in 720 BCE.[36] Na'aman takes a different view, contending that, while according to the *pax Assyriaca* borders within the empire were open, Judea's borders during the seventh century were "largely closed."[37]

### 1.1.4.2. Is the *Gēr* from a Non-Israelite and Non-Judahite Kingdom?

As already noted, Awabdy has recently defended the view that the *gēr* in Deuteronomy is a non-Israelite.[38] Ebach argues similarly in her recent monograph.[39] Also, Achenbach is among the most lucid of the recent literature in arguing that the *gēr* "stands outside the federation of Israel."[40]

---

33. Alfred Bertholet, *Die Stellung der Israeliten und der Juden zu den Fremden* (Leipzig: Mohr, 1896), 123–78; Roland de Vaux, *Ancient Israel: Its Life and Institutions* (London: Darton, Longman & Todd, 1961), 74–76; D. Kellermann, "גּוּר," *TDOT* 2:445; Moshe Weinfeld, *Deuteronomy and the Deuteronomic School* (Oxford: Clarendon, 1972), 90–91.

34. Lohfink, "Poverty," 41.

35. E.g., Na'aman, "Sojourners," 258, 277.

36. Lester L. Grabbe, *Ancient Israel: What Do We Know and How Do We Know It?* (London: T&T Clark, 2007), 169–70.

37. Nadav Na'aman, "Population Changes in Palestine Following Assyrian Deportation," in vol. 1 of *Ancient Israel and Its Neighbors: Interaction and Counteraction: Collected Essays* (Winona Lake, IN: Eisenbrauns, 2005), 215.

38. Awabdy, *Immigrants*.

39. Ebach, *Fremde*, 41.

40. Achenbach, "Eintritt," 242: "die außerhalb des Verbandes Israels stehen." This view is also defended by Van Houten, *Alien in Israelite Law*, 107–8; Rainer Albertz, "From Aliens to Proselytes: Non-Priestly and Priestly Legislation Concerning Strangers," in Achenbach, Albertz, and Wöhrle, *The Foreigner and the Law*, 61, 55; Donald

Significantly for this view, two occurrences of *gēr* in Deuteronomy have the contextual meaning of a person who is outside of the Yahwistic community (Deut 14:29; 28:43–44). A cultic context of the "national" assembly in 29:9–14 and 31:9–13 also seems to support this view. Further, a "flat" reading of the *gēr* in the Pentateuch may drive the view that the *gēr* is non-Israelite, by which the clear foreignness of the *gēr* in the HC is generalized to Deuteronomy. According to this reconstruction, the term *gēr* in Deuteronomy is in opposition to the term נכרי, who is a foreigner of independent means who is not assimilated into the community.[41] A related view, popular in earlier scholarship, is that the *gēr* is someone displaced from the land due to the Israelite conquest.[42]

### 1.1.4.3. Is the *Gēr* a Displaced Judahite?

Others have advocated the view that the term *gēr* in Deuteronomy primarily refers to Judahites who have been displaced from their own land due, for example, to invasion or indebtedness.[43] Separated from land and from kindred, the displaced Judahite no longer receives the protection that kinship and patrimony afford and is therefore vulnerable to exploitation and

---

E. Gowan, "Wealth and Poverty in the Old Testament: The Case of the Widow, the Orphan, and the Sojourner," *Int* 41 (1987): 343; Dion, "Israël et l'Étranger"; Zehnder, *Fremden*; John R. Spencer, "Sojourner," *ABD* 6:103–5; Joel N. Lohr, *Chosen and Unchosen: Conceptions of Election in the Pentateuch and Jewish-Christian Interpretation*, Siphrut 2 (Winona Lake, IN: Eisenbrauns, 2009); Jeffrey H. Tigay, *Deuteronomy*, JPSTC (Philadelphia: The Jewish Publication Society, 1996), 12; Timo Veijola, *Das 5. Buch Mose Deuteronomium: Kapitel 1, 1–16, 17*, DATD 8/1 (Göttingen: Vandenhoeck and Ruprecht, 2004), 27; Jenny Corcoran, "The Alien in Deuteronomy 29 and Today," in *Interpreting Deuteronomy: Issues and Approaches*, ed. David G. Firth and Philip S. Johnston (Downers Grove, IL: InterVarsity, 2012), 234; Joseph Blenkinsopp, "Yahweh and Other Deities: Conflict and Accommodation in the Religion of Israel," *Int* 40 (1986): 354–66; Carly Crouch, *The Making of Israel: Cultural Diversity in the Southern Levant and the Formation of Ethnic Identity in Deuteronomy* (New York: Brill, 2014), 216–23; Kidd, *Alterity*, 46.

41. The term נכרי is discussed in §6.10.1.

42. E.g., T. J. Meek, "The Translation of *Ger* in the Hexateuch and Its Bearing on the Documentary Hypothesis," *JBL* 49 (1930): 173; de Vaux, *Ancient Israel*, 74–76; and more recently Van Houten, *Alien in Israelite Law*, 16.

43. E.g. Bultmann, *Fremde*, 55; Philip J. King and Lawrence E. Stager, *Life in Biblical Israel*, LAI (Louisville: Westminster John Knox, 2001), 40; Braulik, "Deuteronomy and Rights," 138; Na'aman, "Sojourners."

abuse.[44] According to this reconstruction, the term *gēr* in Deuteronomy is in opposition to the term זָר, which in Deuteronomy refers to a person from outside of the local kinship grouping and who is economically independent:[45] "There is another layer of individual, free, dispossessed people, who are dependent on these farmers to claim their labour."[46] As already noted, Bultmann cites social stratification as a dynamic in seventh-century Judah that eroded the ability of Judahite kin groupings to protect their own. Recently, Na'aman, in his study of the *gēr* in Dtn legislative texts, has concluded that Sennacherib's campaign of 701 BCE was the cause of massive domestic displacement in seventh-century Judah. The Assyrian conquest would have given rise to a class of poor and landless people that did not exist on such a scale before.[47]

## 1.1.5. Emerging Issues

Certain issues emerge in these monographs that call for further research. There is little agreement in the scholarship on the *gēr* regarding how this may relate to the composition history of Deuteronomy. Van Houten's methodology for discerning redaction layers in the DC is unusual and has been critiqued by Kidd as simplistic.[48] Kidd himself briefly offers a treatment of historical-critical issues that aligns more closely with critical scholarship on Deuteronomy.[49] Awabdy briefly attempts to apply his exegesis to scholarship on the composition history of the Pentateuch, criticizing the generally accepted conclusions of critical scholarship.[50] Ebach engages in redaction criticism more thoroughly, locating her approach within recent German scholarship on the composition history of Deuteronomy and of the Pentateuch.[51] The variety of methodologies used to discern redaction layers as well as the variety of conclusions in these studies invites further

---

44. Scholars who advocate for this position usually contend nonetheless that the *gēr* in the HC is a foreigner (see further §2.2).

45. The term זָר is discussed in §6.10.1.

46. Bultmann, *Fremde*, 214: "steht eine andere Schicht von einzelnen, freien, besitzlosen Personen, die darauf angewiesen ist, daß diese Bauern ihre Arbeitskraft beanspruchen."

47. Na'aman, "Sojourners," 277.

48. Van Houten, *Alien in Israelite Law*, 77–80; Kidd, *Alterity*, 9.

49. Kidd, *Alterity*, 35–36, 40–41.

50. Awabdy, *Immigrants*, 108–9, 157–61.

51. Ebach, *Fremde*, 76, for example.

investigation. Also, while the most recent scholarship broadly agrees that that the *gēr* is a foreigner, some scholars dispute this consensus. This question of the identity of the *gēr* will be addressed in the analysis of the following chapters. Most surprisingly, the tools offered by cultural anthropology—scholarship on, for example, ethnicity, kinship, and feasting—are largely unused in these studies. To be sure, critical theory on race and ethnicity has been appropriated within the field of Hebrew Bible studies, but this has substantially influenced an analysis of the *gēr* only in a few places.[52] This needs further attention. The most important issue to arise from the scholarship for the present study, however, is the nature and breadth of the inclusion of the *gēr* that Deuteronomy envisages. On the one hand, Awabdy concludes that Deuteronomy calls the community to include the *gēr* socially and religiously. On the other hand, Mark Sneed argues that the social ethics of the Hebrew Bible merely serve the class interests of the biblical writers. Sneed argues, for example, that 10:17–19 legitimizes Yahweh's reign as the patron of the vulnerable, while paradoxically reinforcing the status quo.[53] This question of inclusivism in Deuteronomy will be explored throughout this study. Finally, the theory that an ethic for including the stranger increases in its intensity through redactional layers of Deuteronomy has persisted for many decades and has been reiterated recently by Awabdy and Ebach. This too needs further discussion.[54]

## 1.2. The Aims of This Study

The present work investigates the aforementioned issues emerging in the scholarly conversation on the *gēr* in Deuteronomy in six ways. This study:

---

52. Though see Ebach, *Fremde*, 9–17. Kenton Sparks' treatment of the *gēr* is also a possible exception to this critique; see *Ethnicity and Identity in Ancient Israel: Prolegomena to the Study of Ethnic Sentiments and Their Expression in the Hebrew Bible* (Winona Lake, IN: Eisenbrauns, 1998). For a substantial treatment of ethnicity in the Hebrew Bible, see Dermot Anthony Nestor, *Cognitive Perspectives on Israelite Identity*, LBS (New York: T&T Clark, 2010).

53. Mark Sneed, "Israelite Concern for the Alien, Orphan, and Widow: Altruism or Ideology?," *ZAW* 111 (1999): 502–3. Deuteronomy 10:17–19 is examined in §4.3 and §6.2, and Sneed's argument is addressed there.

54. See Awabdy, *Immigrants*, 66–83, 123–25, 242, and Ebach, *Fremde*, 312. Awabdy mostly adopts a final form approach.

1.  develops and applies an integrative methodology to an inves-
    tigation of the *gēr* in Deuteronomy (explained in what fol-
    lows). An integrative approach that brings together, for exam-
    ple, insights from the social sciences and Israel's social history,
    is urgently needed in research on the *gēr*;
2.  intervenes in the conversation around the inclusion of the *gēr*
    by inquiring into how Deuteronomy's ethics of protection and
    of inclusivism may be operating in the domain of kinship; it
    considers how kinship and ethnicity may be both formed and
    transformed;
3.  employs tools of cultural anthropology and exegesis to ana-
    lyze ethnicity in Deuteronomy in an attempt to clarify the
    identity of the *gēr*;
4.  structures exegesis according to legal subgroups, namely,
    social law, judicial law, festal stipulations, and the covenant
    texts of the frame of Deuteronomy, attending to the peculiar
    characteristics of each law-group and to the peculiar function
    of each law-group in relation to the *gēr*;
5.  examines the ways in which Deuteronomy's ethic of inclusion
    for the *gēr* is embedded theologically and within Israel's own
    narrative;
6.  engages with the developing scholarship on the social history
    of Israel in order to consider how Deuteronomy may have
    addressed contexts of massive displacement.

The remainder of this chapter outlines the means by which these aims will
be pursued.

## 1.3. Methodology

### 1.3.1. An Integrative Methodology

This study adopts an integrative methodology,[55] bringing together legal,
social-scientific, comparative, literary, theological, social-historical, and
literary-historical approaches. These approaches mutually inform a close

---

55. This is my phrase. An integrative approach is crucial if we are to understand
the social, political, and religious significance of these laws in their original context.

exegesis of the texts in Deuteronomy dealing with the *gēr*. An explicitly legal approach, that is "the kind of analysis and categories that legal scholars would apply to most legal systems,"[56] is integral to this methodology, and tools of anthropology can illuminate the social background of the text and the intended function of laws. Also, comparative analysis that encompasses both ancient Near Eastern legal texts and ancient Near Eastern social and economic background provides a background for association and for contrast. A literary approach is key as "legal pronouncements have clear meaning only in the context of the entire legal document of which they are a part."[57] Literary-historical analysis is crucial as the legislative program of both Israel and also of the ancient Near East was a self-conscious process of legal revision, and new legislation was composed in light of new circumstances while also in dialogue with the tradition.[58]

## 1.3.2. A Method for Studying Kinship

Clarifying a methodology for studying kinship and ethnicity is crucial for hearing clearly how Deuteronomy was shaping the people of Yahweh to respond to those who were without kin.

### 1.3.2.1. Kinship in Communal Cultures

In communal cultures, people share a collective identity. Marshall Sahlins describes this as a "mutuality of being,"[59] an "intersubjective solidarity."[60] Marilyn Strathern writes of the traditional Melanesian people: "They contain a generalized sociality within. Indeed, persons are frequently constructed as the plural and composite site of the relationships that produced them. The singular person can be imagined as social microcosm."[61] Anne

---

56. Raymond Westbrook and Bruce Wells, *Everyday Law in Biblical Israel* (Louisville: Westminster John Knox, 2009), 129.

57. Frank Crüsemann, *The Torah: Theology and Social History of Old Testament Law*, trans. Allan. W. Mahnke (Minneapolis: Fortress, 1996), 9.

58. See further, Eckart Otto, "Aspects of Legal Reforms and Reformulations in Ancient Cuneiform and Israelite Law," in *Theory and Method in Biblical and Cuneiform Law: Revision, Interpolation and Development*, ed. Bernard M. Levinson, JSOTSup 181 (Sheffield: Sheffield Academic, 1994), 160–96.

59. Sahlins, *What Kinship Is*, 19–31.

60. Sahlins, *What Kinship Is*, 43.

61. Marilyn Strathern, *The Gender of the Gift: Problems with Women and Problems*

E. Becker describes Melanesian culture before Western contact: "The traditional Melanesian's self-awareness was as a set of relationships. Experience
was diffused among persons, not considered specific to the individual."[62]

This communal self-awareness is expressed in what ethnographers
refer to as the "kinship I," which Sahlins describes as "the fellowship in
contrast to the individual life."[63] The pronoun "I" is used in various ways,
to refer to the speaker him/herself, to the whole group, or to an ances-
tor with whom they may identify. Solidarity may also be experienced in
a "mystical interdependence" of bodies. Mourning rituals that symbolize
a shared death, such as mutilation or tearing of clothing, are common.[64]
Sahlins writes concerning the Nyakyusa of the African Rift Valley, "'The
essential fact is that relatives are believed to be mystically affected by the
very fact of their relationship.' A son who does not participate in the death
rituals for his father can go mad; a uterine nephew who fails to drink med-
icines at the birth of twins to his maternal uncle may see his own children
swell up and die."[65]

In communal cultures a person is not undividable; rather, there is the
"dividable" or "dividual" person who also expresses the whole community.
As Julian Pitt-Rivers puts it, "The majority of the world's population do *not*
share the individualism of the modern West and have no need to explain
what appears to them evident: the self is not the individual self alone, but
includes, according to circumstances, those with whom the self is conceived as solidary, in the first place, his kin."[66]

## 1.3.2.2. The Communal Culture of Deuteronomy

"Mutuality of being" is visible in Deuteronomy, for example, in pronouncements of generational benediction and malediction (see, for example,

with Society in Melanesia (Berkeley, CA: University of California Press, 1988), 13, cited
in Carsten, After Kinship, 93–94.

62. Anne E. Becker, Body, Self, and Society: The View from Fiji (Philadelphia: University of Philadelphia Press, 1995), 5.

63. Sahlins, What Kinship Is, 36.

64. Sahlins, What Kinship Is, 46.

65. Sahlins, What Kinship Is, 46, citing Monica Wilson, "Nyukyusa Kinship," in
African Systems of Kinship and Marriage, ed. A. R. Radcliffe Brown and Cyril Daryll
Forde (London: Oxford University Press, 1950), 126.

66. Julian Pitt-Rivers, "The Kith and the Kin," in The Character of Kinship, ed. Jack
Goody (Cambridge: Cambridge University Press, 1973), 90 (italics original).

Deut 5:9–10, 7:9). The promise that the sins of the fathers will fall upon the children until the third and fourth generation has parallels in communal cultures today.[67] Numerous customary connections, rights, and duties of kinsfolk, weaved together, formed the social fabric of the ancient Near Eastern world. These included genealogical connection (Deut 29:10–12), sharing a connection to the land (for example, Deut 26:1–11), an "expectation to be loving, just, and generous to one another,"[68] an expectation not to demand equivalent return (for example, Deut 1:16–17, 15:7–8), submission to the elders and the paterfamilias (for example, Deut 21:18–21), an obligation to provide mourning rites and burial or inhumation for the corpses of the dead,[69] and an obligation to provide protection and military solidarity, both in defense and in offense.[70] This is not only true of ancient Israel but also of the broader cultural milieu. "The social organization of West Semitic tribal groups was grounded in kinship. Kinship relations defined the rights and obligations, the duties, status, and privileges of tribal members, and kinship terminology provided the only language for expressing legal, political, and religious institutions."[71] Scholars generally recognize that clan structures obtained throughout the monarchic period.[72] And, where clan structures were disrupted (in particular through the devastation of the Babylonian conquest and its aftermath), nuclear households and (to a lesser degree) "adoptive" clans were, nevertheless, the primary groupings within which social relationships were negotiated (see §6.3.3).[73] Further, as J. David Schloen writes, "It is now widely recognized that kinship networks have remained important in the Near East up

---

67. Sahlins, *What Kinship Is*, 49.

68. Meyer Fortes, *Kinship and the Social Order: The Legacy of Lewis Henry Morgan* (Chicago: Aldine, 1969), cited in Frank Moore Cross, *From Epic to Canon: History and Literature in Ancient Israel* (Baltimore: John Hopkins University Press, 1998), 5.

69. See further Gabriel Barkay, "Burial Caves and Burial Practices in Judah in the Iron Age," in *Graves and Burial Practices in Israel in the Ancient Period* [Hebrew], ed. Itamar Singer (Jerusalem: Yad Izhak Ben Zvi/Israel Exploration Society, 1994), 96–164.

70. See further Cross, *From Epic to Canon*, 4.

71. Cross, *From Epic to Canon*, 4.

72. See discussion in Avraham Faust, *The Archaeology of Israelite Society in Iron Age II* (Winona Lake, IN: Eisenbrauns, 2012), 10–11.

73. On kinship in the post-exilic period, see Hugh Williamson, "The Family in Persian Period Judah: Some Textual Reflections," in *Symbiosis, Symbolism and the Power of the Past: Ancient Israel and Its Neighbors from the Late Bronze Age through*

to the present day, not only in rural villages but also in urban neighbor-hoods, where patterns of residence and of economic cooperation reflect extended-family and 'clan' ties (real or fictional)."[74]

### 1.3.2.3. Western Kinship

Western-enculturated readers of Deuteronomy might easily miss how this text was originally both written and heard within a social construct of col-lective identity. Compared with the majority of cultures globally, Western culture is, as Sahlins puts it, hyper-individualistic. A Western person is a "self-fashioning, self-interested individual,"[75] the author of his or her own life with both the capacity and also the responsibility to exercise his or her individual agency. In contrast, agency in communal cultures "is an act of we-ness."[76]

Westerners are, of course, aware of kinship, though they tend to refer simply to "family" rather than the complex of relations that characterize communal cultures. David M. Schneider isolates two irreducible elements of Western kinship: first, shared bio-genetic substance and, second, a code for conduct between kinspersons. From here, Schneider identifies three primary categories for Western kinship, as it is conceived in the social imaginary: "When both elements occur together the category of blood relative is formed; when the code for conduct element occurs alone and without the shared bio-genetic substance element the category of relatives-in-law or relatives by marriage if formed; and, finally, when the shared bio-genetic substance is present alone the category of relatives in nature is formed."[77] As kinship is established largely by blood, it is also thought of as

---

*Roman Palestine*, ed. William G. Dever and Seymour Gitin (Winona Lake, IN: Eisen-brauns, 2003), 469–85.

74. See discussion in David Schloen, *The House of the Father as Fact and Symbol: Patrimonialism in Ugarit and the Ancient Near East*, SAHL 2 (Winona Lake, IN: Eisen-brauns, 2001), 70. This point has been made with respect to early Mesopotamian states by Robert McC. Adams, *The Evolution of Urban Society: Early Mesopotamia and Pre-hispanic Mexico* (New Brunswick: Aldine Transaction, 1966). Schloen argues that in Ugarit many of the corvée laborers who worked on royal farms nonetheless dwelt in traditional villages nearby (Schloen, *House of the Father*, 236–39).

75. Sahlins, *What Kinship Is*, 52.

76. Sahlins, *What Kinship Is*, 53.

77. David M. Schneider, "What Is Kinship All About?," in *Kinship and Family: An*

involuntary (except for marriage) and unchanging.[78] Since people from all cultures tend to think of their own kinship categories not as symbols but as bare facts, "it is difficult at times to convince an American that blood as a fluid has nothing in it which causes ties to be deep and strong."[79]

### 1.3.2.4. Mutable and Adaptable Kinship

We have observed that Westerners, at least among white majority communities, tend to conceive of kinship in terms of blood-ties. Related to this is the Western presumption that kinship is fixed: families are *given*, for better or for worse! In communal cultures, however, kinship is almost universally thought of as adaptive and mutable, and kinship creation may even be emphasized. "One may be kin to another by being born on the same day (Inuit), by following the same tabus (Arawete), by surviving a trial at sea (Truk) or on the ice (Inuit), even by mutually suffering from ringworm (Kaluli)."[80] Mac Marshall describes how a Trukese man may speak of another as "my sibling from the same canoe," referring to a man with whom he survived a life-threatening experience on the ocean.[81]

In fact, mutability and complexity in kinship is often experienced in the West, even if it is not recognized as such. For example, Janet Carsten studied adults who had been adopted at birth as they sought to make connections with their birth parents. The most common explanation that these adults gave for their desire to reconnect displays the strength of blood-connection in Western culture: "to know where I came from," "to be complete," or the like.[82] Nonetheless, many of Carsten's interviewees also expressed the privileged place of adoptive parents in their lives. One adoptee stated, "I wasn't after another mother; I have one."[83] Thus, "Normal exchanges of kinship are not an automatic right, but a privilege that is earned through the demonstrated hard effort that goes into nurtur-

---

*Anthropological Reader*, ed. Robert Parkin and Linda Stone (Mulden, MA: Blackwell, 2004), 263.

78. See further, Carsten, *After Kinship*, 15, 114.

79. Schneider, "What Is Kinship All About," 268.

80. Sahlins, *What Kinship Is*, 68.

81. Sahlins, *What Kinship Is*, 29, citing Mac Marshall, "The Nature of Nurture," *AmE* 4 (1977): 643–62.

82. Carsten, *After Kinship*, 147.

83. Carsten, *After Kinship*, 149.

ing and caring for a child." Further, Carsten and others have examined the ways in which reproductive technology has shifted Western assumptions about kinship, citing sperm donation as one way in which the perceived exclusive role of blood-ties for defining kinship has been disrupted. Similarly, Linda Stone's study of Western soap operas traces how, while biology continues to define kinship, both within this television genre and also in real life, "biogenetic kinship is also fiercely contested, even denounced, and it is rivaled by a new dimension of kinship constructions—individual choice, or will."[84]

The incorporation of outsiders into kinship groups, important to the present study, should be understood in terms of the meanings and symbols of a culture itself. For the Langkawi people who Carsten studied, for example, "A fetus is said to be composed of the blood of the mother and the semen of the father. After birth, however, a child's blood is progressively formed through the consumption of food cooked in the house hearth. As the inhabitants live together in one house over time and eat meals together, their blood becomes progressively more similar."[85] Carsten surmises: "If food is gradually transformed into blood in the body, and those who live together come to resemble each other as well as develop emotional closeness, then in the long term this is surely a quite literal process of creating kinship."[86] For the Langkawi, sharing in food was a means of incorporating foster children and new spouses into the household. Outsiders, too, were enfolded as kindred through cohabitation and food consumption. The way in which sharing food may constitute kinship will be shown to be significant for understanding Deuteronomy's feasting texts in chapter 5. In many cultures, food conveys new life to the eater, and it also imparts the life of the giver into the eater.[87] Historically, the Langkawi have been dependent upon their ability to enfold new immigrants into kinship networks, through in-marriage and fostering. Carsten writes that, "An ideal guest is one who stays for a long time and eventually settles, marries, and has children on the island."[88] "It is very notable that villagers have a strong desire to describe any guest—

---

84. Linda Stone, "Has the World Turned? Kinship and Family in the Contemporary American Soap Opera," in Parkin and Stone, *Kinship and Family*, 397.

85. Carsten, *After Kinship*, 41.

86. Carsten, *After Kinship*, 139.

87. Sahlins, *What Kinship Is*, 29.

88. Carsten, *After Kinship*, 138.

from a young man brought home for a few days as a friend of an adult son, to visiting students working on projects for a week or so—in the idiom of fostering."[89] As for the Langkawi, very many groups globally and historically exhibit a willingness to incorporate outsiders into the kinship grouping.[90]

There are seemingly endless ways in which kinship is forged, apart from blood descent. In fact, in some cultures genetics plays a very minimal role in determining kinship.[91] Evocative for this study of Deuteronomy are the ways in which sharing land is constitutive of kinship in some cultures.[92] Another domain in which strangers appear in Deuteronomy is the household, and the kin-producing function of the household and specifically the "hearth" of the household, in some cultures, has been explored by cultural anthropologists. For example, Carsten observes that for the Zafimaniry, houses "acquire bones." She explains: "The image could hardly be more redolent of the corporeal quality of houses and their link to the bodies of the inhabitants they contain."[93] Food consumed in the hearth of the house is where kinship is forged among the Zumbagua of Ecuador. In this community, a large proportion of kinsfolk are adopted, not as a last resort, but as a commonplace. " 'The Zumbagua family consists of those who eat together,' and 'the hearth … supplants the marriage bed as the symbol of conjugal living and the bond of blood as the emblem of parenthood.' "[94] Other nodes of kinship creation are nurture, giving and sharing in food, name-sharing, working together, mutual assistance, sharing in migration, and especially the hard work, effort, and commitment of living together for the long-haul.[95]

In the early- and mid-twentieth century, studies referred to kinship that was not sealed in blood as "fictive kinship." During the revitalization of kinship studies through the 1980s, however, this term was critiqued as overly influenced by Western presumptions about kinship. In anthropol-

---

89. Carsten, *After Kinship*, 138.

90. See, for example, Sahlins, *What Kinship Is*, 65, 87.

91. Sahlins, *What Kinship Is*, 74–86.

92. Sahlins, *What Kinship Is*, 5–6, citing Francesca Merlan and Alan Rumsey, *Ku Waru: Language and Segmentary Politics in the Western Nebilyer Valley, Papua New Guinea* (Cambridge: Cambridge University Press, 1991).

93. Carsten, *After Kinship*, 44.

94. Carsten, *After Kinship,* 139, citing Mary Weismantel, "Making Kin: Kinship Theory and Zumbagua Adoptions," *AmE* 22 (1995): 693.

95. Sahlins, *What Kinship Is*, 29, 71; Carsten, *After Kinship*, 149.

ogy, it is now agreed that there are many ways by which kinship is constructed across cultures and that these are not mere metaphors for kinship. Rather, they may be equally meaningful as genetic associations or even more meaningful. In light of these insights, the term "adoptive kinship" is now preferred. Sahlins argues that, "all [of these] means of constituting kinship are in essence the same."[96]

### 1.3.2.5. Mutable and Adaptable *Ethnicity*

Schneider's monumental study of American kinship has emphasized how kinship functions as a system of symbols and meanings. He discerns, thereby, how American kinship is experienced with a high degree of correspondence across a number of cultural domains, namely, the family, the nation, religion, and perhaps education. These domains are structured by the same terms: "motherland," "fatherland," the "founding fathers," and so forth. To illustrate, Schneider observes parallels between the two primary ways in which nationality may be constituted, either by birth or by naturalization, and the two primary elements that constitute familial Western kinship, birth and in-law.[97] While Schneider's observation of the process of "naturalization" is notable for this study, even more important is his observation of how ethnicity functions as a social construct. Ethnicity is not natural or fixed as is commonly conceived. In line with the observed malleability of local-kinship, a crucial insight of cultural studies has been the concept of "racial formation." Over against the view that ethnicity is "a homology between a culture, a people, or a nation and its particular terrain,"[98] it is observed that ethnicity is "defined and contested throughout society."[99] Michael Omi and Howard Winant state:

> Racial categories themselves are formed, transformed, destroyed and reformed. We use the term *racial formation* to refer to the process by which social, economic and political forces determine the content and

---

96. Sahlins, *What Kinship Is*, 29.

97. Schneider, "What Is Kinship All About," 263–64.

98. Smadar Lavie and Ted Swedenburg, "Introduction: Displacement, Diaspora, and Geographies of Identity," in *Displacement, Diaspora, and Geographies of Identity*, ed. Smadar Lavie and Ted Swedenburg (Durham: Duke University Press, 1996), 1.

99. Michael Omi and Howard Winant, *Racial Formation in the United States: From the 1960s to the 1990s* (New York: Routledge and Kegan Paul, 1986), 61–62.

importance of racial categories, and by which they are in turn shaped by racial meanings.[100]

Conceiving of ethnicity as a process makes space for cultural concepts such as hybridization, a process of a blending of host and diasporic cultures, and creolization, the intermix of cultures in order to produce new identities.[101] These dynamics are observable in biblical law. Consider, for example, Jethro the Midianite's well-known instructions on public offices in Israel (Exod 19:1–27). Lesser known is the adoption of Jethro's advice within the law of offices and the judiciary in Deut 1:8–18.[102]

In this study, by conceiving of kinship and ethnicity as a process, we may encounter not only imaginative ways of incorporating the gēr within Israel but also the inclusion of the "other" as constitutive for what it means to be/become Israel. The gēr himself or herself may contest and define what it means to be/become Israel. With this possibility in mind, crucial to this investigation will be the question of how ethnicity and religion interrelate and the relationship between external religious boundary markers and internal boundary markers (see especially §§5.10 and 5.11).

### 1.3.2.6. Multiple Corresponding Cultural Domains for Kinship

Schneider's conception of kinship within corresponding cultural domains raises the question of various cultural domains, or levels, of kinship in Deuteronomy. Much of the scholarship on the gēr considers ethnicity in exclusively national categories.[103] "Israel" is a clearly defined group in the eyes of all actors and the primary identification of the members of the community is as "Israel," yielding a simple binary distinction: Israel/not-Israel. However, race and ethnicity theory have interrogated such essentialist conceptions of ethnicity, providing a corrective lens for exegesis.[104] Theorists have observed the influence of colonialism upon the tendency in

---

100. Omi and Wimant, *Racial Formation*, 61. Nestor has applied theory on racial formation to biblical studies (*Cognitive Perspectives*, 192–215).

101. Paul Gilroy, *The Black Atlantic: Modernity and Double Consciousness* (Cambridge, MA: Harvard University Press, 1993), 2; Lavie and Swedenburg, "Introduction," 7–8.

102. See the exegesis of Deut 1:16–17 in §4.2.

103. Bultmann, *Fremde*, and Na'aman, "Sojourners," are notable exceptions.

104. For a definition of "race" and "ethnicity," see Ralph E. Rodriguez, "Race and Ethnicity," in *The Johns Hopkins Guide to Literary Theory and Criticism*, ed. Michael

Western culture to view societies in terms of an "absolute sense of ethnic difference."[105] Colonialism went hand-in-hand with a binary logic: "'They' were supposed to be 'there' and 'we' were supposed to be 'here.'"[106] "Such binaries radically distinguished as well as hierarchized 'home' and 'abroad,' the West and the Orient, the center and the margin, and the subject of study and the disciplinary object of study."[107] This historical essentializing impulse has, in some cases, become the uninterrogated method for analysis of the *gēr*. The *gēr* is considered within a "binaristic linear narrative"[108] of *Israel* and the *foreigner*. For example, Awabdy consistently translates the term אח, "brother-sister," as "countryman," projecting a simple binary opposition between an Israelite and a non-Israelite *gēr*. However, as Lothar Perlitt has demonstrated, "brother" in Deuteronomy varies in its reference, signifying kinship connection at a variety of social levels, including at the clan level.[109] This study will investigate the possibility that an "Israelite" may have identified herself or himself as belonging at a number of social levels. We will also inquire into whether an "Israelite" may have identified with the extended family or a clan just as strongly or even more strongly than with the nation. We will inquire, in turn, about whether a person who was from another clan/settlement may have been considered just as much an outsider as a non-Israelite. Finally, building upon Schneider's work, we will be alert to the possibility that there may be a coherence in Deuteronomy's conception of kinship across corresponding cultural domains, namely, the "nation," the clan, and the household.

### 1.3.2.7. The Present Investigation

Scholarship on the *gēr* in Deuteronomy has sought to discern the spheres in which the *gēr* should be included within the community and also the degree of such inclusion. A key question in the scholarship, for example,

---

Groden, Martin Kreiswirth, and Imre Szeman, 2nd ed. (Baltimore: Johns Hopkins University Press, 2005), 788–89.

105. Gilroy, *Black Atlantic*, 3.

106. Lavie and Swedenburg, "Introduction," 1.

107. Lavie and Swedenburg, "Introduction," 1.

108. Lavie and Swedenburg, "Introduction," 5.

109. Lothar Perlitt, "Ein einzig Volk von Brüdern," in *Deuteronomium-Studien*, FAT 8 (Tübingen: Mohr Siebeck, 1994), 50–73. See also the extensive analysis of אח in this study, at §4.2.3.

has been whether Deuteronomy's various redactions required that the *gēr* be included either socially or religiously.[110] While not ignoring these questions, this study will examine Deuteronomy through the lens of kinship, not simply as an alternative sphere for inclusion (vis-à-vis the social and religious sphere), but as a key social institution, the comprehension of which should shift our view of Deuteronomy's goals entirely. In a seminal study on kinship, Carsten reflects upon the imagination and creativity that people invest in new possibilities for kinship: "I take it as fundamental that creativity is not only central to kinship conceived in its broadest sense, but that for most people kinship constitutes one of the most important arenas for their creative energy." She continues: "It is, among other things, an area of life in which people invest their emotions, their creative energy, and their new imaginings. These of course can take both benevolent and destructive forms … kinship involves not just rights, rules, and obligations but is also a realm of new possibilities.[111] The creativity that Deuteronomy may invest in order to nourish the enfolding of displaced and vulnerable people as kindred is of particular interest for this study.

### 1.3.3. Dating the Law Corpus

In order to proceed using an integrative hermeneutic, it will be helpful to outline some contours for dating the DC. A consensus exists among critical scholars that the DC represents an original Deuteronomic layer (hereafter Dtn), though scholars differ as to exactly which texts and phrases constitute this layer.[112] Wellhausen distinguished between Urdt, which comprised the law code of Deut 12–26 and a twofold frame: Deut 1–4, 27 and 5–11, 28–30; this distinction remains key to the present scholarly

---

110. Some examples of this common approach are: Crouch, *Making of Israel*, 219; Ebach, *Fremde*, 312; Awabdy, *Immigrants*, 122–23.

111. Carsten, *After Kinship*, 9.

112. Otto suggests 6:4–5; 12:13–27; 13:2–12; 14:22–15:23; 16:1–17; 16:18–18:5; 19:2–13, 15–21, 23; 22:1–12, 13–29; 23:16–26; 24:1–4, 6; 25:4, 5–10, 11–12; 26:2–13, 20–44; see Eckhart Otto, "The History of the Legal-Religious Hermeneutics of the Book of Deuteronomy from the Assyrian to the Hellenistic Period," in *Law and Religion in the Eastern Mediterranean*, ed. Anselm C. Hagedorn, and Reinhard G. Kratz (Oxford: Oxford University Press, 2013), 213–14. See also, Karel van der Toorn, *Scribal Culture and the Making of the Hebrew Bible* (Cambridge: Harvard University Press, 2007), 150–52; Reinhard Kratz, *The Composition of the Narrative Books of the Old Testament*, trans. J. Bowden (London: T&T Clark, 2005), 126.

discussion.[113] For Wellhausen, the primary aim of Urdt is the centralization of worship.[114] However, in chapter 5, I will demonstrate that Dtn's goals cannot be reduced solely to this, for Dtn concerns nothing less than the renewal of the family of Yahweh. Dtn references the *gēr* in the feasting texts (14:22–29, 16:1–17) and in various social laws (24:14–15, 17, 19–21; compare these with 23:16–17).

Reinhard Kratz suggests three criteria for determining Dtn texts, the *Numerusweschel* (the law corpus is composed in the second person singular), centralization, and a relation to the CC. Kratz asserts that the presence of all three criteria identifies a text as Dtn.[115] To be sure, these three criteria are relevant, yet the results are not so clear, for, deliberate reuse of formulas and of lexical and syntactical fields abounds in Deuteronomy's redactions. Further, later redactions may revise the CC in fresh ways (see the exegesis of 5:12–15). As a further indicator, the absence of P material characterizes Dtn and Dtr texts; P material may be incorporated into post-Dtr texts.[116] Historical criteria are also relevant. For example, on the basis of the relation of Deut 28 and of various family laws in the DC to the Vassal Treaty of Esarhaddon and Middle Assyrian Laws, Otto dates an original Deuteronomic core to the range of 672–612 BCE.[117] We will explore another potential distinction between the DC and the

---

113. For a detailed discussion of the date of the DC, see Peter Altmann, *Festive Meals in Ancient Israel: Deuteronomy's Identity Politics in Their Ancient Near Eastern Context*, BZAW 424 (Berlin: de Gruyter, 2011), 5–15.

114. Julius Wellhausen, *Prolegomena to the History of Israel: With a Reprint of the Article* Israel *From the Encyclopedia Britannica* (New York: Meridian, 1957), 76. See more recently Bernard M. Levinson, *Deuteronomy and the Hermeneutics of Legal Innovation* (New York: Oxford University Press, 1997).

115. Kratz, *Composition*, 132.

116. Lothar Perlitt, "Priesterschrift im Deuteronomium," *ZAW* 100 Supp 1 (1988): 65–88; repr. as pages 123–43 in *Deuteronomium-Studien*; Nihan, *From Priestly Torah*, 20–58, esp. 20–30.

117. Eckart Otto, *Das Deuteronomium: Politische Theologie und Rechtsreform in Juda und Assyrien* (Berlin: de Gruyter, 1999), 6. Though, Alexander Rofé defends a pre-eighth century date for the original text of much of the frame; see Rofé, "The Covenant in the Land of Moab (Deuteronomy 28:69–30:20): Historico-Literary, Comparative and Formcritical Considerations," in *Das Deuteronomium: Entstehung, Gestalt und Botschaft*, ed. N. Lohfink, BETL 68 (Leuven: Leuven University Press, 1985), 310–20; repr. in *A Song of Power and the Power of Song: Essays on the Book of Deuteronomy*, ed. Duane L. Christensen (Winona Lake, IN: Eisenbrauns, 1993), 269–80. See further, §§4.9 and 6.1.1.

framework of Deuteronomy, namely, that the DC fosters the incorporation of the *gēr* within a household and a clan, while the framework of
Deuteronomy fosters the incorporation of the *gēr* within Israel. Otto's
assertion is apropos: "The Dtn reform program is a response to the social
upheavals caused by the Assyrian crisis and the consequent uprooting
of many individuals."[118] Critical scholarship generally assigns the framework of Deuteronomy (Deut 1–11, 27–34) to the various redactions that
are broadly categorized as Deuteronomistic (hereafter Dtr) and as post-
Deuteronomistic (hereafter post-Dtr).[119] Some key characteristics of the
redactions within Deuteronomy's framework are examined in §6.1.1.

This study will categorize various texts as Dtn, Dtr, and post-Dtr
(listed from earliest to latest). It will also categorize some material as pre-
Dtr (these texts come between Dtn and Dtr). It will probe apparent differences in the treatment of the *gēr* in each of these redactional layers. The
study will propose possible dating scenarios for these layers on the basis
of the analysis, also offering hypotheses regarding the social-historical
situations of displacement that the text may be addressing. As a whole,
this study contributes to a new and potentially fruitful approach to dating
Deuteronomy, on the basis of economic and social history.[120]

### 1.3.4. Legal Revision

Some comments concerning legal revision will be helpful as we set out to
investigate the *gēr* in Deuteronomy using an integrative hermeneutic. There
is a consensus within historical-critical scholarship that the DC revises the
CC in order to address the particular circumstances "in front of the text,"
according to its particular goals.[121] Further, scholarship has long observed
that legal revision was characteristic of the ancient Near Eastern law corpora.
A number of scholars have contributed significantly to our understanding

---

118. Otto, "גֵּר," 15:382. For further differentiation between Dtn, Dtr, and post-
Dtr texts see Otto, *Politische Theologie,* 203–378.

119. See Otto, "History of the Legal-Religious," for an explanation of Dtr and of
post-Dtr.

120. See §3.9. Other examples of this approach are Na'aman, "Sojourners"; Axel
Ernst Knauf, "Observations on Judah's Social and Economic History and the Dating of
the Laws of Deuteronomy," *JHS* 9 (2009): 2–8.

121. See Konrad Schmidt, *The Old Testament: A Literary History,* trans. Linda M.
Maloney (Minneapolis: Fortress, 2012), 97–98.

of the process of legal revision by analyzing the various recessions of ancient Near Eastern legal texts, and this work has demonstrated that the redaction techniques displayed in ancient Near Eastern law corpora are similar to the redaction techniques applied to Israelite law.[122] It would seem, on the basis both of internal indicators and also the evolution of those ancient Near Eastern texts for which we have various redactions in our possession (such as Gilgamesh), that Deuteronomy has developed in a few major stages rather than by many minor accretions.[123]

Of course, if the opposite were true of biblical law, were it unchanging, this would suggest that the relevance of the law for a particular society was unimportant—for a society, that is, other than that of the original audience. "They were continuously changing laws ... because they were a mirror of ever changing life in human society."[124] Indeed, this is the case with legislation in the modern world.

The Pentateuch preserves the older law (the CC) together with its revision (the DC). Levinson and others posit an antithetical relationship between the DC and the CC, contending that the authors of the DC intended to gain legitimation for the DC as authoritative law by presenting it as an authentic revision of the CC, all the while subversively *displacing* the CC with radically different goals.[125] Otto, among others, has responded that the DC is not intended as a replacement of the CC but is to be read alongside the CC.[126] I will consider the ways in which the DC not only appropriates the stipulations of the CC for its new context but also assumes the regulations of the CC, in a complex legal dialogue between the various redactions.[127]

---

122. See David Carr, *The Formation of the Hebrew Bible* (New York: Oxford University Press, 2011), 37–101; Otto, "Aspects of Legal Reforms"; Jeffrey H. Tigay, *The Evolution of the Gilgamesh Epic* (Philadelphia: University of Pennsylvania Press, 1982). James W. Watts, *Reading Law: The Rhetorical Shape of the Pentateuch* (Sheffield: Sheffield Academic, 1999), observes that the process of legal innovation is explicit in certain places within the Hebrew Bible itself. In Lev 24, "the case of the half-Israelite blasphemer prompts Yahweh to enunciate a new legal principle, 'you shall have one law for the alien and for the citizen: for I am Yahweh your God'" (Watts, *Reading*, 104).

123. Carr, *Formation*, 145; Van der Toorn, *Scribal Culture*, 149.

124. Otto, "Aspects of Legal Reforms," 196.

125. Levinson, *Deuteronomy and the Hermeneutics*, 145–46.

126. E.g., Otto, "History of the Legal-Religious," 218–19.

127. Similarly, Otto, "History of the Legal-Religious," 220.

Further, Deuteronomy's later redactions translate the received Deuteronomic tradition for a new context.[128] So, a common religious and ethical thread runs through the various redactions of Deuteronomy. Given that legal revision is a part of the character of biblical law and that various stages of legal development stand alongside each other in the Hebrew Bible, a cautious reconstruction of composition history contributes toward a full picture of the message of Deuteronomy regarding the *gēr*.[129]

## 1.4. Outline of the Work

The balance of this study probes Deuteronomy's ethic regarding the *gēr*. It examines the specifics of this ethic by focussing in on three subgroups of law (chs. 3–5) and then by examining Deuteronomy's framework (ch. 6). Each reference to the *gēr* in Deuteronomy is examined in detail, and broader concerns are explored within the textual analysis. Chapter 3 considers the ways in which social law may protect and also enfold displaced people. Chapter 4 investigates the ways in which law of judicial procedure may enable the *gēr* to participate in the social and economic life of the community. Chapter 5 examines instructions concerning feasting and tithing, considering how cultic feasting may foster the grafting in of the *gēr* as kindred into a household and into a clan. Chapter 6 investigates how the framework of Deuteronomy (Deut 1–11, 27–34) may foster the incorporation of the *gēr* within the kinship grouping of Israel and of her divine kinsperson.

## 1.5. Conclusion

In order to investigate an ethic of inclusivism for the *gēr* as found in Deuteronomy, I will adopt an integrative methodology that brings together legal, social-scientific, comparative, literary, theological, social-historical, and literary-historical approaches. The analysis of the text will be sensitive

---

128. Similarly Ebach (*Fremde*, 314) states: "Das deuteronomische Gesetz bildet die vorexilische Grundlage des Deuteronomiums. Alle weiteren Textpassagen setzen neue Akzente, behalten jedoch das ältere Gesetz bei und setzen sich kommentierend mit diesem auseinander" ("The Deuteronomic law forms the basis of preexilic Deuteronomy. All other texts set new accents but keep the old law, operating as commentary on the old law").

129. See further Otto, "Aspects of Legal Reforms," 192.

to dynamics of kinship, with an awareness of the mutability of kinship across cultures, as explained by cultural anthropology.

The following chapter begins to clarify the meaning of *gēr* in Deuteronomy by examining cognates of *gr* and by observing the diverse meanings of *gēr* in the Pentateuch.

# 2

# *GR*: Cognates and Use in Other Texts

This brief chapter moves toward clarifying the meaning of *gēr* in Deuteronomy. It first explores cognates of *gr* and then examines the diffuse meanings of *gēr* in the law corpora of the Pentateuch.

## 2.1. Cognates to *Gēr*

We begin by examining cognates of *gr*. Akkadian *gērû* has the sense of "foe, adversary,"[1] and Akkadian *girru* is related to journeying.[2] The association of foreignness with hostility may relate these two meanings.[3] Northwest Semitic cognates are more closely associated with the use of *gēr* in the Hebrew Bible. The distinction between lexical meaning and contextual meaning is critical for the following analysis of Northwest Semitic cognates of *gēr*. Following Johannes P. Louw, the lexical meaning of a word describes what the word in and of itself contributes to the sense of a phrase in which it is used. The contextual meaning of the word, on the other hand, is determined largely by the information provided in the context in which the word is used. "It is extremely important in semantics to determine what comes from a lexical item and what comes from the context."[4]

### 2.1.1. The Moabite Inscription (*KAI* 1.181.16)

The use of *gr* in the inscription of the Moabite king Mesha is significant both for the use of the feminine form (alongside the masculine), which does not occur in the Hebrew Bible, and for its use in a list (compare this

---

1. *CAD* 5, s.v. "gērû."
2. *CAD* 5, s.v. "girru."
3. Kellerman, "גּוּר‎," 2:440.
4. P. Louw, "How Do Words Mean—If They Do?," *EFN* 4 (1991): 133.

with the household list in Deuteronomy, 16:11, 14). The text lists categories of people who make up the seven thousand killed in King Mesha's
conquest of נבה, Nebo, and dates to around 835 BCE.[5]

שבעת אלף ג[ב]ר וגרן וגברת וג[ר]ת ורחמת
>seven thousand men and women, both natives and aliens, and female
>slaves[6]

Gibson reasons that (ת)גר refers to non-Israelite persons on the basis
that רחמת signals that the list deals with social categories.[7] Aḥituv's
interpretation of (ת)גר as "boy/girl" on the basis of "lion-cub" seems
less likely given the presence of the Hebrew term *gēr* in similar lists in
the Hebrew Bible (e.g., Deut 5:14) and given the text's interest in enu-
merating social categories.[8] The text describes the population within the
general area of the walled settlement of נבה. The seven thousand men
and women likely came from numerous settlements,[9] and these were
likely rural, kinship based communities. The population is portrayed
with broad brushstrokes, using just three categories. In light of the clan-
based structure of rural settlements, (ת)גר probably refers to people who
are nonnative in the sense of being outside of the traditional clan based
kinship groupings and who therefore dwell as clients or dependents of
some kind. Identity and displacement here is at the clan level rather than
the nation.[10] So *gr* in the Mesha inscription corresponds somewhat to
the use of *gēr* in Deuteronomy.

---

5. "The Inscription of King Mesha," trans. K. A. D. Smelik, *COS* 2.23:137–38.

6. *KAI* 1.181.16; trans. by John C. L. Gibson, *Hebrew and Moabite Inscriptions*,
vol. 1 of *Textbook of Syrian Semitic Inscriptions*, 2nd ed., 3 vols. (London: Oxford University Press, 1971), 76.

7. Gibson, *Hebrew and Moabite Inscriptions*, 80–81.

8. Shmuel Aḥituv, *Echoes from the Past: Hebrew and Cognate Inscriptions from the
Biblical Period* (Jerusalem: Carta, 2008), 394, 409.

9. See Andrew Dearman, "Historical Reconstruction and the Mesha Inscription,"
in *Studies in the Mesha Inscription*, ed. Andrew Dearman (Atlanta: Scholars Press,
1989), 180–81.

10. *KAI* rigtly translates (ת)גר as client (2.181.16). The clan-based kinship grouping of rural settlements is discussed in §5.5.1. The *DNWSI* reflects the interpretation
given here (see DNWSI, s.v. "gr," 232).

## 2.1.2. Phoenician (*KAI* 1.37.A16, B10)

*Gr* appears in a Phoenician text detailing temple rations for temple workers and oblates. The relevant line appears identically on both sides of the tablet:[11]

לכלבם ולגרם קר 3 ופא 3

For the temple pederast and the client, three QR and three P'.

The context suggests that the *gr* is a temple client of some kind. The interpretation of *gr* as a temple prostitute is also possible given the immediate context.[12] Their status, whether free, semifree, or unfree, is unclear. Within a different Phoenician inscription, a personal name, גר מלקרת, demonstrates the use of *gr* with the sense of a client of a deity.[13]

## 2.1.3. Ugaritic

A variety of references for *gr* appear in Ugaritic texts. *Gr* occurs with the sense of tarrying in a foreign town in the myth of King Keret: *w gr . nn . 'rm . šrn*.[14] In the legend of Aqhat, the son of Dan'el is referred to as *gr* as he dwells in his death in the submarine abode of El.[15] *Brḥ* is parallel to *gr* in the following line, with the sense "fugitive."[16] A third occurrence of *gr* in Ugaritic clearly refers to foreigners within a ritual text of atonement that is discussed in more detail below:

*w ṯb . l mspr . m[š]r . bt . ủgrt. w npy . gr*

---

11. *KAI* 1.37.A16, B10.

12. A. van den Branden, "Notes Phéniciennes," *BMB* 13 (1956): 92.

13. G. A. Cooke, *A Textbook of North-Semitic Inscriptions: Moabite, Hebrew, Phoenician, Aramaic, Nabataean, Palmyrene, Jewish* (Oxford: Clarendon, 1903), 63; *CIS* 1.47.

14. *KTU* 1.14:iii:6 = *RS* 3.414 = *RS* 3.344 = *RS* 3.324. Following John C. L. Gibson, *Canaanite Myths and Legends*, 2nd ed. (London: T&T Clark, 2004), 85. Gibson notes the possible translation, *garû*, "attack the villages" (85 n. 3).

15. *KTU* 1.19:iii:47 = *RS* 3.366 = *RS* 3.349 = *RS* 3.325 = *RS* 3.322. Here I follow Baruch Margalit, "Lexiographical Notes on the AQHT Epic (Part II: *KTU* 1.10)," *UF* 16 (1984): 156.

16. Gregorio del Olmo Lete and Joaquín Sanmartín, *A Dictionary of the Ugaritic Language in the Alphabetic Tradition*, 2 vols., HOS 67 (Leiden: Brill, 2003), 1:236.

> And to return to the recitation of "rec[tit]ude": rectitude of the daughter
> of Ugarit: and well-being of the foreigner.[17]

Finally, in a partially preserved administrative text *gr* may refer to a client
of some kind, although this is uncertain: *k gr . pr*[…].[18]

## 2.1.4. Other Languages and Dialects

A Palmyrene inscription demonstrates that *gr* may mean "host" (as well
as guest or client) in some dialects.[19] In Ethiopic, the verb *gwr* has the
sense "to dwell together in a neighbourly way, to live in the vicinity." The
Ethiopic noun *gōr* has the sense "neighbor" or "neighborhood."[20] Closer to
the Hebrew Bible, de Vaux observes that *jar* in Arabic was "the refugee or
lone man who came seeking the protection of a tribe other than his own."[21]

## 2.1.5. Conclusions from Cognates

It is instructive to return to the discussion of semantics at this point. Consider the four examples from Ugarit. Each of these four contexts requires a
different translation for *gr*. Nonetheless, a common lexical meaning seems
to hold in all cases: the *gr* is operating in a sphere outside of his or her kinship grouping or circle of affiliation. Thus while the term *gr* may be translated with various glosses, such as "fugitive," "tarrying one," "foreigner,"
or "client," these meanings are only possible where the context supplies
additional information.[22] These various translations are not basic to the
lexical meaning of the term *gr*. The term *gr* in and of itself simply refers to
the quality of a person as an outsider. The common element in the use of *gr*
in the various Northwest Semitic dialects discussed above is the sense of a
subject's dwelling or working as an outsider, without a natural connection

---

17. *KTU* 1.40.35 = *RS* 1.002 = *UT* 2. Transliteration and translation taken from
Dennis Pardee, "The Structure of RS 1.002," in *Semitic Studies in Honor of Wolf Leslau*,
ed. A. S. Kayne, 2 vols. (Wiesbaden: Harrassowitz, 1991), 2:1187. Two characters in
the text are uncertain. *Gr* appears in a similar context in lines 18 and 26.

18. *KTU* 7.31 = *KTU* 4.28 = *RS* 2.[028].

19. Cooke, *Textbook*, 304–5. For other citations see *DNWSI*, s.v. "gr," 232.

20. Wolf Leslau, *Comparative Dictionary of Ge'ez (Classical Ethiopic)* (Wiesbaden:
Harrossowitz, 1991), 207.

21. De Vaux, *Ancient Israel*, 74.

22. Louw, "How Do Words Mean," 136–37.

to the kinship grouping or context.[23] In this light, Hoftijzer's delimitation of *gr*[1] ("client") and *gr*[2] ("resident alien") in Northwest Semitic is a valid delimitation only in terms of contextual meaning or usage, not in lexical meaning.[24]

These observations about Northwest Semitic cognates may help to clear a number of blockages in the scholarly discussion of *gēr* in the Hebrew Bible. First, foreignness is not by any means germane to the lexical meaning of *gr* in Northwest Semitic cognates. While many scholars hold that the *gēr* in Deuteronomy was a non-Israelite, cognates of *gēr* in Northwest Semitic texts suggest that foreignness is not germane to the lexical meaning of the word. Comparative analysis suggests that *gēr* has the capacity to refer to various levels of displacement. It is the context that is determinative. The social level at which displacement occurs is clarified by the context rather than by the term *gr* itself. So, in a temple text the *gr* may have relocated from outside of the temple household. In a cultic context the *gr* may be of another ethnicity and deity. In an urban context the *gr* may be a foreigner. In a rural context the *gr* may be from the village located over the next hill. Significantly, both the non-Israelite within Israel and the internally displaced Judahite are located outside of the kinship associations of their new context.

This point is pertinent for the analysis of the *gēr* in a holiness text in Deuteronomy just discussed (Deut 14:21, see §3.8). On the one hand, this study argues that *gēr* in Deuteronomy should be translated with the gloss "dependent outsider," referring in part to a person who is displaced at the level of the clan. On the other hand, in 14:21 the *gēr* may be non-Israelite,[25] and *gēr* here could be translated with the gloss "vulnerable foreigner." This is a difference in contextual meaning rather than in lexical meaning. These observations also cast new light upon the various uses of *gēr* across the law corpora of the Pentateuch. As I will observe, in the HC *gēr* most often refers to a foreigner of independent means. Contrary to the common

---

23. I am not here arguing for a "core meaning" for *gr* in Northwest Semitic dialects, nor am I making an argument from etymology. For the methodological problems with these approaches, see Louw, "How Do Words Mean," 129; James Barr, *The Semantics of Biblical Language* (Oxford: Oxford University Press, 1961), 107–60. Rather, I am making a tentative generalized observation upon the lexical meaning of *gr* on the basis of usage in extant Northwest Semitic texts.

24. *DNWSI*, s.v. "gr," 232.

25. See the analysis of Deut 14:21 in §3.8.

assumption that this sense entails a different lexical definition for *gēr* to that in Deuteronomy,[26] these may be differences in contextual meaning rather than lexical meaning. Further clarity on the meaning of *gēr* will be attained throughout this study through observation of semantic markers in the contexts where the term occurs.

## 2.2. The *Gēr* in the Law Corpora of the Pentateuch

To define *gēr* in Deuteronomy, we must trace the shifting reference of the term in the law codes of the Pentateuch. Entire monographs have been compromised by a failure to discern these changes. For example, Van Houten's "flat" reading of *gēr* in the Pentateuch discerns an increasing inclusivism through the historical development of the law codes.[27] However, her observations are more correctly explained by the shifting definition of the term *gēr*. Therefore, we shall now cursorily observe the identity of the *gēr* and the stipulations concerning her or him in the law codes of the Pentateuch, in the order of their likely literary development.

### 2.2.1. The *Gēr* in the CC

The *gēr* appears four times in the CC (Exod 22:20; 23:9 [2x], 12), which is considered by most scholars to precede the DC and the HC.[28] In the CC the term *gēr* refers to a displaced person who is also a dependant in a new context, as in the DC. The *gēr* is associated with the אלמנה ויתום (Exod 22:20–23), but the triad גר יתום ואלמנה does not appear until the DC. The structuring of the laws signifies the import of ethics regarding the *gēr* for the CC. The *gēr* forms an inclusion that brackets a group of laws concerning the protection of the vulnerable (22:20–23:9).[29] The CC stipulates that the *gēr* may not be oppressed (22:20). The *gēr* is protected in

---

26. E.g., Bultmann, *Fremde*, 212–16.

27. Van Houten, *Alien in Israelite Law*, 164.

28. Eckart Otto, *Wandel der Rechsbegründungen in der Gesellschaftsgeschichte des antiken Israel: eine Rechtsgeschichte des "Bundesbuches" Ex XX 22–XXIII 13*, StudBib 3 (Leiden: Brill, 1988), 49–51; Crüsemann, *Torah*, 215.

29. Reinhard Achenbach, "*Gêr – nåkhrî – tôshav – zâr*: Legal and Sacral Distinctions Regarding Foreigners in the Pentateuch," in *The Foreigner and the Law: Perspectives from the Hebrew Bible and the Ancient Near East*, ed. Reinhard Achenbach, Rainer Albertz, and Jakob Wöhrle, BZABR 16 (Wiesbaden: Harrassowitz, 2011), 30; Lohfink, "Poverty," 40–41; Otto, *Wandel*, 38–44.

judicial proceedings (23:6–9), and the Sabbath law dignifies the *gēr* along with the household by giving the *gēr* rest from labor (23:12; cf. 20:10). The protective social and religious inclusion of the *gēr* within a household and village that characterizes the DC has not yet emerged. Thus in the CC the *gēr* is not mentioned in relation to the festivals (23:14–17), and certain key phrases that form Deuteronomy's semantics of integration are missing, such as בשעריך, גרו, גרך, and בקרבך.[30] Nonetheless, given the prominence of the *gēr* in the CC, it seems likely that widespread displacement was already a social reality at the time that the CC was produced.

## 2.2.2. The *Gēr* in the DC

The noun *gēr* appears twenty-two times in Deuteronomy, with thirteen of these occurrences in the DC. As with the CC, in Deuteronomy the term *gēr* consistently refers to a person who is both displaced and also dependent in a new context. Thus Deuteronomy offers by far the most extensive treatment of displaced persons in the Hebrew Bible (*gēr* in the HC has a different reference, as we shall see). It is generally accepted that the DC appropriates and revises the CC for its new context and purposes.[31]

## 2.2.3. The *Gēr* in the HC

The *gēr* appears as a prominent figure in the HC (Lev 17–26), and the noun *gēr* occurs twenty times within these ten chapters.[32] The noun appears thirteen more times in what has been called the "holiness redaction"[33] and twice more in other Priestly material.[34] According to the critical scholarly consensus, the HC is a revision of the DC for an exilic or a postexilic context.[35] Albertz and others bring precision to an analysis of the *gēr* in the

---

30. The phrase בשעריך is discussed at §5.5.2; גרך at §3.3.5; ובקרבך at §5.3.3.2.

31. The DC's revision of the CC is discussed in §§1.3.3 and 1.3.4. See also L. Schwienhorst-Schönberger, *Das Bundesbuch (Ex 20, 22—23, 33): Studien zu seiner Enstehung und Theologie*, BZAW 188 (Berlin: de Gruyter, 1990), 288–414; Otto, "History of the Legal-Religious," 212–23.

32. Lev 17:8, 10, 12, 13, 15; 18:26; 19:10, 33, 34 (2x); 20:2; 22:28; 23:22; 24:16, 22; 25:23, 35; 47 (3x).

33. Exod 12:19, 48, 49; Lev 16:29; Num 9:14 (2x); 15:14, 15 (2x), 16, 26, 29, 30. On the "Holiness Stratum," see Nihan, *From Priestly Torah*, 569–72.

34. Num 19:10, 35:15.

35. Jeffery Stackert, *Rewriting the Torah: Literary Revision in Deuteronomy and*

HC by clearly distinguishing between two meanings of the term occurring in the HC and in the holiness redaction.[36] The less common meaning of *gēr* in the HC references displaced and dependent people, reflecting the usage in the CC and the DC. It is with this less common meaning that the HC commands Israel to "love the stranger as yourself" (Lev 19:33–34), which is parallel to the command to "love your neighbor as yourself" (Lev 19:18). This stipulation is reminiscent of, and probably also dependent upon, a similar expression in the DC (Deut 10:18–19). The gleaning laws (Lev 19:9–10, 23:22) similarly are parallel to and probably dependent upon similar laws in the DC (24:19–22). The social signification of the term *gēr*, however, is no longer dominant in the HC, for "the poverty of the resident aliens seems to be no longer the main problem."[37]

The second and dominant use of *gēr* is new with the HC. This figure is not a dependent.[38] The *gēr* is not seeking a clan or a household to belong to. The *gēr* may be of some means, including possibly owning Israelite slaves (Lev 25:35–38; cf. 17:8, 22:18).[39] The HC is particularly concerned with the proper participation of this figure in the cultus (17:8, 10, 12, 13; 20:2; 22:18; 24:16). The term *gēr* is paired with the term אזרח, and this pairing generally emphasizes what the *gēr* and the אזרח have in common.[40] Both equally are subject to blasphemy laws (24:16), and both may be defiled, according to purity laws (17:15, 18:26). Nonetheless, while there are efforts to live in social and religious harmony with the *gēr* in the HC, Albertz represents the consensus when he writes: "It was not the wish to integrate aliens into the 'people of God' as much as

---

the Holiness Legislation, FAT 52 (Tübingen: Mohr Siebeck, 2007), 114–15; Christophe Nihan, "Resident Aliens and Natives in the Holiness Legislation," in *The Foreigner and the Law: Perspectives from the Hebrew Bible and the Ancient Near East*, ed. Reinhard Achenbach, Rainer Albertz, and Jakob Wöhrle, BZAR 16 (Wiesbaden: Harrassowitz, 2011), 111–34.

36. Albertz, "From Aliens to Proselytes," 57–58; Nihan, "Resident Aliens," 112; Jan Joosten, *People and the Land in the Holiness Code: An Exegetical Study of the Ideational Framework of the Law in Leviticus 17–26*, VTSup 67 (Leiden: Brill, 1996), 54–72.

37. Albertz, "From Aliens to Proselytes," 57.

38. Rendtdorff, "Ger," 81.

39. See D. Vieweger, "Vom 'Fremdling' zum 'Proselyt': Zur sakralrechtlichen Definition des גר im späten 5. Jahrhundert v. Chr," in *Von Gott reden: Beiträge zur Theologie und Exegese des Alten Testaments; Festschrift für Siegfried Wagner zum 65. Geburtstag*, ed. D. Vieweger and E. J. Waschke (Neukirchen-Vluyn: Neukirchener, 1995), 274–75.

40. Rendtorff, "Ger," 81–82.

possible."[41] Na'aman writes that the term *gēr* referred to "a person whose membership of the religious community in the province of Yehud and in the exile was uncertain, as opposed to the citizen whose membership was unquestioned."[42] In short, the term *gēr* in the HC most commonly designates a non-Israelite, meaning outside of the Yahweh-group, who was economically independent. As observed in the preceding discussion of cognates of the term *gēr*, it is more helpful to view these differences in the use of *gēr* in the DC and in the HC as a variation in contextual meaning rather than in lexical meaning.

The *gēr* also appears in later layers. Three references to the *gēr* in the holiness redaction include the provision for and the regulation of the participation of the *gēr* in the Passover.[43] The main objective of references to the *gēr* in the later Priestly layers is "simply to include the *gēr* in all those ritual innovations that had been developed after the implementation of the Holiness Code."[44]

Further clarity on questions of translation and definition must await a close exegesis of texts relating to the *gēr*. These questions will be revisited after an examination of Deuteronomy's social law in chapter 3.

---

41. Albertz, "From Aliens to Proselytes," 62; similarly Nihan, "Resident Aliens," 112.

42. Na'aman, "Sojourners," 257.

43. Concerning later layers, see Nihan, *From Priestly Torah*, 559–75.

44. Albertz, "From Aliens to Proselytes," 64; Nihan offers a similar analysis ("Resident Aliens," 111).

# 3
# The *Gēr* in Social Law

This chapter probes the social law of Deuteronomy in order to understand the protection and inclusion of the *gēr* in this law. Speaking generally, Deuteronomy's social law is aimed to protect vulnerable people against exploitation, restraining a creditor's power to accumulate indentured workers and slaves. It addresses especially practices surrounding labor and production. This chapter will examine social law that concerns the *gēr*, being alert to three issues: Is the *gēr* included within Deuteronomy's brother-sister ethic in any way? Are there ways in which the *gēr* may also share in the gift of the land and its abundance? Do these texts in any way nourish the participation of the *gēr* within the community of Yahweh?

This chapter is the first of three that concern the *gēr* within a specific law type: social law, judicial law, and festal law. Chapter 6 then examines the *gēr* in Deuteronomy's framework (Deut 1–12, 27–34). This approach of examining laws according to the various subgroups of law is a distinctive approach within scholarship on the *gēr*. Awabdy, in a recent monograph, repudiates the validity of grouping laws, resulting in a significantly weakened analysis.[1] Distinct laws in Deuteronomy share functional, lexical, conceptual, and ethical domains. Laws within groups operate in harmony with one another, and the various groups of laws also function together to achieve the goals of Deuteronomy's social program. A part of the hermeneutical approach of this study is to inquire into the symbiotic relationship of the laws within each subgroup and between subgroups.

The present chapter begins by exploring the nature of displacement and landlessness in the ancient Near East, then explores the humanitarian character of the law corpus. There follows a detailed exegesis of texts

---

1. Awabdy, *Immigrants*, 106–7.

concerning the *gēr* in Deuteronomy's social law. Finally, in light of the exegesis, the meaning of the term *gēr* is discussed.

### 3.1. Comparative Observations: Economic Displacement and Alterity

### 3.1.1. Economic Displacement in the Ancient Near East and in Israel

Assuming the identity of the *gēr* in Deuteronomy as a displaced and vulnerable person, a number of features of ancient Near Eastern society are salient for comparative investigation: progressive land alienation, the erosion of kinship groups, and the various semifree arrangements by which vulnerable people may be bonded to a household.[2] Of course, there are limitations upon the degree to which social and economic trajectories within a Mesopotamian city-state can be correlated with those in ancient Israel. Nevertheless, the three dynamics listed above are observable in both, in differing degrees, so the comparison is illuminating. The emergence of the city-state in Mesopotamia precipitated a process of land alienation and a concentration of land ownership within the temple household, the palace household, and the private households of wealthy officials. Ignace J. Gelb suggests that in the third and early second millennium many clan groupings probably stayed intact; however, they no longer owned land, and they were thus unable to give the assistance that traditionally they had.[3] The early second millennium witnessed a shift whereby land was owned by large proprietors, and land-lease contracts proliferate for this period. Contracts of sale for the Fara and pre-Sargonic periods include both individual sellers and multiple sellers, and the latter is likely evidence of the sale of the patrimony of large kinship groupings.[4] Many clan groupings were dissolved, and "the landless poor had no option but to enter into the service of the state households."[5] The *mīšarum* decrees were a response to perva-

---

2. For this section, I am indebted to personal email correspondence with Bruce Wells.

3. Ignace J. Gelb, "Household and Family in Early Mesopotamia," in *State and Temple Economy in the Ancient Near East: Proceedings of the International Conference Organized by the Katholieke Universiteit Leuven from the 10th to the 14th of April 1978*, ed. E. Lipiński, OLA 5 (Leuven: Deptartment Orientalistiek, 1979), 56–58.

4. Gelb, "Household and Family," 68–71.

5. Ignace J. Gelb, "From Freedom to Slavery," in *Gesellschaftsklassen im Alten Zweistromland und den angrenzenden Gebeiten: XVIII; Rencontre assyriologique inter-*

sive indebtedness and land alienation,[6] as were various laws restricting the power of creditors.[7]

Many people who did not own land or other forms of capital fell prey to famine slavery and other forms of voluntary slavery.[8] As for famine slavery, an impoverished person facing starvation contracted his or her labor for a lifetime in exchange for the basic necessities of life. Also, debt slavery was a likely end for those without land and without the protection of kin in Mesopotamia. For example, Carlo Zaccagnini asserts of Nuzi, "Sales of wives, children, relatives, or oneself, due to financial duress, are a recurrent feature of the Nuzi socio-economic scene, which is characterized by an overall process of impoverishment of the peasant family groups, mainly as a result of the fiscal burden exerted by the central state apparatus."[9] It would seem that Deuteronomy's stipulations regarding the *gēr* aimed, in part, to avert the dire circumstances that could lead to voluntary or involuntary slavery (see, e.g., 14:28–29, 26:12–15, and §5.4 below).

These dynamics of land alienation and the erosion of kinship groups shed light upon the socioeconomic forces that the DC seeks to address. In Syria-Palestine, progressive land alienation characterized the Northern Kingdom in the late ninth century and Judah during the eighth century.[10] These data are relevant to our study, for the *gēr* in Deuteronomy is by definition dislocated from both land and kinship groupings. So, throughout this study we will be alert to ways in which Deuteronomy may be seeking to prevent such dislocation from occurring and, when dislocation occurs, to reinstate displaced people as full participants in the community.

---

nationale, München, 29. Juni bis 3. Juli 1970, ed. D. O. Edzard, ABAW 75 (Munich: Verlag der Bayerischen Akademie der Wissenschaften, 1972), 87.

6. Jacob J. Finkelstein, "Ammiṣaduqa's Edict and the Babylonian 'Law Codes,'" *JCS* 15 (1961): 101; Gregory Chirichigno, *Debt-Slavery in Israel and the Ancient Near East*, JSOTSup 141 (Sheffield: JSOT, 1993), 55–58.

7. E.g., Laws of Hammurabi 48, 241.

8. On famine slavery, see Raymond Westbrook, "Slave and Master in Ancient Near Eastern Law," in *Law from the Tigris to the Tiber: The Writings of Raymond Westbrook*, ed. Bruce Wells and Rachel Magdalene, 2 vols. (Winona Lake, IN: Eisenbrauns, 2009), 178–80, 189–92.

9. Carlo Zaccagnini, "Nuzi," in vol. 2 of *A History of Ancient Near Eastern Law*, ed. Raymond Westbrook, 2 vols. (Leiden: Brill, 2003), 585.

10. Rainer Kessler, *The Social History of Ancient Israel: An Introduction* (Minneapolis: Fortress, 2008), 98.

### 3.1.2. Alterity and Vulnerability

A proportion of those designated *gēr* in Deuteronomy were likely non-Israelites (see further §3.7.2). Other scholars have investigated the social and economic vulnerability of foreigners at length, so the present discussion is brief.[11] "Foreigners in the ancient Near East were in a precarious situation."[12] Foreigners had limited legal protection, and they could be enslaved against their will or even killed. The wife-sister narratives in Genesis demonstrate a foreigner's vulnerability to oppression, forced marriage, and even murder (12:10–20, 26:6–11). In some texts, disparaging speech demonstrates distain for foreigners. For example, Asshurnasirpal declares that the people of Zipermena "chirp like women" as they talk.[13] To be sure, it was in the interest of the state to protect foreign merchants, and this is treated as a matter of the utmost importance in law codes and in interstate correspondence.[14] However, this privilege would not have applied to a poor and displaced person. An Ugaritic atonement ritual is likely evidence both of a positive social norm concerning the just treatment of foreigners and also of the frequency with which that norm was violated:

> *w ṯb . l mspr . m[š]r . bt . ủgrt . w npy . gr*
> And to return to the recitation of "rec[tit]ude": rectitude of the daughter
> of Ugarit: and the well-being of the foreigner.[15]

Westbrook notes that a foreigner who was fortunate may have obtained status as a resident alien; such a figure would best correspond to the *gēr* in the HC (see §2.2.3). This would have protected a foreigner from enforced

---

11. See Awabdy, *Immigrants*, 228–37; Karel van Lerberghe and Antoon Schoors, eds., *Immigration and Emigration within the Ancient Near East: Festschrift E. Lipiński* (Leuven: Peters, 1995); Jack R. Lundbom, *Deuteronomy* (Grand Rapids: Eerdmans, 2013), 394 and citations there; Raymond Westbrook, "The Old Babylonian Term, '*naptārum*,'" *JCS* 46 (1994): 41–46.

12. Westbrook, "Slave and Master," 171; for the following, see also 174, 192.

13. V. Haas, "Die Dämonisierung des Fremden und des Feindes im Alten Orient," *RO* 41 (1980): 40.

14. E.g., Laws of Hammurabi, 5. See further Gary Beckman, "Foreigners in the Ancient Near East," *JAOS* 133 (2013): 205–7.

15. *KTU* 1.40.35 (= *RS* 1.002 = *UT* 2); transliteration and translation from Pardee, "Structure of *RS* 1.002," 1187. Two characters in the text are uncertain. *Gr* appears in a similar context in lines 18 and 26.

slavery, but it did not necessarily guarantee further provisions of social justice.[16] In this light, it is evident that Deuteronomy's provision for the *gēr* is highly unusual in the ancient world. As Elias J. Bickerman reflects, an Athenian would have been bewildered to be told that he or she had to love the metics, something that would have been demanded by the command in Deuteronomy, "you shall love the *gēr*" (10:17–19).[17]

Furthermore, we are observing that in ancient Israel people from a different clan grouping may have been seen as an "outsider." The suspicion and antagonism due to "foreigners" would certainly have been also applied to those outside of the clan grouping. As Bruce Malina observes, while norms of reciprocity determine behavior within clan groupings, it is honorable to deceive and even to murder an "outsider," since such people are considered as nonpersons.[18]

### 3.2. The Humanitarian Character of the Law Corpus

A bird's eye view of the content and the structure of the DC clarifies the remarkable humanitarian ethic of Deuteronomic law.[19] Israelite law, first appearing in the CC, is characterized by a combination of three literary types: ancient Near Eastern "statutory" law,[20] Israelite cultic law, and Israelite social law.[21] The following brief description of the literary types within the CC will go far toward establishing the character of Deuteronomic law. I follow Crüsemann in this analysis.

---

16. Westbrook, "Slave and Master," 171.

17. Elias J. Bickerman, *From Ezra to the Last of the Maccabees: Foundations of Post-Biblical Judaism* (New York: Schocken Books, 1962), 19.

18. Bruce J. Malina, *The New Testament World: Insights from Cultural Anthropology*, 3rd ed. (Louisville: Westminster John Knox, 2001), 42, 45, 63. Malina's analysis concerns first-century Syria-Palestine; however, his analysis of concepts of honor-shame and kinship would apply equally to the era of Deuteronomy (see, for example, Don C. Benjamin, *The Social World of Deuteronomy: A New Feminist Commentary* [Cascade: Oregon, 2015]).

19. A recent fresh and thorough study that asserts both the strong ethical trajectory of Deuteronomy's social law and also the relation of Deuteronomy's ethics to theology is Daisy Yulin Tsai, *Human Rights in Deuteronomy with Special Focus on Slave Laws*, BZAW 464 (Berlin: de Gruyter, 2014).

20. I am aware of the difficulties of this designation for ancient Near Eastern law.

21. Crüsemann, *Torah,* 191.

1. Formal law, the *mišpāṭîm* (Exod 21:1–22:16). The *mišpāṭîm* is a collection of casuistic legal stipulations that is only found in the CC within the Hebrew Bible. It follows an established pattern in cuneiform law of a simple legal case that is expanded by variations upon the initial case. The examples tend to be hypothetical and were probably intended for training professional judges.[22] The *mišpāṭîm* "had the same function as comparable collections of cuneiform laws."[23] The *mišpāṭîm* are laws for the good ordering of society and balance the needs of the perpetrator and the victim, with compensation as the guiding principle.[24]

2. Cultic law (Exod 20:24–26, 22:17–19). The scribes who authored the CC included a small amount of cultic law, including the altar law (Exod 20:22–26) and brief stipulations regarding sorcery, bestiality, and sacrifices to other gods (Exod 22:17–19). Cultic law is not found in extant ancient Near Eastern law corpuses. The 6/1 schema (Exod 21:1, 23:12) frames the CC within the exclusive lordship of Yahweh, casting Yahweh as the guarantor of the legislative program.[25]

3. Social law (Exod 22:20–23:9). There is a collection of social laws in the CC that is distinctive among ancient Near Eastern law corpuses for its relentless concern to protect the most vulnerable. Stipulations concerning the *gēr* frame the social law (Exod 22:20, 23:9), and the second half of the social law is a block concerning judicial process that focuses on the weakest in the community (see §3.1.2). "They appear, unlike the Mishpatim or other ancient Near Eastern law, as commandments from God and they rely expressly on the action of God as their standard and foundation (especially Exod 22:26; 23:7)."[26] Crüsemann suggests that the social law

---

22. Eckart Otto, "The Study of Law and Ethics in the Hebrew Bible/Old Testament," in *Hebrew Bible/Old Testament: The History of Its Interpretation*, ed. Magne Saebø, 3 vols. (Göttingen: Vandenhoeck & Ruprecht, 1996–2015), 3.2:602; Westbrook and Wells, *Everyday Law*, 27–31; Raymond Westbrook, "Biblical and Cuneiform Law Codes," *RB* 92 (1985): 251.

23. Otto, "Study of Law and Ethics," 602.

24. Crüsemann, *Torah*, 168–69.

25. The pattern 6 + 1 = 7 signifies the divine. See the exegesis of Deut 5:12–15 (§3.7).

26. Crüsemann, *Torah*, 191; Erhard S. Gerstenberger's thesis that the apodictic laws had their origin in the family setting has been widely accepted; see *Wesen und Herkunft des »apodiktischen Rechts«*, WMANT 20 (Neukirchen-Vluyn: Neukirchener, 1965).

functions in relation to the *mišpāṭîm* in a way analogous to the role of human rights charters in relation to statutory law today.[27]

Crüsemann observes:

> The book of the covenant is shaped by the thought that the rights of aliens, the poor and other exploited people are demands of God to his people that have the same importance as the basic religious principles of the exclusive veneration of God (together with the regulations regarding sacrifice and celebrations). The literary development of this connection is the birthplace of Torah, and it is a central event for biblical theological history and its conception of God.[28]

The DC is a revision of the CC that does away with much of the formal law. The DC contains a minimum of cultic law (Deuteronomy's festal law has a high social ethic), no *mišpāṭîm* as such (family law has a similar function in Deuteronomy), and no laws concerning civil damages that are prominent in the *mišpāṭîm* and in ancient Near Eastern law corpora.[29] Further, there is a greatly expanded collection of social laws, including extensive provisions for the release of debts (Deut 15:1–11) and of slaves (15:12–18), a reallocation of the tithe to the people and every third year to the poor (14:22–29, 26:12–15), expanded provisions for the inclusion of the most vulnerable in legal processes (1:16–17, 24:17a), and new laws for the full participation of the weakest in society that were not imagined in the CC, in particular in the feasts. Otto states:

> The book of Deuteronomy, being a reformulation of the Covenant Code, based itself on the latter's commandments of social ethics and developed Exod 23:4–5 into the main principle of all the Deuteronomic ethics, demanding brotherly conduct even toward the enemy (Deut 22:1–4).[30]

The DC is, in a sense, a socially oriented covenant charter bearing some semblance to a human rights charter. Its purpose is not to reproduce a

---

27. Crüsemann, *Torah*, 195.

28. Crüsemann, *Torah*, 191. See too Seth L. Sanders, *The Invention of Hebrew* (Urbana: University of Illinois Press, 2009), 163.

29. The family law of the DC corresponds to ancient Near Eastern formal law. See further, Crüsemann, *Torah*, 257.

30. Otto, "Study of Law and Ethics," 605. See also Weinfeld, *Deuteronomy and the Deuteronomic School*, 283–84.

book of statutory law but radically to reorder society according to its sister-brother ethic.[31] Consistent with Deuteronomy's concern for the most vulnerable is its unique delimitation of the roles of public offices, so that even the king is severely restricted in his responsibilities and in his capacity to accumulate resources.[32] "The authors of the book of Deuteronomy could refer to the social ethics of the priestly authors of the Covenant Code and develop an even more intensive programme than that of the Covenant Code."[33] This explains why Deuteronomy has often been associated with the prophetic tradition. S. R. Driver, for example, called Deuteronomy a "prophetical law-book."[34] In Deuteronomy, a prophetic ethos is embedded within the ethical trajectory of the exodus.

Scholars have observed the limitations of law to express ethical standards. Law corpuses tend to be concerned with the outer limits of behavior rather than with core ideals, due to their utilitarian function in ordering society.[35] Deuteronomy, however, expresses ethical ideals with full force in some legal texts, for example in the stipulation to provide sanctuary for a fleeing slave (24:15–16), in inclusive feasting that includes the *gēr* and other vulnerable people within the kinship grouping (14:22–27, 16:1–17, 26:1–11), and in the intolerance of poverty stipulation (15:4). Fretheim explores how Deuteronomic law is placed alongside other material such as motivation clauses that frame the law as an outworking of Yahweh's own actions. "That the law is developed as an exegesis of divine action means that believers are always being called to go beyond the law. The range of God's actions is not legally circumscribed. God is always doing new

---

31. See further Weinfeld, *Deuteronomy and the Deuteronomic School*, 284.

32. Levinson, *Deuteronomy and the Hermeneutics*, 138–43; Crüsemann, *Torah*, 222–24.

33. Otto, "Study of Law and Ethics," 605.

34. S. R. Driver. *A Critical and Exegetical Commentary on Deuteronomy*, ICC (Edinburgh: T&T Clark, 1896), xxvi; Schmidt, *Old Testament*, 97–98.

35. Eryl W. Davies, for example, argues that law has a utilitarian function that is concerned with the outer limits of behaviour rather than with ideals. So, it is possible to keep the commands but still come under the denunciation of the prophets; see *Prophecy and Ethics: Isaiah and the Ethical Tradition of Israel*, JSOTSup 16 (Sheffield: JSOT, 1981), 27. See also Gordon J. Wenham, *Psalms as Torah: Reading Biblical Song Ethically* (Grand Rapids: Baker Academic, 2012), 80. On the nature of ancient Near Eastern law and of biblical law and their relation to legal procedure, see Westbrook and Wells, *Everyday Law*, 25–27.

things."[36] Thus Fretheim rightly points to the "open-endedness" of many of the laws. Deuteronomy 15:7b–9 is a good example of law that is offered in a way that invites creative generosity:

> You shall not harden your heart or shut your hand against your poor brother, but you shall open your hand to him and lend him sufficient for his need, whatever it may be. Take care lest there be an unworthy thought in your heart. (ESV)

The DC is "preached law" that "addresses the reader directly."[37] The peculiar formulation of Deuteronomy suggests that the book was, from the earliest layer, a social and religious reform document. This observation connects with generally accepted observation that the law corpora of the Hebrew Bible, as with cuneiform law corpora, operate in a similar way to wisdom literature in containing cases and stipulations from which general principles for communal ethics may be deduced and by which judges may be trained. This is opposed to a view of the law corpora as formal "legislation" for judges to apply.[38]

### 3.2.1. The Structure of the Law Corpus of Deuteronomy

The structure of the DC (Deut 12–26) is notoriously difficult to discern. McBride discerns a five-part structure based upon the two phases: "When the LORD your God cuts off before you the nations…" (12:29, 19:1 [ESV]) and "When you come to the land" (17:14, 26:1 [ESV]).[39] Crüsemann proffers a chiastic structure.[40] Stephen Kaufman, Georg Braulik, and others perceive the Decalogue as the key to unlocking the structure of the DC.[41]

---

36. Terence E. Fretheim, "Law in the Service of Life: A Dynamic Understanding of Law in Deuteronomy," in *A God So Near: Essays on Old Testament Theology in Honour of Patrick D. Miller*, ed. Brent A. Strawn and Nancy R. Bowen (Winona Lake, IN: Eisenbrauns, 2003), 193, 195–97.

37. Fretheim, "Law in the Service of Life," 195.

38. See Bernard Jackson, *Wisdom-Laws: A Study of the Mishpatim of Exodus 21:1–22:16* (Oxford: Oxford University Press, 2006).

39. Dean S. McBride Jr., "Polity of the Covenant People: The Book of Deuteronomy," *Int* 41 (1987): 239 n. 26.

40. Crüsemann, *Torah*, 207.

41. Stephen A. Kaufman, "The Structure of the Deuteronomic Law," *Maarav* 1–2 (1978–1979): 105–58.

For Braulik, the DC *interprets* the Decalogue.[42] For Kaufman, the connection is one degree further removed: the DC is, in a sense, *authorized* through its correspondence to the Decalogue.[43] The lack of a clearly discernible structure for the DC is consistent with our present inability to understand the logic behind the structure of the extant ancient Near Eastern law corpuses.[44]

Two further organizational devices are crucial for exegesis. First, the DC is composed of a number of law subgroups. The laws within each subgroup are related to one another conceptually and lexically and are often spread about the law code, namely, social law (15:1–18; 22:1–12; 23:16–26; 24:6–25:4, 13–19), laws of judicial procedure (1:9–18; 16:17–20; 17:2–13; 19:1–13, 15–21; 24:17a), family law (21:15–17, 18–21; 22:13–30; 24:1–5; 25:5–10), laws regarding warfare (20:1–20, 21:10–14), laws of public office (17:14–18:22), feasting/tithing (related to social law; 14:22–29, 16:1–17, 26:1–15), and laws of divine privilege (chs. 12 and 13; 26:16–19). This study is structured according to subgroups of laws: social law (the present chapter), judicial law (ch. 4), and feasting/tithing (ch. 5). Second, a very general thematic movement through the law corpus may be traced, beginning with laws of divine privilege (12:1–14:21), followed by a first block of social laws (14:22–16:17), laws concerning public offices including the law courts (16:18–18:22), laws concerning the preservation of life (19:1–21:9), laws concerning family/sexuality (21:10–23:15), and, finally, a second block of social laws (23:15–26:15).

### 3.2.2. A System of Protection for the *Gēr*

While the structure of the DC is elusive and multifaceted, the cumulative force of its social law is clear. Lohfink has argued that the social law in the DC operates as a "system," with the goal of doing away with poverty alto-

---

42. Georg Braulik, "Die Abfolge der Gesetze in Deuteronium 12–26 und der Dekalog," in *Das Deuteronomium: Entstehung, Gestalt und Botschaft*, ed. N. Lohfink, BETL 68 (Leuven: Leuven University Press, 1985), 272.

43. Kaufman, "Structure," 125. Otto suggests a pentalogical structure for the Decalogue and for the DC ("History of the Legal-Religious," 230). See recently, Karin Finsterbusch, "The Decalogue Orientation of Deuteronomic Law: A New Approach," in *Deuteronomium: Tora für eine neue Generation*, ed. Georg Fischer, Dominik Markl, and Simone Paganini, BZABR 17 (Wiesbaden: Harrassowitz, 2011), 123–46.

44. Samuel Greengus, *Laws in the Bible and in Early Rabbinic Collections: The Legal Legacy of the Ancient Near East* (Eugene, OR: Cascade, 2011), 9.

gether.[45] For example, there are laws aimed to decrease the likelihood of the peasant farmer falling into debt (e.g., 14:28–29; 24:6, 10–15; 26:12–15), while other laws provided a means of recovery for when debt occurs (e.g., 15:1–3; 12–18).

This system of protection is visible from another angle, in the interplay between the subgroups of laws just observed, and I focus here on the *gēr*. First, the social laws protect the *gēr* and other vulnerable people from economic practices that prioritize wealth accumulation over the wellbeing of the poor (see Deut 15:1–18; 22:1–12; 23:16–26; 24:6–25:4, 13–19). These laws enable the weakest to participate within the community (the subject of the present chapter). Second, the laws of judicial procedure insist upon justice and kindness toward the *gēr* in legal processes (see ch. 4). Third, the feasting texts (14:22–29; 16:1–17; 26:1–15) foster the inclusion of the *gēr* within the family life of the household and of the settlement (see ch. 5). Fourth, the laws of public office (17:14–18:22) provide an egalitarian baseline for society by delimiting the responsibility and authority of public office holders.[46] Fifth, the centralization command carves Deuteronomy's social vision on the conscience of the community through ritual. Also, the centralization command provides accountability for the implementation of Deuteronomy's reform program before the divine judge.[47]

What follows is an exploration of each occurrence of the term *gēr* in Deuteronomy's social law.

## 3.3. The *Gēr* as Hireling (Deut 24:14–15)

### 3.3.1. The *Gēr* within the Text Block 24:6–25:4

The noun *gēr* occurs five times in a block of social laws (24:6–25:4) that is the clearest and most forceful expression of Deuteronomy's brother-sister ethic for the sake of the most vulnerable, comparable in force perhaps only to 15:1–18. Before turning to the treatment of the *gēr* in this text block, some comments on the section are in order. In regard to the integrity of this text block, it is framed by two blocks of family law (24:1–6, 25:5–10). It is internally linked via five laws concerning pledges (24:6, 7, 10–13, 17), three references to the exodus (24:9, 18, 22), a pervasive concern for the

---

45. Lohfink, "Poverty," 43, 44, 47.
46. See McBride, "Polity."
47. See the exegesis of Deut 16:1–17 in §4.2.

poorest in society, and especially a strong connection to the social laws of the CC (Exod 22:20–23:9).[48] These laws bear witness to various classes of people in Israelite society—the day laborer, gleaner, landowner, debtor, creditor—and the text block is concerned to restrain economic accumulation at the expense of the vulnerable. Ethics of inclusion for the *gēr* operate within the three spheres: household, clan/township, and all Israel.

The laws are embedded theologically via a pair of motivation clauses characteristic of social laws: the slavery/exodus motif (24:9, 18, 22) and the contingency of blessing upon justice (24:13, 19). These two clauses bind together the diversity of social laws in the DC. Two less common motive clauses are the preservation of the community from association with evil (24:7, 16) and Yahweh's responsive attention to both the blessings and the curses verbalized by the oppressed (24:13b, 15b), discussed below.

A network of literary connections in this text block signals that the laws are somewhat interchangeable. Each law applies, more or less, to every vulnerable person in the community.[49] For example, regarding the hireling stipulations (24:14–15), the lexeme עני and the motif of the sun going down connect the law with the preceding stipulation concerning pledges (12:12–13). The opening prohibition, לא תעשק, connects with the opening prohibition regarding legal justice for the *gēr* and the fatherless, לא תטה in 17a, and חטא connects with the stipulation concerning the death penalty (24:16). Therefore, we may conclude that the hired worker (who must receive his wage before nightfall, 24:14–15) also should not be oppressed in matters of distraint (24:12–13) and that the fatherless who deserves legal protection (24:17a) should also be paid promptly (24:14–15). In this way, the text block functions as a network of protection, and all of these laws become relevant to the protection of the *gēr*. More broadly still, the collection of laws nurtured the society toward a general posture of compassion, subordinating economic advancement to the wellbeing of the vulnerable.

Now we examine in detail three stipulations in this section: the hireling stipulation (24:14–15), the gleaning laws (24:19–22), and a stipulation regarding the *gēr* in judicial procedure (24:17).

---

48. Kaufman relates Deut 24:8–25:4 to the ninth "word" concerning false witness, under the rubric of "fairness to one's fellow as regards both his substance and his dignity" ("Structure," 41–42).

49. See also Lundbom, *Deuteronomy*, 690–91.

### 3.3.2. *Gēr* as Hireling: Legal and Socioeconomic Analysis

> 14 Do not oppress a needy and destitute hired laborer, whether one of your brothers or your stranger who is in your land and within your gates.15 You shall give him his wage in his day, before night comes upon him, for he is poor, he is always in dire need of it, so he will not call out against you to Yahweh and you will incur guilt.

We begin our close analysis of the *gēr* in Deuteronomy's social law with the law of the hireling in Deut 24:14–15. The passage consists of two parts: a general prohibition against oppressing a day laborer and instructions to pay a day laborer on the day of work. We learn here that a *gēr* often found employment as a hireling. A hireling was among an ancient Near Eastern society's poorest. His or her work was demanding (Job 7:1); the hireling worked under the watchful eye of the foreman (Job 14:6); dependence upon a day's wage entailed vulnerability to exploitation (Deut 24:14–15, Job 7:2); and the possibility of debt bondage lurked. Difficult as it was, such work was essential for a *gēr*'s subsistence.[50]

Most commonly references to the שכיר in the Hebrew Bible involve terms of hire that are longer than a day (Lev 25:6, 40, 50, 53; Deut 15:18; Is 16:14; 21:16). Terms of one year (Lev 25:53) and three years are mentioned (Isa 16:1). In the present text, however, payment on the day of work suggests that hire is on a day-to-day basis: ביומו תתן שכרו ולא תבוא עליו השמש (see also Job 7:2, Mal 3:5). Shorter terms of hire seem to have been common around harvest time.[51] Day laborers lacked the security of a long-term contract and therefore were highly susceptible, along with their families, to starvation; day laborers depended upon a daily wage for survival. This stipulation provides a window into the perilous existence of a שכיר in ancient Israel, also giving us a picture of the extreme vulnerability of many *gēr*.

---

50. In many cases hirelings worked and lived under conditions preferable to those of a slave, for the שכיר was free or semifree. So the HC demands that slave owners treat a עבד as one would a שכיר (Lev 25:40). Nonetheless, in some circumstances, slavery within a household of some means may well have been preferable to the impoverished existence of a day laborer. See further Karen Radner, "Hired Labor in the Neo-Assyrian Empire," in vol. 5 of *Labor in the Ancient World*, ed. Piotr Steinkeller and Michael Hudson (Dresden: ISLET, 2015), 329–43.

51. Radner, "Hired."

We should be alert to the likelihood that many of the hired laborers were women. Cultural anthropology makes clear that women's work in the pan-Mediterranean world is not confined to the private sphere of the household and that women work long hours in the field, including making bricks, picking fruit, and caring for animals. However, it is men who most often appropriate the economic benefits from their labor.[52]

### 3.3.3. Literary and Theological Analysis

The law of the hireling is linked lexically to the preceding law on pledges, and both are concerned to restrain the use of economic and social power at the expense of the weakest. A similar law in Leviticus is brief, without a relative clause or a motivation clause: לא תלין פעלת שכיר אתך עד בקר (Lev 19:13). The comparison brings into relief Deuteronomy's distinctive parenetic and theological style: this is preached law. Nonlegal, parenetic features include the phrases עני ואביון and בארצך בשעריך. These phases have an emotive tenor that is legally redundant and are designed to persuade the hearer.[53] The distinction between the brother and the stranger, however, has legal import, considering the significance of class in extant ancient Near Eastern law corpora.[54]

The opening exhortation likely represents an ancient law or custom: לא תעשק שכיר.[55] The word שכיר, "hireling," is a substantive adjective. The LXX and 1QDeut[b] has "wages" (μισθός, שכר) in the place of שכיר, rendering "do not withhold the wages of the poor and needy." However, עשק always has a personal collective as its object in the Hebrew Bible, so the MT is likely correct. The verb עשק ("to oppress") refers to the exploitation of a weaker party for economic gain.[56] Its scope includes behavior that is strictly legal but ignores the vulnerable circumstances of the weaker

52. David D. Gilmore, "Anthropology of the Mediterranean Area," ARA 11 (1982): 196.

53. Cf. Dale Patrick, "Casuistic Law Governing Primary Rights and Duties," JBL 92 (1973): 182.

54. On the role of class in Hittite Laws, see Martha T. Roth, Law Collections from Mesopotamia and Asia Minor, WAW 6 (Atlanta: Society of Biblical Literature, 1995), 72.

55. Similarly, Richard Nelson, Deuteronomy, OTL (Louisville: Westminster John Knox, 2002), 291. See, by comparison, Instruction of Amenemope 14.5–9 (Miriam Lichtheim, The New Kingdom, vol. 2 of Ancient Egyptian Literature: A Book of Readings [Berkeley: University of California Press, 1973], 154–55).

56. J. Gordon McConville, Deuteronomy, ApOTC 5 (Leicester: Inter-Varsity

party (compare this with Deut 24:17b, Mic 2:2, Amos 4:1). Three pairs of phrases qualify the initial prohibition: poor/needy, brother/*gēr*, and land/gates (24:14). Extant texts witness to seasonal laborers who are not destitute, who may even farm their own land but are working to pay off outstanding debts.[57] However, the reference to עני ואביון ("poor and needy") signals that the present text concerns the most destitute. Nonetheless, the phrase עני ואביון may be an addition,[58] and the probable original phrase לא תעשק שכיר (without the adjectives) testifies to the general vulnerability and impoverishment of hirelings and their families.

The phrase מאחיך או מגרך clarifies that this stipulation applies both to kindred, מאחיך, and to those who are displaced and who seek sustenance within the clan, מגרך.[59] While treating *kindred* with compassion is a natural human impulse, as observed above, strangers in the ancient Near East were regularly exploited and had no legal recourse. The DC is concerned that the displaced person receives the same compassion and justice, as would a brother-sister. Thus the DC incorporates the *gēr* within Deuteronomy's brother-sister ethic. In regard to justice and compassion, then, the stranger is equal to the brother-sister.[60]

"Your *gēr*" and "your brother/sister" are said to be בארצך בשעריך. Usage in Deuteronomy clarifies that the phrase בארצך בשעריך qualifies both the *gēr* (see 26:1, 11; 16:14) and the brother (see 15:7, 11; 23:21; 25:7). The fourfold use of the second-person suffix "your" emphasizes the close association between the *gēr* and the landed kinsfolk in order to motivate hearers to compassion: מאחיך או מגרך אשר בארצך בשעריך. Land gift (בארצך) and the gift of a settlement in which to dwell (בשעריך) are the

---

Press, 2002), 362. עשק does not occur in the CC, and it has its biblical roots in prophecy and cultic texts.

57. Radner, "Hired," 333.

58. This is explained in what follows.

59. On the את in Deuteronomy, see §4.2.3. On the settlement as the likely setting for some of Deuteronomy's social laws, see §5.5.1. The "min" particle operates as a partative marker: the expression references *some of* the *gēr* and some of the brothers (see Bruce K. Waltke and Michael Patrick O'Connor, *An Introduction to Biblical Hebrew Syntax* [Winona Lake, IN: Eisenbrauns, 1990], 212–13).

60. Achenbach states: "Der Fremde wird hier den Brüden gleichgestellt. Das für die dtn Sammlung charakteristische Bruderethos erhält so seine Bedeutung auch für die, die außerhalb des Verbandes Israels stehen" ("Eintritt," 242: "The stranger is equal to the brothers here. For the Dtn corpus is characterized by an ethic of brotherhood that also has implications for the one standing outside of the association of Israel")

theological grounds for justice and kindness. Yahweh has given generously to his people, and the purpose of Deuteronomy's law is to extend
this divine gift out into all the highways and byways of the community.

The phrase בשעריך reflects the reality that this stipulation will be
applied at the local level of a settlement, town, or city.[61] That the responsibility for the *gēr* is to be borne at a local level should alert us to the likelihood that the *gēr* is also "alien" at this local level. The *gēr* does not belong
to the kinship grouping or the place in which she or he resides. As for the
provenance of this figure, this text does not hint at from whence the *gēr*
has come nor whether the *gēr* is a foreigner or a Judahite. The critical con-
sideration is that this figure has been uprooted from a kinship grouping
and from patrimony and is now dependent upon the local kin grouping
for his or her livelihood.

A specific form of oppression is then addressed: ביומו תתן שכרו ולא
תבוא עליו השמש. Because an impoverished day laborer depends upon
wages for survival, prompt payment is critical. The hireling's desperation
renders her or him easy prey for exploitative employers, and the vulnerability is exacerbated for the *gēr* who has no kindred as advocates.

The text gives two motivation clauses to inspire obedience, but no
legal penalties are recorded. Thus it may be that this stipulation is difficult
to enforce in a legal dispute. Rather, Yahweh is the court of appeal. First,
compassion is stirred by an expression of the dire circumstances of the
hireling: כי עני הוא ואליו הוא נשא.[62] The word נשא is a present participle
denoting an ongoing circumstance with repeated actions,[63] reflecting the
hireling's daily need. Second, mistreatment may prompt the hireling to
call down imprecations upon the employer: ולא יקרא עליך אל יהוה והיה
בך חטא.[64] This voice of the poor was expressed positively in the previous
stipulation concerning pledges:

Deut 24:13b (pledge law)

וברכך ולך תהיה צדקה לפני יהוה אלהיך

---

61. Similarly, Lundbom considers that 24:6–25:22 address the context of rural
settlements (*Deuteronomy*, 689). On the phrase בשעריך, see §5.5.2.

62. Lundbom interprets נפש as "desire" here; cf. Hos 4:8, Jer 22:27, 34:16, 44:14,
Ezek 24:25, Ps 24:4 (*Deuteronomy*, 692).

63. See Waltke and O'Connor, *Syntax*, 626.

64. Cf. Nelson, *Deuteronomy*, 291–92.

Deut 24:15b (hireling law)

ולא יקרא עליך אל יהוה והיה בך חטא

The two texts are related. In the hireling law, "bless" becomes "cry out," and "righteousness" becomes "guilt."[65] Yahweh's ear is attentive to the needy and is responsive to their cries, cries of both blessing and curse. The hireling law's correspondence with the following stipulation via חטא leaves no doubt that the cry of the oppressed worker is a legal plea where Yahweh plays the role of judge.[66] In Israel, as in the ancient Near East, the very real possibility of recompense from the divine judge for failure to do right was generally assumed. Indeed, the divine judge functioned as a tier of the legal system.[67]

### 3.3.4. Composition History of the Hireling Laws

Neither עשק nor שכיר occur in the CC.[68] "Within your gates" is characteristic of Dtn.[69] The sentence "you shall give him his wage in his day" seems to be original, since Dtn prefers specific stipulations to general injunctions (cf. 24:12–13a).[70] Similarly, Merendino reconstructs the original text: "Do not oppress a hired laborer. You shall give him his wage in his day."[71] Contra Merendino, however, the motif of supplying the needy

---

65. קרא occurs as a cry of the oppressed that is directed to Yahweh only here and in Ezek 8:18. The texts likely are not associated compositionally.

66. The seriousness of Yahweh's judgement is underlined by the repeated use of חטא, which connects the hireling law with the death penalty (24:16).

67. Wells and Westbrook, *Everyday Law*, 45–49.

68. On the composition of the hireling law, see Christoph Levin, "Rereading Deuteronomy in the Persian and Hellenistic Periods: The Ethics of Brotherhood and Care for the Poor," in *Deuteronomy–Kings as Emerging Authoritative Books: A Conversation*, ed. Diana V. Edelman (Atlanta: Society of Biblical Literature, 2014), 66. Levin argues that the phrase עני ואביון is an addition ( "Rereading," 52). On the tendency for legal revisions to expand law, see Otto, "Aspects of Legal Reforms," 167–68. For this tendency in other ancient Near Eastern text types, see Carr, *Formation*, 65–99.

69. This motif is characteristic of the DC, appearing in texts clearly dated to Dtn (e.g., 16:11, 14). Similarly, Levin, "Rereading," 53–55; Kratz, *Composition*, 123. For an extensive discussion of the phrase בשעריך, see §5.5.2.

70. The originality of this phrase stands in contrast to the position of A. D. H. Mayes, *Deuteronomy*, NCB (Grand Rapids: Eerdmans, 1979), 325.

71. Rosario Pius Merendino, *Das deuteronomische Gesetz: Eine literarkritische, gattungs- und überlieferungsgeschichtliche Untersuchung zu Dt 12–26*, BBB 31 (Bonn:

before sundown is likely original. This motif occurs in the CC concerning pledges (Exod 22:15). It is appropriated by Dtn in the preceding stipulation concerning pledges (24:12–13a; note the common reversal of motifs in the revision, השמש, שוב in 24:13a) and also here (24:15).[72] *Gēr* with a pronominal suffix is likely a part of a Dtr redaction, and I will demonstrate in the next section that the pair מאחיך או מגרך is likely a Dtr addition.

The word בארצך is a late addition. It involves a highly unusual duplication of locations, בארצך and בשעריך. The words ארץ and גר do not appear together in Deuteronomy except in 24:14b (cf. 26:1, 11). In addition, there are textual anomalies. The word בארצך (MT and SP) is probably a harmonizing plus vis-à-vis the LXX, in light of a parallel expression in Dtn (15:7); as such, it is probably very late.[73] This late harmonizing addition of ארץ completes the pattern of triple pairs (24:14). The addition of בארצך may reflect an enhanced sense of the brotherhood of all Israel present in later redactions, as I explore in chapter 6.

The composition history demonstrates the strong social ethic of the earliest version of Deuteronomy. Dtr introduces the phrase, מאחיך או מגרך, and I will observe below that Dtr rearticulates and strengthens Dtn's concern for the stranger.[74] Three loci of inclusion occur explicitly here, likely from three different authorial processes:

---

Hanstein, 1969), 303: "Erpresse nicht einen Löhner: an seinem Tag gib ihm seinen Lohn."

72. Levin ("Rereading," 66) and Mayes (*Deuteronomy*, 325–26) also consider that the sundown motif is a part of the Dtn original. Most critical scholars hold that a text that revises the CC is more likely to be from the early stratum of Deuteronomy (see, e.g., Kratz, *Composition*, 117, 130). But this is not certain; see my exegesis of 5:12–15. The tendency for motifs to be reversed in a revision is known as Seidel's law (Levinson, *Deuteronomy and the Hermeneutics*, 18).

73. See Carr regarding harmonization of this kind (*Formation*, 93). Levin takes ארץ as a part of the redaction concerning the brother and stranger ("Rereading," 66 n. 66). However, the awkwardness of the addition as well as the textual corruption suggests that this is more likely a result of assimilation and a following harmonization.

74. The ways in which Dtr rearticulates and strengthens Dtn's concern for the stranger is demonstrated in the exegesis of 5:12–15 (§3.7) and especially in chapter 6, concerning Deuteronomy's framework.

Table 3.1. Loci of Inclusion in 24:14–15

| Phrase | Locus of inclusion | Redaction layer |
|---|---|---|
| מגרך | the household | Dtr |
| בשעריך | the settlement | Dtn |
| בארצך | all Israel[75] | late harmonization |

In sum, the hireling law offers a glimpse into the likely circumstance of a *gēr* in Israel who worked as a day laborer. The law incorporates the *gēr* within Deuteronomy's brother-sister ethic. Before moving to the function of the gleaning stipulations in relation to the *gēr* (24:19–22), we turn aside to consider the function and composition history of the noun *gēr* with a pronominal suffix.

### 3.3.5. The Noun *Gēr* with a Pronominal Suffix

The reference to the *gēr* as a hireling is one of five references to the *gēr* involving a pronominal suffix: גרך in 5:14, 24:14, 29:10, 31:12, and גרו in 1:16. The pronominal suffix motif is one of a number of integration formulas in Deuteronomy (see also בשעריך and בקרבך). The social location of the *gēr* signified by this motif varies between the household (5:14) and the clan grouping (29:10). The pronominal-suffix form is unique to Deuteronomy, as Perlitt has recognized.[76] For example:

24:14 (the hireling stipulation)

מאחיך או <u>מגרך</u> אשר בארצך בשעריך

5:14 (the Sabbath stipulation of the Decalogue)

אתה ובנך ובתך ועבדך ואמתך ושורך וחמרך וכל בהמתך <u>וגרך</u> אשר
בשעריך

The peculiarity of these phrases is evident when set in relief to the customary household list, where the *gēr* appears without the pronominal suffix:

---

75. All Israel becomes an important motif in the frame of Deuteronomy, which is dated to Dtr and to post-Dtr (see ch. 6).

76. Perlitt, "Ein einzig Volk," 63. The pronominal suffix form in Exod 20:10 is an interpolation from Deut 5:12.

16:11a

ושמחת לפני יהוה אלהיך אתה ובנך ובתך ועבדך ואמתך והלוי אשר
בשעריך <u>והגר</u> והיתום והאלמנה אשר בקרבך

In this last text (similar to 16:14), the male and female slave receives the
pronominal suffix, whereas the gēr does not. In 16:11, 14 the pronominal
suffix seems to designate the slave as the property of the paterfamilias.
Thus it is remarkable that some of these texts refer to the gēr with the
pronominal suffix (1:16, 5:14, 24:14, 29:10, 31:12). Ownership is clearly
not in mind in these texts, as someone with nonfree status would be designated a slave rather than as a gēr (עבדך ואמתך). The suffix must reference
a strong association with the household, such as contracted labor, indentured labor, or a less formal participation.

With the exception of the hireling stipulation (24:14), all of these references are a part of the framing texts of the DC and likely postdate the
law corpus.[77] On this basis, the reference to the gēr in the hireling stipulation is probably also a later redaction. The pronominal suffix phrase perhaps emerged as a part of the Decalogue redaction.[78] These references to
the gēr involving the pronominal suffix are remarkable for their inclusive
ethic. For instance, the participation of the gēr in Sabbath rest dignifies
the gēr with the right to rest, to enjoyment of the goodness of the land
(5:14). Texts of covenant ratification (29:10) and the seventh-year reading
of Torah (31:12) include the gēr within the family of Yahweh.

What is the impetus of this change of reference to the gēr? In terms
of composition history, the pronominal suffix form likely signals either a
historical change in the relationship between the gēr and the settlement/
household, a change in the composition of the settlement/household itself,
or a change in both. Possibly, the pronominal suffix form for gēr emerged
in response to the new social reality created by the collapse of kinship
groupings in the wake of the Babylonian conquest at the end of the Iron
Age. This event included the destruction of almost all of the urban centers
and the destruction or abandonment of the vast majority of villages and
farms.[79] Extended kinship groupings were broken through processes of

---

77. See the discussion of the composition history of the frame in §6.1.1.

78. On the Decalogue redaction, see the analysis of 5:12–15 in §3.7.

79. Avraham Faust, *Judah in the Neo-Babylonian Period: The Archaeology of Desolation*, ABS 18 (Atlanta: Society of Biblical Literature, 2012), 71, 138, 147, 234. Faust
challenges the so-called "continuity school" that argues for a fair degree of social con-

mass execution, exile, famine, disease, and emigration that resulted from the conquest.[80] Other clear examples of terminological shifts in the social domain also respond to these social, historical circumstances of upheaval. For example, during the Persian period the house of the father may be referred to in the plural, בית אבות (Ezra 2:59).[81] Hugh Williamson suggests that a group of households rather than the *house of the father* would have been the primary social identity for those who remained in the land.[82] Also, the reference of משפחה seems to have shifted in Chronicles and Ezra-Nehemiah from referring to kinship groupings to a variety of groupings, including guilds.[83] Faust asserts that "those social changes were clearly the result of the collapse of the Judahite society in the sixth century."[84] The suffixed form of *gēr* may be another term in the social domain reformulated for a new context. The redactor is signaling that Dtn's ethic of inclusivism for the stranger is being applied to new social circumstances. The terms גרך in 5:14, 24:14, 29:10, and 31:12 and גרו in 1:16 associate the *gēr* with a household, perhaps specifically a nuclear family, in the new social context of Judah during the Neo-Babylonian period and beyond, when consanguineous clan groupings had been largely destroyed.[85] Perhaps due to the sheer number of displaced people during this period, the designa-

---

tinuity between the late Iron Age and the Neo-Babylonian period in rural Judea and in the urban areas of Benjamin and of the Northern Highlands. Examples of this school include Rainer Albertz, *Israel in Exile: The History and Literature of the Sixth Century B.C.E.*, trans. David Green, StBibLit 3 (Atlanta: Society of Biblial Literature, 2003); Oded Lipschits, *The Fall and Rise of Jerusalem: Judah under Babylonian Rule* (Winona Lake, IN: Eisenbrauns, 2005). I follow Faust here.

80. Faust, *Judah*, 106–8. Faust convincingly challenges the assertion of Albertz and others that kinship groupings in rural areas were more or less left intact (cf. Albertz, *Israel*, 135; Lipschits, *Fall*, 295).

81. Williamson, "Family," 472, 475; Williamson argues that family structure in the Persian period exhibited some variety ("Family," 477).

82. Williamson, "Family," 474–75. Often in Ezra and Nehemiah, primary allegiances were determined by concerns other than family (475–76).

83. David Vanderhooft, "The Israelite *Mishpaha* in the Priestly Writings, and Changing Valences in Israel's Kinship Terminology," in *Exploring the Long Duree: Essays in Honor of Lawrence E. Stager*, ed. D. Schloen (Winona Lake, IN: Eisenbrauns, 2009), 491.

84. Faust, *Judah*, 174.

85. Albertz suggests that the addition of the pronominal suffix to the noun *gēr* signals a patron-client relation that is different from the more family-based relationships within the settlements that is evident in earlier texts in Deuteronomy ("Aliens," 56).

tion "your *gēr*" was necessary in order to emphasize the responsibility of landed groups to include these people. To be sure, this interpretation is by no means certain. Nonetheless, given that the suffixed form of *gēr* is restricted to post-Dtn layers, a change in social context of some kind is likely reflected there.

More must be said regarding the remarkably inclusive ethic of texts containing the pronominal suffixed form of *gēr* observed here. The pronominal suffix takes its place among Deuteronomy's formulas for integration. The close association of the *gēr* and the household and settlement referenced in the phrase גרך, combined with the deep ethic of protection and inclusion in these texts (1:16, 5:14, 29:10, 31:12), may suggest that the DC is fostering a new kind of belonging and even a new kind of status for the *gēr*. Still, the association is evocative rather than explicit. The mere fact of the DC's persistent expectation that the household and clan may not treat the *gēr* as cheap labor but must care for and provide for a *gēr* is a signal to us that Deuteronomy is moving along this groove, since "kinsfolk are expected to be loving, just and generous to one another and not to demand strictly equivalent return of one another."[86] Outside of the kinship group, though, such behavior is altruistic—and indeed highly unlikely in a Mediterranean communal context.[87] Significantly, pronominal suffixes are never attached to the terms נכרי and זר, and this contrast signals the characteristic dependence of the *gēr* and also Deuteronomy's intention for the incorporation of such people.

An exploration follows of the *gēr* in stipulations to leave the residue of the harvest.

### 3.4. Gleaning Stipulations (Deut 24:19–22)

19 Supposing that you reap your harvest in your field and you accidently leave behind a sheaf in the field, do not return to get it. It shall be for the stranger, the fatherless, and the widow,[88] in order that Yahweh your God may bless you in all the work of your hands.

---

86. Fortes, *Kinship and the Social Order*, cited in Cross, *Epic*, 5.

87. Cross, *From Epic to Canon*, 5.

88. The LXX adds τῷ πτωχῷ ("poor") at the beginning of the list of the vulnerable to harmonize with Lev 19:10 and 23:22.

20 When you beat off your olives, do not search through[89] the branches afterward. It shall be for the stranger, the fatherless, and the widow. 21 When you cut the grapes[90] of your vineyard do not glean it afterward. It shall be for the stranger, the fatherless, and the widow. 22 Remember that you were a slave in the land of Egypt. Because of this I command you to keep this law.

## 3.4.1. Analysis

The noun *gēr* occurs three times within three parallel stipulations that concern leaving the residue of the harvest for the vulnerable (24:19–21). During the harvest, the landed farmer was not to go over the field, vineyard, and olive trees a second time in order to gather the residue. The poor were to be given the opportunity and the dignity of harvesting some of the produce for their own sustenance. In this way, the poorest could avoid the shame of begging.[91] The full phrase לגר ליתום ולאלמנה יהיה is repeated three times, making the vulnerable triad the focal point of the text by virtue of legal redundancy. The *gēr* is emphasized by its placement at the beginning of the list and also by the appearance of the exodus motive clause that associates in particular to the *gēr*.[92] This text functions in conjunction with the three previous stipulations as a powerful call to protect and to provide for the *gēr* (the hireling, 24:14–15; judicial law, 24:17a; pledges, 24:17b).

Similarly, the Instruction of Amenemope teaches compassion toward widows who are gleaning:

---

89. פאר is a denominative form of פארה branch (see *HALOT*, s.v. "פאר," 3:908). Olives were picked, shaken free, or made to fall by beating with a stick (King and Stager, *Life*, 96).

90. בצר: vineyards were harvested by removing branches with shears; cf. Akk. *baṣāru*, "to tear off, to tear apart" (*CAD* 2:134).

91. Lundbom, *Deuteronomy*, 696. A personal anecdote illustrates the importance of procuring one's own food for one's dignity. A gentleman with a physical disability attends a weekly community meal that is offered by my worshiping community. Every person who attends is considered a host and is invited to contribute to the meal in one way or another. This gentleman walks with a frame, and yet he is able to take out the recycling at the end of the evening. He expresses how meaningful it is for him to play a valuable role in hosting the meal.

92. See the discussion in §3.4.3.

Do not pounce on a widow when you find her in the fields and then fail to be patient with her reply.[93]

Read alongside Deut 24:19–22, the Instruction of Amenemope suggests that gleaning was an ancient and widespread practice of the poor in antiquity. Nonetheless, we may conclude from the Instruction that gleaning was not necessarily a legal right of the poor. Farmers had an economic interest in methods that were time-efficient and thorough (Jer 6:9). The narrative of Ruth illustrates a gleaner's vulnerability to abuse (Ruth 2:9).

The majority of casuistic laws in the Hebrew Bible are remedial, concerning an offense against a party, but the gleaning laws do not address a prior offense. Dale Patrick calls this type of law "casuistic law governing primary rights and duties."[94] The law asserts that the *gēr* has a primary right to the residue of the harvest and that the landowner has a corresponding duty to leave the residue for the *gēr*. This legal right is reflected in the categorical assertion: "It is for the *gēr*, the orphan, and the widow." This legal right is expressed emphatically both by the triple *lamed* prefix, לגר ליתום ולאלמנה יהיה, and by the triple repetition of the whole clause. Should the landowner fail to leave the residue for the *gēr*, this would constitute a breach of the stipulation. Following such stipulations is not simply a duty of charity or of generosity; it is a matter of justice—it concerns rights. Luke Glanville describes the nature of rights and duties in this way: "It is not only right to perform them but it is wrong to not perform them."[95]

The text has a three-part structure arranged according to the three elements of the so-called Mediterranean triad of foodstuffs: grain, olive oil, and wine. A literary pattern is repeated three times. כי introduces the protasis, "when you harvest the crop in your field" and so forth; לא introduces three prohibitions against collecting the residue.

Establishing an olive orchard or a vineyard took some time, and Deuteronomy's demand that the *gēr* share in these valuable resources (24:20, 21) demonstrates that the *gēr* was to be treated as a participant in the community and as a co-recipient of Yahweh's gifts. Such participation is especially remarkable given that a displaced person has no traditional

---

93. Instruction of Amenemope 28.1–2 (Lichtheim, *New Kingdom*, 161).

94. Patrick, "Casuistic," 181.

95. Luke Glanville, "Christianity and the Responsibility to Protect," *SCE* 25 (2012): 315. Glanville is analyzing international norms for a *responsibility to protect*. Ebach also refers to the "rights" of the *gēr* in Deuteronomy (*Fremde*, 45).

connection with the land. Olive presses (usually cut into rock) were often located in the vicinity of a plantation,[96] and it is possible that some farmers lent the use of the olive press to the vulnerable gleaners in order that they could extract olive oil. Olive oil was used by both rich and poor for staple food, for its medicinal qualities, and for burning in lamps.[97]

The literary style of these stipulations is expansive in contrast to the stipulations that precede them. While the other laws studied in this chapter contain some legally redundant parenetic material, extensive repetition characterizes the gleaning laws. In terms of the sheer amount of textual material and the use of literary devices, these laws have closer parallels with some ancient Near Eastern cultic and royal texts.[98] The liturgical and highly parenetic style supports a shift from laws concerned to restrain oppressive behavior (24:6–18) toward positive acts of kindness in the present law. The style is designed to influence the reader, especially though mnemonic effect.[99] The priority of the *gēr* in the list of the vulnerable enhances the mnemonic effect in favor of the stranger. This rhetoric attempts to motivate more than mere compliance to the letter of the law; it aims to arouse deep compassion and create a shift in the reader's conscience by repeating with lyrical cadence that the harvest belongs to all.

The *gēr* is also highlighted in the list of the vulnerable in that a *waw*-conjunctive joins the fatherless and the widow, but not the *gēr*, in the three occurrences of the list in both the MT and SP. The LXX differs (also 26:12), probably assimilating with other references to the triad (16:11, 14), and the MT should be accepted as the *lectio difficilior*.[100] As observed above, the phrase "the fatherless and the widow" functions as a metonymy for impoverished people, while the figure of the *gēr* is marked as representing the distinctive social problem of displacement in the world of the author.

A motive clause follows both the stipulation concerning the grain and also the final stipulation concerning the vineyard.[101]

---

96. King and Stager, *Life*, 96.

97. King and Stager, *Life*, 97.

98. E.g., Instruction of Amenemope 11.1–6 (Lichtheim, *New Kingdom*, 154–55); *RS* 1.003/*RS* 18.056 cited in Dennis Pardee, *Ritual and Cult at Ugarit*, WAW 10 (Atlanta: Society of Biblical Literature, 2002), 59–65.

99. On the rhetorical function of repetition, see Watts, *Reading*, 71.

100. See further Awabdy, *Immigrants*, 97 n. 176.

101. The LXX adds the Egypt motive clause at the end of the second stipulation regarding olives. Such duplication, however, is unusual for Deuteronomy.

24:19 (following the grain harvest stipulation)

למען יברכך יהוה אלהיך בכל מעשה ידיך

Yahweh's blessing is contingent upon nonoppressive behavior in a prior stipulation, (24:13). Here the blessing is further contingent upon active compassion (24:19b).[102] It is not enough to avoid blatant exploitation; landholders must ensure that everyone in the community shares in the blessing. Tigay observes that the blessing motif qualifies stipulations that require landowners to prioritize the welfare of the poorest above their own economic gain: "Lest the Israelites fear that these sacrifices will cause economic hardship, he is assured that, on the contrary, they will ultimately lead to greater prosperity."[103]

As observed in regard to the hireling stipulation (§3.3), the Deuteronomic responsibility for the *gēr* is to be fulfilled locally. The addressee here is first the paterfamilias; however, the whole kinship grouping must fulfill the burden of this stipulation. Again, this should alert us to the reality that the term *gēr* here is circumscribed locally. It concerns an impoverished person without roots in his or her place of residence. The text does not indicate the provenance of the displaced people (e.g., whether they are displaced Judahites or displaced foreigners). Kinsfolk must show compassion to people who are without kin, whoever they are and wherever they are from.

### 3.4.1.1. Cultural Analysis

What is the cultural meaning of the gleaning law? At the very least, this law communicates a responsibility toward vulnerable people. Yet for whom did communal Mediterranean people have responsibility? Approaching this issue negatively, Mediterranean people had no responsibility toward "outsiders." Indeed, outsiders were viewed with suspicion, often as a threat. Oftentimes, outsiders could be harmed and even killed with impunity, an action that could increase the honor of the killer![104] Consider, for example, the violent aggression toward Lot and his guests (Gen 19). The vulnerability of outsiders is also illustrated in the wife-sister narratives of the patriarchs in Egypt (12:10–20, 26:6–11). Hospitality protocol was a means

---

102. This motive clause associates with 14:29b. This is likely purposeful given the thematic association. The third year tithe text (14:29a) adds ואכלו ושבעו.

103. Tigay, *Deuteronomy*, 144.

104. Gilmore, "Anthropology," 178–79.

of temporarily neutralizing the cultural suspicion and aggression toward outsiders. To add, Israelites apparently could be reluctant to fulfill their responsibilities even toward clanspeople, and the strength of this obligation seems to have been vague. The narrative of Zelophehad's daughters, for example, projects a context where clansmen were often unwilling to preserve the name and patrimony of a deceased relative (Num 27, 36; see also Deut 1:16–17, Ruth 4:5–6).

In light of these cultural assumptions, we may shift our understanding of the gleaning law from a question of charity or human rights toward questions of responsibility and solidarity. The issue of solidarity is explicit in the requirement of the hireling law that brothers be treated as brothers and that strangers also be treated as brothers (24:14–15). Solidarity is also behind the gleaning laws (24:19–22), which may be viewed in terms of sharing possessions with others in order that they may subsist. We may observe how kinship is experienced in sharing of possessions in many texts in the Hebrew Bible, such as Abraham and Lot's sharing livestock and land (Gen 13:8–9; cf. Gen 20:14, 21:25–30, Exod 19:5–6, Deut 33:1–29). Set within this cultural context, by invoking a willingness to share the harvest with the poor, the gleaning laws are also nourishing a sense of kinship solidarity with vulnerable people. The flip side of taking responsibility for the fatherless, widow, and stranger is an experience of shame should such people not be able to subsist—for these are your kindred.

Evidently, then, these social laws address the question: To whom do we have responsibility? Who must we protect? Who must we enfold? With whom shall we share our possessions? These social laws, in other words, were heard and experienced across the field of kinship—who is my kin? Moving upstream, the social problems that these laws addressed were kinship problems: the stranger, fatherless, and widow needed a clan who would take responsibility for them, within which they would find belonging, subsistence, and protection.

### 3.4.1.2. The *Gēr* and Landlessness

Some scholars suggest that the reality that the *gēr* in Deuteronomy does not possess property is evidence of Deuteronomy's intention to maintain the outsider status of the *gēr*.[105] (To be sure, in Leviticus the *gēr* may own

---

105. E.g., Sneed, "Israelite," 505–7.

land, yet the identity of the *gēr* is different in Leviticus from Deuteronomy, as discussed above.) In the *gēr*'s relation to patrimony, the *gēr* was distinguished from the primary addressee of Deuteronomy, the paterfamilias, who is the "you" of the household list of Deuteronomy (e.g., 16:11, 14). Nonetheless, the relationship of the *gēr* to the land in the text of Deuteronomy is dynamic rather than static, liminal rather than institutional. While Deut 24:19–22 in no way signals that the *gēr* has land title, so to speak, the syntax of the text nevertheless signals a close association of the *gēr* to the land. Indeed, the concept that the gift of land and its abundance is for the *gēr*, too, is expressed not only here but also in numerous texts that are analyzed below (e.g., 5:12–15, 26:1–11, 29:9–14). Deuteronomy's vision is that displaced people are, eventually, incorporated into the clans and thereby connected to patrimony. However, the term *gēr* by definition refers to landless people, and at such a time when a displaced person is adopted into a clan he or she ceases to be a *gēr*.

## 3.4.2. Composition History

Merendino suggests that the stipulation concerning the grain harvest (24:19) is independent of the stipulations concerning the oil and grapes (24:20–22) on the basis that "weist v. 19a eine längere Form auf."[106] In contrast to Merendino and Mayes, I suggest that all three stipulations of the gleaning law belong to Dtn, for the passage is structured according to the Mediterranean triad of foodstuffs. The grain, oil, and wine motif appears in a pre-Dtr redaction of the CC, a text concerning the Sabbath year (Exod 23:10–11), with strong thematic and ethical associations with the present text.[107] The triad also appears in a number of Dtn texts (12:17, 14:23, 18:4, 24:19–22). Consequently, it appears likely that the three stipulations concerning the grain, olive, and grape harvest operated as a unified whole in Dtn. The first motivation clause may well be a part of the original layer (24:19b), though the clause בכל מעשה ידיך in 24:19bβ predominantly occurs in the frame, raising the possibility that it is a later redaction.[108]

---

106. Rosario Pius Merendino, *Das deuteronomische Gesetz: Eine literarkritische, gattungs- und überlieferungsgeschichtliche Untersuchung zu Dt 12–26*, BBB 31 (Bonn: Peter Hanstein, 1969), 307–8: "v. 19a has a longer form."

107. See further Otto, "History of the Legal-Religious," 212; Kratz, *Composition*, 117, 130.

108. Deuteronomy 2:7, 14:29, 16:15, 28:12, 30:9, 31:9. Altmann, among others,

### 3.4.3. The *Gēr* and the Egypt Motive Clause

The gleaning stipulation is positioned in between two "remember Egypt" motive clauses (24:18–22), framing the stipulation within Israel's own narrative of Yahweh's redemption. The exodus appears around fifty times in Deuteronomy, and eleven of Deuteronomy's twenty-two references to the *gēr* relate directly to the exodus and related motifs. According to Rifat Sonsino's categorization, 111 of Deuteronomy's 225 prescriptions are supported by a motive clause, amounting to 50 percent of Deuteronomy's laws.[109] This may be compared with 16 percent of laws in the CC and 51 percent of laws in the HC.[110] The abundance of motive clauses in Deuteronomy itself is a testimony to the oft-cited "democratic" quality of Deuteronomy.[111]

Cyril Rodd contends that the exodus motive clause relates particularly to laws concerning the *gēr* and slaves, relating to other *personae miserable* such as orphans and widows only secondarily.[112] Here Rodd has isolated a pattern neglected in other discussions of the exodus in motive clauses, and I will review the data for Rodd's thesis. In Deuteronomy, fourteen of 111 motive clauses concern the exodus or Israel's sojourn in Egypt. The following observations may be made:

---

observes that motifs within the DC that are predominantly found within the frame may be post-Dtn; see Peter Altmann, "Feast, Famine, and History: The Festival Meal *Topos* and Deuteronomy," *ZAW* 124 (2012): 557 n. 6.

109. Rifat Sonsino, *Motive Clauses in Hebrew Law* (Chico, CA: Scholars Press, 1980), 93. Sonsino defines a motive clause as "a dependent clause or phrase which expresses the motive behind the legal prescription or an incentive for obeying it" (*Motive Clauses*, 65). The first extended analysis of motive clauses was provided by Berend Gemser, "The Importance of the Motive Clause in Old Testament Law," in *Congress Volume: Copenhagen, 1953*, ed. G. W. Anderson. VTSup 1 (Leiden: Brill, 1953), 50–66; repr. as pages 96–115 in *Adhuc Loquitur: Collected Essays by B. Gemser*, ed. A. van Selms and A. S. van der Woude, POS 7 (Leiden: Brill, 1968). See also Cyril Rodd, *Glimpses of a Strange Land: Studies in Old Testament Ethics* (Edinburgh: T&T Clark, 2001), 109–25.

110. Sonsino, *Motive Clauses*, 221.

111. "Instead of self-authenticating oracular pronouncements or stark apodictic decrees bearing the stamp of royal office, we find this legislation making liberal appeal to the experiences and interests of an Israelite public" (McBride, "Polity," 238).

112. Rodd, *Glimpses*, 182–83.

- The exodus motive clause is related to a small number of themes. The clause is strongly related to laws concerning social justice and social inclusion (5:14–15; 10:18–19; 15:12–15; 16:11–12; 24:19–22; 26:5, 11; cf. 17:16). It is strikingly absent from laws with other concerns, such as war, tithes, sexual relations, and so forth.
- The exodus motive clause is peculiarly related to slavery (5:14–15, 15:12–15, 16:11–12) and to the *gēr* (5:14–15; 16:11–12; 24:19–22; 29:11, 16).
- The *gēr*-in-Egypt clause is highly related to ethics of inclusivism, especially for the *gēr* (10:18–19, 23:8, 26:5).[113]
- The exodus motive clause appears in laws relating to the Passover (16:1, 3), identifying the community as those who have been emancipated by Yahweh with latent ethical implications.[114]
- In 10:18–19, the exodus associates with the *gēr* over and against the fatherless and widow. This pattern also appears in the CC (Exod 22:21, 23:9).
- Four uses undergird warnings against idolatry. The *hiphil* of יצא ("who brought you out") highlights Yahweh's claim over Israel as their new master, by virtue of Yahweh's redeeming them (5:6, 6:12, 13:6, 11).
- Five of these motive clauses include the motive of remembering Egypt, זכר (Deut 5:14–15, 15:12–15, 16:3, 24:17–18, 24:19–22).

In sum, Rodd has perceptively isolated a particular, though not exclusive, connection of the exodus motive clause to laws concerning the *gēr* and slavery. The categories of *gēr* and the slave are not unrelated: there is threatening danger for a *gēr* to fall into slavery through oppression or debt or both, evidenced in Israel's own experience in Egypt. The connection of the Egypt-exodus motifs with the *gēr* and the slave seems to be one of identity, of Israel's identifying with these categories through its own history. Israel was first *gēr* in Egypt (Deut 10:18–19, 23:8, 26:5) and then enslaved in Egypt. The call to "remember" slavery-exodus frames

---

113. The *gēr*-in-Egypt formula is discussed at length at §5.3.3.5.
114. See further the exegesis of 16:17 in §5.2.

the stipulation to leave the residue of the harvest (24:18, 22), clarifying that the act of "remembering" is not merely cognitive but also ritualized in practices.

The association between the *gēr* and slave and the exodus event is most importantly grounded in theology: Yahweh's own actions in delivering oppressed people that is exemplified in the exodus event and embodied in legislation. In this vein, the catechetical credo of Deut 6:21–25 states:

> We were Pharaoh's slaves in Egypt. And Yahweh brought us out of Egypt with a mighty hand. And Yahweh showed signs and wonders, great and grievous, against Egypt and against Pharaoh and all his household, before our eyes. And he brought us out from there, that he might bring us in and give us the land that he swore to give to our fathers. And Yahweh commanded us to do all these statutes, to fear Yahweh our God, for our good always…. (ESV, modified)

First, then, Israel, having been brought out from under the rule of Pharaoh, is "brought into" a new allegiance to Yahweh their deliverer, in Yahweh's land. Deuteronomy 6:12–13 signals this change of alliance by juxtaposing Israel's identity as Pharaoh's slaves מבית עבדים with a new identity serving (עבד) Yahweh.[115] Second, Israel was "brought out" to form a new society, in contradistinction to Egypt's oppression, shaped by Yahweh's statutes and commandments. The giving of law is presented as a theological-political issue: it is constituted by a change of king.

The exodus motive clause in Deuteronomy, then, composed as it is of only a few words, evokes the entire narrative of slavery, emancipation, land gift, and service to Yahweh (cf. 26:5b–10). If there should be any doubt about the capacity for phrases or even individual words to evoke an entire narrative, we may recall that these texts emerge within what Malina refers to as "high context" societies. That is, they were low in detail and high in contextually derived symbolism.[116] In this light, since the exodus motive clause evokes a whole narrative of slave emancipation, we may conclude that the exodus motif is imbibed with a strong ethical trajectory at all

---

115. Walter Brueggemann observes this pattern in the book of Exodus; see "Pharoah as Vassal," *CBQ* 57 (1995): 35. See also David Daube, *The Exodus Pattern in the Bible* (London: Faber and Faber, 1963), 42–46; Jon D. Levenson, "Exodus and Liberation," *HBT* 13 (1991): 134–74, esp. 150.

116. Bruce J. Malina, *The Social Gospel of Jesus: The Kingdom of God in Mediterranean Perspective* (Minneapolis: Fortress, 2001), 2–4.

times in this book (see further §§5.3.3.4, 5.3.3.5). This trajectory is ultimately grounded in the character and work of Israel's new master, Yahweh, as Brueggemann states:

> Yahweh is characteristically a God who enacts exoduses, and who does so in many places, perhaps everywhere. Wherever people are in oppressive situations and are helpless to extricate themselves, there this God might be engaged.[117]

Thus the eleven passages that undergird an ethic of inclusion for the *gēr* with the *gēr*-in-Egypt/slave-in-Egypt motive clauses evoke narrative history of enormous ethical freight. We turn now to the *gēr* in law concerning judicial procedure (24:17).

## 3.5. Pledges (Deut 24:17)

### 3.5.1. Two Related Stipulations

Deuteronomy 24:17a is a further provision for the stranger, now in the sphere of procedural law. This is a third law concerning the *gēr* within a block of social laws (Deut 24:6–25:4), and it is analyzed in detail in the following chapter as a law of judicial procedure. Of interest here is the association of this law with the following prohibition against taking a widow's garment in pledge (24:17b).

Deut 24:17

לא תטה משפט גר יתום ולא תחבל בגד אלמנה

> Do not pervert the justice due to the *gēr* and the fatherless. Do not take a widow's garment in pledge.

These two stipulations are linked by the interpolation of the second prohibition within the formulaic triad of the vulnerable. "The protection law regarding pledges for the widows (24:17b) is immediately associated with 24:17a, so that its validity can be assumed for strangers."[118] Indeed, as I

---

117. Walter Brueggemann, *Theology of the Old Testament* (Minneapolis: Fortress, 1997), 178.

118. Achenbach, "Eintritt," 242: "Das Schutzgebot im Pfandungsfall für Witwen

observed earlier in the chapter, the literary interconnectedness throughout Deut 24:6–25:4 indicates that all of the laws in this text block apply, more or less, to all categories of vulnerability.

A widow was uniquely vulnerable, and her outer garment doubled as a protection from rain during the day and a blanket at night.[119] Due to the importance of the outer garment, in the Yavneh-Yam inscription a worker in Israel entreats a governor/commander regarding its confiscation by a supervisor. Wells and Westbrook suggest that the man may have been a day laborer who, out of desperate need, received his wage at the beginning of the day, giving his garment as a pledge for the coming day's work. The laborer's plea is that his fellow workers could testify that he had brought the full amount into the granary.[120] Amos also witnessed the practice of taking a garment in pledge against a loan: "They lay themselves down beside every altar on garments taken in pledge" (Amos 2:8 ESV). The CC had stipulated that the garment of an impoverished person must be returned before sundown (Exod 22:26–27). The DC expanded this stipulation into a series of pledge laws that form the first half of this text block (Deut 24:6–13).[121] Here is a further expansion: a widow's garment must not be taken in pledge *at all*. At its heart, this stipulation requires that God's people consider the circumstances of a vulnerable person (including the *gēr*) and place that person's basic needs over their own economic progress.

### 3.5.2. The *Gēr* Included within a Traditional Literary Trope

The *gēr* in Deuteronomy often appears within the triad of the vulnerable (והגר והיתום והאלמנה), which occurs for the first time in Deuteronomy (10:18; 24:17, 19, 20, 21; 27:19). Deuteronomy's triad/quartet of vulnerable people appears in 24:17 in broken form (as it does in 10:17–18). This formula is now examined, observing the transformation of a traditional literary trope for the poor to include the *gēr*.

While past scholarship rightly characterizes the *gēr*, fatherless, and widow as landless groups, the triad's commonality is more fundamentally

---

(24:17b) wird unmittelbar an 24:17a angeschlossen, so das dessen Gültigkeit auch für die Fremden angenommen werden kann."

119. King and Stager, *Life*, 269.

120. Westbrook and Wells, *Everyday Law*, 115; Aḥituv offers an alternative suggestion (*Echoes*, 158).

121. See Lundbom, *Deuteronomy*, 678–80.

located in an absence of kinship ties and the concomitant lack of means for sustaining themselves.[122] This list also commonly occurs as a quartet, with the Levite listed as the first of four dislocated categories of people (14:29; 16:11, 14; 26:11, 12, 13), and this most frequently in the original Dtn layer. In some occurrences of the list of vulnerable people, only one or two categories are listed, which is sufficient to reference all vulnerable people who may associate with the household and the settlement (see, e.g., 26:11). Contrary to the view of Awabdy, who suggests the various configurations of the list "are applied without apparent reason or for aesthetic purposes,"[123] the list is shaped according to the literary or theological context of each occurrence (regarding 26:11, see §4.3.3). The appearance of the quartet of the vulnerable in household lists indicates their belonging within the household, most markedly in feasting texts (14:27; 16:11, 14; 26:11; see also 1:16, 5:14).

We now trace the historical development of the triad. The couplet of "the fatherless and the widow" appears in many ancient Near Eastern texts, especially from Mesopotamia. The oldest extant reference to the fatherless and the widow is in the reform texts of Urukagina:

> Urukagina made a covenant with Ningirsu
> That a man of power must not commit an (injustice)
> against an orphan or widow.[124]

Another early example is in the epic of Aqhat from Ugarit. Fensham summarizes: "While Daniel the king was waiting for the god of Crafts, Kothar-wahasis, to bring a bow for Aqhat, his son, he was busy judging the cause of the widow and orphan."[125] The couplet אלמנה ויתום appears in the CC (Exod 22:21, 23). Here the *gēr* is referenced alongside the couplet (22:20–21), but the *gēr* is not fully integrated into the triad until the Dtn redaction. "Both times the same order is used: (1) *'lmnh*, (2) *ytwm* (Exod

---

122. See further Kristine Henriksen Garroway, *Children in the Ancient Near Eastern Household* (Winona Lake, IN: Eisenbrauns, 2014), 92.

123. Awabdy, *Immigrants*, 119.

124. In Samuel Noah Kramer, *The Sumerians: Their History, Culture and Character* (Chicago: University of Chicago Press, 1963), 319. See F. Charles Fensham's discussion in "Widow, Orphan, and the Poor in Ancient Near Eastern Legal and Wisdom Literature," *JNES* 21 (1962): 130.

125. Fensham, "Widow," 134.

22:21, 23). This order is reversed in all references in Deuteronomy, to (1) *ytwm*, (2) *'lmnh*."[126]

The insertion of the term *gēr* into the couplet אלמנה ויתום is an innovation of Deuteronomy. On the one hand, the *gēr* fits easily with the couplet, as the *gēr* has in common a severance from kindred and from a means of sustenance. On the other hand, the two categories listed in the traditional couplet, אלמנה ויתום, are especially vulnerable, for there is no male laborer in the family. Thus the common claim in scholarship that the triad והגר והיתום והאלמנה is "the poor *par excellence*"[127] lacks precision. Furthermore, the fact that the *gēr* comes first in the triad of the vulnerable is significant, for given the legacy of the duo fatherless-widow, one would expect otherwise. So, it would seem that widespread displacement is *the* pressing social issue in the community before Deuteronomy. Through this transformation of an established literary trope, Deuteronomy is able to articulate its ethics regarding the *gēr* in terms of the already established literary tradition of Israel and of the ancient Near East regarding the poor.

Three further remarks are in order in regard to the triad in Deuteronomy. First, Kidd has catalogued other class nouns that occur in ancient Near Eastern texts along with the pair יתום ואלמנה. Kidd observes that the stranger does not appear in any extant texts, highlighting the significance of the appearance of the *gēr* in Deuteronomy.[128] Second, the *gēr* and the Levite are often emphasized among these vulnerable categories in Deuteronomy by their emphatic placement (10:18–19, 14:29) or by the frequent omission of the other categories of vulnerable people (1:16, 5:14, 14:17, 26:11, 29:10, 31:12). Third, following from this, it seems that in Deuteronomy the couplet יתום ואלמנה has a generic quality as a reference to the poor, while the *gēr* and Levite are of peculiar social and theological concern for Deuteronomy. This will be born out in the exegesis of the following chapters.

Vulnerable people commonly participated in the life of ancient Near Eastern households as inexpensive labor and so were vulnerable to exploitation. In many cases, Deuteronomy may not be so much *initiat-*

---

126. Thomas Krapf, "Traditionsgeschichtliches zum deuteronomischen Fremd-ling-Waise-Witwe-Gebot," *VT* 24 (1984): 88–89: "Beide Male die nämliche Reihen-folge (1.) *'lmnh*, (2.) *ytwm* gebraucht wird (V. 21, 23). Deise Reihenfolge wird in allen Deuteronomiumtexten vertauscht zu (1.) *ytwm*, (2.) *'lmnh*."

127. Garroway, *Children*, 92.

128. Kidd, *Alterity*, 35–40.

*ing* relationships between the vulnerable and landed households as much as *transforming* relationships already established. We are beginning to see that Deuteronomy alters the status of vulnerable people, fostering their participation within the people of God, specifically within the household and within the village. This strategy is clarified in the following discussion of the law of the fleeing slave and the function of this law within Deuteronomy's system of protection for the *gēr*.

### 3.6. The Fleeing Slave and the *Gēr* (Deut 23:16–17 [Eng. 23:15–16])

Deuteronomy 23:16–17 can be translated as follows:

> 16 You shall not turn[129] over a slave to his or her master, who seeks refuge from him with you. 17 The slave shall dwell with you, in your midst, at the place the slave may choose in one of your settlements, wherever suits the slave. You shall not treat the slave poorly.

### 3.6.1. Legal Analysis

While the noun or verb *gr* does not appear in the law concerning the fleeing slave, this text is nonetheless linked lexically and conceptually to laws concerning the *gēr*. In contrast to ancient Near Eastern slave law, Deuteronomy here asserts the rights of the slave rather than of the slave owner.[130] It also asserts a legal and moral duty for Israelite communities to offer a home to a fleeing slave, who may reside wherever the slave chooses. This law disrupts slavery as an institution: slavery will continue only so long as it continues to be of benefit to an individual slave.[131]

---

129. אַל suggests the translation "deliver" rather than apprehend, though both senses may be implied (so Greengus, "Laws," 116).

130. Chirichigno suggests that this law refers to chattel slaves in particular, as debt slaves would likely have had other ways of addressing mistreatment (*Debt-Slavery*, 184).

131. Rabbinic scholars and many modern interpreters understand this law as referring to a slave who has fled into Israel from another kingdom (see, e.g., Greengus, "Laws," 117–18; Tigay, *Deuteronomy*, 387 n 58; Tsai, *Rights*, 62–63). I suggest that, while this may have been the reference of the law in a former context, in its present context in the DC Deut 23:15–16 is a part of a system of slave laws that address the circumstances of slaves who reside within Israel (see also 15:12–18). Against the argument that the slave here is never referred to as "brother" (e.g., Tsai, *Rights*, 63), Deut

A number of extant ancient Near Eastern law corpora legislate against harboring runaway slaves. Penalties for being found with a slave who is owned by another include paying the owner the cost of the slave's labor (Hittite Laws 24), paying the owner the full price of a slave (Lipit-Ishtar Laws 12–13), and the death penalty (Laws of Hammurabi 16–20). Rewards for returning runaway slaves were also specified (Hittite Laws 22–24; Laws of Hammurabi 17).[132] Treaties commonly included clauses stipulating the return of fleeing slaves and of other fugitives. "Slaves were deprived of the freedom of transition from one authority to another in the ancient world."[133]

The core stipulation of this text, לא תסגיר עבד אל אדניו, directly repudiates the ancient Near Eastern norm of slave return that is stipulated in law corpora and treaties.[134] The phrase אשר ינצל אליך מעם אדניו in 23:16b is legally superfluous, adding a personal dimension and introducing the following stipulation concerning an escapee's right to reside in whatever town is desired.[135] Resumptive repetition of אדניו in 23:16a, b may signal that 23:16b is a later addition.[136] Deuteronomy 23:16–17 would probably have been difficult to enforce in judicial procedure, as responsibility rests with a whole community; thus the stipulation is probably best described as a divine imperative rather than substantive law.

### 3.6.2. The Relation of This Stipulation to the *Gēr*

The escaped slave is displaced within a new context, without kindred and without means, so the fleeing slave becomes, in effect, a *gēr*.[137] The lexical and conceptual field of Deut 23:16–17 associates with laws concerning the *gēr* rather than with slave law. The phrase בקרבך in 23:17 is applied to

---

23:16–17 adopts the lexical and conceptual field of texts concerning the *gēr*, and this figure is never referred to as אח (see §4.2.3).

132. Greengus, *Laws*, 119–121; Tsai, *Rights*, 132–33.

133. One function of Egyptian fortification lines was to arrest escaping slaves; see Nili Wazana, *All the Boundaries of the Land: The Promised Land in Biblical Thought in Light of the Ancient Near East* (Winona Lake, IN: Eisenbrauns, 2013), 53.

134. Deuteronomy 23:16a and 23:17b may comprise an original stipulation.

135. Regarding legally superfluous material, see Patrick, "Casuistic," 183.

136. Contra Braulik, "Rights," 143. Resumptive repetition may be an intentional marker of additional material (Carr, *Formation*, 44; Levinson, *Deuteronomy and the Hermeneutics*, 18).

137. Braulik also makes this observation ("Rights," 143).

the *gēr* elsewhere (16:11, 26:11, 28:43, 29:10, Josh 8:35). The final stipulation, לא תוננו, concerns the treatment of the escaped slave once the slave is accepted into the community. Likely, ינה is a deliberate echo of the opening stipulation in the social law of the CC that also concerns the *gēr*.[138]

Exod 22:20

וגר לא תונה ולא תלחצנו כי גרים הייתם בארץ מצרים

*Gēr* and ינה are also paired in P (Lev 19:33) and in two prophetic texts (Jer 22:3; Ezek 22:29). Further, in 23:17 the escaped slave is באחד שעריך, identifying the slave with the landless. The formula אשר בשעריך is among Deuteronomy's integrative formulas, with the function of incorporating vulnerable people into the clan.[139] In a sense, the escaped slave benefits from the ethic of integration that Deuteronomy provides for the *gēr*.

By associating the escapee with the *gēr*, the text recasts the unfree slave as a free person. The immense social, legal, and economic implications of this law can hardly be overstated: a slave may procure a change in status from unfree to free simply by fleeing! This implication is by no means lost on the text, for the former master's ownership (אדניו) is referenced twice in 23:16. Thus this stipulation disrupts the institution of slavery. Further, the law implicitly rejects the economic assumptions that lay behind slavery, such as slave as property, the priority of debt repayment over freedom, and the priority of the rights of the slave owner. I would only add that this law, in its present context, is intended to be read alongside the Dtn social laws regarding debt release and slave release that preserve the *residual* rights of slaves (Deut 15:1–18), as well as the more conservative statutory law of the *mišpāṭîm* (Exod 21:2–11).[140]

Deuteronomy 23:16–17 augments the developing mosaic of theology and ethics in this study of the *gēr* in Deuteronomy in at least five ways:

1. We learn regarding the social origins of displacement that a *gēr* may be a slave who has fled his or her owner, probably due to mistreatment.

---

138. Exod 22:20 and Exod 23:9 frame the CC social law.

139. See the discussion of בשעריך in §5.5.2.

140. I have argued that the laws of the DC operate together as a legal and ethical system, at times even in tension with one another. They are designed to be read alongside the laws of the CC (see §§1.3.4 and 3.2).

2. Deuteronomy 23:17 is abundant with associations of land gift, implying that the *gēr*/escapee is also a recipient of Yahweh's gifts (e.g., ישב). The phrase במקום אשר יבחר echoes the altar-law formula: "Deut 23:16–17 arguably treats the whole land of Israel as a sanctuary offering permanent asylum."[141]

3. There is a threefold expression of the relation of the *gēr*/escapee with the settlement and the household in 23:17: עמך ישב, בקרבך, באחד שעריך. These three expressions of integration, in rapid succession, are a most intimate expression of association.

4. There are three expressions of the agency of an escapee in choosing a place to dwell in 23:17: באחד, במקום אשר יבחר, בטוב לו, שעריך. By extrapolation, this exhortation to welcome the *gēr*/escapee in whatever town he or she chooses applies to every *gēr* that Deuteronomy addresses. Regarding במקום אשר יבחר, Yahweh is the subject of all other occurrences of *bḥr* with this form. Clear echoes of Yahweh's *choice* of a place reinforce the sense of the agency and of the dignity of the *gēr*/slave.

5. This law is reinforced by its association with the preceding laws of admission (23:1–8), via the hospitality motif. Nathan MacDonald suggests that the restrictions upon the admission of Ammonites and Moabites into the assembly is in light of their failure to enact cultural norms of hospitality (23:3–6); an Egyptian's positive reception is due to the hospitality that Egypt extended to Israel when Israel itself was *gēr* (23:7).[142]

In sum, a displaced person may expect a brotherly-sisterly welcome in whatever Israelite city or settlement that she or he desires to call home. Once again, the integrative impulse of the text is to be enacted at a level of a local kinship grouping. "The integrative direction of the Dtn commandments with regard to the *gēr* and the other needy, is, therefore, based upon individual localities, within which no one is directly obliged to secure his

---

141. Tsai, *Rights*, 63.

142. Nathan MacDonald, *Not Bread Alone: The Uses of Food in the Old Testament* (Oxford: Oxford University Press, 2008), 93–96.

livelihood (in view that *gēr* is a stranger to the locality)."[143] We turn now to the *gēr* in the Sabbath stipulation of the Decalogue.

### 3.7. The Sabbath (Deut 5:12–15)

The Sabbath stipulation in Deut 5:12–15 reads as follows:

> 12 Observe the Sabbath day and keep it holy as Yahweh your God has commanded you. 13 Six days you shall labor and do all of your work, 14 but the seventh day is a Sabbath to Yahweh your God. Do not do any work, you, your son or daughter, your male or female servant, your ox or your ass or any of your cattle, or your stranger who is within your gates, in order that your male and female servant may rest as well as you. 15 Remember that you were a slave in the land of Egypt and Yahweh your God freed you from there with a mighty hand and an outstretched arm; because of this Yahweh your God has commanded you to keep the Sabbath day.[144] (ESV, modified)

#### 3.7.1. Canonical Significance and Ancient Near Eastern Background

Deuteronomy 5:14 joins together the divine character of Sabbath, שבת ליהוה אלהיך, with a social ethic for the stranger and other vulnerable people. While the Sabbath command belongs to the frame of Deuteronomy, the command is investigated in the present chapter rather than chapter 6, as it reflects, in part, the lexical and conceptual domain of the DC. Discussing the Sabbath (5:12–15) with the social law reflects a prior decision to be sensitive to the various subgroupings of law in Deuteronomy. In a similar way, 1:16–17 will be analyzed as law of judicial procedure.

This stipulation presupposes that the household head has authority over the *gēr*, at least in regard to labor, as is reflected in the phrase גרך in 5:14. The pronominal suffix signals that the *gēr* here is closely associated with the household, perhaps as an indentured laborer or as a contracted

---

143. Bultmann, *Fremde*, 215: "Die integrative Tendenz, die den dtn Geboten bezüglich des ger und der übrigen Bedürftigen zugrundeliegt, ist deshalb an den einzelnen Ortschaften orientiert, in denen zumal im Blick auf den ger als einen Ortsfremden niemand unmittelbar verpflichtet wäre, ihm den Erwerb seines Lebensunterhalts möglich zu machen."

144. The LXX has καὶ ἁγιάζειν αὐτήν, and 4Q Deut[n] (4Q41) adds לקדשו, "to keep it holy," forming an inclusion with 5:12a.

laborer (see §3.3.5). Indentured laborers and slaves in Mesopotamia were required to work almost every day. A Nuzi *tidennūtu* contract (cited in full in §2.1) stipulated: "But if Taena departs from the work of Tulpunnaya for a single day, Uqari must give one mina of copper, his hire (for a replacement) per day to Tulpunnaya."[145] Many a displaced person in Mesopotamia would have worked without a day of rest. "The uniquely biblical conception of the week and the sabbatical cycle stands out equally by virtue of its pervasiveness in biblical laws and letters, as by its absence from the surrounding Near East."[146] In chapter 5 I observe how ancient Near Eastern lunar festivals reinforced the divine sanction for royal rule. "Here, then, two of the great contrasts between biblical Israel and its Near Eastern matrix meet: sabbatical cycles versus lunar calendars, and divine versus royal authority."[147]

In Deuteronomy, the Decalogue stands at the beginning of the longest of Moses's speeches (Deut 5–26), and, along with the Exodus Decalogue, it records the words that Yahweh spoke to the people directly (now retold by Moses).[148] Lohfink argues that the Sabbath command achieved the utmost prominence in the final form of the Pentateuch as the central command of the Decalogue of Deuteronomy.[149] Key words in the Sabbath command link to the beginning and the end of the Decalogue, and the use of the conjunctive particle brings together the social commands, locating Sabbath at the center, so that Sabbath is "the principle commandment" in the Decalogue of Deuteronomy. The *gēr* here is highlighted by the absence of the pairing והיתום והאלמנה, and the appearance of the *gēr* is evidence of a large number of displaced people in the period of the text.

---

145. Robert H. Pfeiffer and E. A. Speiser, "One Hundred New Selected Nuzi Texts," *AASOR* 16 (1936): 87, lines 10–14.

146. W. W. Hallo, "New Moons and Sabbath: A Case Study in the Contrastive Approach," *HUCA* 48 (1977): 15.

147. Hallo, "New Moons," 17.

148. Dominik Markl, "The Ten Words Revealed and Revised: The Origins of Law and Legal Hermeneutics in the Pentateuch," in *The Decalogue and Its Cultural Influence*, ed. Dominik Markl, HBM 58 (Sheffield: Sheffield Phoenix, 2013), 19–20.

149. See further Norbert Lohfink, *Theology of the Pentateuch: Themes of the Priestly Narrative and Deuteronomy* (Minneapolis: Fortress, 1994), 254–59. Also Braulik, "Rights," 138.

### 3.7.2. Composition History

A majority of critical scholars believe that the Decalogue is a literary work postdating the law codes; my analysis takes this position as well. As will be demonstrated, the Decalogue uses literary tropes that appear to have their deepest roots in the law codes, namely, the CC and the DC. It is possible that the Decalogue was a part of the first of two major exilic redactions, and it seems logical that the DC was somewhat reordered in accordance with the Decalogue at this time.[150] Scholarship continues to disagree upon whether the Exodus Decalogue or the Deuteronomy Decalogue was the prior one, though there is some preference for the priority of the Exodus Decalogue.[151] The composition of the Decalogue and of the Sabbath command in particular has been the subject of intense debate over the past twenty years.[152] For the sake of clarity, this study will confine its analysis to Deut 5:12–15 as a redaction of Exod 23:12. This approach is valid, since Deut 5:12–15 inserts key motifs from Exod 23:12 that were omitted in the Exodus Decalogue, in particular the ox-donkey motif and the למען ינוח clause.

### 3.7.3. Legal Revision and the Intention of the Sabbath Command

The Decalogue of Deuteronomy recasts the seventh day rest as "Sabbath," both enhancing its social imperative and representing the Sabbath as a practice that takes place "before Yahweh." Prior to the Deuteronomic Decalogue, the seventh day of rest was referred to with the verb שבת (see, e.g., Exod 23:12). The Deuteronomic Decalogue uses the noun שַׁבָּת and thereby institutes the weekly "Sabbath."[153] In 5:12, the injunctive שמור connects with Dtn cultic law (16:1), casting Sabbath rest as a cultic ordi-

---

150. Braulik, "Abfolge"; Markl, "Ten," 13; Otto, "History of the Legal-Religious," 229–231; Schmidt, *Old Testament*, 137–38.

151. Erhard Blum, "The Decalogue and the Composition History of the Pentateuch," in *The Pentateuch: International Perspectives on Current Research*, ed. T. B. Dozeman, FAT 78 (Tübingen: Mohr Siebeck, 2011), 289; Reinhard D. Kratz, "Der Dekalog im Exodusbuch," *VT* 44 (1994): 205–38.

152. For a summary of the scholarship, see Markl, "Ten," 13–14 n. 1; Blum, "Decalogue," 289–301.

153. Some scholars suggest that the seventh day of rest stipulation initially applied to the time of the harvest (see Exod 34:21) and was extended from there to the entire year (Otto, *Deuteronomium*, 739; E. Haag, "שַׁבָּת," *TDOT* 14:390).

nance.[154] "The Horeb-Decalogue in Deut 5:12–15 is the oldest clearly visible instance of the connection between the institution of a day of rest and Sabbath."[155]

A sanctioned day of rest within a seven-day cycle also appears in non-legislative texts of the Hebrew Bible.[156] Likely early references are Amos 8:4 and Hos 2:11. It is possible that "Sabbath" appears in the Yavneh-Yam inscription, which would be a pre-Dtr nonlegislative occurrence.[157] If so, this would mean that during the late monarchy a Sabbath was enjoyed by at least some of the vulnerable in Judah, in the case of the Yavneh-Yam inscription, probably a day laborer. While the seventh-day rest likely predated the law corpuses, the legislative material of the CC and of Deuteronomy intensifies the social element of this tradition for the sake of the least.

### 3.7.3.1. The 6/1 Schema: Theology and Ethics

The prominence of the 6/1 schema in Deuteronomy's social program for the *gēr* warrants discussion of this schema's development. The following discussion is indebted in particular to Otto's analysis.[158] In legislative texts, form-critical observations suggest that the seventh day of rest stipulation has its literary roots in the Feast of Unleavened Bread stipulation with its 6/1 schema (initially Exod 23:15a, 34:18, and later, with the "6[7] days you shall eat formula," in Deut 16:8 and Exod 13:6).[159] The 6/1 schema has a prehistory in ancient Near Eastern cultic law, and in Israelite law

---

154. שמור is characteristic of Dtr (cf. 6:17, 11:22, 27:1).

155. Otto, *Deuteronomium*, 739: "Dafür ist der Horebdekalog in Dtn 5, 12–15 der älteste Beleg, der die Verbindung von Ruhetagsinstitution und Sabbat noch deutlich zu erkennen gibt." The Sabbath may have some association with a celebratory ritual on the full moon day (see, e.g., Isa 1:13, 66:23, Ezek 46:1). See further Moshe Weinfeld, *Deuteronomy 1–11*, AB 5 (New Haven: Yale University Press, 1991), 302; Eckart Otto, *Deuteronomium 1–11*, 2 vols, HThKAT (Freiburg: Herder, 2012), 1.2:738–39.

156. Concerning the Sabbath outside of legislative texts, see Haag, "שַׁבָּת," 14:391–92; Carr, *Formation*, 302–3.

157. So Aḥituv, *Echoes*, 161. Aḥituv dates the Yavneh-Yam inscription to the time of Josiah. "And your servant harvested and finished/measured and stored in the granary as always before the Sabbath" (lines 5–6; Aḥituv's translation). Dennis Pardee, however, argues that שבת here simply refers to ceasing work; see his "Judicial Plea from Meṣad Ḥashavyahu (Yavneh-Yam): A New Philological Study," *Maarav* 1 (1978): 44.

158. Eckart Otto, "שָׁבַע," *TDOT* 14:336–67.

159. Otto, *Deuteronomium*, 738; Haag, "שַׁבָּת," 14:390.

the schema is also theologically motivated. "The separation for Yahweh acknowledges the reign of Yahweh over the area that is separated."[160] In the literary-historical development of the 6/1 schema, then, the theological dimension appears before the social dimension. The social ethic of the schema first appears in the stipulation of a seventh-day rest in the pre-Dtr cultic law of the CC, Exod 23:12, which is the primary source text for the Sabbath command of the Deuteronomic Decalogue.[161] "Starting with the festival of unleavened bread, the heptadic system gains importance for the whole Old Testament festival calendar tradition."[162]

### 3.7.3.2. Exodus 23:10–12: The Primary Source Text for Deuteronomy 5:12–15

Exodus 23:10–12 and Exod 21:2–11 frame the law corpus according to the 6/1 schema. This encloses the CC within the interwoven themes of Yahweh's reign (indicated by the 6/1 schema) and of care for the weakest in society.[163]

Exod 23:12

ששת ימים תעשה מעשיך וביום השביעי תשבת למען ינוח שורך וחמרך
וינפש בן אמתך והגר

Exodus 23:12a is made up of a 6/1 schema of work and rest. The motive clause (12b) clarifies the social aim of the stipulation, and the 6/1 schema embeds the law within the exclusive worship of Yahweh. The pair שורך וחמרך is taken from Exod 23:4, a stipulation that is the rhetorical climax

---

160. Otto, *Deuteronomium*, 738: "Die Aussonderung für JHWH drückt die Anerkenntnis der Herrschaft JHWHs über den Bereich der Aussonderung aus."

161. With Otto, "History of the Legal-Religious," 212; Otto, *Deuteronomium*, 738–39; F. L. Hossfeld, *Der Dekalog: Seine späten Fassungen, die originale Komposition und seine Vorstufen*, OBO 45 (Freiburg: Göttingen, 1982), 53–57. Contra Weinfeld, *Deuteronomy*, 305. Bultmann, *Fremde*, 64, 166, and Haag, "שַׁבָּת," 14:387–97, take the Decalogue as prior to Exod 23:12. However, the relation between Exod 23:12 and Deut 5:12–15 follows a pattern whereby the DC intensifies the social dimension of the CC.

162. Otto. *Deuteronomium*, 738: "Vom Mazzotfest ausgehend gewinnt das Heptadensystem Bedeutung für die gesamte alttestamentliche Festkalendertradition." In Deut 16:1–15 temporal organization is grouped according to the number seven a total of seven times (Otto, "שֶׁבַע," 14:355).

163. Otto, "Aspects of Legal Reforms," 186–89.

of the (earlier) social law of the CC.[164] In its earlier context, the pair signified the weakest in the community. The household of the paterfamilias is
the context for the unusual phrase וינפש בן אמתך והגר ("and that the son
of your slave woman and the stranger may be refreshed"). Deuteronomy
5:12–15 is a revision of Exod 23:12, and a close analysis of the redaction is
warranted for an investigation of the *gēr* in Deuteronomy.

### 3.7.3.3. Deuteronomy 5:12–15: Redaction and Kerygma

I have observed throughout this chapter that the DC intensifies the social
ethics of the CC, and this same pattern is evident in the Sabbath stipulation. Deuteronomy inserts three blocks of text into the source text, at
the beginning, at the *sof-passuq*, and at the *attnah* of Exod 23:12 (the text
appropriated from Exod 23:12 is underlined below). Deuteronomy 5:12–
15 is also dependent upon Deut 16:8 and upon P material, but this will
only be observed where relevant.[165]

Table 3.2: Deut 5:12–15 as a Redaction of Exod 23:12

| Exod 23:12 | Deut 5:12–15 |
|---|---|
| | שמור את יום השבת לקדשו כאשר צוך יהוה אלהיך |
| ששת ימים תעשה מעשיך וביום השביעי תשבת | ששת ימים תעבד ועשית כל מלאכתך ויום השביעי שבת ליהוה אלהיך לא תעשה כל מלאכה אתה ובנך ובתך ועבדך ואמתך ושורך וחמרך וכל בהמתך וגרך אשר בשעריך |
| למען ינוח שורך וחמרך וינפש בן אמתך והגר | למען ינוח עבדך ואמתך כמוך |
| | וזכרת כי עבד היית בארץ מצרים ויצאך יהוה אלהיך משם ביד חזקה ובזרע נטויה על כן צוך יהוה אלהיך לעשות את יום השבת |

This redaction uses several of the literary tropes that form Deuteronomy's
vocabulary for social ethics. For example, the pair ושורך וחמרך is symbolic
in legislative texts of the justice that is due to the weakest. The reception

---

164. See the discussion of Exod 23:1–8 in §3.2.
165. Regarding the use of P in Deut 5:12–15, see Weinfeld, *Deuteronomy*, 304–5.

of this pair, ושורך וחמרך, from the earliest social law to the Deuteronomic Decalogue may be outlined:

Exod 23:4 (just judicial processes) → Exod 23:12 (seventh-day rest) → Deut 5:14 (Decalogue Sabbath, compare with Deut 22:4)

Four observations will help clarify the aim of 5:12–15. First, the text creates a dialectic between renewing work and exploitative work. Deuteronomy 5:13 revises Exod 23:12a. The root עבד (cf. תעשה in Exod 23:12) is a highly unusual expression for work in Deuteronomy (also 15:19; cf. מעשה in 14:29, 15:10, 27:15, 31:29 and מלאכה in 16:8). The expression contributes to Deuteronomy's goal of framing the Sabbath in terms of slavery-exodus (note also the double occurrence of ועבדך ואמתך [Deut 5:14b, c] and the slavery-exodus motive clause, Deut 5:15).[166] The use of עבד curiously suggests that work is exploitative, if there is no provision for rest, opening up a dialectic between "good work" and "bad work." The latter takes Israel back to Egypt, and the former is experienced in Canaan. We might reflect that bad work requires deliverance, while good work requires rest.

> Sabbath marks the definitive separation between slavery in Egypt and the epoch that is formally inaugurated at Sinai…. The Sabbath imperative suggests that the basis on which work may be judged "good" goes beyond its direct products … marking Israel's domestic economy as a renewing economy … in contrast to an industrial economy that exhausts workers and material goods.[167]

Second, Deut 5:14 holds in tension the divine character of Sabbath, שבת ליהוה אלהיך (5:14a), and Sabbath's social orientation. It recasts the seventh-day stipulation of Exod 23:12 in terms of the cultic ritual formula of Dtn (e.g., ועשית חג שבעות ליהוה אלהיך, 16:10aα):

Exod 23:12: תשבת → Deut 5:14a: שבת ליהוה אלהיך

Moreover, Deut 5:14 recasts the seventh day of rest according to the extended Dtn formula for cultic feasts, with the elements in order (Deut

---

166. Weinfeld notes that while מעשה (used in Exod 23:12) seems to refer only to agricultural work, מלאכה seems to refer to any kind of work (*Deuteronomy*, 305).

167. Ellen F. Davis, *Scripture, Culture, and Agriculture: An Agrarian Reading of the Bible* (Cambridge: Cambridge University Press, 2009), 143.

14:16; 16:11, 14a; 26:11; cf. 12:17, 12; 16:8): ritual name (noun, e.g., חג) + "to the Lord your God" + injunctive (verbal form, e.g., שׂמח) + household list.[168] Thus Deuteronomy at once reframes the seventh day of rest as a cultic ritual before Yahweh, even as it enhances its social orientation for the most vulnerable.

Third, class distinctions are disrupted. The participant list enumerates those who live under one roof. This includes the domestic animals that lived in the stalls on the "ground floor" of a four-room house.[169] The entire household was to participate in this divine ordinance of rest from labor. In the MT, a *waw*-conjunctive links the sons and daughters to the vulnerable (ועבדך) that is omitted in the Exodus Decalogue (ובנך ובתך עבדך, Exod 20:10). The *waw* is omitted in LXX and SP Deuteronomy; however, the principle of *lectio difficilior* applies in this case, and the *waw* should be accepted.[170] The *waw* links consanguineous kindred and the landless within the household seamlessly, disrupting class distinctions within the household list. (I am not here suggesting that the Sabbath command removes hierarchy, which would be anomalous in any Mediterranean communal culture.)

Fourth, the two motive clauses include the *gēr* within Israel's own journey from slavery to flourishing. The first motive clause, למען ינוח עבדך ואמתך כמוך, revises a similar clause in Exod 23:12, and both clauses confirm that the goal of the Sabbath is rest for the most vulnerable (cf. למען ינוח שׁורך וחמרך וינפשׁ בן אמתך והגר, Exod 23:12). The revision highlights slaves in line with the observed goal of Deut 5:12–15 to frame Sabbath in terms of the slavery-exodus motif (cf. Deut 5:6).[171] The noun נוח ("rest") refers to weekly rest from labor and is also a key word in Deuteronomy's narrative of displacement, slavery, conflict, and settlement.[172] The word נוח evokes settling in the land, receiving peace from enemies, and, by exten-

---

168. The injunctive is recast as the work prohibition formula in Deut 5:14, לא תעשׂה כל מלאכה (cf. 16:8). Phrases in Deut 5:14 are appropriated from Deut 16:8 (Dtn) and Exod 13:6 (pre-Dtr). The work prohibition formula is found in a different form in P (see Weinfeld, *Deuteronomy*, 304).

169. King and Stager, *Life*, 28–35.

170. We may presuppose a disposition toward harmonizing the Exodus Decalogue and the Deuteronomy Decalogue.

171. Reference to both male and female slaves (also Exod 23:12) may distinguish between work in the field and in the settlement compound with the point that the Sabbath command encompasses all types of work and of workers.

172. See my discussion of Israel's narrative in the exegesis of 26:1–11 in §5.3.3.

sion, enjoying the fruits of the land (Exod 33:14, Deut 3:20, 12:10, 25:19, 28:65).[173] Thus slaves and the *gēr* are not mere economic functionaries but co-heirs of the blessings of the land. The phrase כמוך, missing from Exod 23:12, emphasizes that the *gēr* is a *partner* in the "rest" that is the fruits of the gift of land and its produce.

### 3.7.4. Theology and Ethics of Inclusivism in the Sabbath Stipulation (Deut 5:12–15)

> Sabbath sets a boundary to our best, most intense efforts to manage life and organize land for our security and well-being. The Sabbath is not only a social arrangement for maintaining humanness, but it is a theological affirmation of Yahweh's ownership of the land and of history.[174]

Deuteronomy 5:12–15 recasts the seventh-day stipulation of Exod 23:12 in terms of the cultic ritual formula, joining together the divine character of Sabbath, שבת ליהוה אלהיך (5:14a), and Sabbath's social orientation. At a comparative level, the Sabbath disrupts the normal course of the lunar month and year. Sabbath is an unpredictable intrusion that insists, on the basis of Yahweh's liberation, upon a 6/7 rhythm of work and rest even for the stranger and even during the harvest, when ceaseless work might be expected. The Sabbath was associated with the exodus from its literary origins in Massot (Exod 23:15, 34:18). "Israel does not owe its (agrarian) life to the mythic power of the earth but to having been freed by God from all systems of exploitation and oppression."[175] In light of the uniqueness of the Sabbath command in the ancient Near East, perhaps no single law expresses the social revolution of Deuteronomy more forcefully. The "awkwardness" of this seventh-day disruption is perhaps amplified by the presence of the *gēr*, who at both a literary level and "on the ground" is the unlikely companion, reminding Israel of its unlikely deliverance.

---

173. The basic meaning in the *qal* is "settle down" (F. Stolz, "נוח," *TLOT* 2:722).

174. Walter Brueggemann, *The Land: Place as Gift, Promise and Challenge in Biblical Faith*, OBT (Philadelphia: Fortress, 1977), 63.

175. See Braulik, "Rights," 137.

### 3.7.5. The Social-Historical Context for Dtr's Ethics of Inclusion for the *Gēr*

In the following chapter I will argue that Dtr may be tentatively dated to Neo-Babylonian Judah, on the basis of social-historical considerations (see §4.9.3). Assuming the validity of this argument, it is illuminating to consider the Sabbath command in this light. Faust argues that the Babylonian conquest of Judah and the resulting assassination, exile, famine, emigration, and disease created a "postcollapse society."[176] Faust estimates that, in the years following the conquest, the Judahite population decreased to around 10 percent of the levels at the end of the Iron Age, increasing to around 20 percent in the late sixth century.[177] The majority of cities and of rural settlements were destroyed, and there was no polity or centralized economy of which to speak.[178] "The population must have subsisted on simple agriculture."[179] The massive death toll and the resulting destruction of kinship groupings would have produced widespread displacement.[180] The provisions for the *gēr* in the Sabbath command and in other Dtr texts rearticulates and intensifies for this new context the ethic of inclusion for the stranger that was formerly expressed in Dtn. The exile of the elite landowners would have created some social mobility, for the best of the land was now available to the reduced and mostly peasant population (see, e.g., Jer 39:10, 52:16).[181] This possibility of land holdings would have been an opportunity for the *gēr* that was unimaginable during the monarchic period. This new opportunity, combined with harrowing need, necessitated a recontextualization of Dtn's egalitarian program for sixth-century Judah.[182] Perhaps the Dtr redaction of the judicial laws (1:16–17; discussed in the following chapter) was ordered to protect the rights and autonomy of displaced people in light of this new opportunity. The rule of

---

176. Faust, *Judah*, 170.

177. Faust, *Judah*, 138–47. Recovery was remarkably slow, typical of post-collapse societies. Two and a half centuries after the event the population was still 33–35 percent of the levels at the end if the Iron Age (*Judah*, 138).

178. Faust, *Judah*, 235–39.

179. Faust, *Judah*, 237.

180. On the erosion of kinship groupings during the Neo-Babylonian period, see §4.7.3.

181. Faust, *Judah*, 174, 237; Albertz, *Israel*, 92.

182. Cf. the strong echoes of Deuteronomy's social program in Ezek 18:5–24, 33:10–20.

Yahweh, which transforms society in line with the ethical trajectory of the exodus, was the theological reality that undergirded this recontextualization of ethics. Here I diverge from Bultmann's assertion that there was continuity in social relations beyond the Babylonian conquest, and my reconstruction of the goals of Dtr in relation to the *gēr* differs from Bultmann's as a result.[183]

### 3.7.6. The *Gēr* is a Liminal Figure

Having observed the *gēr* in four social laws, it is clarifying to take a step back in order to reconsider this figure, the *gēr*. It is evident from the above that *gēr* in Deuteronomy designates a liminal category of people, on the threshold between one social status and another. The *gēr* is neither independent (for the *gēr* provides cheap labor for a household and/or a clan, also dwelling with this group), nor is the *gēr* incorporated within a kinship network (the *gēr* is not a "brother," as in 24:14–15; cf. 1:16). The participation of the *gēr* in the Sabbath provision illustrates, at least incipiently, how Deuteronomy is seeking to transform the relationship between the *gēr* and the kinship grouping, fostering incorporation of the *gēr* into the household. Almost all scholarly reconstructions of the *gēr* either ignore this dynamic or inadvertently oppose it. Richard Nelson, for example, describes the *gēr* as being in a patron-client relationship with the host.[184] While not without some truth,[185] this metaphor has the sense of a static hierarchical arrangement that ignores the movement toward inclusivism within Deuteronomy's social vision. Clearer still, MacDonald states, "For Deuteronomy the resident alien remains a resident alien."[186] Similarly, according to Van Houten, "no way was open for aliens to become members of the Israelite community."[187] These studies characterize the social status of the *gēr* in Deuteronomy as static.

183. Bultmann, *Fremde*, 215.

184. Nelson, *Deuteronomy*, 83.

185. The more a *gēr* was incorporated within a household, the more thoroughly the honor of the *gēr* would be embedded in the honor of the paterfamilias and the more thoroughly the identity of the *gēr* would be a communal identity shared with the whole household.

186. MacDonald, *Not Bread Alone*, 99.

187. Van Houten, *Alien in Israelite Law*, 107.

Otto accurately isolates the basic need of the *gēr*: "The landless and their families needed to be integrated into the clans."[188] While only modest assertions may be made at this early point in the study, participation in the community is envisioned, for example, in that the *gēr* is included within Deuteronomy's brother-sister ethic (observed above regarding 24:14–15), in that the *gēr* had a primary right to the residue of the harvest (24:19–22), in the apparent integration of the fleeing slave within a settlement (23:16–17), in the participation of the *gēr* in Sabbath rest (5:12–15), and in the phrases בשעריך (24:14), גרך (24:14), and בקרבך (23:16–17).[189] We shall observe with increasing clarity throughout this study that Deuteronomy's goal is that the *gēr* not be exploited as cheap labor; rather, the *gēr* is to be a full participant in the life of the household and the settlement. So, *gēr* in Deuteronomy designates a liminal category of people on the threshold between one social status and another.

Nonetheless, the *gēr* is not yet a brother-sister. Awabdy rightly observes that parallelism brings the *gēr* and the sister-brother into association (e.g., 1:16–17, 24:17):

> You shall not oppress a hired worker who is poor and needy, whether he is one of your brothers or one of the sojourners who are in your land within your towns. (Deut 24:17)

However, Awabdy's assertion that "'your countrymen' [brothers] include the Israelite *and* his gr" lacks nuance.[190] *Gēr* is never explicitly designated a brother in Deuteronomy, as the absence of affiliation is definitional for the *gēr*! More accurately, the *gēr* is a liminal figure, and Deuteronomy is *fostering* the inclusion of displaced people as kin. So, on the one hand, in certain texts the *gēr* appears in apposition to the אח. On the other hand, the law stipulates that the *gēr* is to be protected as one would protect a kinsperson.

Perhaps surprisingly, a stipulation within Deuteronomy's food law (14:21) also belongs with Deuteronomy's social law concerning the *gēr*, and we turn to this text before considering the broader implications of our analysis.

---

188. Otto, "שער," 15:380.
189. See §§3.3.5, 5.3.3.2, and 5.5.2.
190. Awadby, *Immigrants*, 41, emphasis original.

## 3.8. Food for the *Gēr* (Deut 14:21)

> Do not eat any carcass that has not been properly slaughtered. You may give it to the *gēr* who is in your gates and the *gēr* may eat it, or you may sell it to the foreigner, for you are a holy people to Yahweh your God.

Kinsfolk may give the carcass of a clean animal to the *gēr* that she or he may eat (14:21a; cf. Exod 22:30). The word נבלה is most commonly translated with the sense of "anything that dies of itself." However, Sparks interprets נבלה in the context of 14:1–21 as "the carcass of a clean species which has not been properly slaughtered," on the basis that this is the class of animal flesh that has not been dealt with in the preceding stipulations (12:10–14, 14:3–20).[191]

The broader context is food laws in which limitations upon edible foods are enumerated, beginning with ground-dwelling creatures (14:4–8), then sea creatures (14:9–10), and, finally, creatures that dwell in the air (14:11–20). True to Deuteronomy's practical concern for the life of the community, these instructions are memorable, "easy-to-follow rules of thumb."[192] The phrase כי עם קדוש אתה ליהוה אלהיך frames the section (14:2a, 21b). The distinction between clean and unclean foods symbolizes the character of Israel as children of Yahweh (14:1), functioning as an identity marker of the community. In relation to the demanding ethics that follow in the law corpus (14:21, 15:1–18, 16:9–15), the food laws seem to operate as a kind of rehearsal, in a mundane area of life, for the distinctive ethical and religious life of the community.

Regarding composition history, 14:1–21 does not connect to the centralization command that unites Deut 12–17, and Mayes rightly takes the plural address as an indication of a Dtr hand (14:1, 4–21).[193] Veijola is likely correct that the food laws were composed by the same exilic hand that composed the profane slaughter exemption (Deut 12), for both texts

---

191. Kenton Sparks, "A Comparative Study of the Biblical נבלה Laws," *ZAW* 110 (1998): 596.

192. Nelson, *Deuteronomy*, 176.

193. Mayes, *Deuteronomy*, 237. The original DC was likely composed in the singular address.

concern clean food that is eaten away from the sanctuary.[194] Deuteronomy 14:3–21 and Lev 11 seem to draw from a common source text.[195]

Behind the prohibition of eating a creature that has not been properly slaughtered is the principle of not eating blood (cf. Deut 12:15–28, Exod 22:30). While the carcass of swine may not even be touched (14:8), the carcass of a clean animal that would normally be eaten for food may be given to the *gēr* (14:21a). The prohibition is given in the plural address (14:21aα), consistent with 14:4–20. However, the address changes to the singular at 14:21aβ for the provision of the *gēr* (underlined below), which associates with the Dtn social law. The singular is maintained throughout the tithing law that follows (14:22–29), which is also a part of Deuteronomy's system of social protection. The *Numeruswechsel* flags that an aim of 14:21a is the relief of the vulnerable stranger:

14:21a (singular underlined)

לא תאכלו כל נבלה <u>לגר אשר בשעריך תתננה ואכלה או מכר לנכרי כי</u> עם קדוש אתה ליהוה אלהיך

A literary play on the verb אכל casts the consumption of unclean meat by the *gēr* as a right and valid partaking in the abundance of the land, gifted by Yahweh. The *waw*-singular verb construction, ואכלה (14:21aβ) associates with the tithe feast that follows (ואכלת, 14:26; both phrases are in the singular address), and it contrasts to the sixteen prior references in the food laws of permission, תאכלו, and prohibition, לא תאכלו (14:3–20). Numerous other literary connections between 14:22–29 and 14:1–21 associate the *gēr*'s meal with the description of the tithe, which is the most lavish description of festal repast in Deuteronomy: "Spend the money for whatever you desire—oxen or sheep or wine or strong drink, whatever your appetite craves" (14:26 ESV). By association with the tithe feast and with the theology of Yahweh's abundant supply for Israel unfolded in that text (14:22–29), the נבלה meal is represented as a part of the *gēr*'s portion of the divine blessing in the land.[196] To add, the use of אכל without שמח indicates that the *gēr*'s נבלה repast is a mundane meal eaten locally rather than a cultic feast (cf. 12:7; 14:26, 29; see ch. 5). Finally, the *inclusio* כי עם

---

194. Veijola also argues that the mourning rites, 14:2, were a later addition (*Das 5. Buch Mose*, 295).

195. Nelson, *Deuteronomy*, 177; Mayes, *Deuteronomy*, 237.

196. See the analysis of 14:22–27 and of 14:28–29 below.

קדוש אתה ליהוה אלהיך (14:2a, 22aβ) frames the act of supplying the נבלה
for the *gēr* as a distinctive characteristic of the people of Yahweh.

Regarding 14:21, Nelson asserts that "Deuteronomy manages to blend
its humane social ethics with its insistence on a sharp ethnic boundary."[197]
Albertz's assertion on the basis of 14:21 that "the Deuteronomic legislators
did not regard the *gērīm* as members of Israel" reflects the near scholarly
consensus on this text.[198] Indeed, the provision that the *gēr* may consume
the נבלה, exempting the *gēr* from the principle of not eating blood, signifies that the *gēr* is not included within the identification: כי עם קדוש אתה
ליהוה אלהיך (14:2a, 22aβ).

The sense of *gēr* in 14:21 as referring to a figure who stands outside of
the community of Yahweh should be put into dialogue with texts already
observed where the *gēr* is displaced in relation to a local kinship group.
This variety of portraits suggests that the term *gēr* has capacity to refer to
otherness at various social levels and that the contextual meaning of *gēr*
may indeed vary in Deuteronomy.

However, it bears reflecting on how internally displaced persons may
also find themselves in this text. A displaced person may be so poor that
survival trumps cultic purity.[199] This idea is supported by the strong social
ethic within the text itself. Bultmann, in his exegesis of 14:21, sustains his
theory that the *gēr* is a locally displaced Judahite, contending that the *gēr* is
here free from the prohibition, since the *gēr* is not a part of the constituting
layer of the "*Jahwevolk*," which is constituted of landed people. Indeed, dislocation from a lineage group may be sufficient to bring one's membership
within the worshiping community into question.[200]

Whatever the provenance of the *gēr* in 14:21, there is a deliberate tension in this text between dynamics of inclusion, namely, the *gēr* participating in the divine supply for God's people and the otherness of the *gēr*
that is signified in the eating of the נבלה. This is a tension inherent to the
term *gēr*, however, for this is a liminal figure on the threshold between
one social status and another. Finally, I observe that, while the *gēr* may be
offered the נבלה, the *gēr* is not required to receive it, and we might assume

197. Nelson, *Deuteronomy*, 181.

198. Albertz, "Aliens," 55. Similarly, Lundbom, *Deuteronomy*, 476.

199. A point made by Altmann, *Festive*, 190 n. 234, and Bultmann, *Fremde*, 88–89.

200. Consider the importance of tracing lineage in Ezra-Nehemiah (Ezra 2; 8:3–
14; Neh 7; 11:4–20). This is discussed further in chapter 6.

that the *gēr* who associates himself or herself within the worshiping community may choose not to receive it.

### 3.9. Translation of the Term *Gēr* in Deuteronomy

Having observed the term *gēr* in social law and in cognates, we are in a position to explore the question of translation. Spina has suggested in an influential article the translation "immigrant," stating that "*gēr* should be translated by a word that underscores not simply the outsider status in the adopted social setting, but in addition those factors and conditions related to the emigration in the first place."[201] This suggestion is challenged, though, on the basis that *gēr* is a legal term that references the present dislocation of an individual or family and does not distinguish regarding the circumstances behind the displacement.[202] Awabdy has recently advocated for the translation "immigrant" on the basis that the *gēr* is from a kingdom other than Judah and other than the Northern Kingdom.[203] Below I interrogate this theory regarding the origins of the *gēr*. Van Houten and many others suggest the translation "resident alien."[204] While this translation may be appropriate for the *gēr* in the HC, it is not suitable for Deuteronomy. In every reference to the *gēr* in Deuteronomy, across the redactional layers, the *gēr* is not only resident in a new context but also dependent in that context. Dependency is visible in the *gēr*'s labor within the household and the settlement (5:14, 24:14), in her or his inclusion within the triad of the vulnerable (16:11a, 14), in the reference גרך (5:14, 29:10), in the phrase בקרבך,[205] and in the local provision for the *gēr*'s sustenance (14:28–29, 26:12–15). Van Houton's translation "resident alien" is only admissible based upon a "flat" reading of the term *gēr* in the Pentateuch that assumes a single definition throughout.

---

201. "Israelites," 323.

202. Similarly Ebach (*Fremde*, 312) asserts, "Dabei treten seine Herkunft, sen Geschlecht und seine kulturelle Prägung in den Hintergrund" ("His origins, his gender, and his cultural background recede into the background"). I establish in §3.10 that *gēr* is a legal term.

203. Awabdy, *Immigrants*, 110–16.

204. Van Houten, *Alien in Israelite Law*, 16; James K. Hoffmeier, *The Immigration Crisis: Immigrants, Aliens and the Bible* (Wheaton, IL: Crossway Books, 2009), 52; MacDonald, *Not Bread Alone*, 99.

205. Regarding the phrase בקרבך, see §5.5.2.

Naʾaman correctly identifies three characteristics of the *gēr* in Deuteronomy. The *gēr* is dependent, landless, and on the lowest stratum of the social ladder.[206] A better translation is "dependent stranger." Throughout the remainder of this study I will shorten this phrase simply to "stranger." The *gēr* has left kinship ties, village, and land, and the *gēr* now dwells within a community within which the *gēr* has no blood relations or patrimony. The *gēr* is therefore without the protection and privileges that kin ties and place of birth afford. The *gēr* is in social limbo. On the one hand, the *gēr* is free and not a slave; on the other hand, the *gēr* is landless and without meaningful connection. The *gēr* is easily oppressed, as there are no family members to be outraged at any injustice that may be perpetrated against the *gēr*. Relegated to the fringe of society, the *gēr* would ideally attach himself or herself to a beneficent patron for protection.

### 3.9.1. Female Gender for the *Gēr*?

The male *gēr* may exist alone or together with his nuclear family.[207] We should be alert to the possibility that androcentric pronouns may incorrectly bias readers to assume that the *gēr* pertains exclusively to males. The presence of the female אלמנה in the lists of the vulnerable may contribute to this error, giving the impression that, given that the widow is female, the *gēr* must be male. Cultural anthropology of the pan-Mediterranean area has shown that, in many cases where there is weak economic attachment to land, including among landless laborers, women are relatively dominant and families are matrifocal. The opposite is also true. Agricultural and pastoral populations with a strong economic attachment to patrimony tend to be patralineal.[208] My point here is not to propose a social structure for the *gēr* but merely to remind readers that landless populations are constituted by both genders and that women may be just as vital to the social organization of these people as men, even more so. Indeed, the most extended phrase for the *gēr* in Deuteronomy, "From woodcutter to water-drawer" (29:10b) is most likely a reference to women and may be evidence of a relatively dominant role for women among those designated *gēr* (see the discussion of 29:10b, at §6.3.3.4). It is clarifying to consider

---

206. Naʾaman, "Sojourners," 258.

207. Sneed, "Israelite," 500; *HALOT*, s.v. "גר," 1:201.

208. Jeremy Boissevain et al., "Towards a Social Anthropology of the Mediterranean [and Comments and Reply]," *Cultural Anthropology* 20 (1979): 83–84.

gender in the context of the list of the vulnerable: "You, your son, your daughter, your male slave, your female slave, the Levite who is in your gates, the stranger, the fatherless, and the widow who is in your midst" (16:11a). The אלמנה, generally glossed as "widow," is a woman who lacks the protection of male kindred.[209] On the one hand, an אלמנה may belong to the clan with which she resides (e.g., Naomi in Ruth 1:19) or may be an outsider in relation to a clan within which she seeks to subsist. On the other hand, a female *gēr* is from outside of the clan grouping in which she seeks to subsist. A female *gēr* may or may not be attached to male kindred. The following table relates these terms for vulnerable women to their social location.

Table 3.3: Terms for Vulnerable Women: אלמנה and גר

|  | Protected by male kin | Not protected by male kin |
|---|---|---|
| belongs to the clan | daughter, woman, wife | אלמנה or, if unmarried, יתום |
| does not belong to the clan | גר (limited protection; shared vulnerability with male kin) | may be referred to as גר, אלמנה, or, if unmarried, יתום |

The distinction between these terms seems to be less relevant in Dtr and post-Dtr texts. In later texts, אלמנה and יתום as categories of vulnerability fade from the text, and the term *gēr* is uniquely prominent. It appears that displacement was so prevalent in the communities that these texts addressed (see §4.9) that every displaced person was referred to as a *gēr*. This study will, where possible, use both genders for personal pronouns that reference the term *gēr*. The character of the term *gēr* in Deuteronomy is further clarified by considering the legal nature of this word.

---

209. Paula S. Hiebert, "'Whence Shall Help Come to Me?': The Biblical Widow," in *Gender and Difference in Ancient Israel*, ed. Peggy L. Day (Minneapolis: Fortress, 1989), 125–41.

## 3.10. *Gēr* versus *Gwr* and the Legal Nature of *Gēr*

We may add to the characterization of the *gēr* in Deuteronomy as a dependent stranger by observing the legal nature of the term *gēr*. Scholarship has assumed a correspondence between the noun גֵּר and the verb גּור, such that both words refer to displaced people seeking a new home. Kidd has brought greater precision to a definition of the noun גֵּר by investigating its relation to the verb גּור. The verb גּור tends to be used in narrative texts to refer to "specific events in the lives of concrete characters,"[210] while the noun גֵּר tends to be used in legal texts. This is significant for the scholarly discussion for three reasons. First, while texts such as 2 Sam 4:3, Ruth 1:1, and Isa 16:4 are examples of displacement that would fit the common understanding of the noun גֵּר, the noun form of *gr* is altogether missing in these texts. Ignoring this distinction, *HALOT* cites these texts as illustrating the noun.[211] The same error is made by Spina in his influential article, where it is stated that Ruth "becomes a ger," making no distinction between the verb and the noun.[212] However, גֵּר is not found at all in the book of Ruth. Rather, the noun גֵּר is most often used in legal texts to denote people attempting to make a home *in Israel*.[213] Where the noun גֵּר does appear in narrative, the legal function often remains important.[214] Second, the term גֵּר consistently appears in the singular; this is the fixed form of the noun within legal texts.[215] This is a significant point, not least as scholarship persists in referring to the *gēr* as *gērîm*.[216] While there are indeed many designated as *gēr*, the technical use of the term in legal texts is nonetheless in the singular. Third, the legal use of *gēr* also exposes a flaw in Spina's innovation in translating the term *gēr* as "immigrant" in order to reflect the original troubled circumstances of the *gēr* from which he

---

210. Kidd, *Alterity*, 15.

211. *HALOT*, s.v. "גֵּר," 1:201.

212. Spina, "Israelites," 324.

213. Kidd, *Alterity*, 14, 23–24. Kidd also suggests that the verb גּור only refers to those who leave Israel, whereas the noun גֵּר only refers to those who enter Israel (*Alterity*, 20–26). However, this distinction in usage has more to do with the disproportionate occurrence of גֵּר in legal texts than with semantics, and the distinction does not hold in all cases.

214. E.g., Gen 15:13, 23:4, Deut 26:6.

215. גֵּר appears in the plural only once in Deuteronomy, in a later text (10:19b). All plural references are an adaptation of the earlier singular legal form (see §4.9.1).

216. E.g., Achenbach, "Eintritt," 251; Sparks, *Ethnicity*, 240.

has fled.[217] Against Spina, *gēr* is a legal term that references the present dislocation of the *gēr* in his new context; the word *gēr* does not comment upon the origins of the displacement.[218] Kidd's important observation of the legal sense of the term *gēr* has been entirely ignored in subsequent scholarship, so far as I am aware.[219]

### 3.10.1. The *Gēr* and Legal Status

Given that *gēr* is a legal term, we turn now to the necessary task of differentiating between *gēr* as a technical legal term used in law corpora and *gēr* as a designation of legal status authorizing residence in a new setting. The former is affirmed by this study, while the latter is rejected (contrary to Kidd and Awabdy, among others).[220] Scholars have often argued that the *gēr* is a person who is given the legal authority to reside within a community and who therefore has the right to benefit from the protections that are prescribed in Deuteronomy. This question is crucial, as entire theses have been built upon the (in my view incorrect) assumption that the *gēr* has, in James K. Hoffmeier's words, "followed legal procedures to obtain recognized standing as a resident alien."[221] First, the confusion seems to arise in light of the (incorrect) assumption that the *gēr* is exclusively a foreign migrant, which, at least for Hoffmeier, introduces the question of border control.[222] However, I argue in this study that a proportion of those designated *gēr* in the Judahite community were internally displaced people, so the question of state borders is irrelevant.

Second, I argue in §5.5.1 that Deuteronomy's response to the *gēr* addresses, for the most part, rural agricultural contexts. Cheap farm labor was sought in the ancient Near East, for a person's labor was worth more than his or her bread.[223] Thus the concern of the DC was not the legal

---

217. Spina, "Israelites," 324.

218. See for example 24:14, 17, 19–22.

219. Awabdy notes Kidd's assertion that the term *gēr* signifies legal status (a contention that this study challenges). However, Awabdy neglects Kidd's more fundamental observation that the noun *gēr* is a legal term (Awabdy, *Immigrants*, 4).

220. Kidd, *Alterity*, 16; Awabdy, *Immigrants*, 3; Hoffmeier, *Immigration*, 52.

221. Hoffmeier, *Immigration*, 52.

222. Hoffmeier, *Immigration* 38–46.

223. See further Gelb, "Household," 23–24. Yet in times of destitution, dependents were a burden, and we would expect that under these circumstances there would be little capacity to support non-family members ("Household," 61).

admission of vulnerable workers into a settlement, town, or city—that much was assumed—but that vulnerable laborers were not exploited.

Third, this theory may also be challenged at the level of Deuteronomy's broader social vision. If the *gēr* is one who had "followed legal procedures to obtain recognized standing as a resident alien," then a displaced person who had *not* obtained such legal standing goes unrecognized in Deuteronomy, yet such a category of people would be among the most vulnerable in Judahite society. Thus the common assertion that the term *gēr* refers to legal admission is misleading. Rather, *gēr* is a legal term that applies to an individual or to a family by virtue of the *gēr*'s displacement as a vulnerable stranger within a kinship setting that is not her or his own.

Two points of clarification are in order. First, to be sure, the term *gēr* does indeed signify social status. The term *gēr* signifies that a (vulnerable) resident has origins elsewhere. This, however, is a different concept from legal admission into a community. Second, a legal *term* does not necessarily signify legal *status*. By contemporary analogy, the term *foreign national* is a legal term that emerged in contemporary legal contexts and that occurs in contemporary legislation, yet *foreign national* does not signify legal status in the same way that the terms *refugee, citizen, designated foreign national,* or *permanent resident* do.[224]

### 3.11. Conclusion

This chapter has investigated the social law in Deuteronomy regarding the *gēr*. The hireling law (24:14–15) incorporates the *gēr* within Deuteronomy's brother-sister ethic, מאחיך או מגרך. The gleaning laws (24:19–22) insist that the harvest is to be shared by the whole community, including the *gēr*. Yahweh's surprising logic of blessing ensures that sharing the bounty of the land will lead, not to less economic productivity, but to further abundance. The law concerning a fleeing slave (23:16–17) is connected lexically and conceptually to laws concerning the *gēr*. This law contains a most intimate expression of integrating landless people within an Israelite settlement, town, or city. The participation of the *gēr* in the Sabbath command of the Deuteronomy Decalogue disrupts the class distinctions between the stranger and the landed household, and it incorporates the *gēr* as a co-

---

224. These terms are used, for example, in Canada's 2001 Immigration and Refugee Protection Act.

heir of the gifts of land and its bounty and as partner in the "rest" that is
the result of this gift. In 14:21, the singular address signals that an aim of
14:21a is the relief of the vulnerable stranger. We observed that, in the
communal Mediterranean context, outsiders were viewed with suspicion
and antagonism. In this highly parochial context, these social laws address
the question of to whom we have responsibility. Whom must we protect?
These social laws, in other words, were heard and experienced across the
field of kinship: Who is my kin?

This exegesis challenges the recent claim of Crouch, for example, that
the social laws of the DC concerning the *gēr* are "solely legally and economically orientated" and "impl[y] nothing about the incorporation of
the גר into the Israelite community."[225] Crouch is, of course, correct to
state that social laws are legally and economically motivated—that is the
nature of social law. Further, we must await the discussion of feasting texts
(ch. 5) for a fuller picture of inclusivism. Yet even here in the social law, we
see that the Deuteronomist is fostering the participation of the *gēr* within
the community.

Deuteronomy's ethic for the stranger in these texts operates in three
related spheres: economic, social, and religious:

1.  Economic: These laws are concerned to ensure that the
    stranger also enjoys the fruit of the land. A creditor's ability
    to accumulate indentured workers and slaves is restrained, for
    human flourishing takes precedence over economic produc-
    tivity.
2.  Social: The *gēr* is included within three spheres of the com-
    munity: the household (24:14–15), the clan/town (23:16–17),
    and the people of Israel (5:12–15). These laws have fundamen-
    tally altered the relation of the *gēr* within these communities,
    for the *gēr* may not be used merely for cheap labor. The DC
    has disrupted class distinctions (5:12–15), and it has dignified
    the stranger as a co-recipient of the gift of land and its abun-
    dance (24:19–22).
3.  Before Yahweh: The DC's social ethic is performed and is
    secured before the face of Yahweh. The 6/7 schema unites

---

225. Crouch, *Making*, 222. Crouch's interpretation of the *gēr* in Deuteronomy
(*Making*, 216–23) seems to be predetermined by her larger thesis of the ethnic exclusivity of the tradents of Deuteronomy.

worship and ethics. The Sabbath command recasts rest for the stranger as a cultic ordinance. Yahweh, the divine judge, is attentive to the voice of the stranger, both to bless and to curse. The *gēr* is caught up in Yahweh's act of redemption for Israel, and the exodus narrative compels Israel to ensure for the *gēr* freedom, subsistence, and belonging.

The following chapter introduces a fourth sphere, the judicial. In turn, chapter 5 introduces the cultic sphere via analysis of Deuteronomy's feasting texts.

# 4

# The *Gēr* in Law of Judicial Procedure

The *gēr* appears in four texts within Deuteronomy's compendium of laws regarding legal processes: 1:16–17, 10:17–19, 27:19, 24:17a. This chapter will investigate the function and intention of these laws. Chapter 3 (social law), the present chapter (law of judicial procedure), and chapter 5 (feasting law) investigate the *gēr* within various subgroups of law. Chapter 3 has shown how Deuteronomy's social law fosters the inclusion of the *gēr* in the economic sphere, the social sphere, and, to some degree, the religious sphere. The present chapter will analyze Deuteronomy's provision for the stranger in the judicial sphere.

## 4.1. The Nature and Function of Procedural Law

The laws of judicial procedure require that the *gēr* have recourse to the legal system, along with the kinsperson (1:16–17, 10:17–19, 27:19, 24:17a). A consistent lexical and conceptual field links Deuteronomy's judicial law texts to one another.[1] In this chapter I will demonstrate that law of judicial procedure was the most important legal category for the protection and inclusion of the stranger within the community.

Bernard M. Levinson and Frank Crüsemann, among others, have contributed studies of the judicial law of the Pentateuch and specifically of Deuteronomy.[2] However, as far as I am aware, there is no substantial study

---

1. I am indebted to comments on an earlier version of this research of Richard Averbeck and also Bruce Wells. Laws concerning just legal proceedings in Deuteronomy are 1:9–18; 10:17b–18; 16:18–20; 17:2–13; 19:15–21; 24:8–9, 17a; 27:19.

2. Crüsemann, *Torah,* 238–40; Levinson, *Deuteronomy and the Hermeneutics,* 325–404; Levinson, "Deuteronomy's Conception of Law as an 'Ideal Type': A Missing Chapter in the History of Constitutional Law," in *'The Right Chorale': Studies in Biblical Law and Interpretation,* ed. Bernard M. Levison (Tübingen: Mohr Siebeck,

of the function of procedural law in Deuteronomy's system of protection for the *gēr*. The great significance of the laws of judicial procedure concerning the *gēr* is demonstrated by their location at key points in Deuteronomy: Deut 1:16–17 is the headmost stipulation in Deuteronomy, and 10:17–19 and 27:19 are located within sections that together frame the law corpus (Deut 12–26).[3] The importance of judicial law in Deuteronomy is also evident by its being repeatedly associated with the centralization formula of Deut 12 (e.g., 1:17; 17:8, 10) and with the exclusive worship of Yahweh (*Privilegrecht*) via the phrase ובערת הרע מקרבך (13:6; cf. 17:7, 12; 19:19).[4]

The motive clauses differentiate Deuteronomy's law of judicial procedure from other subgroups of law, displaying a distinctive theological and ethical focus. While the social laws are undergirded by motive clauses concerning the exodus (e.g., 5:15, 24:21) and of blessing and land gift (e.g., 24:19, 26:1), the core laws of judicial procedure (16:18–20; 17:2–13; plus 19:19, 20) are undergirded by the concern ובערת הרע מקרבך (17:7; cf. 19:19, 20),[5] which connects with the exclusive worship of Yahweh (13:6) and by a concern that punishment for offenders would set an example (17:13, 19:20).

A relative egalitarianism is one key component in Deuteronomy's law of judicial procedure. The *community* was responsible to appoint judges, undermining the usual privilege of the king as the chief justice: שפטים ושטרים תתן לך (16:18).[6] Having appointed judges, the responsibil-

---

2008), 58–68; see also Hans Jochen Boecker, *Law and the Administration of Justice in the Old Testament and Ancient Near East* (Minneapolis: Augsburg, 1980); Herbert Niehr, *Rechtsprechung in Israel: Untersuchungen zur Geschichte der Gerichtsorganisation im Alten Testament*, SBS 130 (Stuttgart: Katholisches Bibelwerk, 1987); Robert R. Wilson, "Israel's Judiciary in the Pre-Exilic Period," *JQR* 74 (1983): 229–48; Ze'ev W. Falk, *Hebrew Law in Biblical Times* (Utah: Brigham Young University Press, 2001), 47–82; Westbrook and Wells, *Everyday Law*, 35–52; Moshe Weinfeld, "Judge and Officer in Ancient Israel and in the Ancient Near East," *IOS* 7 (1977): 65–88; Greengus, *Laws*, 274–76.

3. The significance of the position of 1:16–17 is explored below. Deuteronomy 27:19, regarding judicial procedure, is the sole reference to social law in the Shechem curse list, giving this stipulation emphasis.

4. Crüsemann, *Torah*, 238.

5. This clause is highly associated with substantive law that refers to legal proceedings in Deuteronomy (21:21; 22:21, 22, 24; 24:7) and is distinctively Deuteronomic.

6. Keith W. Whitelam argues that the king had authority over the judicial system

ity to maintain justice remained nonetheless with all of the population (16:19–20). Deuteronomy's core stipulations concerning judicial procedure (16:18–17:13) are a part of a corpus of laws concerning public office (16:18–18:22), which were concerned to distribute power and responsibilities among the various public roles, limiting the power of any individual office.[7] "The complete transfer of all power to the free people of the land means a tremendous break with the great authorities of ancient Near Eastern and also Israelite-Judean society."[8]

Wells and Westbrook discern in Israel three levels of tribunal that corresponded to three levels of administration.[9] The king was the supreme judge "who had the military and political power to enforce royal law."[10] Officials presided at a provincial level. At a local level, the elders and/or a city council provided judgment. Judgment at the local level often would have required securing the approval of a majority in the community.[11] A number of the DC's laws seem to reflect a more traditional kin-based legal procedure that likely characterized rural settlements and towns, where elders presided (e.g., 19:1–21; 21:1–9, 18–21; 22:13–21; 25:4–10). A fourth level of judiciary is the divine judge who in the DC is most visible in motive clauses attached to the laws (e.g., 24:7b, 9, 13b, 13c, 15b).[12]

---

from an early date; see *The Just King: Monarchical Judicial Authority in Ancient Israel* (Sheffield: JSOT, 1979), 229. On Deuteronomy's challenge to the judicial responsibility of the king, see Levinson, "Law as an 'Ideal Type,'" 76.

7. McBride, "Polity," 241–42; Joshua Berman, "Constitution, Class, and the Book of Deuteronomy," *HPS* 1 (2006): 523–48.

8. Crüssemann, *Torah*, 247. Robert R. Wilson suggests that "the laws that deal specifically with the judiciary are best understood as attempts to reform the sort of hierarchical legal system attributed to Jehoshaphat" ("Israel's Judiciary," 246).

9. Westbrook and Wells, *Everyday*, 35. On the correspondence between the judiciary and administrative authority, see 1:14. See further, Wilson, "Israel's Judiciary."

10. Westbrook and Wells, *Everyday Law*, 240.

11. Westbrook and Wells, *Everyday Law*, 36; Wilson, "Israel's Judiciary," 236. Otto argues that the laws concerning the local proceedings held at the gate of a settlement have Canaanite roots ("שַׁעַר," 15:398–99). There are various views on the relation between the texts describing traditional contexts that involved elders to the judicial texts that required centralization. See Levinson, "Law as an 'Ideal Type,'" 72 n. 52.

12. In the Hebrew Bible, Yahweh may be approached for judgment through oaths and oracles (Exod 22:6–8, 9–10; Deut 1:17; Josh 7:10–18). See Westbrook and Wells, *Everyday Law*, 45–49; Levinson, *Deuteronomy and the Hermeneutics*, 113.

### 4.1.1. The Vulnerability of Displaced People in the Law Courts, in Israel, and in the Ancient Near East

Displaced people receive extraordinary attention within Deuteronomy's law of judicial procedure. This must be because such people could have had a perilous relationship with the judiciary, both in Israel and in the ancient Near East. Their vulnerability is displayed in a proto-Genesis text within the Abraham narrative, Gen 19:9.[13] The men of Sodom exclaim of Lot: "This fellow came to sojourn [האחד בא לגור], and he has become the judge!" The paradox within the phrase itself is that a stranger with few legal privileges would assume for himself the role of judge. Within the narrative, Lot's helplessness before the mob illustrates how a person without kinship connection may have had no legal recourse.[14] Indeed, Westbrook states that foreigners "had no legal rights outside of their own country or ethnic group unless they fell under the local ruler's protection."[15] The legal vulnerability of foreigners is illustrated in the wife-sister narratives of the patriarchs in Egypt (12:10–20, 26:6–11). Involuntary slavery was a danger for displaced people, as a Babylonian proverb reflected: "A resident alien in another city is a slave."[16] A contrasting dynamic may be visible in new texts from the archives of two Judean communities in exile in Babylonia in the Tigris corridor. These texts seem to indicate that these communities had complete access to the legal system.[17] It may be that communities such as these were less vulnerable than a lone displaced individual or a nuclear

---

13. Carr designates these as "proto-Genesis;" see *Reading the Fractures of Genesis: Historical and Literary Approaches* (Louisville: Westminster John Knox, 1996), 306, 339; cf. Schmid, *Literary*, 161. See further §5.3.3.5. Here, I am not suggesting that Lot is a *gēr*; rather, I am demonstrating the vulnerability of displaced people generally.

14. For an analysis of Gen 19 in terms of otherness, see Elizabeth Robertson Kennedy, *Seeking a Homeland: Sojourn and Ethnic Identity in the Ancestral Narratives of Genesis*, BibInt 106 (Leiden: Brill, 2010), 142–70: "What the narrative makes most clear is the jarring contrast between Lot's address to the townspeople as *brothers*, and their response in v. 9 that he is a *sojourner*" (159). "The men of Sodom communicate with their statement that it is inappropriate for a sojourner to take a role in the communal process of judgment" (163).

15. Westbrook, "Slave," 171.

16. Westbrook, "Slave," 171.

17. Laurie Pearce and Cornelia Wunsch, *Documents of Judean Exiles and West Semites in Babylonia in the Collection of David Sofer* (Ithaca, NY: Cornell University Press, 2014).

family; these Judean groups had the means to access traveling legal scribes, for example. In regard to judicial rights, then, a general distinction should be made between communities of foreigners and displaced and impoverished individuals and families.

Not only displacement but also poverty and social class could render a person powerless in litigation. Recall, for example, the episode of Naboth's vineyard (1 Kgs 21:1–29). Similarly, the prophet Amos decried unjust litigation processes:

> They hate him who reproves in the gate, and they abhor him who speaks the truth ... you who afflict the righteous, who take a bribe, and turn aside the needy in the gate. Therefore he who is prudent will keep silent in such a time, for it is an evil time. (Amos 5:10–13 ESV)

Through unjust judicial process, wealth could become consolidated power in ancient Israel, crushing both the needy and the middle class.[18]

The needy lacked influential advocates and could easily have their lawsuits ignored, not the least because officials were appointed from influential families and enjoyed a network of relationships with the elite.[19] Thutmose III describes the qualities of a just judge to his vizier Rekhmire:

> He is the one who does not make himself a friend of anyone ... it is an abomination to God to show face (rdi hr [=show partiality]). This is an instruction ... regard him whom you know like him whom you do not know.[20]

The *gēr* was twice removed from legal protection, being both displaced and impoverished. It is no wonder, then, that the *gēr* is the focus of Deuteronomy's social stipulations concerning judicial procedure (1:16–17, 24:17a).

---

18. The barriers facing the poor at the gate may have extended even beyond corruption to sociological barriers. In a discussion of social stratification in pre-revolution Ethiopia, Nega Mezlekia observes that morality inhered to class and role. Mezlekia observes that corrupt judges were considered to be moral people simply because of their standing in the community; see Mezlekia, *Notes from the Hyena's Belly* (New York: Picador, 2000), 48. On this point, see also Malina, *Social World*, 46. This possibility, that moral distinctions inhere to class, deepens the significance of the command לֹא תַכִּירוּ פָנִים (1:17, 16:19).

19. Crüsemann, *Torah*, 82.

20. Weinfeld, *Deuteronomy*, 141.

### 4.1.2. Judicial Law in the CC and in the DC

The judicial law of the CC is the primary source for Deuteronomy's compendium of texts regarding legal procedure:

1    You shall not spread a false report.
     You shall not join hands with a wicked man to be a malicious witness.
2    You shall not fall in with the many to do evil, nor shall you bear witness in a lawsuit, siding with the many, so as to pervert justice,
3    nor shall you be partial to a poor man in his lawsuit.
4    If you meet your enemy's ox or his donkey going astray, you shall bring it back to him.
5    If you see the donkey of one who hates you lying down under its burden, you shall refrain from leaving him with it; you shall rescue it with him.
6    You shall not pervert the justice due to your poor in his lawsuit.
7    Keep far from a false charge, and do not kill the innocent and righteous, for I will not acquit the wicked.
8    And you shall take no bribe, for a bribe blinds the clear-sighted and subverts the cause of those who are in the right.[21] (Exod 23:1–8 ESV)

The primary function of the text, highlighted by sheer repetition, is to fortify the legal process against the influence of those with power. "The pressure that arises from the mixing together of rumors (Exod 23:1), majorities (23:2), power (23:1), money (23:8), etc. becomes apparent in these verses."[22] The text has a unified chiastic structure that moves from influential people in the frame to vulnerability at the center. The text's frame concerns resisting people of means who exert their power in order to influence litigation processes (23:1, 7). The inner frame concerns the poor, warning both against perverting the justice that is due to them and also against ignoring unjust processes in their favor (23:3, 6). The center stipulations concern stray and suffering animals that belong to one's enemy (23:4–5). These center stipulations symbolize the compassion and the kindness that ought to characterize judicial procedure for the weakest. Reference to the *gēr* in the following verse, Exod 23:9, brings the *gēr* within the protective circumference of this text.

---

21. Moshe Weinfeld observes similarities between Exod 23:1–8 and Hittite instructions for officials ("Judge and Officer," 76–77).
22. Crüsemann, *Torah*, 190.

In Deuteronomy there is a set of core laws of judicial procedure that are distinct by virtue of their location within a group of stipulations concerning public offices (16:18–18:22), by the motive clauses attached to them (17:7; cf. 19:19, 20; 17:13; see further 19:20), and by their common concern for impartiality. The core texts are distinct from the texts that concern the *gēr* (1:9–18, 10:17–19, 24:17a, 27:19).

- ◆ Within Deut 16:18–20,[23] verse 19 appropriates Exod 23:6, 8 (underlined): לֹא תַטֶּה מִשְׁפָּט לֹא תַכִּיר פָּנִים וְלֹא תִקַּח שֹׁחַד כִּי וְלֹא תִקַּח הַשֹּׁחַד יְעַוֵּר עֵינֵי חֲכָמִים וִיסַלֵּף דִּבְרֵי צַדִּיקִם. The clause שֹׁחַד exhibits the tendency for revisions to reverse the original text (cf. Exod 23:8a).[24] The revision supplements the original with the appointment of the judges while also asserting responsibility of the whole community to uphold justice. It (unusually) subtracts the reference to the poor in legal processes (cf. לֹא תַטֶּה מִשְׁפָּט אֶבְינְךָ בְּרִיבוֹ, Exod 23:6).

- ◆ Deut 17:2–7 connects the judicial system with the exclusive worship of Yahweh, emphasizing the required integrity of witnesses.

- ◆ Deut 17:8–13 concerns the authority of the supreme court located at the central sanctuary.

---

23. Lohfink and Braulik, who adopt a block model of redaction, ascribe most of 16:18–17:13 and 19:15–21 to the early exilic period; see Lohfink, "Distribution of the Functions of Power: The Laws Concerning Public Offices in Deuteronomy 16:18–18:22," in *A Song of Power and the Power of Song: Essays on the Book of Deuteronomy*, ed. Duane L. Christensen (Winona Lake, IN: Eisenbrauns, 1993), 336–52; repr., "Die Sicherung der Wirksamkeit des Gotteswortes durch das Prinzip der Schriftlichkeit der Tora und durch das Prinzip der Gewaltenteilung nach den Ämtergesetzen des Buches Deuteronomium (Dt 16,18–18,22)," in *Great Themes from the Old Testament*, trans. Ronald Walls (Chicago: Franciscan Herald, 1981), 55–75; Georg Braulik, "Abfolge," 252–72). However, Levinson argues cogently that 16:18–20 is unified compositionally with 16:1–17 (*Deuteronomy and the Hermeneutics*, 99). Further, the prominence of the centralization command in the text as well as its revision of Exod 23:1–8, 14–17 suggest that it may be assigned to Dtn. Similarly, Otto offers good reasons for ascribing much of 16:18–17:13; 19:15–21 to Dtn (Otto, "שָׁעַר," 15:375–77; Otto, "History of the Legal-Religious," 215–20).

24. Levinson cites this pattern as Seidel's law (*Deuteronomy and the Hermeneutics*, 18).

◆   Deut 19:15–21 concerns just witnesses and seems to assume
the detailed description of corrupt witnesses in the CC (Exod
23:1–2, 7–8).[25]

The core judicial texts are concerned with impartiality—what has been
called "blind justice"—a fair hearing and impartial judgment. [26] The goals
of these core texts include the marginalization of the king in judicial processes and the delimitation of roles and of power across public offices.
These core texts mute the explicit emphasis upon the most vulnerable of
the CC, a dynamic that is highly unusual in that the legal revisions of the
Dtn characteristically enhance the social ethic of the CC. (Nonetheless,
judicial probity itself protects the most vulnerable.) The judicial texts in
Deuteronomy that concern the *gēr* augment the concern for impartiality
exhibited in the core texts with Deuteronomy's particular concern for the
stranger. I turn now to these texts that are explicitly socially oriented.

### 4.2. A Social Redaction of Judicial Law (Deut 1:16–17)

1:16 And I commanded your judges at that time: "Hear cases between
your brothers-sisters,[27] and judge justly between a person and his or her
brother-sister and his or her *gēr*.… 17 Do not show bias in judgment, but
hear the great and the weak alike. Do not fear a person, for judgment is
God's. Bring the case that is too difficult for you to me, and I will hear it."
(Deut 1:16–17)

The contribution of this text, the first in Deuteronomy's compendium of
texts concerning litigation, is to insist that the *gēr* has recourse to the legal
system along with the kinsperson.[28] Deuteronomy's system of protection for *gēr* in substantive law will have little effect unless the *gēr* also has
recourse to justice at the gate via procedural law. The command is marked
by its position as the first stipulation in the book of Deuteronomy. Indeed,
its location as the headmost stipulation in Deuteronomy corresponds to

---

25. On witnesses, see Greengus, *Laws*, 274, 277–79.

26. Blind justice is traditionally symbolized by the figure of *Justitia*.

27. "Brother-sisters": both men and women had the right to give testimony at the
gate (e.g., 21:18–20).

28. For this section, I am indebted to personal email correspondence with
Eckart Otto.

the priority of procedural law also in the Laws of Hammurabi,[29] for in the law corpora of both Israel and Mesopotamia, law of judicial procedure is a cornerstone of social order.[30] Nonetheless, while the Laws of Hammurabi are concerned with judicial probity, reflecting here Deuteronomy's core judicial texts, 1:16–19 and the other texts examined in this chapter are concerned with just procedure for the most vulnerable and especially for the stranger.[31] This reflects Deuteronomy's high social ethic vis-à-vis the ancient Near Eastern law corpora.

### 4.2.1. A Social Redaction of the Dtn Procedural Law Texts

Explicit protection for the most vulnerable in judicial processes was emphasized in the CC (Exod 23:3, 6) and was later muted in the core judicial texts of Dtn, as observed above.[32] Deuteronomy 1:16–17 emphatically returns to this theme, as a later redaction.[33] In the larger text block (Deut 1:9–18), Moses organizes the tribes, appointing leaders for administrative, military, and judicial functions. The larger text block is structured in three parts, each section beginning with the speech formula "And I spoke/commanded you on that day, saying" (1:9, 16, 18). The text concerning just judgment for the *gēr* (1:16–17) is the rhetorical climax of the text block, for it stands at the center of this structure, it is most closely related to the CC, it likely concerns a ritual oath of integrity for the judges,[34] and it receives a motivation clause.

The core Dtn texts concerning just processes (16:18–20) revise the CC:[35]

---

29. Laws of Hammurabi, laws 1–5 (Roth, *Law*, 81–82).

30. See further, Levinson, "Law as an 'Ideal Type.'"

31. Levinson states: "In Israelite law, just as in cuneiform law, formal matters like textual sequence can thus amount to meta-legal reflections on the priorities of the legal system" ("Law as an 'Ideal Type,'" 60).

32. Though, the vulnerable are explicitly protected in one Dtn law of judicial procedure, 24:17a.

33. Deuteronomy 16:18–20 was composed prior to 1:16–17. As a general rule, the law corpus is assigned to Dtn, while the framework of Deuteronomy is designated as Dtr (see §6.1.1). In the following discussion, 1:16–17 is assigned to late Dtr.

34. So Weinfeld, *Deuteronomy*, 138.

35. See especially Levinson, *Deuteronomy and the Hermeneutics*, 325–404.

### Table 4.1. Deut 16:19 as a Redaction of the Covenant Code

| Exod 23:6 | Deut 16:19a |
|---|---|
| לא תטה משפט אבינך בריבו | לא תטה משפט |

| Exod 23:8 | Deut 16:19b |
|---|---|
| ושחד לא תקח כי השחד יעור פקחים | ולא תקח שחד כי השחד יעור עיני |
| ויסלף דברי צדיקים | חכמים ויסלף דברי צדיקם |

The Dtn revision (16:18–20) aims to reform the judiciary according to the goals of centralization and according to an egalitarian ethic, while reaffirming the concern of the CC for just legal processes.[36] It is significant that the reference to the poor in Exod 23:6 is omitted in Deut 16:19. Such an unusual deletion highlights the narrow goals of the core procedural law texts.[37]

Deuteronomy 1:16–17 is a social redaction of the earlier Dtn procedural law texts. The present text places justice for the *gēr* in legal processes front and center, quite literally.[38] Deuteronomy 1:9–18 is well known as an appropriation of Exod 18:13–27, which concerns the judicial reform that is precipitated by Jethro.[39] Similarly, there is a clear relationship between Deut 1:9–18 and Num 11:11–17, 24b–30, though the direction of dependence is less clear.[40] However, the dependence of Deut 1:16–17 upon Deut 16:18–20 is fundamental for understanding Deuteronomy's procedural law.[41]

---

36. The core texts for judicial reform include the themes of the delimitation of the roles and influence of public offices, the implicit marginalization of the king, and the *Yahweh Privelegrecht* (16:18–20, 17:2–13, 19:15–21).

37. There is one Dtn procedural law text that explicitly reaffirms the concern of the CC for the poor in judicial processes (24:17a), analyzed in the next section.

38. With Veijola, I find no evidence that 1:16–17 is a secondary addition with the larger text block of 1:9–18 (*Das 5. Buch Mose Deuteronomium,* 22).

39. To be sure, there are many significant associations between Deut 1:9–18 and Exod 18:13–27, e.g., Exod 18:21b, 25b and Deut 1:15; Exod 18:22b, 26b and Deut 17b; Exod 18:21a and Deut 1:13a.

40. See, e.g., Nelson, *Deuteronomy,* 20.

41. Dependence upon Deut 16:18–20 is acknowledged in the analysis of Veijola, *Das 5. Buch Mose*; Otto, *Deuteronomium,* 349–53; Christoph Levin, *Die Verheissung des neuen Bundes: In ihrem theologiegeschichtlichen Zusammenhang ausgelegt,* FRLANT 137 (Göttingen: Vandenhoeck & Ruprecht, 1985), 85. It is ignored by some other studies, including that of Weinfeld, *Deuteronomy,* 139–40.

Table 4.2. Sources for Deut 1:16–17

| Exod 18:16a | Deut 1:16b |
|---|---|
| <u>ושפטתי בין איש ובין</u> רעהו | שמע בין אחיכם ושפטתם צדק בין איש |
| | ובין אחיו ובין גרו |
| Deut 16:18b | |
| ושפטו את העם <u>משפט צדק</u> | |

| Deut 16:19 | Deut 1:17a |
|---|---|
| <u>לא תכיר פנים</u> | לא תכירו פנים במשפט כקטן כגדל |
| | תשמעון |

In both 1:16 and 1:17 the revision expands the sources in order to emphasize the right of the vulnerable to an equitable trial.[42] In 1:16 שפט is augmented with שמע, highlighting the right of the stranger to a hearing at the
gate. The stipulation against judicial corruption in the core text (16:18–20)
assumes that both parties will receive a hearing—in this text corruption
threatened at the point of judgment. Deuteronomy 1:16, however, considers the plight of the stranger, and it may by no means be assumed that the
stranger's case will even receive a hearing, so שמע (1:16) is added; אחיו
replaces רעהו, according to Deuteronomy's brother-sister ethic. A remarkable insertion regarding equitable judgment for the stranger follows:

1:16b

שמע בין אחיכם ושפטתם צדק בין איש ובין אחיו ובין גרו

In 1:17a the requirement for impartiality is augmented to address issues
of wealth, power, and status: בקטן כגדל תשמעון. The addition of במשפט
(1:17a) creates a chiasm with the preceding sentence (1:16).

Three conclusions have been established at this point. The core procedural law texts revise the CC according to Deuteronomy's goals of the centralization of worship and of egalitarianism, somewhat muting the CC's
explicit concern for the poor in judicial procedure. Deuteronomy 1:16–17
is a socially oriented redaction of Dtn core texts regarding legal procedure
and as such emphasizes that the *gēr* is on an equal footing with the kinsperson. The placement of procedural law here in the opening act of the

---

42. Interestingly, the redactors of 1:16–17 appropriated phrases from 16:18–19
that are not found in the CC.

drama of Deuteronomy (1:9–18) marks the theme of justice for the *gēr* in judicial proceedings as having the utmost importance.[43]

In searching for a social context for 1:16–18, one can see that 1:16–18 must be dated in relation to 16:18–20. Deuteronomy 1:9–18 functions within Deut 1–3, suggesting that it follows 16:18–20.[44] The text reflects Dtr's enhanced concern for displaced persons, vis-à-vis Dtn, that will be observed especially in chapter 6. The text is consistent also with Dtr's focus upon all Israel,[45] comporting with Otto's suggestion that 1:9–18 is a part of the exilic Moab redaction.[46] The availability of unused land during the Neo-Babylonian period[47] would have created opportunity for the *gēr* that was unimaginable during the monarchic period, opening the possibility of land holdings and of upward mobility. Perhaps this social redaction of the judicial laws (1:16–17) was ordered to protect the rights and autonomy of displaced people in light of this new opportunity.

### 4.2.2. The Right to a Hearing and to Just Judgment, Exegesis of 1:16–17

The third-person suffix form of the noun גרו ("his/her *gēr*") occurs only here (cf. גרך in 5:14, 24:14, 29:10, 31:12; on the pronominal suffix form of *gēr*, see §3.3.5). The unique form גרו, vis-à-vis גרך, is due to the unique form of address in this text. Here the judge rather than the paterfamilias is the addressee of Moses's speech (cf. 5:14). The third-person suffix in this context expresses the same social reality as the second masculine singular suffix in other contexts. The suffix indicates a close and perhaps formal association with the household. Possible arrangements may include contractual labor (free status), labor in payment of debt (semifree status), and less formal associations.[48] We might infer from this verse that the relationship between a kinsperson and "his *gēr*" was often contentious (1:16; see further 1:12, 24:14–15). A dispute between these parties may have concerned unmet obligations of the landowner owed to the *gēr* or of the *gēr* owed to the landowner. Or disputes may have concerned attempts to

---

43. On the significance of the ordering of laws, see Jacob J. Finkelstein, *The Ox That Gored*, TAPS 17/2 (Philadelphia: American Philosophical Society, 1981).

44. On dating the frame of Deuteronomy (Deut 1–11, 27–34), see §6.1.1.

45. See further, chapter 6.

46. Otto, *Deuteronomium*, 250.

47. Faust, *Judah*, 174, 237; Albertz, *Israel*, 92.

48. The *gēr* must have been free or semifree, in distinction to the אמה and the עבד.

curtail the freedom of the *gēr* or to ensnare the *gēr* in debt (compare this with the complaint of the hired worker in the Yavneh-Yam inscription, discussed in §3.5.1). Of course, in the normal course of events such disputes were easily "settled," for the stranger had no legal recourse.

The text makes mention of two stages in a trial, the hearing of testimonies and the verdict, "hear ... judge," requiring that the *gēr* is treated justly in both.[49] "The first condition for a fair trial is that the judges give both parties a hearing in accordance with the law."[50] The infinitive absolute שמע functions as a command (cf. 5:12, 6:17). The phrase בין אחיכם is an abbreviated expression, and the dative is enumerated fully in the following phrase: בין איש ובין אחיו ובין גרו. So the phrase שמע בין אחיכם intends that the testimony of the *gēr* as litigant is also heard. These associated phrases are the closest that Deuteronomy comes to referring to the *gēr* as brother-sister. If it is doubted that the *gēr*, too, had the right to a legal hearing, the command is repeated: כקטן כגדל תשמעון (1:17).

The requirement for a just verdict is then addressed: ושפטתם צדק בין איש ובין אחיו ובין גרו. The author highlights the social tension that this law entails, for, on one hand, the triple בין within balanced clauses underlines the need for an equal platform for the *gēr* in a legal dispute.[51] On the other hand, in the same sentence the third-person suffix גרו highlights the dramatic social and legal distinction between the *gēr* and the sister-brother. The vulnerable stranger, dependent though she or he may be, shares equally in the protection of the judiciary.

The next verse (1:17) forms a chiasm with 1:16 via repetition of "hear" and "judge":

1:16

שׁמע בין אחיכם ושׁפטתם צדק בין איש ובין אחיו ובין גרו

1:17

לא תכירו פנים במשׁפט כקטן כגדל תשׁמעון

---

49. On stages of a trial, see Greengus, *Laws*, 275.

50. Veijola, *Das 5. Buch Mose*, 26: "Die erste Bedingung für einen gerechten Prozess liegt darin, dass der Richter beiden Parteien rechtliches Gehör gibt."

51. The repetition is the result of redaction from Exod 18:16. The triple occurrence of בין is emphatic. Cf. Gen 3:15; 9:12; Lev 10:10; 1 Sam 20:42.

The chiasm confirms the dual intention of 1:16. First, every person in Israel has the right to give testimony at the gate.[52] Second, kinship or wealth may not bias legal verdicts. This law will require a judge to decide a case against his own clansperson for the sake of a stranger. Such judicial inclusivism had implications for the social structure of ancient Israel. Law codes generally have the function of stabilizing interclass relationships.[53] The judicial rights given to the *gēr*, however, protect the *gēr* in his of her economic endeavors, protecting the *gēr*'s status as "free" as well as the *gēr*'s honor. It also resists efforts of the wealthy elite to acquire cheap labor via strategies of debt.

The inclusive ethic for the *gēr* found in 1:16–17 is deepened by the concerns of the larger text block. Deuteronomy 1:9–18 projects a forceful egalitarian ethic right at the outset of the book of Deuteronomy. "It portrays the leader, Moses, as engaged in consultation with the people concerning national policy. In Deut 1:9–18, Moses recounts the need he felt to decentralize his regime. He notes explicitly that he did not take unilateral action, but rather described his feelings on the subject to the people, suggested a plan, and then sought and received their approval."[54] The *gēr*, too, is enfolded within this ethic. The logic of the text includes the *gēr* within the multiplication of Israel, which is the stated problem that opens the section: יהוה אלהיכם הרבה אתכם והנכם היום ככוכבי השמים לרב (1:10). The *gēr* also contributes to טרחכם ומשאכם וריבכם (1:12). Thus the *gēr* is also a part of the fulfillment of the promise (1:10). Also, displacement and ethnicity are foregrounded in the larger context, allying Israel with the *gēr*. In a source text (Exod 18:13–27), Jethro, a non-Israelite, is the progenitor of judicial reform, and in the immediate narrative context, Israel itself is sojourning (נסע, פנה, 1:7; cf. Exod 18:3). Therefore, a part of Deuteronomy's answer to the question of what it means to be the people of Yahweh is that Israel itself is a community on a journey, a community that is made up of the displaced. This is a community, then, in which the *gēr* may be

---

52. Two paragogic nuns occur in 1:17, תשמעון and תקרבון. Following J. Hoftijzer, the form marks contrast; see Hoftijzer, *The Function and Use of the Imperfect Forms with Nun Paragogicum in Classical Hebrew*, SSN 21 (Assen: Van Gorcum, 1985); cited in Waltke and O'Connor, *Syntax*, 516. תשמעון may emphasize the surprising inclusion of the stranger in judicial processes over against a kinsperson, and תקרבון may mark the distinctive authority of the centralized judiciary (cf. 17:8–13).

53. Weinfeld, *Deuteronomy*, 64.

54. Berman, "Constitution," 534.

at home, receiving justice at the gate, inclusion within a community, and economic mobility.

### 4.2.3. The אח and the *Gēr* in Deuteronomy

Deuteronomy's brother-sister ethic, essential for the logic of 1:16–18, is central within the social and theological vision of the whole book. Clarifying its function will also elucidate Deuteronomy's vision for the stranger. The word אח occurs forty-eight times in Deuteronomy, and thirty-five of these occurrences are in the DC. It does not appear in the CC, demonstrating that the brother-sister ethic is key part of the Deuteronomic social innovation.[55] This ethic is a means of safeguarding against a hierarchical and oppressive society[56] and doing so within the broader scheme of the family of Yahweh.

There is a degree of confusion regarding the אח motif in the scholarship. First, scholarship tends to collapse the varied references of אח into the single concept of the fraternity of all Israel.[57] Second, the common contention that Deuteronomy enfolds the *gēr* as אח requires nuance. Veijola expresses these two premises together: "'Your brothers' means 'all of Israel as a fraternal people'; in this case the 'stranger' is included (v 16b)."[58] While these two premises are not entirely inaccurate, Deuteronomy's sister-brother theme is multivalent, and its pregnant ethic is located within a complex of references. Further, Awabdy's assertion that these assump-

---

55. Perlitt ascribed the "Bruderschicht" to the Dtn ("Ein einzig Volk," 55–57). So also Eckart Otto, "The Book of Deuteronomy and Its Answer to the Persian State Ideology: The Legal Implications," in *Loi et Justice dans la Littérature du Proche-Orient ancient*, ed. Olivier Artus, BZAR 20 (Wiesbaden: Harrassowitz, 2013), 113; Otto, "History of the Legal-Religious," 219–20. Christoph Levin has recently argued that the "bruderschicht" is a secondary Persian redaction ("Rereading"). However, Sparks has plausibly argued that the equation of brotherhood with the poor predates the exile, on the basis of its influence upon Jeremiah (*Ethnicity*, 237 n. 41).

56. J. Gordan McConville, *God and Earthly Power: An Old Testament Political Theology*, LHBOTS 454 (London: T&T Clark, 2006), 66.

57. See recently Crouch, *Making*, 204–11.

58. Veijola, *Das 5. Buch Mose*, 26: "Mit 'euren Brüdern' ist die Gesamtheit Israels als 'brüderliches' Volk gemeint, das in diesem Fall auch die 'Fremden' einschließt (v. 16b)."

tions confirm that the *gēr* is a foreigner is problematic even as the assumptions are problematic.[59]

The use of cognates and of אח in other Hebrew literature suggests that אח is a highly flexible term whose reference may vary according to the context. For example, in the Meṣad Ḥashavyahu ostracon, a worker complains that a supervisor has seized his cloak unjustly. He writes: "All of my companions [*'ḥay*] will testify for me." Dennis Pardee argues that this is a reference to the testimony of fellow workers.[60] The word אח has a range of references in Deuteronomy. A number of times the term אח refers to the male progeny of the same parent(s), Perlitt's original "bruderschicht."[61] A common reference for אח concerns the relations within a clan or settlement.[62] In certain contexts אח has an intratribal (e.g., 18:7) or an intertribal reference (e.g., 3:18, 20; 10:9; 18:2; 33:16: 33:24). Dustin Nash has recently observed parallels in the use of *ahum* in Mari texts for describing intergroup relations.[63] The word אח also commonly refers to all of Israel (e.g., 1:28; 17:15, 20; 18:15, 18; 22:1, 2, 3, 4) or even to the kingdom of Edom (e.g., 2:4, 8; 23:7).[64]

Scholarship is more or less agreed that ancient Israelite society was organized at three main levels.[65] The foremost affiliation was the "house of the father." Next was the clan, משפחה. Last, the tribe played an important organizational role in early Israel.[66] The identity of all Israel is especially prominent in Deuteronomy's frame (see ch. 6). A person was associated

---

59. Awabdy, *Immigrants*, 110–16.

60. Meṣad Ḥashavyahu (Yavneh-Yam), Line 10a. Pardee's translation from "Judicial Plea," 37, 49.

61. Perlitt, "Brüdern," 53–54. E.g., 13:7; 25:5, 6, 7, 9; 28:53–54.

62. E.g., 1:16; 19:18, 19; 23:20, 21; 24:7, 14; 25:11. It is demonstrated that many of these references reflect a rural context (§5.5.1).

63. Nash refers to ARM XXVI 358, ARM XXVII 68, FM II 116, A.3572, and A.3577; see Nash, "The Representation of Inter-Group 'Brotherhood' in the Hebrew Bible and the Mari Archives: The Akkadian Evidence and Its Biblical Implications," (paper presented at the Annual Meeting of the Society of Biblical Literature, Baltimore, 24 November 2013).

64. Perlitt holds that the reference to the Edomite as brother is a late seventh century addition ("Brüdern," 53–54).

65. See Norman K. Gottwald, *The Tribes of Yahweh: A Sociology of the Religion of Liberated Israel, 1250–1050 BCE*, BibSem 66 (Sheffield: Sheffield Academic, 1999), 237–92; Faust, *Archaeology*, 8–12.

66. Scholars are more or less agreed that during the monarchy kin-based tribal structures were largely fictional and that the tribe was formed rather by common

within the community at all of these levels, and different levels of social grouping may become more or less important at different times.[67] Accordingly, the term אָח may apply to any of these levels of kinship, its reference depending upon the context.

### 4.2.3.1. The Clan as Brother-Sister, in Relation to the *Gēr*

The primary social identification of common people was within a household and the clan. In the Instruction of Amenemope, "brother" identifies close kin relations: "Do not refuse your oil jar to a stranger, / Double it before your brothers" (16.11–12).[68] Similarly, אח in Deuteronomy often refers to the relations within a settlement/clan/town, also fostering group identity in terms of sisterhood-brotherhood.

> If among you one of your sisters-brothers should become poor, within any of your towns/settlements [באחד שעריך] within your land that Yahweh your God is giving you…. (15:7; see, similarly, 24:14)

Here the gate represents the (local) bounds of the social grouping. While the literary context is all Israel, the stipulation nonetheless applies locally so that אח is again identified at the level of the clan, as in the following:

> And I commanded your judges at that time: "Hear cases between your brothers-sisters and judge justly between a person and his or her brother-sister and his or her *gēr*." (1:16)

The theological scope of this passage is all Israel (1:10), even as the social relations that are being addressed are locally bound.

Three related dynamics are present regarding the *gēr* in relation to the term אח. First, the *gēr* is by definition not a sister-brother: absence of affiliation defines the *gēr*. Indeed, the *gēr* is placed in apposition to the אח in numerous texts (e.g., 1:16; 24:17). Second, the *gēr* is nonetheless included within the protective circle of Deuteronomy's brother-sister ethic. Third,

---

geography, shared history, or shared agricultural interest (e.g., Gottwald, *Tribes*, 256; Faust, *Archaeology*, 9).

67. Thomas Hylland Erikson, *Ethnicity and Nationalism: Anthropological Perspectives*, 2nd ed. (Sterling, VA: Pluto Books, 2002), 30–31.

68. Translated by Miriam Lichtheim (*COS* 1.47:121).

dialogism is crucial, whereby within a single text brotherhood-sisterhood is identified both at the level of the clan and at the level of all Israel. Correspondingly, the *gēr* is located both at a local level and also conceptually or theologically within all Israel.[69] The multivalence of the term אח recalls Schneider's conception of the correspondence of kinship structures across a number of cultural domains (see §1.3.2.6). Diffuse domains may be structured by the same kinship terms and concepts, Schneider suggests.[70] These associations create enduring relationships of solidarity and collective identity both between social domains and also within them. The symbol of brotherhood signifies the values of cohesion and ethical responsibility through creating a correspondence between the social domains of the household, clan, and nation.

### 4.2.3.2. All Israel as Brother-Sister in Relation to the *Gēr*

Deuteronomy, especially within the frame texts (Deut 1–12, 17–34), addresses the whole of Israel as אח, as family. The family metaphor is utilized in order to foster group identity and solidarity at a "national" level. In Deuteronomy we observe "the retreat of tribal divisions," toward the idea of a "trans-tribal people."[71] This shift is observed, for example, in the use of אח to refer to all of Israel (1:28; 17:15, 20; 18:15, 18), in the use of the second masculine singular address, and in the phrase "Hear, O Israel" (4:1; 5:1; 6:3, 4; 9:1; 10:12; 27:9). Deuteronomy "permeates the entire social system with fraternal structures."[72] Thus the king is לבלתי רום לבבו מאחיו, and an (Israelite) slave is an אח, as well as the person seeking a loan (23:20), and they are to be treated accordingly. The unity of all of Israel as family includes within its scope the vulnerable, namely, the fatherless, the widow, the slave, and the *gēr*.[73] Perlitt states, regarding the laws of remission, "In

---

69. This is especially clear in 1:16–18.

70. David M. Schneider, "Kinship, Nationality, and Religion in American Culture: Towards a Definition of Kinship," in *Symbolic Anthropology: A Reader in the Study of Symbols and Meanings*, ed. Janet L. Dolgin and David M. Schneider (New York: Columbia University Press, 1977), 67.

71. McConville, *God*, 93. Otto notes, "Deuteronomy was, from its origin in the late Assyrian epoch, a book that served the aim to define Judah's identity more intensively than any other book in the Hebrew Bible" ("Deuteronomy and Its Answer," 112).

72. Braulik, "Deuteronomy and Human Rights," 147.

73. McConville, "Singular Address in the Deuteronomic Law and the Politics of Legal Administration," *JSOT* 97 (2002): 33–34.

Deut 15, the brother is not, therefore, a blood relative, friend, or colleague but the neighbor, the poor, and Hebrew, in short, the fellow human being."[74] Thus, Deuteronomy's brother-sister ethic calls upon the family of Yahweh to protect the most vulnerable among them as kindred—as אח. According to Deuteronomy's theological and ethical vision, the *gēr* is on the way to being enfolded within this fraternity: "The term 'the family of Yahweh' is aimed at the mystery of divine affection especially toward needy, poor and oppressed people."[75]

### 4.2.3.3. Inclusivism, Sisterhood-Brotherhood, and the *Gēr*

We have observed a parallelism that brings the *gēr* and the sister-brother into association (e.g., 1:16–17, 24:17). However, as stated above, Awabdy's assertion that " 'your countrymen' includes the Israelite *and* his gr" lacks nuance.[76] *Gēr* is not explicitly designated a brother in Deuteronomy, as the *gēr* is identified precisely by a lack of kinsfolk. Rather, Deuteronomy's brother-sister ethic *extends* to the *gēr*.[77] In this way, Deuteronomy is *fostering* the inclusion of displaced people as kin—the *gēr* is a liminal figure. So, while in certain texts the *gēr* appears in apposition to the אח, nonetheless the law stipulates that the *gēr* is to be protected as one would protect a kinsperson, for example:

> You shall not oppress a hired worker who is poor and needy, whether he is one of your brothers or one of the strangers who are in your land within your towns. (Deut 24:14)

The fact that the linguistic distinction between the *gēr* and the "brother" remains throughout in Deuteronomy does not thereby undermine the

---

74. Perlitt, "Brüdern," 56: "In Dtn 15 ist der Bruder also nicht der Blutsverwandte, Freund, oder Kollege, sondern der Nächste, der Arme, der Hebräer, kurz: der Mitmensch."

75. Norbert Lohfink, "Gottesvolk: Alttestamentliches zu einem Zentralbegriff im konziliaren Wortfeuerwerk," in *Unsere großen Wörter: Das Alte Testament zu Themen dieser Jahre* (Freiburg: Herder, 1977), 124: "Der Ausdruck 'Jahwefamilie' zielt auf das Geheimnis der göttlichen Zuneigung gerade zu den notleidenden, armen und unterdrückten Menschen."

76. Awabdy, *Immigrants*, 41, emphasis original.

77. The inclusion of the *gēr* as kin within the household and settlement is explored especially in the analysis of feasting texts below: §5.2.3; §5.2.4.

inclusive dimension. This is a matter of definition: *gēr* is a legal term that refers to vulnerable and clan-less people. Thus, as Deuteronomy's ethic of incorporation is put into practice, there will be no longer be any *gēr*.

By way of summary, I make seven observations:

1. Deuteronomy's sister-brother ethic is multivalent; this is critical for interpretation.
2. The term *gēr* identifies a vulnerable person who is from outside the core family; the *gēr*, by definition, is not a brother-sister within the clan grouping.
3. Deuteronomy's brother-sister ethic extends to the *gēr*.
4. In this way, Deuteronomy is *fostering* the inclusion of the *gēr* as kin, as brother-sister.
5. The *gēr* is a liminal figure; by definition, once a stranger is incorporated within the community as kin, he or she is no longer a *gēr*.
6. According to Deuteronomy's theological and ethical vision, the *gēr* is on the way to being incorporated within the fraternity of all Israel.
7. The multivalent use of אח is a rhetorical strategy that blurs the boundaries between a household or clan and the nation. It associates these domains of sociality, creating enduring relationships of solidarity and collective identity.

### 4.3. Yahweh the Just Judge for the *Gēr* (Deut 10:17–18)

17 For Yahweh your God, he is God of gods and Lord of lords, the great God, mighty and terrible, who is impartial in judgment, who does not accept a bribe, 18 the one who secures justice for the fatherless and the widow, and who loves the stranger, giving him or her food and clothing. 19 So you are to love the stranger, for you were strangers in the land of Egypt.

Deuteronomy 10:17b–18 characterizes Yahweh as the guarantor of just judicial processes for the most vulnerable. While in contemporary discourse 10:17–19 is perhaps the most popular biblical text for displaying an ethic of inclusivism, I am not aware of any writing, popular or scholarly, that probes into the contribution of 10:17–19 to Deuteronomy's corpus of judicial law for the *gēr*.

The present analysis investigates 10:17–19 as judicial law, and a thorough analysis of the *gēr* in 10:17–19 is provided in chapter 6. Loving the *gēr* (10:18) must include the provision of a fair hearing and of fair judgment. Two statements of the kingship of Yahweh provide the theological backdrop for Israel's election (10:14, 17a). The second of these, "God of God and Lord of Lords," is qualified by a relative particle אשר, which links with two nonperfective verbs of prohibition (10:17b; underlined) and with two participial clauses (10:18; verbs are underlined). The participles (עשה משפט ואהב) are active-fientive,[78] depicting the ongoing activity of Yahweh, which previously has been demonstrated in his delivering Israel (cf. 10:21–22).

10:17b

אשר לֹא יִשָּׂא פנים וְלֹא יקח שחד

10:18

עשה משפט יתום ואלמנה וְאַהֵב גר לתת לו לחם ושמלה

The first three clauses concern judicial process (10:17bα, β, 18a). These clauses associate lexically and conceptually with both Dtn judicial law and Dtn social law. The parallelism between 10:18a and 10:18b confirms that Yahweh's just judgment applies for the *gēr*, too.

The needy lacked influential advocates and easily could be ignored in their lawsuits, not least as officials were appointed from influential families and enjoyed a network of relationships within elite circles. The initial clause, אשר לֹא יִשָּׂא פנים, a characteristic legal formula of the DC (see also Lev 19:15, Deut 24:17a), assumes the syntax of the nonperfective of prohibition.[79] The phrase is common in instructions for judiciary; for example, Thutmosis III advised his new vizier Rekhmire:

> He is one who does not turn his face towards officials and councilors, and who does not make himself a fri[end] of anyone.… It is an abomination of God to show face.[80]

---

78. See Waltke and O'Connor, *Syntax*, 37.3b.

79. See Waltke and O'Connor, *Syntax*, 31.5d. Targums Onkelos and Pseudo-Jonathan strengthen the call for impartiality: דלית קדמוהי מסב אפין ואף.

80. Weinfeld, "Judge," 79.

Yahweh models for Israel's officials a right refusal to be swayed by those of means and connection, a trait that Yahweh has also displayed in the exodus (10:19b).

In the ancient Near East, the divinity was considered to be a very real tier of the judicial system. The intervention of the deity, should justice not be done, was feared, and the divine judge therefore had a tangible impact on judicial process. Yahweh fulfills this role not only by modeling but also by securing just legal processes for the most vulnerable:

10:18

עשה משפט יתום ואלמנה

Yahweh's kinship with the *gēr* is the context for his action on the *gēr's* behalf as the divine judge (ואהב גר, 10:18bα).[81] Cross explains that "properly vengeance is proscribed within the kinship group."[82]

In this text Yahweh displaces the human ruler as the just king (10:17b–18).[83] During the monarchy, "judicial authority ultimately lay in the hands of the king"[84] (see 1 Sam 14:24–46). Similarly, in the ancient Near East the king was the chief justice; Hammurabi postures himself as the *šar mīšarim*, the "king of justice."[85] However, the biblical lawmakers "transformed precedent by making the royal legislator of biblical law the divine monarch, Yahweh."[86] Yahweh delegates the responsibility for justice not to the king but to the whole community (10:19a; 1:13; 16:18). "Yahweh is not only powerful, but he exercises his power as an ideal worldly king to establish social justice, which manifests itself in impartiality and incorruptibility, especially for the sake of marginalized groups in society."[87]

---

81. On "love" and kinship, see the analysis of 10:17–19 in §6.2.

82. Cross, *Epic*, 4.

83. Berman, "Constitution," 534.

84. Wilson, "Israel's Judiciary," 240, see also 240–245.

85. Laws of Hammurabi, xlvii.77 and xlviii.7. On this epithet of Hammurabi, see Roth, *Law*, 142 n. 49. However, J. Nicholas Postgate states, "To sum up, then, no instance survives of an Assyrian king's intervention directly in individual legal cases, whether in Assyria or Babylonia, but it seems likely that in both countries they were in theory able to do so" (*The Land of Assur and the Yoke of Assur: Studies on Assyria 1971–2005* [Oxford: Oxbow, 2007], 55).

86. Levinson, "Law as an 'Ideal Type.'" 59.

87. Veijola, *Das 5. Buch Mose*, 256–57: "Jahwe ist aber nicht nur machtvoll, sondern übt seine Macht wie ein idealer weltlicher König aus, um die Gerechtigkeit

The first three clauses regarding judicial process (10:17bα, β, 18a) are found in Deut 16:19, though there is also dissimilarity. The phrase לא ישא פנים associates most closely with the HC (Lev 19:15); עשה משפט יתום ואלמנה (10:18a) is an unusual phrase that associates most closely with 24:17a (Dtn).[88] For the composition history of 10:17–19, see §6.2.1.

This exegesis strongly challenges the deconstructive readings of Mark Sneed and others, who argue that the Hebrew Bible's social ethics serve the class interests of the biblical writers. Sneed argues that the present passage legitimizes Yahweh's reign as the patron of the vulnerable, while paradoxically reinforcing the status quo. Sneed compares this text to Hammurabi's legitimizing claim to be the defender of the orphan and the widow in the prologue of the Laws of Hammurabi.[89] However, Sneed's comparison is flawed. In the Laws of Hammurabi, a tension exists between Hammurabi's claims to just rule in the prologue and epilogue and the absence of meaningful care for the vulnerable in the law corpus itself.[90] In contradistinction, within Deuteronomy the characterization of Yahweh as the divine-royal judge (10:17–18) underpins the social goals of Deuteronomy's judicial law. Just judicial procedure has potential to disrupt processes of unjust indebtedness and enslavement for the stranger.

## 4.4. A Socially Oriented Dtn Judicial Law (Deut 24:17a)

Deuteronomy 24:17a is a third text in Deuteronomy that stipulates that the *gēr* is to be protected in legal procedure (for 24:17b, see §3.5).

Deut 24:17[91]

לא תטה משפט גר יתום ולא תחבל בגד אלמנה

Do not pervert the justice due to the *gēr* and the fatherless. Do not take a widow's garment in pledge.

---

zu verwirklichen, die sich in Unparteilichkeit und Unbestechlichkeit manifestiert und besonders den marginalisierten Gesellschaftsgruppen zugute kommt."

88. See the analysis of 24:17a, above.

89. Sneed, "Israelite," 502–3.

90. See Lohfink, "Poverty," 34–38.

91. The LXX adds a conjunction before יתום and χήρας to the first injunction (24:17a). Both of these variants are assimilations to the more usual expression of the trio (cf. 16:11a, 14; 27:19).

Compare with Exod 23:6:

לא תטה משפט אבינך בריבו

While the CC concerns the דל ("poor, powerless") and the אבון ("poor"),
the DC identifies more precisely the *gēr* (1:16, 24:17a) and the fatherless
(24:17a), in line with Deuteronomy's distinctive concern for the stranger.
In addition, while 1:16–17 is a later redaction of 16:18–20, the present text
likely belongs to Dtn and is thus contemporary with the core procedural
law texts (16:18–20, 17:2–13, 19:15–21). This is consistent with the concern for the *gēr* that is evident in other Dtn texts (e.g., 16:1–17, 24:19–22).
In regard to the literary shape of the DC, however, 24:17a is not a part of
the core judicial texts. Both stipulations here (24:17a, b) revise the CC
and, as such, likely belong to Dtn. The triad of the vulnerable is appropriated from the CC, appearing in broken form here (Exod 22:21, 23:9).
While Mayes raises the possibility that יתום is a late addition,[92] this is
unlikely, as Dtn seems to prefer the full triad (cf. 14:28; 16:11a, 14; 26:12,
13). Achenbach notes that "clear efforts for the increased protection of
the stranger are observable in the older Deuteronomic stipulations within
Deuteronomy."[93]

The stipulation לא תטה משפט גר יתום addresses the whole community:
judges, litigants, witnesses, and, in clan-based contexts, the consenting
community. The verb נטה appears in the CC in the context of perverting
or misguiding justice (Exod 23:2, 6) and is a characteristic phrase of the
prophets (Amos 5:12) and of Proverbs (17:23, 18:5). The *hiphil* form of
נטה displays the sense of the *hiphil*, to cause an event, whereby the object
or second subject participates in the event.[94] In this case, an action (e.g.,
bribery) of a perpetrator (the first subject) initiates a sequence of events
that leads to justice (the second subject) running off course, thus: "Do not
misguide the *course* of justice" (Exod 23:6, Deut 16:19, 24:17a). The verb
נטה in 16:19 concerns fair legal process that pursues "truth" (17:4), that
involves diligent inquiry (1:16, 17:4), and that is free from influence (1:17,
16:19). Thus נטה has to do with parity in judicial process. Its use in 24:17a

---

92. Mayes, *Deuteronomy*, 326.

93. Achenbach, "Eintritt," 243: "Es ist also im dtn Dtn gegenüber älteren Bestim-
mungen deutlich das Bemühen um eine verstärkte Absicherung der Fremden erkennbar."

94. Waltke and O'Connor, *Syntax*, 433–36.

and 27:19 brings vulnerability to the fore, requiring that the vulnerable are to receive equal and fair treatment at the gate in a case against a kinsperson. This requirement would at times require a judge or elder to decide in favor of a stranger in his or her case against the kin of the elder himself. McConville states, "This is the clearest requirement of [the *gēr's*] inclusion in the public life of Israel."[95]

Furthermore, the composition history of 24:17a clarifies its ethical impulse. Three texts in Deuteronomy appropriate Exod 23:6: Deut 16:19, 24:17a, and 27:19. Deuteronomy 16:19 appears within Deuteronomy's core stipulation concerning just legal processes (16:18–20), and the reference to the poor is omitted (לא תטה משפט), for these texts are concerned with judicial probity more generally. Deuteronomy 24:17, however, reflects and enhances the concern of the CC for just legal procedure for the vulnerable (Exod 23:3–6). Thus the full thrust of Exod 23:1–8 is represented in Dtn by the two texts, Deut 16:18–20 and 24:17a, together. The Deuteronomist probably intended for Exod 23:6 (of the CC) and Deut 24:17a (of the DC) to be read together. The longer text, Exod 23:1–8, unfolds the dynamics of favoritism and influence. "The pressure that arises from the mixing together of rumors (Exod 23:1), majorities (23:2), power (23:1), money (23:8), etc. becomes apparent in these verses."[96] Deuteronomy 24:17a sharpens the ethical imperative of the CC for the most vulnerable. The strength of the ethical imperative of 24:17a is seen in that Dtn's revision does not contain the balancing phrase ודל לא תהדר בריבו (Exod 23:3). Further, 24:17a occurs within a section that is perhaps more concerned than any other collection of ancient law with the dignity of the vulnerable over against the accumulation of those with means. Deuteronomy 24:17a is located here in order to emphasize that just legal procedure for the stranger is critical for the implementation of Deuteronomy's social program. Further, some stipulations in this block insist that the unique circumstances of a vulnerable person be considered, even extending requirements beyond what could have been enforced in a court of law (see, e.g., 24:17b and 24:19–21). In its context, then, the phrase לא תטה משפט גר יתום entails more than restraint upon corrupt legal procedure; it promotes compassionate judgments that consider the circumstances and

---

95. McConville, *Deuteronomy*, 363. McConville's comment stands also for the other references to the *gēr* in judicial law (1:16–18; 10:16–18; 27:19).

96. Crüsemann, *Torah*, 190.

needs of the *gēr* (cf. 24:17b). Just judicial process for the poorest restricts, somewhat, the expansion of consolidated power.

An extended motivation clause concerning slavery in Egypt follows, evoking awareness of the defenselessness of the *gēr* at the gate and even the very real possibility of enslavement should the *gēr* not receive a hearing or a fair judgment. All three occurrences of the phrase ויפדך יהוה אלהיך משם concern laws that dignify vulnerable strangers and slaves as participants in the community (also 5:15, 15:15). Yahweh's redemption (פדה) establishes an ethical trajectory for Israel. Would-be oppressors must become redeemers.

## 4.5. Judicial Rights of the *Gēr* Protected in a Curse Ceremony (Deut 27:19)

The judicial rights of *gēr* are protected not only in stipulations but also by a curse within the Shechem covenant-renewal ceremony (27:1–26).

ארור מטה משפט גר יתום ואלמנה ואמר כל העם אמן

Cursed be anyone who perverts the justice due to the *gēr*, orphan, or widow. And all the people shall say, "Amen." (Deut 27:19, ESV modified)

It is remarkable that the single curse in the Shechem curse list (27:15–26) that relates to Deuteronomy's social laws highlights judicial process for the marginalized. Unjust procedures aided oppressors, resulting in indenture and loss of freedom for the *gēr*. Injustice in legal procedure may be hidden from the eyes of the community, but the significance of the curse of 27:19 is that Yahweh, the divine judge, observes this evil and intervenes. In Israel, as in the ancient world, "curses and blessings were perceived as powerful forces that shaped human destinies."[97] As described above, the *hiphil* of נטה in 27:19 has the sense "misguide the *course* of justice." The curse formula appropriates the syntax of the nonperfective of prohibition, a characteristic legal formula of the DC used in the parallels (see Exod 23:6, Deut 16:19aα, 24:17a).[98]

---

97. Melissa Ramos, "Spoken Word and Ritual Performance: The Oath and the Curse in Deuteronomy 27–28" (PhD diss., University of California Los Angeles, 2015), 1.

98. See Waltke and O'Connor, *Syntax*, 31.5d.

This text is discussed further in chapter 6, and there I observe that numerous clear associations with material from the HC and the interweaving of Dtr and Priestly concerns signals that 27:15–26 postdates these strata. In light of the analysis throughout this chapter, the literary development of 27:19 may be traced through the redaction layers of Deuteronomy in the way I have laid it out below, though certainty eludes us:

1. Exod 23:6. The CC.

לא תטה משפט אבינך בריבו

Do not pervert the justice due to your poor in his or her lawsuit. (ESV modified)

2. Deut 16:19aα. Dtn: reference to the poor is omitted.

לא תטה משפט

Do not pervert justice…

3. Deut 24:17. Dtn: in judicial law the vulnerable triad first appears here (in broken form).[99]

לא תטה משפט גר יתום ולא תחבל בגד אלמנה

Do not pervert the justice due to the *gēr* and the fatherless. And do not take a widow's garment in pledge.

4. Deut 27:19. Post-Dtr: curse formula.

ארור מטה משפט גר יתום ואלמנה ואמר כל העם אמן

Cursed be anyone who perverts the justice due to the *gēr*, fatherless, or widow. And all the people shall say, "Amen." (ESV modified)

The unit 27:1–26 forms an *inclusio* with 11:26–32 around the law corpus.

## 4.6. Synthesis of Literary Layers

A general pattern of literary development emerges from the discussion above. This is visible most simply by comparing the law of judicial procedure in the law corpus (Deut 12–26) with the texts from the frame (Deut 1–11; 27–34).

---

99. See again n. 91 above.

- **Dtn or early Dtr:** The procedural law of the CC is the primary source for Deuteronomy's group of texts regarding legal procedure (Exod 23:1–8). The core Dtn judicial texts (16:18–17:13, 19:15–21) deleted the reference to the poor present in the CC, focusing upon judicial probity. There is, however, one Dtn law concerning just judicial process for the *gēr* and the fatherless: 24:17a. In regard to the literary shape of the DC, however, 24:17a is not a part of the core judicial texts.
- **Dtr and post-Dtr:** There is repeated explicit protection of the *gēr* in the law of judicial procedure in Dtr and post-Dtr texts (1:16–17, 10:17–18, 27:19), over against Dtn texts. Two texts that are likely post-Dtr, 10:17–19 and 27:19, emphasize the theme of Yahweh as the divine judge.

The preceding exegesis suggests that the periods in which Dtr and post-Dtr were produced were likely contexts of massive internal displacement. The *gēr* also appears in other, nonjudicial Dtr and post-Dtr texts, including 26:1–15, 29:9–14, and 31:9–13 (these texts are explored in chapters 5 and 6). Deuteronomy's frame, which renews and reconstitutes Israel, also protects displaced people at the law courts as a key objective (other categories of vulnerability diminish in importance in these texts; see §4.9.). On the basis of the texts explored here, we may conclude that law of judicial procedure was a key legislative instrument for the protection of displaced people.

This literary-historical analysis will be picked up later in the chapter, concerning Israel's social history and the dating of texts. First, however, the provenance of the *gēr* is discussed.

### 4.7. The Provenance of the *Gēr*: Social History and Deuteronomy

It was noted in the introduction that there are three primary contending views in the scholarship for the origin of the *gēr*, and we now return to examine this question directly. The three views are: a refugee in the wake of the Assyrian invasion of the Northern Kingdom, a foreigner from a kingdom other than either Judah or the Northern Kingdom, or a displaced Judahite. These three views are now interrogated, and an alternative, integrative, model is suggested. As we proceed, we must bear in mind that, given the sheer number of references to the *gēr* in Deuteronomy and also the literary and theological emphasis within these texts, the periods in which the redaction strata of Deuteronomy were produced must have been contexts of massive displacement.

### 4.7.1. Is the *Gēr* a Refugee in the Wake of the Destruction of Samaria?[100]

The relationship between Judah and Israel is complex and debated. To be sure, by the seventh century Israel and Judah had been separate politically for over two hundred years.[101] Nonetheless, Avraham Faust has demonstrated that "the clear cultural boundaries reflected in the archaeological record serve as an independent evidence for affinity between most of the inhabitants of the two kingdoms."[102] In this light, given Deuteronomy's conception of the brotherhood-sisterhood of all Israel, if those designated *gēr* were largely northerners, then some indication of this would be expected in Deuteronomy. Yet there is nothing in texts concerning the *gēr* in Deuteronomy to suggest that the *gēr* was from the Northern Kingdom over and against anywhere else. A further problem with this view is that Dtr and post-Dtr texts, which many scholars claim emerged from within exilic Judah and Persian Yehud, respectively,[103] demonstrate an enhanced ethic of inclusion and protection for the *gēr* over and beyond that of Dtn (see, e.g., 1:16–17, 5:12–15, 29:9–14). Now, if the *gēr* in the seventh century (Dtn) is a displaced northern Israelite, then the *gēr* in the sixth century and beyond must be of a totally different origin. However, there is no hint of such a shift in the former identity of the *gēr* in the text. Na'aman contends that, while according to the *pax Assyriaca* borders within the empire were open, Judea's borders during the seventh century were "largely closed."[104] However, Israel Finkelstein has recently disputed

---

100. This theory was discussed in §1.1.4.1, and the relevant scholarship was cited there.

101. Recently, some scholars have argued that the concept of a united monarchy is a post-720 BCE invention, e.g., Israel Finkelstein, "State Formation in Israel and Judah: A Contrast in Context, A Contrast in Trajectory," *NEA* 62 (1999): 35–52.

102. Avraham Faust, "Between Israel and Judah: Politics, Economy and Identity" (paper presented at the Annual Meeting of the Society of Biblical Literature, San Diego, 25 November 2014), 10.

103. E.g., Otto, *Deuteronomium*, 243–48.

104. Na'aman, "Population," 215. Grabbe, however, suggests that one reason for the expansion of Jerusalem during the seventh century was immigration following the conquest of Samaria in 720 BCE (*Ancient Israel*, 169–70).

this on the grounds of archaeology and the transmission of northern texts to Judah.[105]

Assuming a seventh-century context for Dtn, some of those referred to as *gēr* in Dtn were probably northerners, but not the majority. Depending upon how one views the affinity between Judah and Israel, the view that the *gēr* is a refugee fleeing south from the Northern Kingdom may be, in a sense, a variation upon the view that the *gēr* is from another "nation" altogether.

### 4.7.2. Is the *Gēr* from a Non-Israelite and Non-Judahite Kingdom?[106]

Migration patterns in the seventh century support the contention that only a small number of those designated *gēr* were from a kingdom other than Judah or the Northern Kingdom. Judah was never an Assyrian province, and its population accordingly was not subject to deportation and to the influx of deportees during the seventh century, as were the surrounding territories. Assyrian deportations into the surrounding area, including the Philistine coast and Samaria, are attested in inscriptions and in the book of Ezra.[107] These brought population flux and a diversity of ethnicities and cultures within the proximity of Judah during the seventh century. Esarhaddon's offensive on the Philistine coast (680–669 BCE) and his campaigns against Egypt[108] may have caused some refugee movement into Judah. Excavation at Tel Batash, near Ekron, have revealed a mixture of Judahite, Phoenician, Assyrian, and Transjordan small finds.[109] Thus Crouch has recently concluded, "The economics and populations of Philistia and Judah were closely intertwined during the long seventh century."[110] Also, the material culture at sites such as Ḥorvat Qitmit and Ḥorvat ʿUza indicate the likelihood of migration from the Transjordan into the eastern Negev during the seventh century.[111] In the seventh century, then, "to a

---

105. Israel Finkelstein, "Migration of Israelites into Judah after 720 BCE: An Answer and an Update," *ZAW* 127 (2015): 188–206.

106. This theory was discussed in §1.1.4.2, and the relevant scholarship was cited there.

107. See Naʾaman, "Population," 212.

108. Naʾaman, "Population," 212.

109. George L. Kelm and Amihai Mazar, *Timnah: A Biblical City in the Sorek Valley* (Winona Lake, IN: Eisenbrauns, 1995), 164–68.

110. Crouch, *Making*, 41.

111. Crouch, *Making*, 52–57.

degree unfamiliar from the past, Judah's residents found culturally distinctive individuals and groups traipsing through, even resident in, their own backyard."[112] Nonetheless, Judah did not experience the massive interstate population shifts that incorporation into the empire entailed until the time of the rise of the Babylonian Empire. Thus migration from outside of the kingdom of Judah cannot be the primary social affect behind the large population of those labeled *gēr* that is the concern of Dtn, though it doubtless contributed to it. Foreign immigration was especially limited within Persian Yehud, and the "harsh realities of life" in Yehud, which included widespread socioeconomic stratification and poverty, has led some scholars to conclude that Persian Judah was "undesirable as a location for immigration"[113] (this is explored in §§4.7.3, 6.4.3, and 6.4.5.1).

We will observe in the following section that there was massive internal displacement through the periods within which Deuteronomy was probably written; assuming that this was so, it would be strange if Deuteronomy made provisions for displaced people from other nations but none for internally displaced people. Although the view that the *gēr* was exclusively a foreigner is defended in many recent publications, it is more likely that non-Judahites/non-Israelites were only a portion of those designated *gēr* in the redaction strata of Deuteronomy.

### 4.7.3. Is the *Gēr* a Displaced Judahite?[114]

The possibility that the *gēr* in Deuteronomy may be a displaced Judahite has been opened by the analysis of cognates of *gēr* above (§2.1). There it was observed that foreignness is not germane to the lexical meaning of *gr* in Northwest Semitic cognates. The social level at which displacement occurs is clarified by the context rather than by the term *gr* itself. There is also a correspondence between internal displacement in Judah during the periods to which the literary strata Deuteronomy are often

---

112. Crouch, *Making* 57.

113. John Kessler, "Diaspora and Homeland in the Early Achaemenid Period: Community, Geography and Demography in Zechariah 1–8," in *Approaching Yehud: New Approaches to the Study of the Persian Period*, ed. Jon L. Berquist, SemeiaSt 50 (Atlanta: Society of Biblical Literature, 2007), 165.

114. This theory was discussed in §1.1.4.3, and the relevant scholarship was cited there.

dated[115] and provision for the *gēr* in the corresponding literary strata; this is now explored.

### 4.7.3.1. Displacement in Judah

### 4.7.3.1.1. Displacement in Judah during the Seventh Century

Below (§4.9.1) I will observe that legislative protection for the *gēr* comes into full flower in Dtn, which far outstrips the earlier attempts of the CC to provide protection and succor for the *gēr*. Critical scholars most commonly date Dtn to the seventh century,[116] and there are two likely causes of massive internal displacement in this century.

First, during the eighth century Judah moved toward more comprehensive structures of statehood, lagging about a century behind the Northern Kingdom in these developments.[117] With statehood came increasing social stratification and widespread, permanent indebtedness. The books of Isaiah and Micah denounce the landed elite and the central aristocracy for their excessive opulence and their exploitation of the population (see Isa 3:14–15, 5:11–12). Kessler asserts, "The crucial change that led to the conditions evident from the eighth century onward is the transition from 'normal' indebtedness to an irreversible debt overload." Indebtedness led, in turn, to loss of land and then to slavery for many. "The mechanism of heavy indebtedness, once set in motion, allows scarcely any to escape."[118] A good many of those whom Dtn sought to protect were likely displaced from their land through this system of indebtedness. Dynamics of urbanization, of loss of land, and of enslavement eroded kinship groups,[119] which were the most important system of protection. In turn, these dynamics enhanced the process of displacement. This phenomenon is visible in the משפה laws, which seek to break the cycle of indebtedness

---

115. On dating Deuteronomy, see §§4.9, 6.1.1.

116. The date of Dtn is discussed further in §4.9. For a differentiation between Dtn, Dtr, and post-Dtr texts, see Otto, *Das Deuteronomium: Politische Theologie*, 203–378.

117. See further Kessler, *Social History*, 98.

118. Kessler, *Social History*, 111–12.

119. Baruch Halpern, "Jerusalem and the Lineages in the Seventh Century B.C.E.: Kinship and the Rise of Individual Liability," in *Law and Ideology in Monarchic Israel*, ed. Baruch Halpern and Deborah W. Hobson, JSOTSup 124 (Sheffield: JSOT Press, 1991), 71–89.

and land loss (Deut 15:1–18). Indeed, the whole system of social laws in the DC addresses a cycle of deepening indebtedness and enslavement in Judahite society.

The other likely cause of massive domestic displacement is Sennacherib's campaign of 701 BCE, as argued most prominently by Na'aman. In light of Hezekiah's leadership in the anti-Assyrian coalition, Sennacherib aimed to weaken Judah, which was the most powerful state near the border with Egypt. Sennacherib demolished most of the major Judahite sites and deported tens of thousands of residents. Jerusalem was the only major urban center left in seventh-century Judah.[120] As far as we know, of the 354 settlements destroyed by the Assyrians at this time, only thirty-nine were rebuilt in the seventh century.[121] Na'aman observes that the Assyrian conquest would have given rise to a class of poor and landless people that did not exist on such a scale before.[122]

### 4.7.3.1.2. Displacement in Judah during the Sixth Century

The Dtr redactions are most commonly dated to the sixth century in critical scholarship. The massive displacement in Judah produced by the Neo-Babylonian conquest and its aftermath is a likely context for the ethics of Dtr regarding the *gēr*. Faust argues that the Babylonian conquest of Judah and the resulting assassination, exile, famine, emigration, and disease created a "post-collapse society."[123] Chapters 5 and 6 will demonstrate Dtr's enhanced concern for displaced persons vis-à-vis Dtn.[124] Dtr texts such as the Sabbath command (5:12–15) rearticulate and intensify for this new context the ethic of inclusion for the stranger that was formerly expressed in Dtn (see §3.7.5).

---

120. Na'aman, "Population," 209–12; Grabbe, *Ancient Israel*, 179.
121. Grabbe, *Ancient Israel*, 167.
122. Na'aman, "Sojourners," 277.
123. Faust, *Judah*, 170.
124. This is discussed in more detail in the exegesis of 5:12–15 in §3.7.

4.7.3.1.3. Displacement in Persian Yehud

Post-Dtr texts regarding the *gēr* may have responded to the social fragmentation that characterized the period of Persian Yehud.[125] There was division between rich and poor during this period (e.g., Neh 5:1–13, Mal 3:5).[126] After the Neo-Babylonian invasion, an upper class that was connected to the Babylonian elite rose quickly within Judah, and with this hierarchy came indebtedness, land alienation, and enslavement.[127] Also, the return of the exiles produced conflict over patrimony and further land alienation. These social forces may have produced much of the displacement behind post-Dtr's concern for the *gēr* (as explored in §§4.7.3, 6.4.3, and 6.4.5.1).

The foregoing social-historical analysis suggests that, while many or most of those designated *gēr* were internally displaced Judahites, a blended model is likely, whereby some were northerners and some of were non-Judahite and non-Israelite. The question of the provenance of the *gēr* is now examined from another angle, that of social identity and "otherness" across diffuse social domains.

### 4.8. The Provenance of the *Gēr*: Social Location of "Otherness"

4.8.1. The Social Location of "Otherness" in the Hebrew Bible

It should be reiterated at this point that the term *gēr* itself does not identify the provenance of displacement. This point has been made via a study of Northwest Semitic cognates of *gēr* as well as exegesis. I have been building the case that, from the point of view of the kinsfolk, the term *gēr* simply identifies a vulnerable person who is from outside of the core family. The preceding discussion has made the case that the periods within which

---

125. For further analysis see §5.3. On the dating of post-Dtr, see Achenbach, "Eintritt," 251; E. W. Nicholson, *Deuteronomy And Tradition* (Philadelphia: Fortress, 1967), 22; Otto, "History of the Legal-Religious," 234–39.

126. See Kessler, *Social*, 134–36.

127. Daniel L. Smith, "The Politics of Ezra: Sociological Indicators of Postexilic Judean Society," in *Second Temple Studies 1: Persian Period*, ed. Philip R. Davies, JSOT-Sup 117 (Sheffield: JSOT, 1991), 92–93. See further Lester L. Grabbe, *Yehud: A History of the Persian Province of Judah*, vol. 1 of *A History of the Jews and Judaism in the Second Temple Period*, LSTS 47 (London: T&T Clark, 2004), 172, 191–94.

Deuteronomy witnessed massive internal displacement, and other causes of displacement in Judah/Yehud would have included foreign immigration and refugees from the Northern Kingdom. This discussion now turns to questions of social identity.

The observed prominence of the household and clan groupings in Deuteronomy's legislation demonstrates that the primary identity of an Israelite was found in association with the extended family.[128] "An Israelite identified himself, using the gentilic pattern, with a *bayit* or *bet 'ab* ('house of one's father')."[129] Illustrative is the narrative of Achan. While the muster includes the tribe, clan, and lineage group, ultimately Achan and his household are stoned (Josh 7:14–26). Similarly, responsibility for redemption falls to the kinship group, and blood vengeance is a duty of kinsfolk.[130] The extended family remained the dominant social structure in the rural sector during the late monarchy.[131] Indeed, Schloen observes

> in recent decades a number of researchers have observed—in opposition to the view held by an earlier generation of anthropologists and historians—that localized kinship networks did not disappear as an effective force with the advent of complex urban society. It is now widely recognized that kinship networks have remained important in the Near East up to the present day, not only in rural villages but also in urban neighborhoods, where patterns of residence and of economic cooperation reflect extended-family and "clan" ties (real or fictional).[132]

Consequently, "In a lineage-based agrarian society the immigrant from another tribe or even the next village is just as much of an outsider."[133] The

---

128. See Faust, *Archaeology*, 11.

129. Lawrence E. Stager, "The Archaeology of the Family in Ancient Israel." *BASOR* 260 (1985): 21–22.

130. See further, Cross, *Epic*, 4–5.

131. Faust, *Judah*, 174; Shunya Bendor, *The Social Structure of Ancient Israel: The Institution of the Family* (beit'ab) *from the Settlement to the End of the Monarchy* (Jerusalem: Simor, 1996), 216–24. For the view that kinship structures are retained in the late monarchy, see Faust, *Archaeology*, 162; Schloen, *House*; Na'aman, "Sojourners," 276 n. 99. For an opposing view, see Halpern, "Lineage," 71–89.

132. Schloen, *House*, 70, and citations. This point has been made with respect to early Mesopotamian states by McC. Adams, *Evolution*. Schloen argues that in Ugarit many of the corvée laborers who worked on royal farms nonetheless dwelt in traditional villages nearby (*House*, 236–39).

133. Walter Houston, *Contending for Justice: Ideologies and Theologies of Social*

*gēr* appears in relation to the household (observe the household list, for example, "You and your sons and your daughters, your male and female slaves, the Levites resident in your towns, as well as the strangers, the orphans, and the widows who are among you," 16:11, 14) and to the clan (בשעריך, Deut 16:11a, 14; cf. 5:14; 14:21, 29; 16:14; 24:14; 26:12; 31:12). Deuteronomy is cultivating the inclusion of a displaced person at this local level of the household and the clan, and otherness is also constituted at this local level.[134]

More evidence is Bultmann's observation that in narrative texts the root *gr* has capacity to refer to displacement both at a "national" level and in terms of the territorial area of one's own people. An example of the latter is a reference to the Beerothites, who are said to be *gērim* within Gittaim, to which they had fled: ויהיו שם גרים עד היום הזה (2 Sam 4:3b). Both Gittaim and Beeroth belong to Benjamin.[135] Bultmann also observes narrative examples of the use of *gr* in contexts of "national" displacement. However, Bultmann demonstrates with nuance that even in these texts the term *gr* itself does not provide the sense of foreignness. For example, regarding Moses's sojourn in Midian (Exod 2), Bultmann states:

> In Midian, Moses is a "national" stranger to the extent that he is regarded as אִישׁ מִצְרִי (v. 19).…. In the context of this distinction of ethnic affinities as required by the course of the narrative, the expression בְּאֶרֶץ נָכְרִיָּה in v. 22b takes the "national" aspect. The fact that being a *gēr* is not the same as being a national stranger is also shown by the fact that the word ישב is also used for this kind of residence (v.15b: וַיֵּשֶׁב בְּאֶרֶץ־מִדְיָן).[136]

Bultmann concludes from his analysis: "Foreignness is not an aspect of the term *gēr* itself, in the sense of foreign origin. The verb is to be inter-

---

*Justice in the Old Testament* (London: T&T Clark, 2006), 108.

134. The inclusion of the *gēr* within the household and the clan is discussed in §§5.2.3 and 5.2.4.

135. Bultmann, *Fremde*, 21–22.

136. Bultmann, *Fremde*, 18: "In Midian ist Mose insofern ein 'national' Fremder, als er als אִישׁ מִצְרִי betrachtet wird (v. 19).…. Im Kontext dieser vom Gang der Erzählung geforderten Unterscheidung von ethnischen Zugehörigkeiten trägt in v. 22b der Ausdruck נָכְרִיָּה den 'nationalen' Aspekt. Daß das גר-Sein nicht mit dem Ansässig-Sein als national Fremder gleichbedeutend ist, geht umgekehrt auch daraus hervor, daß für diese Weise des Aufenthalts auch das Wort ישב gebraucht wird (v.15bβ: וַיֵּשֶׁב בְּאֶרֶץ־מִדְיָן)."

preted as being-in-residence: one is a 'stranger' in terms of the place of residence."[137]

To be sure, the kerygma of Deuteronomy, especially in Deuteronomy's framework (Deut 1–12, 27–34), fosters the cohesiveness of the Yahweh community, and all Israel is a dominant group identity in the framework (see the exegesis of 29:9–14 below). Essentializing categories such as עמוני (23:4), מואבי (23:4), אדמי (23:8), and מצרי (23:8) nourish group "insider-ism" at this level. However, the term *gēr* is a generic descriptor that associates within a different lexical and conceptual domain (e.g., the household list formula and the "gates" formula). The *gēr* is simply a vulnerable person who seeks a living within a core family that is not the *gēr*'s own. As Na'aman states, "Traditional society in Judah was based on family solidarity, on the leadership of the elders and notables, and its economy rested primarily on land. Integrating into such a traditional society was a major hurdle for displaced people who had been torn from their own former family structures, and had neither land nor means of production to provide them with self-sufficient subsistence."[138] When the *gēr* appears in the context of all Israel in the framework of Deuteronomy (Deut 1–11, 27–34), this figure is nonetheless explicitly identified in the text in connection with the household and the clan, as explored below (see §§6.3 and 6.4). I will explore how, where the *gēr* is incorporated within Israel via covenant-renewal ceremonies and other "national" rituals, the *gēr* appears not by virtue of his or her foreignness but because severance from kin and patrimony also calls into question an association within the assembly.[139]

A point that is ignored in the discussion is that a foreign identification for a noun is obvious where foreignness is genuinely signified. The five uses of the term נכרי in Deuteronomy, for example, appear in contexts that highlight the distinction between the נכרי and the native Israelite (14:21, 15:3, 17:15, 23:21, 29:21). This is the case also for the term *gēr* in the HC. It is true, too, of the gentilics: עמוני (23:4), מואבי (23:4), אדמי (23:8), and מצרי (23:8); compare ארמי (26:5). In Deuteronomy, however, the *gēr* is consis-

---

137. Bultmann, *Fremde*, 22: "daß in dem Begriff *ger* selber kein Aspekt von Fremd-heit im Sinne ausländischer Herkunft liegt. Bei der Erklärung des Wortes ist von dem Verb *gûr* auszugehen, das ein Ansässig-Sein bedeutet, das vom Ort des tatsächlichen Aufenthalts aus als das eines 'Fremden' erscheint."

138. Na'aman, "Sojourners," 276–77.

139. For a further discussion of this dynamic, see the exegesis of 29:9–14 and 31:9–13 (§§6.3 and 6.4).

tently referenced at the level of the household, settlement, town, or city—
the *otherness* of the *gēr* clusters at that local level.

### 4.8.2. Otherness at the Level of Family and Clan in Ancient Near Eastern Texts

Otherness is similarly identified at the level of the nuclear family or the
extended kinship grouping in many extant ancient Near Eastern texts. The
Instruction of Amenemope identifies a "stranger" as one who is not near
kin: "Do not refuse your oil jar to a stranger, / Double it before your brothers" (28.3–4).[140] Also, the *matūtu* (adoption) tablets from Nuzi may refer
to the adoptee as "stranger," *na-ka-ra*,[141] citing the adoptee's former location outside of the kinship group. Indeed, Akkadian *nkr*, "stranger," may
refer to someone who is simply from a different household. In a text from
Nuzi, a man, Zigi, gives his property to his wife Zilipkiashe. Upon Zilipkiashe's death, his sons will own the property. The clause is added, "She
shall not give anything to strangers [*nakari*]."[142] Here otherness is defined
in terms of a relation to the house of the paterfamilias. Back to the Hebrew
Bible, we may imagine a scenario where a *gēr* was a displaced farmer from
a settlement situated just over the hill, so to speak, though this would not
be the only scenario behind the term *gēr*. The definitive factor is that the
*gēr* is separated from the protection that kinsperson and land afford and
that the *gēr* is seeking sustenance within a משפחה that is not the *gēr*'s own.

### 4.8.3. Ambivalences Surrounding the Term *Gēr*

The term *gēr* has the capacity to refer both to internal displacement and
external displacement, depending upon the context (see §2.9). *Gēr* refers
to a foreigner in two texts in Deuteronomy: 14:21 (Dtr) and 28:43–44 (pre-
Dtr). (The permission to give the נבלה to the *gēr*, 14:21, is the only text that
Albertz produces to support his claim that the *gēr* in Deuteronomy is a

---

140. Translation from Lichtheim, *New Kingdom*, 161.

141. E. A. Speiser, "New Kirkuk Documents Relating to Family Laws," *AASOR*
10 (1928–1929): 30. Speiser is translating line 14 of text 60 in Edward Chiera, *Texts
of Varied Contents*, Harvard Semitic Series 5 (Cambridge: Harvard University Press,
1929).

142. Moshe Weinfeld, "The Covenant of Grant in the Old Testament and in the
Ancient Near East," *JAOS* 90 (1970): 190, and see n. 45.

foreigner.)[143] These texts suggest that at least *some* of those designated *gēr* were foreigners, though not necessarily all.[144]

Further evidence that term *gēr* includes foreigners in its scope is that the term נכרי consistently refers to a foreigner of *independent means* (see §6.10.1) and that there is no other term (apart from *gēr*) in Deuteronomy for *impoverished* foreigners. We conclude on this basis that the term *gēr* includes foreigners who are displaced and impoverished. On this point, I diverge from Bultmann, for although he is correct to state that Deuteronomy addresses contexts of internal displacement,[145] there are good reasons for thinking that many of those designated *gēr* were also from outside of Judah/Yehud. Again, in terms of definition, the *gēr* is simply a displaced and dependent person in the context of the kinship group within which the *gēr* now resides.

We must add to these observations dynamics of the text's reception. We have suggested that that Dtn originally addressed a context of massive internal displacement, yet this does not eliminate the possibility of the same texts being interpreted in a later period (or in a different location) as addressing a new context of immigration at a "national" level. If it be objected that the original intention of the text has exclusive privileges for interpretation, we must recall that revision and reinterpretation is germane to the production of the text itself. Thus inevitably throughout the periods of the production of Deuteronomy and also beyond, the term *gēr* has rightly been interpreted as referring to a wide range of circumstances of displacement, both internal and external.

## 4.9. Social History and Literary History

Having investigated the texts concerning the *gēr* in social law and judicial law and having explored the social-historical provenance of the *gēr* in Deuteronomy, we may step back to explore the development of the noun *gēr* and the composition history and social history of these texts.

---

143. Albertz, "Aliens," 55.

144. The contention of Achenbach and others that the *gēr* is not mentioned in the Passover-Massot text (16:1–8) because of their foreignness is discussed, below, at §5.2.8.

145. Bultmann, *Fremde*, 213.

4.9.1. Stages of the Development of the Noun *Gēr*

First I will sketch some contours in the composition history of the noun *gēr* up to and including its use in Deuteronomy.[146] A small number of occurrences of the verb גור precede the law corpora. Some pre-Dtn traditions within the book of Genesis narrate the sojourning of the patriarchs using the verb גור. Two references occur within what seems to be a self-contained proto-Genesis Jacob narrative in which the motif of travel and return is prominent.[147] In the first, God commands Isaac גור בארץ הזאת (26:3) within the Isaac wife-sister narrative that modifies the Jacob material (26:1–33).[148] In the second, Jacob's words to Esau, עם לבן גרתי ואחר עד עתה, are part of early linking material within the Jacob narrative (32:5).[149] Two other early references are found in material connected with the Abraham tradition, namely, in the Abraham wife-sister narrative and in reference to Lot in the city of Sodom (Gen 12:10, 19:9).[150] Many scholars conclude that Dtn was produced independently of these texts.[151] There are no uses of the noun *gēr* in the Pentateuch that predate the law corpora.[152] Outside of the Pentateuch, both the verb and the noun appear in passages that may well be dated earlier (e.g., 2 Sam 4:3, Isa 16:4).

---

146. I gratefully acknowledge Peter Altmann's comments on an earlier draft of this section.

147. "Proto-Genesis" designates the original book of Genesis, which was in part a compilation of earlier traditions. See Carr, *Reading*, 177, 218. On the proto-Genesis Jacob narrative, see Carr, *Reading*, 177, 256–289; Erhard Blum, *Die Komposition der Vätergeschichte*, WMANT 57 (Neukirchen-Vluyn: Neukirchener, 1984), 7–151. גור also appears in texts likely to be later: Gen 35:27 and 47:4. On these later texts, see Carr, *Reading*, 106, 273.

148. Carr, *Reading*, 177, 205, 257; Carr, *Formation*, 475.

149. Carr, *Reading*, 258. Other references in the Jacob story are probably later: 35:27 is likely P; 47:4 is later than the Joseph material that surrounds it (see Carr, *Reading*, 106, 273).

150. Carr designates these as "proto-Genesis" (*Reading*, 306, 339); cf. Schmid, *Old Testament*, 161. Other occurrences of גור in the Abraham material (20:1, 21:23, 21:34) are likely later (see Carr, *Reading*, 20–21; Carr, *Formation*, 485; Schmidt, *Old Testament*, 86–87).

151. E.g., Schmidt, *Old Testament*, 125.

152. The two occurrences of the noun *gēr* in the Patriarchal narratives likely postdate both the CC and Dtn. The first is a reference to Israel as *gēr* in Egypt with strong Deuteronomistic connections (Gen 15:13). This reference is thought by many to be late, non-P material (Carr, *Reading*, 163–67; Moshe Anbar, "Genesis 15: A Conflation

A second stage that may be observed is the appearance of the noun in the CC as a technical legal term (Exod 22:20; 23:9, 12).[153] I have argued, following Kidd, that the noun *gēr* in the Pentateuch is in most occurrences a legal term. This legal sense of the noun must have developed with the law corpora themselves or else within prior legal material, either written or oral, upon which the corpora drew. The characteristic dependence of the *gēr* that is visible in the CC and the DC is introduced to the lexeme at this point, a characteristic that is not present in the Genesis texts.

In a third movement, the noun *gēr* appears in Dtn, where it maintains its technical legal sense. At this point the Pentateuch's ethical vision for the vulnerable stranger comes into full flower. In Deuteronomy the term *gēr* is appended to the fatherless-widow doublet and is also subsumed within the brother-sister ethic of Deuteronomy in order to address a context in which displaced and vulnerable people are a pressing social concern. The rigorous ethic concerning the vulnerable stranger is thoroughly embedded in Deuteronomy's theology and narrative.

In a fourth movement, the motif of Israel as *gēr* in Egypt is added into the Dtr tradition (10:19, 23:8, 26:5; this is discussed at length at §5.3.3.5).[154] This motif is distinct from the slavery motif, and it refers to an initial period in Egypt when Jacob and his household received hospitality. The insertion of this motif perhaps took place within the so-called exilic Moabite redaction.[155] At around the same time, the motif of Israel as *gēr* in Egypt may have been appended to laws concerning the *gēr* in the CC.[156]

---

of Two Deuteronomic Narratives," *JBL* 101 [1982]: 39–55). Abraham's self identification as *gēr* in the second text (Gen 23:4) is likely later as well (Carr, *Reading*, 111–12, 339–40).

153. There are some further textual connections between the Genesis texts referenced above and a block of social law in the CC that is framed by the noun *gēr* (22:20–23:9). Observe: הרג (Gen 12:12, 26:7, Exod 23:7), רעע (Gen 19:7, Exod 23:3), צעקה (Gen 19:13, Exod 22:22), and משכרת, שכר (Gen 29:15, 31:7, Deut 24:15). These connections may be the natural result of thematic correspondence, as both texts are concerned with the sojourner and other vulnerable categories of people. Or they may be evidence of a more direct literary relationship.

154. See also Ebach, *Fremde*, 200.

155. Otto, "History of the Legal-Religious," 231.

156. See §5.3.3.5.

### 4.9.2. Social History

I have observed that procedural law for the *gēr* is asserted at four points in Deuteronomy, three of these in the framework, here dated to Dtr and post-Dtr (1:16–18, 10:17–19, 27:19). The *gēr* also appears in other Dtr and post-Dtr texts. Other categories of vulnerability are omitted in these two texts, 29:9–14 and 31:9–13, which are analyzed in chapter 6. We have observed in the exegesis of 1:16–17, and we will also observe in chapter 6, that other categories of vulnerability fade in importance in Deuteronomy's later texts, and a concern for the *gēr* comes to the fore. These observations forcefully demonstrate three dynamics that have not been observed in the scholarship:

1. Displacement was the most pressing social issue within the community during the period of Dtr and of post-Dtr (other categories of vulnerability diminish in prominence).[157]
2. In Deuteronomy's framing texts, as Israel was reconstituted, the inclusion of those who had been separated from patrimony and from kindred was a primary goal.[158]
3. Judicial law was a most important legal category for the protection and inclusion of the stranger within the community.

These three points are of staggering significance for the *gēr* in Deuteronomy; the second and third points are developed further in chapter 6. The widespread displacement that characterized the community in front of the text has implications for dating Deuteronomy, and this is discussed now.

### 4.9.3. A Social-Historical Approach to Dating Deuteronomy

The quest to secure a date for Deuteronomy's various redactions is now revisited, and what follows contributes to a new and potentially fruitful approach to dating the book on the basis of economic and social history.[159] Dynamics of internal displacement are the primary historical cue for dating followed here.

---

157. Though, there is reference to slaves (5:12–15) and to the vulnerable triad (10:17–18, 27:19).

158. See further analysis of the framing texts of Deuteronomy in chapter six.

159. See, for example, Na'aman, "Sojourner"; Axel Knauf, "Observations."

We have observed that the original Dtn layer projects a society in front of the text that is confronted with widespread displacement. The displacement is only intensified in Dtr, for the *gēr* is the dominant social issue of Deuteronomy's framing texts (1:16–18, 29:9–14). Displacement remains a pressing social issue in texts that seem to be authored later, referred to as post-Dtr (e.g., 10:17–19, 31:9–13).[160] This analysis suggests that Deuteronomy was authored over connected periods of deep and persistent, but differentiated, internal displacement. In dating Deuteronomy, then, we are searching for a series of sequential sociohistorical settings, each of which had at least a period of widespread social displacement. Among the causes of such displacement may be conquest, famine, disease, socioeconomic disparity, and the erosion of kinship groupings that arises from all of these dynamics.

There are other important indicators for dating Deuteronomy to be taken into account: a strong trend in the scholarship suggests that the infrastructure for sophisticated and ongoing textual development was present from the eighth century onward.[161] Furthermore, Crüsemann observes that the *gēr* does not appear as a social issue in the earlier prophetic works. Instead, widespread displacement seems to be a phenomenon that began in the late eighth century.[162] Also, allowance must be made for the prior development of the CC, with its own pronounced ethic of inclusivism for the *gēr*. Sennacharib's invasion of Judah (701 BCE) is a possible starting point for Deuteronomy's developing response to displacement.[163] Dtn may be dated tentatively to the early seventh century. Dtr may be composed partially in response to the widespread displacement following the Neo-Babylonian conquest and its aftermath. This explains Dtr's heightened ethic for the *gēr* vis-à-vis Dtn. Post-Dtr may respond to displacement created by socioeconomic stratification and by the return of the *golah* in

---

160. See further, §§4.7.3, 6.4.3, and 6.4.5.1.

161. E.g., Sanders, *Invention*, 7; Carr, *Formation*, 304–5; William M. Schniedewind, *How the Bible Became a Book: The Texualization of Ancient Israel* (Cambridge: Cambridge University Press, 2004), 64–90. Carr also postulates a "preliminary literary system" in the ninth and tenth century that is visible in the present Hebrew Bible (*Formation*, 355–85).

162. Crüsemann, *Torah*, 184.

163. The social context for displacement in the seventh century has been explored in §3.7.5.

the Persian period.[164] These three social settings are explained more fully in the following chapters.

### 4.9.4. A Critique of Knauf's Model for Dating Deuteronomy

Ernst Axel Knauf has also used a social and economic method for dating Deuteronomy, recently arguing that Dtn was produced in exilic Judah. He cites, among other proofs, the frequent occurrence of כסף in the CC (eight of eighty-five verses) in comparison with the DC (seven of 345 verses) as evidence that the CC addresses a highly monetized society, whereas the DC addresses a less-developed economy that would fit the exilic period. However, Knauf ignores the fact that seven of eight occurrences of כסף in the CC are within the so-called statutory law of the *mišpāṭîm* (Exod 21:2–23:15). I explained in chapter 3 that the *mišpāṭîm* is a distinctive type of law that closely resembles ancient Near Eastern law corpora and is concerned with property, loans, injury, and the penalties and compensation that these involve; this explains the high frequency of כסף. The DC omits this type of law altogether. Thus, Knauf's argument on the basis of occurrences of כסף cannot be sustained. Knauf rightly points out that the destruction of Judah by Nebuchadnezzar was far more traumatic than that of Sennacherib. He argues that the widespread displacement that followed the Neo-Babylonian conquest of Judah makes better sense of Dtn's concern for the *gēr* than the seventh-century context. However, Knauf's exegesis of texts concerning the *gēr* in Deuteronomy is oversimplified. A reconstruction that makes better sense of the data is that Dtn responds to the displacement created (in part) by Sennacherib's invasion, while the intensified ethic for the *gēr* that is visible in Dtr responds to the comprehensive devastation of society in the Neo-Babylonian conquest and its aftermath. Knauf's model is not able to account for Dtr's intensified concern for the *gēr*.[165]

An alternative view is that Dtn has its origin in the sixth-century diaspora communities. But this seems improbable in that the strong ethic

---

164. See §§4.7.3, 6.4.3, and 6.4.5.1.

165. Juha Pakkala offers nine arguments for a post 586 BCE date for Dtn ("The Date of the Oldest Edition of Deuteronomy," *ZAW* 121 [2009]: 388–401), but see Nathan MacDonald, "Issues in Dating Deuteronomy: A Response to Juha Pakkala," *ZAW* 122 (2010): 431–35; and see also Juha Pakkala, "The Dating of Deuteronomy: A Response to Nathan MacDonald," *ZAW* 123 (2011): 431–36. Otto, too, objects to a Babylonian or Persian date for Dtn ("History of the Legal-Religious," 222).

for displaced people evident in Dtn seems to presuppose a social context that would be difficult for an absent author to imagine. Achenbach and others have suggested that the *gēr* laws reflect Israel's own displaced circumstances in the exile,[166] yet no clear reference to the exilic community as *gēr* exists in the Hebrew Bible.[167] Also, the experience of the Babylonian deportees, who tended to live together in settlements,[168] differs from the use of the word *gēr* in Deuteronomy. In Deuteronomy, *gēr* refers to a vulnerable person or family dwelling in a kinship context that is not native to them. Also, new texts from the archives of two Judean exilic communities in Babylonia cast further doubt on this hypothesis, for these documents also make no reference to Judean law as set forth by Deuteronomy or Ezra, appearing as typical secular Neo-Babylonian texts.[169]

There is good reason to presume that much of the material in Deuteronomy (e.g., much of the family law and some of the original strata of various social laws) was composed well before the seventh century. If my present reconstruction errs, an earlier date is more likely to be correct than a later alternative.[170]

## 4.10. Conclusion

In sum, this chapter has investigated four texts within Deuteronomy's law of judicial procedure that reference the *gēr*: 1:16–17, 10:17–19, 27:19, 24:17a. The highly significant function of the law of judicial procedure in Deuteronomy's system of protection for the *gēr* has not been studied,

---

166. Achenbach, *"gēr,"* 36.

167. Second Chronicles 30:25 refers to refugees from the Northern Kingdom in Judah as *gēr*.

168. Cornelia Wunsch, "Glimpses on the Lives of Deportees in Rural Babylonia," in *Arameans, Chaldeans, and Arabs in Babylonia and Palestine in the First Millennium B.C.*, ed. Angelika Berlejung and Michael P. Streck (Wiesbaden: Harrassowitz, 2013), 249; Kessler, *Social History*, 125.

169. Pearce and Wunsch, *Documents*.

170. Carr argues for an early monarchic, northern, form of Deuteronomy (*Formation*, 479). On the northern origins of Deuteronomy, see recently Stefan Schorch, "The Samaritan Version of Deuteronomy and the Origin of Deuteronomy," in *Samaria, Samarians, Samaritans: Studies on Bible, History and Linguistics; Papers Presented at the Sixth International Conference of the Société d'Études Samaritaines held at Pápa, Hungary in July 17–25, 2008*, ed. József Zsengellér (Berlin: de Gruyter, 2011), 23–37.

as far as I am aware. The chapter began by examining the character and function of judicial law concerning the *gēr*. Biased judicial process was a most significant instrument whereby wealth became consolidated power in ancient Israel and whereby both the needy and the middle class were held down. The *gēr* was twice-removed from legal protection, being both displaced and impoverished.

Four texts have been examined in turn. Deuteronomy 1:16–18 provides that the testimony of the *gēr* must be received and judgment must be delivered such as to give equal weight to the *gēr* in his or her dispute with a kinsperson. Deuteronomy 10:17b–18 characterizes Yahweh as the guarantor of just judicial processes for the most vulnerable. Deuteronomy 24:17 is a Dtn judicial law that reflects and enhances the concern of the CC for just legal procedure for the vulnerable (cf. Exod 23:3, 6). Deuteronomy 27:19 protects via a curse ceremony the judicial rights of the *gēr*. Such judicial inclusivism had implications for the social structure of ancient Israel. Law codes generally have the function of stabilizing interclass relationships. The judicial protection granted to the *gēr*, however, dignifies the *gēr* as a full participant in the community, while also restraining the ability of the elite to ensnare the *gēr* via improper debt strategies.

Judicial law for the *gēr* appears at three points in Deuteronomy's frame (1:16–18, 10:17–19, 27:19). These texts, along with other Dtr and post-Dtr texts (26:1–15, 29:9–13, 31:9–14), illustrate three dynamics that are ignored in the scholarship. First, displacement was *the* pressing social issue within the community in the period of Dtr and of post-Dtr. Second, as Israel was reconstituted, the inclusion of those who had been separated from patrimony and from kindred was a primary goal of Deuteronomy's framing texts. Third, judicial law was the most important legal category for the protection and inclusion of the displaced within the community. A social-historical approach to dating was used in order to determine dates for the various redactions of Deuteronomy, according to three broad periods of displacement in Judah's history.

# 5

# The *Gēr* in Deuteronomy's Feasts

## 5.1. Introduction

### 5.1.1. The *Gēr* in Deuteronomy's Feasts

The *gēr* and other vulnerable categories appear repeatedly in the feasting stipulations (14:22–29, 16:1–17; 26:1–15). These are a subgroup of laws within Deuteronomy, as are social law (ch. 3) and law of judicial procedure (ch. 4). The previous chapter showed how the law of judicial procedure secured the legal rights of the *gēr* in a dispute and also how this opened the possibility of upward mobility for displaced people. The feasting texts, the subject of this chapter, picture the community in festal celebration before Yahweh. These festal texts are related to one another conceptually and lexically, associating in particular to social law and to law of divine privilege (Deut 12 and 13; 26:16–19).

We have observed that the *gēr* in Deuteronomy is a person or family separated from patrimony and from the traditional kinship ties that granted the *gēr* identity, belonging, and security. Relegated to the fringe of society, the *gēr* would ideally attach himself or herself to a beneficent kin grouping for protection. For the *gēr*, slavery was an ever-present threat, since the *gēr* had no land to pledge, had no kinsperson to redeem him or her, and was economically poor. The feasting texts address these vulnerabilities, implicitly addressing the question: What kind of relationship ought the *gēr* to share with the community, with the land, and with Yahweh? Specifically, the feasting texts address this question in three ways:

1. The festival calendar, 16:1–17. *Gēr* as kin: How does the festival calendar transform relationships in the direction of kinship?

2. The Festival of Firstfruits, 26:1–11. Israel as *gēr*: In what ways is an ethic of inclusion for the *gēr* embedded in Israel's own formative narrative of wandering and vulnerability?

3. The third-year tithe, 14:28–29, 26:12–15. Holiness and the *gēr*: What is the significance of the fact that the *gēr* consumes the sacred portion?

This chapter will trace this logic, examining each of these passages. First, however, relevant ancient Near Eastern feasting texts are surveyed as a point of comparison. Second, the capacity of feasting to transform social relations is considered through the lens of cultural anthropology.

### 5.1.2. Feasting in the Ancient Near East: Divine Confirmation of the King

Ancient Near Eastern feasting texts offer a point of comparison. Three pertinent themes for assessment are the festal participants, hierarchy, and ideology. A banquet in the ancient Near East was an occasion for relationship and merriment.[1] It was an event at which serious decisions were made, allegiances were formed, and music and even comical and creative disputation might be presented.[2] Royalty and other elite are prominent in these texts, and banquets were often a means of consolidating royal privilege. The Babylonian Akitu festival, for example, was a twice-yearly celebration held at both the spring harvest and the autumn seeding. It was celebrated in various forms throughout the written history of the ancient Near East, and its various recensions shed light on the role of ritual feasting in giving divine authentication to royal rule. The king was the host of festivities during the Akitu festival. On the fourth day of Nisan, the festival began, and the king was presented with the scepter of kingship. On the eighth day, the king led the procession of the gods from Esagil to the Akitu

---

1. This analysis develops the work of others, in particular Georg Braulik's investigation of Deuteronomy's feasting texts in light of Canaanite harvest festivals ("The Joy of the Feast," in *Theology of Deuteronomy: Collected Essays of Georg Braulik, O.S.B.*, trans. U. Lindblad [N. Richland Hills, TX: Bibal, 1994], 27–66); MacDonald's study of these texts in light of anthropology (*Not Bread Alone*, 70–99); and, most importantly, Altmann's extensive study of Deuteronomy's feasts in light of ancient Near Eastern feasting and anthropology (*Festive*).

2. Herman L. J. Vanstiphout, "The Banquet Scene in the Mesopotamian Debate Poems," in *Banquets d'Orient*, ed. R. Gyselen, Res Orientales 4 (Bures Saint-Yves: Group pour l'Etude de la Civilisation du Moyen-Orient, 1992), 12.

house, located outside the city.[3] The dominance of the king and his city in feasts such as the Akitu both reflected and contributed to the centraliza- tion of authority and of economic resources, a centralization that perme- ated state religion as well as economics and politics.[4]

The royal table in the ancient Near East exemplifies what Michael Dietler has described as the potential of feasting to unite and to divide.[5] Motifs such as banquet contributions, precedence in entering, inclusion and exclusion, and seating arrangements are prominent. Jack Sasson writes, "Their goal was to include those deemed worthy of belonging to [the king's] circles; but also to exclude those unworthy of the honor."[6] Sasson continues: "Court etiquette was strict about who squats, who sits at meals, and who is closest to the presiding lord, all such judgment depend- ing on the prestige of the king a delegation represented and the ranking within a delegation. The potential for public humiliation was infinite."[7] In royal feasts, kinship was also forged: "In a society in which political instability was the norm and loyalty was achieved through formal oaths, sitting together during meals must have created obligations and nour- ished allegiances at all levels of the culture."[8] Meal participants may refer to one another in familial terms, such as father, brother, and son.[9] Some Old Testament feasts are occasions for the divine authentication for royal authority, for example 2 Sam 6:17–19. However, in the DC feasting texts, no human king is mentioned: Yahweh is host and King. Feasting of the general population in the ancient Near East is obscured from us, since clay

---

3. Karel van der Toorn, "The Babylonian New Year Festival: New Insights from the Cuneiform Texts and Their Bearing on Old Testament Study," in *Congress Volume: Leuven 1989*, ed. J. A. Emerton (Leiden: Brill, 1989), 332–35.

4. Victor Turner describes the economic and political benefits of state feasts for the city and its elites; see *Dramas, Fields, and Metaphors: Symbolic Action in Human Society* (Ithaca, NY: Cornell University Press, 1974), 188.

5. Michael Dietler, "Theorizing the Feast: Rituals of Consumption, Commensal Politics, and Power in African Contexts," in *Feasts: Archaeological and Ethnographic Perspectives on Food, Politics, and Power*, ed. Michael Dietler and Brian Hayden (Washington, DC: Smithsonian Institution, 2001), 77.

6. Jack M. Sasson, "The King's Table: Food and Fealty in Old Babylonian Mari," in *Food and Identity in the Ancient World*, ed. Cristiano Grottanelli and Lucio Milano (Padova: S.A.R.G.O.N. editrice e libreria, 2004), 213–14.

7. Sasson, "King's Table," 201.

8. Sasson, "King's Table," 210.

9. Sasson, "King's Table," 214.

tablets tend to preserve the economic records of the temple and royalty. The populace is featured in a small number of texts, such as the Emar seven-year Zukru festival.[10]

Foreigners and vulnerable groups, dominant in the DC's feasts, are rarely mentioned in ancient Near Eastern feasting texts. However, *KTU* 1.40 is an Ugaritic expiation ritual regarding the treatment of foreigners that also includes foreigners as ritual participants. The text contains a repeated prepositional phrase, *lp* ("according to the mouth of")[11] followed by a list of ethnic designations:

> (29′) (21) be it according to the statement of the Hurrian, be it according to the statement of the Hittite ... be it according to the statement of
> (30′) (22) your oppressed ones, be it according to the statement of your im[pov]erished ones...[12]

Pardee interprets the ritual as expiation for sinning against foreigners.[13] Altmann adds, "Like Deut 16:9–15, a primary emphasis here is on the ritual participants, namely, that they include all classes, genders, and ethnicities present in the society."[14]

Notwithstanding these rare instances of inclusion, in general, while ancient Near Eastern texts describe the dining practices of the gods or their sponsored elite, the DC feasting texts center on the household, and the participation of vulnerable people is dominant. Cultural anthropology has observed the capacity of pilgrimage feasts to transform social structures and to create kinship, and this scholarship is now discussed.

---

10. See "The ZUKRU Festival," trans. Daniel E. Fleming (*COS* 1.123:431–36); Daniel E. Fleming, "The Israelite Festival Calendar," *RB* 106 (1999): 8–34.

11. Cf. Hebrew לפי. Johannes C. de Moor and Paul Sanders, "An Ugaritic Expiation Ritual and Its Old Testament Parallels," *UF* 23 (1991): 283–300.

12. Lines 29/21–30/22.

13. Pardee, "Structure of RS 1.002." De Moor and Sanders interpret the text as "sinning like foreigners," that is, committing the kinds of sins that foreign nations commit (de Moor and Sanders, "Ugaritic Expiation," 297). However, Altmann gives good reasons to adopt Pardee's interpretation (*Festive*, 152).

14. Altmann, *Festive*, 153. Altmann observes the connection between *KTU* 1.40 and the declaration of innocence regarding provision for vulnerable people in Deut 26:12–15 (*Festive*, 153 nn. 94–95).

### 5.1.3. Anthropology: The Capacity of Pilgrimage Feasting to Effect Social Relations

Brian Hayden notes that "feasting, like kinship, marriage, and language, is a universal feature of human societies."[15] Feasts may be defined as "any sharing between two or more people of special foods (i.e., foods not generally served at daily meals) in a meal for a special purpose or occasion."[16] Michael Dietler explores the power of food to negotiate relationships:

> Food and drink are highly charged symbolic media because they are "embodied material culture": that is, a special form of material culture produced specifically for ingestion into the body. They are a basic and continual human physiological need, which are also a form of "highly condensed social fact" ... embodying relations of production and exchange and linking the domestic and political economies in a highly personalized way.[17]

Dietler's study is suggestive of the social potency of Deuteronomy's feasts to shape social relations.

Victor Turner has explored the power of pilgrimage feasts to break down social structure and stratification.[18] Citing the work of Arnold van Gennep, he suggests that "in all ritual movement there was at least a moment when those being moved in accordance with a cultural script were liberated from normative demands ... the possibility exists ... of formulating a potentially unlimited series of alternative social arrangements."[19] Pilgrimage involves a "spatial separation from the familial and habitual"[20] and so has power to forge new and creative relations. "It may, in various cultures, have punitive, purificatory, expiatory, cognitive, instructional, therapeutic, transformative, and many other facets, aspects, and functions."[21] Turner suggests that a suspension of social norms and status is a central feature of pilgrimage, producing what he calls *communitas*, a concept that he defines

---

15. Brian Hayden, "Feasting Research," https://tinyurl.com/SBL2638a.

16. Brian Hayden, "Fabulous Feasts: A Prolegomenon to the Importance of Feasting," in Dietler and Hayden, *Feasts*, 28.

17. Dietler, "Theorizing," 72.

18. Turner, *Dramas*.

19. Turner, *Dramas*, 13.

20. Turner, *Dramas*, 196.

21. Turner, *Dramas*, 196.

as "anti-structural ... in that [it is] undifferentiated, equalitarian, direct, nonrational."[22] Within this antistructure of *communitas*, kinship is experienced, matches are made, and friendships are forged, all of which to some degree transcend status lines. Importantly, Turner discusses the potential of pilgrimages to forge *lasting* friendships and to recast social structures and dynamics *permanently*.[23]

Turner's research is a clarifying frame for Deuteronomy's harvest festivals, wherein the whole community shares a pilgrimage feast, forging a communal identity as the people of Yahweh (consanguineous family, Levite, *gēr*, fatherless, and widow alike). Before examining Deuteronomy's feasting texts in turn, a discussion of methodology is in order.

### 5.1.4. Methodology

The present chapter will take a different methodological route from the previous chapters, investigating the text by focusing on the elements that bring coherence to the whole, while also using the tools of anthropology and of the comparative method. While there are exceptions, previous studies of Deuteronomy's feasting texts (especially 16:1–17; 26:1–11, 12–15) have tended to focus on issues of composition history, ignoring the pregnant theology and ethics in the final form of the text.[24] For example, in past decades, studies of 16:1–17 have most often focused on the origins of Passover and Massot and on issues of textual history.[25] The complex interweaving of Deuteronomic motifs and ethics displayed in the final form of 16:1–17 remains underexplored. Similarly, since Gerhard von Rad argued that 26:5b–9 is an ancient creedal summary of salvation history that preceded a developed narrative of Israel's origins, studies of 26:1–11

---

22. Turner, *Dramas*, 47.

23. Turner, *Dramas*, 200–201, 205–6.

24. Exceptions include: Braulik, "Joy"; Altmann, *Festive*.

25. Many major studies of Passover-Massot, 16:1–8, have been driven by questions regarding the historical development of the two rituals. Mayes (*Deuteronomy*, 254–57) and Merendino (*Das deuteronomische Gesetz*, 137–38) argue that Massot was the prior feast. Others argue that Passover is the prior festival, e.g., Gerhard von Rad, *Deuteronomy*, OTL (Philadelphia: Westminster John Knox, 1966), 111; Gottfried Seitz, *Redaktionsgeschichtliche Studien zum Deuteronomium*, BWANT 93 (Stuttgart: Kohlhammer, 1971), 196–98. Jörn von Halbe argues that Massot originated as a facet of Passover ("Erwägungen zu Ursprung und Wesen des Massotfestes," ZAW 87 [1975], 339–40). De Vaux concludes that both are ancient festivals (*Ancient Israel*, 491).

have mostly focused upon the credo and have been concerned with historical-critical issues.[26] These two texts in particular (16:1–17; 26:5b–10) have been fields upon which battles concerning the composition history of the Pentateuch and of the Hebrew Bible have been fought.

In light of this trend, whereby issues of composition history saturate the discussion while the intricate unity of these texts as well as their pregnant ethics and theology is ignored, this chapter will proceed by investigating these ignored features. Indeed, an investigation of the given form of Deuteronomy's festival calendar, 16:1–17, is justified in the light of the unity of the text as an exposition of the Sabbath command, as argued below. Further, the sophisticated verbal patterning within the given text of the Festival of Firstfruits, 26:1–11, brings unity to this text. Deuteronomy's feasting texts are now studied, beginning with the festival calendar, 16:1–17.

## 5.2. Festival Calendar (Deut 16:1–17): *Gēr* as Kin

### 5.2.1. Introduction

This section explores the ways in which Deuteronomy's festival calendar, 16:1–17, may be fostering the inclusion of the stranger as kindred through cultic feasting before Yahweh. Feasts function as communal boundary markers,[27] and the festival calendar reconfirms the group identity of the people of Yahweh through seasonal cultic performances. We will observe the ways in which these feasts are both cohesive and also inclusive.

Passover-Massot (16:1–8) is not a harvest festival as such, occurring just before the grain harvest. It is more somber in tone than the Feasts of Weeks and Booths, in line with the exodus motif. Furthermore, the distinctive character of Passover and Massot is blurred in 16:1–8, and the two feasts tend toward blending into one[28] as, I suggest, a literary means of connecting worship at the sanctuary (the Passover sacrifice) with worship

---

26. Gerhard von Rad, "The Form-Critical Problem of the Hexateuch," in *The Problem of the Hexateuch and Other Essays*, trans. E. W. Trueman Dicken (New York: McGraw-Hill, 1966), 1–78; trans. of *Das formgeschichtliche Problem des Hexateuchs*, BWANT 26 (Stuttgart: Kohlhammer, 1938). See the summary of the discussion of the composition history of 26:1–11, below.

27. Hendel, *Remembering Abraham*, 22.

28. Levinson, *Deuteronomy and the Heremeneutics*, 53–97.

throughout the land (the Feast of Unleavened Bread). The Feasts of Weeks (16:9–12) and Booths (16:13–15) are harvest festivals for which the whole community gathers for joyful feasting in light of the Yahweh's provision. The Feast of Weeks acquires a distinctly celebrative tone in the DC; it is not called a חג in Lev 23:15–21 and Num 28:26–31, but it is here. In this feast, ethics are grounded in the themes of Sabbath, agricultural abundance, and the exodus. The Feast of Booths in the DC is a week of rejoicing in light of the harvest. "As Deut 16:14a and Neh 8:17 show, the Feast of Booths features the motif of joy, thus the root שׂמח."[29] The exodus theme fades, replaced by a most emphatic expression of agricultural blessing (16:15), which is the motivation for generosity and inclusion in Booths.

Regarding composition history, most critical scholars identify an original version of 16:1–17 as Dtn.[30] The text appropriates the cultic calendar of the CC, Exod 23:14–17, both texts following a structure of three festivals with a following summary. Regarding 16:1–8, Massot adapts material from the earlier festival calendars (Exod 23:14–17, 34:18–20), while the Passover material is a Dtn innovation.[31] The Dtn stipulations concerning the Feasts of Weeks (16:9–11) and Booths (16:12–15) also adapt Exod 23:14–17, recasting the festivals as household feasts at the chosen place that include the vulnerable. Two motifs of Deuteronomy's feasting texts are now analyzed: שׂמח and the list of participants.

### 5.2.2. The Meaning of שׂמח in the DC Feasting Texts

The verb שׂמח is a key motif in 16:1–17, as in the other feasting texts. Braulik separates the exhortation שׂמח from the meal itself, suggesting that the DC downplays the significance of eating and drinking in light of the excesses of Canaanite cultic festivity.[32] However, Gary Anderson has since demonstrated that the exhortation שׂמח is not so much calling for an emotion as requiring certain cultic behavior.[33] The verb שׂמח is better

---

29. Merendino, *Das deuteronomische Gesetz*, 34: "Wie Dt 16,14a und Ne 8,17 zeigen, kennzeichnet das Motiv der Freude, also die Wurzel שׂמח, das Laubhüttenfest."

30. E.g., Mayes, *Deuteronomy*, 257. Kratz argues that only 16:16–17 is Dtn (*Composition*, 122). However, see Altmann's rebuttal, (*Festive*, 193).

31. Following Altmann, *Festive*, 194.

32. Braulik, "Joy," 59. Weinfeld removes connotations of feasting altogether in his discussion of Deut 12:7, 18 (*Deuteronomy*, 346).

33. Gary A. Anderson, *A Time to Mourn, a Time to Dance: The Expression of Grief*

translated "celebrate" rather than "rejoice"; שׂמח refers to cultic feasting.[34] This observation can be established on the grounds that the presence of אכל in three of these texts (7:12, 18; 14:26), food lists (14:23b, 26a), and descriptions of agricultural bounty and blessing (14:24, 29b; 16:9, 10, 13, 15b) clarify that food consumption is envisaged. In addition, Altmann notes that שׂמח "recalls the free-flowing wine and generous meat portions in the Ugaritic banquets of the Rephaim, El' s Feast, and the Baal Cycle."[35] Thus, "Deuteronomy not only accepts, but goes so far as to highlight the meal element of the festival."[36] The verb שׂמח in these contexts can be translated simply "feast!"

The present study suggests that שׂמח in Deuteronomy also connotes the inclusivity of the feast, a point rarely drawn out in the scholarship. A compound subject of festal participants follows seven of eight occurrences of שׂמח in these texts (12:12, 18; 14:26; 16:11, 14, 15; 26:11).[37] Indeed, all eight occurrences in the DC feasting texts envisage household feasting that includes these vulnerable people who are associated with the household. Deuteronomy envisages the joy of fraternal unity through which division due to status and economic privilege is overcome. Indeed, "The brotherliness of YHWH's family is not merely proclaimed by Deuteronomy; it is also intended to be experienced."[38] The participant list is a crucial formula in Deuteronomy's feasting trope, and this is now analyzed.

### 5.2.3. The List of Participants (Deut 16:11, 14): Transformed Relationships between the *Gēr* and the Household

> Traditional society in Judah was based on family solidarity, on the leadership of the elders and notables, and its economy rested primarily on land. Integrating into such a traditional society was a major hurdle for the refugees who had been torn from their own former family structures,

---

*and Joy in Israelite Religion* (University Park, PA: Pennsylvania State University Press, 1991), 1, 14–18. Joy "presumes a set of publically recognizable behaviors" (Anderson, *Time to Mourn*, 15).

34. Anderson, *Time to Mourn*, 20.

35. Altmann, *Festive*, 205; see also 180–85.

36. Altmann, *Festive*, 205.

37. The landless are not listed in 12:7, but their inclusion may nonetheless be assumed from the other references.

38. Braulik, "Joy," 58.

and had neither land nor means of production to provide them with self-sufficient subsistence.[39]

For Deuteronomy, it was the household that was given the ultimate responsibility to enfold the *gēr*, less as an outsider than as kin. Faust's assertion that the "most basic unit" of ancient Israelite society was the house of the father, אב בית, is reflected in the prominence of the household in Deuteronomy's social laws.[40] The membership of this social grouping is catalogued in the Deuteronomic motif of the list of festal participants, appearing in both Weeks and Booths.

16:11a

ושמחת לפני יהוה אלהיך אתה ובנך ובתך ועבדך ואמתך והלוי אשר
בשעריך והגר והיתום והאלמנה אשר בקרבך

16:14

ושמחת בחגך אתה ובנך ובתך ועבדך ואמתך והלוי והגר והיתום
והאלמנה אשר בשעריך

The participant lists are prominent in the text by their length and repetition. They are also emphasized by their positions at the center of *waw*-consecutive suffix conjugation verbal chains and by motivation clauses (16:12a, 15b). The lists also appear at the emotional high point of both festal texts, the declaration of a feast: שמח, "feast!"

The list of participants is structured, as it were, in concentric circles of natural connection within the household, progressing from the pater-familias at the center, outward to בן and בת, then to the household slaves, then the Levites, and outward again to the vulnerable who also participated in the life of the household. Thus, in contrast to the ancient Near Eastern feasting texts discussed above, "Deuteronomy founds the festival community on families, so that community is structured from below so to speak, instead of being organized from above."[41] The list of participants envisages a structure of the household that includes the vulnerable along with the nuclear family.

39. Na'aman, "Sojourners," 276–77.
40. Faust, *Archaeology*, 11.
41. Braulik, "Joy," 57.

Reading the list of festal participants in light of the social structure of households in ancient Israel clarifies what the inclusion of the vulnerable may have entailed. In what follows I am addressing a rural context.[42] Some, but not all, family units lived in a multiple family settlement consisting of a small number of extended families.[43] Within such a settlement, each extended family had an independent dwelling that may or may not have been attached to other dwellings by shared walls. Faust offers that the average area of rural four-room houses in Iron Age Israel was around 130 square meters. In light of R. Naroll's suggested ratio of around 10 square meters per person,[44] Faust suggests that rural four-room dwellings contained around thirteen people:

> Based on the size of the buildings in villages and on farms, it is indeed reasonable to assume that they were inhabited by extended families … including parents, married sons and their children, unmarried daughters, unmarried aunts, and other relatives who remained living there for various reasons, slaves (?), agricultural workers, and others.[45]

This arrangement, called the בית אב, was "the ideal type of household organization for small proprietors subsisting off their land."[46]

While the vulnerable people in the list were often not "blood relations," the list indicates they are nonetheless a part of the household. The size of these dwellings indicates that an extended family along with some vulnerable people probably dwelled under the one roof. So, it is likely that at least some of those designated *gēr* shared a roof with an extended family. Faust states:

> The *bet av* often included additions, some of them family members with various degrees of kinship, and others strangers (adopted children, hired

---

42. I argue that the festal participant list fits more naturally in a rural rather than an urban context (see §5.5.1).

43. Braulik, "Joy," 57. Lawrence E. Stager suggests that the nuclear family, rather than the extended family, was the fundamental unit of these settlements ("Archaeology," 20).

44. R. Naroll, "Floor Area and Settlement Population," *AAnt* 27 (1962): 587–89, cited in Faust, *Archaeology*, 110.

45. Faust, *Archaeology*, 160.

46. Faust, *Archaeology*, 20.

staff, foreigners, slaves), such as Jephthah, who belonged to "his father's house" (or at least aspired to belong to it), despite being illegitimate.[47]

The HC provides clear evidence that a *gēr* commonly dwelled within an Israelite household:

> If your brother becomes poor and cannot maintain himself with you, you shall support him as though he were a stranger and a sojourner, and he shall live with you. (Lev 25:35 ESV)

Doubtless the capacity of a household to include vulnerable members would have varied according to a family's life stage, and during times of destitution the capacity to support people outside of the family would have diminished. Indeed, even family members were hired out or sold into slavery in desperate circumstances.[48] Inevitably, the *gēr* subsisted in a variety of living arrangements. Vulnerable people also sometimes lived in quarters within the settlement set apart for their use.[49] Faust suggests that in cities the poor may have been housed in an oblong-shaped building that is found near the gate at many urban developments.[50]

5.2.4. Transformed Relationships between the *Gēr* and the Clan

If the list of participants associates the stranger within the household, the phrase בשעריך (Deut 16:11a, 14; cf. 5:14; 14:21, 29; 16:14; 24:14; 26:12; 31:12) associates the stranger within the clan grouping of a settlement or within a city. We will observe how in Deuteronomy's social laws the gate is not an exclusionary boundary but a demarcation of responsibility (see §5.5.2). In the festival calendar, via the phrase בשעריך, the *gēr* is also being incorporated at the level of the clan grouping. Subsequently, there is no indication whatsoever in Deuteronomy that the *gēr* is a "non-permanent resident" who is "present for an indeterminate length of time," as Crouch has recently claimed.[51] The way in which Dtn fosters the inclusion of the

---

47. Faust, *Archaeology*, 12. Williamson asserts that an Israelite household during the Persian period commonly included vulnerable people who are not consanguineous with the household ("Family in Persian," 474).

48. See Gelb, "Household," 61.

49. See further King and Stager, *Life*, 12.

50. Faust, *Archaeology*, 101–2.

51. Crouch, *Making*, 217.

*gēr* within a household and within a clan through cultic feasting weighs heavily against this hypothesis.

## 5.2.5. Dynamics of Inclusion

In the festival calendar, both the absence of certain common ancient Near Eastern feasting motifs and the presence of others has the effect of diminishing the distinction between the paterfamilias and the *gēr*, tending toward mutuality. First, the host's contributions for the feast are not enumerated, as they are in many ancient Near Eastern feasting texts.[52] Rather, generosity is ascribed to Yahweh. Second, signifiers of status are missing, such as seating arrangements and the host's cup.[53] Third, common motifs for hosting a banquet are missing, such as food preparation, invitations,[54] the meat/wine consumption sequence,[55] and the expression "to give to eat or drink." These distinctive may be explained by the central idea that the DC feasts are kinship feasts that are relatively egalitarian in character, with Yahweh as host. (Of course, this is not "egalitarian" in a modern Western sense but as befits a Mediterranean communal, patriarchal context. To be sure, this is also subversively egalitarian in the political domain.)

I demonstrated in the introduction how people exercise tremendous creativity in forging new kinship relations. It appears that this creativity is exercised at the level of a text in the festival calendar, with the goal to nourish ritual practices of inclusion. Cross states, "In West Semitic tribal societies we know best, such individuals or groups were grafted onto the genealogies and fictive kinship became kinship of the flesh or blood. In a word, kinship-in-law became kinship-in-flesh."[56] Turner's study of the potential of pilgrimage feasting to nourish communitas suggests that a goal of Deuteronomy's pilgrimage feasts was to incorporate the stranger within the protective circumference of a household.

---

52. Compare the extensive enumeration of the king's contribution in the seven-year Zukru festival, discussed above (§5.1.2).

53. See Irene Winter, "The King and the Cup: Iconography of the Royal Presentation Scene on the Ur III Seals," in *Insight through Images: Studies in Honour of Edith Porada*, ed. M. Kelly-Buccelati, P. Matthiae, and M. Van Loon (Malibu, CA: Undena, 1986), 265.

54. On the practice of sending invitations, see Murray Lichtenstein, "The Banquet Motifs in Keret and in Proverbs 9," *JANESCU* 1 (1968): 19–31.

55. See Lichtenstein, "Banquet Motifs."

56. Cross, *Epic*, 7.

We should recall also the kinship-making function of households that was alluded to in the introduction. Carsten explains, "The house brings together spatial representations, everyday living, meals, cooking, and the sharing of resources with the often intimate relations of those who inhabit this shared space." This is a "dense overlay of different experiential dimensions of living together." Carsten reflects that "the very qualitative density of experiences in the houses we inhabit leads many people around the world … to assert that kinship is made in houses through the intimate sharing of space, food, and nurturance that goes on within domestic space."[57] Deuteronomy's inclusivist ethic for the stranger and especially the incorporative function of the feasting texts strongly suggests that Deuteronomy's household lists are deliberately evocative for forging kinship within a household. To put it another way, the festival calendar implicitly yet relentlessly addresses the question: What kind of relationship is to be shared between the vulnerable and the landed? Deuteronomy's pilgrimage feasts foster a transformation of this relationship in the direction of kinship. These people commonly participate in the life of ancient Near Eastern households as inexpensive labor vulnerable to exploitation. So in many cases Deuteronomy may not be so much *initiating* relationships between the vulnerable and landed households as *transforming* relationships that already established.

Significant also for an interpretation of the festival calendar is that the taste and smell of particular foods and particular eating experiences have the capacity to shape the social and cultural memory of a group of people. David Sutton states, "Taste and smell have a much greater association with episodic than semantic memory, with the symbolic rather than the linguistic, and with recognition rather than recall."[58] Food's "synesthetic qualities … are an essential ingredient in ritual and everyday experiences of totality."[59] In regard to the festival calendar, consumption of particular foods in the context of an experience of inclusive feasting creates memories and symbols with the capacity to renorm social identity within the community. The unique intensity of a feast, as opposed to quotidian meals, the emotional intensity of slaughtering cattle,[60] as well

---

57. Carsten, *After Kinship*, 35

58. David Sutton, *Remembrance of Repasts: An Anthropology of Food and Memory* (Oxford: Berg, 2001), 101.

59. Sutton, *Remembrance*, 102.

60. Carol L. Meyers, "The Function of Feasts: An Anthropological Perspective on

as the synesthetic quality of food suggest the potency of the these feasts to renorm relationships between the *gēr* and the household. Together with the core family, the stranger shares in the fellowship, the ritualized time, the smell of boiling meat, the warmth of wine, the tastes of festal recipes, the long pilgrimage with winding conversations, the waiting, fulfillment, liturgical life—all before Yahweh who supplies the harvest! Through feasting together on the abundance that Yahweh has provided, symbols of mutuality are enacted and memories of kinship created that have the power to transform relationships between the household and the *gēr* permanently.

A natural question to ask of this thesis is: If Deuteronomy is so intent upon incorporating the *gēr*, then why is the *gēr* not also called a brother? Indeed, why are these people called *gēr* at all? It is critical that the *gēr* in Deuteronomy is a liminal figure, on the threshold between one social status and another. The *gēr* is not yet a brother-sister, for absence of kinsfolk is definitional for the term *gēr*. The stipulations of Deuteronomy nourish the inclusion of the *gēr* within the life, work, feasting, worship, and, ultimately, kinship of a household and village. As observed above, on the one hand, in certain texts the *gēr* appears in apposition to the אח; on the other hand, the same text stipulates that the *gēr* is to be protected and included as one would protect and include a kinsperson (e.g., 24:14–15).

### 5.2.5.1. "Conversion" to Yahwism?

Our discussion also raises the question of whether the stranger must "convert" to Yahweh as a prerequisite of inclusion into the community, as some scholars have suggested. Sparks, for example, speaks of a figure that he calls an "assimilating *gēr*" as "a foreigner who joined himself to the national God."[61] Our prior discussion of the interconnected life of communal cultures should alert us to the Westernness of this question, which emerges from within an individualistic set of social assumptions. As Marshall Sahlins states regarding communal cultures, "Among kinfolk

---

Israelite Religious Festivals," in *Social Theory and the Study of Israelite Religion: Essays in Retrospect and Prospect*, ed. Saul M. Olyan, RBS 71 (Atlanta: Society of Biblical Literature, 2012), 155–56.

61. Sparks, *Ethnicity*, 264. Van Houten, however, states that "the exclusive relationship that the Israelites had with God meant that no way was open for aliens to become members of the Israelite community" (Van Houten, *Alien*, 107).

neither interest nor agency are individual facts—again in contrast to the self-fashioning, self-interested individual as we know him [in the West]."[62] Rather than conversion, Deuteronomy's vision is that the stranger would be caught up in the joy, the community, the story, the ritual, the abundance, and the gratitude of the family of Yahweh. In other words, Deuteronomy fosters the renewal of Israel in light of the gracious rule of Yahweh, and the stranger is swept up in the divine invitation. To put it another way, who wouldn't want to join a feast?

Alternatively, Harold V. Bennet claims that a distinguishing feature of the *gēr* in the DC is the *gēr*'s "attitude" of nonassimilation. To be sure, it is probable that some of those in the *gēr* group chose to maintain former religious and cultic observances. Nonetheless, the feasting texts seem to assume that most of them will eagerly participate in cultic worship (16:11, 14; cf. 31:9–13). Also, forsaking former cultic practices is not a prerequisite in these texts. Indeed, it seems natural that an individual or a family that is facing starvation and without kinship connection would be receptive to overtures for adoption into their new community and culture.[63] As for Bennett's postulate that the *gēr* is distinguished by his or her attitude of nonassimilation, the covenantal texts of 29:9–14 and 31:9–13 through which the *gēr* is included within covenant ceremonies argues directly against this assertion (see ch. 6 on these texts).

I now turn to four themes in 16:1–17 in order to observe the strength of this incorporative ethic: Sabbath release, the exodus, blessing, and the altar law. It will be observed that this ethic is inseparably interrelated with those key themes and commitments for which Deuteronomy is most famous.

## 5.2.6. Ethics of Inclusion Embedded in Four Themes

### 5.2.6.1. Theme 1: The Sabbath and an Ethic of Participation

The inclusion of the vulnerable within the household is undergirded in 16:1–17 by the theme of Sabbath release. Stephen Kaufman, Braulik, and others who perceive the Decalogue as the key to unlock the structure of

---

62. Sahlins, *What Kinship Is*, 52.

63. Harold V. Bennett, *Injustice Made Legal: Deuteronomic Law and the Plight of Widows, Strangers, and Orphans in Ancient Israel* (Grand Rapids: Eerdmans, 2002), 45–46.

the DC associate the Sabbath command with the context 15:1–16:17.[64] Within this frame, 16:1–17 recasts the feasts in terms of Sabbath, a seven-day rhythm of work and release.

Kaufman notes numerous connections between 15:1–16:17 and the Sabbath command, and I add to Kaufman's analysis the motif of sevens, occurring in a six plus one pattern. Passover-Massot (16:1–8) comprises a six plus one pattern of affliction moving to feasting. The timing of the Feast of Weeks is calculated in groups of seven sevens: שבעה שבעת תספר (16:9). Booths is celebrated for seven days (16:13–15). The number seven is repeated seven times within 16:1–8.[65] There is an ethical dimension within each occurrence of six plus one: a movement from affliction to abundance that is consistent with the Sabbath command.[66]

Thus, intertextuality characterizes the festivals as Sabbath festivals. The life-giving Sabbath rhythm of work and rest (identified in the exegesis of 5:12–15 above) corresponds to the life-giving rhythm of work and festivity within the festival calendar. This rhythm signifies the full and blessed life that the whole community is to share, especially the vulnerable.[67] It incorporates the *gēr* as a co-heir of the gifts of land and its bounty and as a partner in the "rest" that is the result of this gift.[68]

### 5.2.6.2. Theme 2: The Exodus and Ethics of Inclusion

The exodus from Egypt is a second and most important theme in which the inclusion of the vulnerable in the household as kindred, through feasting, is embedded in 16:1–17. The exodus is dominant in 16:1–17, being referred to explicitly five times and also implicitly throughout 16:1–8 through elements of the ritual of Passover-Massot. The motivation clause for inclusive feasting in the Feast of Weeks is: "You shall remember that you were a slave in Egypt" (Deut 16:12a ESV).

---

64. Kaufman, "Structure," 129–33. Kaufman views 14:22–29 as a transitional piece between the third and fourth command ("Structure," 128–29).

65. Deuteronomy 15:1–11 stipulates a seventh-year release of debts. Deuteronomy 15:12–18 stipulates the release of slaves following six years of work.

66. For further discussion of the pattern of sevens in Deut 16:1–17, see Otto, "שֶׁבַע," 14:355.

67. McConville, *Deuteronomy*, 128.

68. See the exegesis of 5:12–15 in §3.7.

It has been observed that the exodus motive clause evokes a whole narrative of Israel's enslavement, emancipation, and new allegiance to Yahweh (see §3.4.3). The exodus motive clause is now examined from another angle: motifs taken from ancient Near Eastern slave law and custom are building blocks for the ethical structure of 16:1–17. Words such as עבד, ריקם, יצא, and עני were full of significance for ancient Israelites, immersed as they were in a slave culture, in a way that may be missed today.[69] To be sure, these words are associated with the exodus narrative. However, these words and concepts also preceded the exodus narrative. David Daube has observed how the exodus narrative itself is shaped by ancient laws and customs concerning slave release. In terms of ancient Near Eastern laws and customs, Daube explains that Pharaoh is presented as "flouting established regulations" regarding the treatment of slaves and their release. Yahweh in effect enforces these ancient obligations and intervenes in "the faithful exercise of a recognized privilege."[70] Daube continues: "In the minds of the authors [of the exodus narrative], their interest lay in their connection with rules concerning the dismissal of a slave."[71] The word עבד in 16:12 is the regular term for slavery in the law corpora.[72] The word יצא (16:3b, 3c, 6), the most common expression for deliverance from Egypt in Deuteronomy, is a legal term for slave release used in the original exodus narrative and appropriated from there to the DC.[73] The word עני, from the phrase לחם עני ("bread of affliction," 16:3b), is a key term for oppression from the exodus story (Exod 3:7, 17; 4:31; Deut 26:7), the prior condition into which Yahweh steps as the great king and enforcer of ancient laws of justice (16:3c). The adjective forms a part of Deuteronomy's vocabulary for social vulnerability and poverty ethics (Deut 15:11; 24:12, 14, 15), and we must understand the injunction to "remember Egypt" (16:3c; 12a) in

---

69. Chirichigno suggests that debt slavery in Israel grew in a similar way to debt slavery in the ancient Near East. After settlement and especially during monarchy, social stratification led to the rise of indebtedness and the alienation of land (*Debt-Slavery*, 101–44).

70. Daube, *Exodus*, 13.

71. Daube, *Exodus*, 23. Mark S. Smith challenges Daube's assertion that these associations between law and the exodus narrative are deliberate on the part of the author; see *The Pilgrimage Pattern in Exodus*, JSOTSup 239 (Sheffield: Sheffield Academic, 1997), 280–81. However, my investigation of the exodus motif in 5:15 (see §3.7) discloses a most intentional use of this motif in redaction.

72. Daube, *Exodus*, 25; Brueggemann, "Pharoah," 35.

73. Daube, *Exodus*, 31; Braulik, "Deuteronomy and Human Rights," 135.

this light. The word לילה (16:1) subtly develops the theme of exodus. It is textually displaced in 16:1, where it is found within a motivation clause for the ritual Passover *meal*. Originally it referred to the time that the first-born of Egypt was struck down (Exod 10:13; 11:4; 12:12, 29, 30). Arguably, then, לילה evokes the theme of Yahweh's judgment upon oppressors.[74] A further motif taken from ancient Near Eastern slave law and custom is the prohibition of sending a slave away ריקם ("empty-handed"). Providing a released slave with cattle and agriculture and even jewelry was a part of ancient Near Eastern slave-release custom.[75] Through the repetition of ריקם in 15:13–14 and 16:16b–17, a rich tapestry of theology and ethics emerges: Israel is not ריקם, for Yahweh has filled Israel with abundance, and in this light and in light of the exodus Israel must not leave the vulnerable in it midst ריקם, nor may Israel appear before Yahweh ריקם. Each of these terms portrays Yahweh as enforcing ancient laws and customs for the sake of the vulnerable.

It must be stressed that these motifs for slavery were related to the daily reality of the original readers. For example, a man who encounters Deuteronomy's injunction וזכרת כי עבד היית במצרים (16:12a) may himself be working with all his might to redeem his son, whom he has given as an anticretic pledge in order to secure a loan taken out to plant a crop. The exodus motif throughout Deuteronomy must have been heard by the original audience as both highly ethical and also highly theological.

Thus the exodus theme in 16:1–17 demonstrates that the list of festal participants is no second thought. This text block is relentlessly occupied with social ethics. So, we must understand the ethics of inclusion for the *gēr* in 16:1–17 as asserted in the strongest possible terms.

### 5.2.6.3. Theme 3: Divine Blessing and Ethics of Inclusion

Divine blessing upon agriculture is a third theme in which the transformation of relationships between the stranger and the household is embedded. The text is characterized by vocabulary associated with blessing, a pattern that also characterizes the tithe (14:22–29): ברך, כל, אכל, נתן. The focus of ברך in Deuteronomy is narrow, referring particularly to the fertility

---

74. Mayes suggests that לילה links the month of Abib to the Passover (*Deuteronomy*, 258). However, לילה is more precisely connected with judgement upon Egypt.
75. Daube, *Exodus*, 47–61.

of agriculture and animals.[76] Deuteronomy 16:1–17 abounds in expressions of farming rhythms and agriculture (16:2a, 9, 13, 15), and the call to inclusive feasting in 16:11a, 14 emerges from within a joyful expression of abundance. Deuteronomy 16:1–17 projects a fundamental commitment regarding blessing: the blessing is given to the whole community, landed and landless alike, and continued blessing is contingent upon the blessing being shared with the least (14:29). "Lest the Israelites fear that these sacrifices will cause economic hardship, he is assured that, on the contrary, they will ultimately lead to greater prosperity."[77]

The principle that the blessing is given to the whole community is expressed simply and powerfully by the inclusion of the landless in the harvest feasts. Anthropological study has demonstrated that in feasting cultures a large proportion of agricultural production is consumed in feasting. Consumption of alcohol and meat is mostly, if not entirely, restricted to feasts in many societies.[78] In ancient Israel, while wine and to a lesser degree meat formed part of quotidian food consumption,[79] a significant proportion of both was consumed at feasts.[80] My point is that the inclusion of the landless in household feasts involved the landless sharing in the best of the harvest. This provision signals that the *gēr* receives the harvest not as charity but as a participant within the Yahweh community—as kindred.

### 5.2.6.4. Theme 4: The Altar Law and Ethics of Inclusion

The altar law is a fourth theme in which the inclusion of the vulnerable as kindred within the household is embedded. Apart from 12:1–28, this law occurs most frequently in the festival calendar (16:2b, 5b, 7a, 11b, 15a). While scholarship analyzes the altar law in relation to "name theology" and to centralization,[81] paying attention to the context of the altar law

---

76. In this vein, ברך is related to the phrases ובכל מעשה ידיך (16:15c), בכל מעשך‎ ובכל משלח ידך (15:10), and to the word group associated with land and soil. Fertility in childbirth is not referenced explicitly in Deuteronomy, though it is an aspect of ברך throughout most of the Hebrew Bible.

77. Tigay, *Deuteronomy*, 144.

78. Dietler, *Theorizing*, 91–92, 96–98.

79. Nathan MacDonald, *What Did the Ancient Israelites Eat? Diet in Biblical Times* (Grand Rapids: Eerdmans 2008), 23, 77–79.

80. King and Stager, *Life*, 101; MacDonald, *Eat*, 92.

81. Discussion of the altar law is often abstracted from its context. See, e.g., Mayes, *Deuteronomy*, 260.

reveals that the formula also plays an integral role within the theology and ethics of 16:1–17. Here the place formula along with the phrase לפני יהוה אלהיך (16:11a, 16) takes its meaning, at least in part, from the ancient Near Eastern motif of the responsibility of the king to uphold justice, especially for the vulnerable.[82]

The king's *presence* is relevant: a person may *appear* before a king for just pronouncement, as expressed, for example, in the epilogue of the Laws of Hammurabi (xlvii.59–78, xlviii.3–19).[83] Similarly, some legal texts in the DC require parties to appear before Yahweh, לפני יהוה, for judgment (19:17; cf. 17:12). A returned pledge will be credit לפני יהוה אלהיך (see also 26:13–15; cf. 21:7–8).[84] This use of the cultic formula לפני יהוה אלהיך indicates that this formula and by extension the altar law itself have an ethical function:

16:11a

ושמחת לפני יהוה אלהיך אתה ובנך ובתך ועבדך ואמתך והלוי אשר
בשעריך והגר והיתום והאלמנה אשר בקרבך במקום אשר יבחר יהוה
אלהיך לשכן שמו שם

One implication of the altar law here is that Israel appears for feasting before the divine king, in whose presence just relations are established between the landed and displaced people.

In what has preceded I have demonstrated the strength of an ethic of inclusion for the stranger in the festival calendar by observing how this ethic is embedded in four themes in 16:1–17: Sabbath release, the exodus, the blessing motif, and the altar law/cultic formula. A key question in the scholarship remains to be discussed however: Is the *gēr* included "religiously" in these texts?

---

82. See, e.g., Moshe Weinfeld, *Social Justice in Ancient Israel and in the Ancient Near East* (Minneapolis: Fortress, 1995), 45–46, 49.

83. Text from Roth, *Law Collections*, 133–34.

84. Related too are the unrelenting injunctions to obey the voice of the Lord, e.g., 13:19, and to keep his commands, e.g., 26:16–19. The relation between justice for the vulnerable and Yahweh's sovereign rule is most emphatically presented in 10:12–22. Ian Wilson has established that the phrase ליהוה אלהיך and the altar law itself are more than locative devices; they refer to Yahweh's presence; see *Out of the Midst of the Fire: Divine Presence in Deuteronomy*, SBLDS 151 (Atlanta: Scholars Press, 1995), 197.

### 5.2.7. The *Gēr* before Yahweh: Religious Inclusion

Crouch insists that the feasting texts do nothing to foster the inclusion of the *gēr* within the Israelite community: "He remains clearly distinguished from Israelites and is excluded from activities relating to Israelite self-definition."[85] She reflects a trend in scholarship that there is only limited inclusion for the *gēr* in Dtn and that this inclusion is enhanced in Dtr and in post-Dtr. Ebach argues that "the גר in the preexilic period is compared with Israel solely as an object for action."[86] In the exilic and post-exilic period, however, the *gēr* is an active member of the people of Yahweh.[87] Awabdy argues that, while in the DC the *gēr* was integrated socially, in the frame of Deuteronomy (Deut 1–11, 27–34) the *gēr* was integrated both socially and religiously.[88] Similarly, Awabdy suggests that the laws of admission (23:2–9) are an interpretative key explaining this difference. On the basis of this text, Awabdy suggests that those who have demonstrated commitment to Yahweh and to his people for three generations are to be admitted into the assembly. Thus, 23:2–9 provides a "religious and social transition from the DC to the P-E [prologue-epilogue]."[89]

First, it seems unlikely that immigrants who had been in the land for three generations would fit the social profile for a *gēr* in Deuteronomy: a stranger dependent on a household and a clan for sustenance, akin to the fatherless and widow. Second, Awabdy's assumption that sociality and religion can be so easily separated within a communal Mediterranean society is simplistic.[90] Third, and most significant, Awabdy, Ebach, and Crouch underestimate the religious significance of the *gēr* appearing in Dtn feasting texts פני יהוה אלהיך (e.g., 16:11, 16; 26:10–11). The so-called cultic formula is *the* expression for worship at the chosen place in Dtn; there is no other. So if the *gēr* is not included in the religious life of the nation in Dtn via the cultic formula, it is difficult to see how Dtn includes anyone in the religious life of the nation. The view that the frame texts create a new religious inclusivism ignores the religious inclusivism of the cultic feasting texts, whereby the *gēr* becomes included within the family of Yahweh.

---

85. Crouch, *Making*, 219.

86. Ebach, *Fremde*, 312: "wird der גר in der vorexilischen Zeit ausschließlich als Handlungsobjekt Israel gegenübergestellt."

87. Ebach, *Fremde*, 200.

88. Awabdy, *Immigrants*, 122–23.

89. Awabdy, *Immigrants*, 66–83, 123–25, 242.

90. See, e.g., Malina, *Social Gospel*, 16–18, 101–2.

Jenny Corcoran errs in the other direction, contending that the fundamental distinction between *gēr* and נכרי is that the *gēr* is open to faith in Yahweh, whereas the נכרי is not.[91] However, in this text allegiance to Yahweh is not a prerequisite to coming before Yahweh but an anticipated result. The phrase שמח plus a compound subject of feasters envisages that the *gēr*, along with the whole household, will be caught up in grateful festal celebration of Yahweh's gifts.[92]

Before leaving the festival calendar, a question that arises in scholarship must be addressed.

### 5.2.8. Does the *Gēr* Participate in Passover-Massot?

Scholars often observe that the *gēr* is omitted from Passover-Massot in 16:1–8, concluding that the stranger is not welcome to this ordinance. The most common explanation offered is that Passover-Massot is a remembrance of the exodus, the constitutive event for the nation, and that this necessarily renders Passover-Massot ethnically exclusive. This is a festival for ethnic Israelites, it is argued.[93] However, this popular idea suffers from misunderstandings on a number of levels. To begin with, if ethnic identity is the explanation for why the *gēr* is not mentioned in Passover-Massot, then 16:1–8 goes too far, as it also fails to mention the Levite, the fatherless, and widow.[94] Stranger still, ובנך ובתך are not mentioned. Indeed, there is no list of participants at all. This observation signals that the omission of the list of participants does not signify the exclusion of the *gēr*, for Israelite בנך ובתך are certainly not excluded a priori from Passover-Massot. This contention is strengthened by the observation that in Deuteronomy the exodus is not a symbol of ethnic particularity but of redemption, justice,

---

91. Corcoran, "Alien," 231.

92. שמח is discussed above at §5.2.2.

93. E.g., Van Houten, *Alien*, 89–90; Crouch, *Making*, 291; Ebach, *Fremde*, 54; Achenbach, "*gēr*," 32; Albertz, "Aliens," 61; Kidd, *Alterity*, 46.

94. Van Houten, having explained the exclusion of the *gēr* from the Passover (16:1–8) on the grounds of ethnicity, then explains the exclusion of the fatherless and the widow from Passover-Massot on different grounds, namely, that only Weeks and Booths contain the "spirit of generosity" that leads to the inclusion of the vulnerable (*Alien*, 90). However, the use of different reasons for the exclusion of different groups from Passover is overly complex and the application of Occam's razor suggests that a better explanation may be available.

and inclusion.[95] Thus the absence of the list of participants is not an indication of exclusion.

The absence of a list of participants, rather, is explained in that Weeks and Booths are harvest pilgrim feasts, and in both cases the list of participants occurs in the context of an exhortation to "feast" (שׂמח) upon the harvest. The list of participants is a part of the feasting formula.[96] Passover-Massot is not a harvest festival; it contains no call to שׂמח. It is instead characterized by remembrance of affliction.[97] Altmann rightly discusses the connection of Passover-Massot (Deut 16:1–8) with Exod 12:1–13:16, observing that in Exod 12:43–49 the outsider may be included in the Passover through circumcision, and in Deut 16:1–8 the stranger may be included in the Passover through participation within an Israelite household.[98]

Crouch has recently argued that the festival calendar clearly distinguishes between the gēr and the Israel group in light of the fact that the gēr is excluded from Passover-Massot. Moreover, the gēr participates in the Feasts of Weeks and Booths only as one with an interest in the harvest but not participate in the Israel group.[99] However, it bears repeating that the cultic formula פני יהוה אלהיך (16:11, 16) is the expression for worship before Yahweh at the chosen place in Dtn. So if the gēr is not included within Israel in Dtn through the cultic formula, it is difficult to see how Dtn includes any person within Israel.

### 5.3. Firstfruits Festival (Deut 26:1–11): Israel as Gēr

The Bible is a story dealing exactingly with a gift.[100]

#### 5.3.1. Introduction

The following analysis probes the gēr in the ritual of Firstfruits (26:1–11). The rhetorical setting of the passage is Moab, and here on the edge of the

---

95. Contrary to Van Houton, *Alien*, 89–90. See the analysis of the exodus motive clause in §§3.4.3 and 4.2.6.2.

96. See the exegesis of Deut 14:22–27 (§5.4).

97. Tigay notes that David Abudraham characterizes the seven weeks between Passover-Massot and the harvest as a time of "quasi mourning," of anxiously waiting for the harvest (*Deuteronomy*, 156).

98. Altmann, *Festive*, 186–90. Altmann identifies Exod 12:43–49 as P or post-P.

99. Crouch, *Making*, 221.

100. Wendell Berry.

land, a ritual is given that anticipates future generations of farmers[101] who will return the firstfruits of the harvest to Yahweh in a ritual of thanksgiving with rejoicing. The firstfruits are placed in a basket and carried on a journey through the land to the place that Yahweh will choose. Two declarations are made before Yahweh, by which each new generation appropriates the gift of land and of redemption for themselves. Two categories of landless people are explicitly named for inclusion in the festival: the *gēr* and the Levite; these journey with the household from the farm to the sanctuary for a celebratory cultic feast, with thanksgiving. Deuteronomy 26:1–11 comprises a frame (26:1–5a, 10–11) with an extended declaration within the frame (26:5b–10), the content of 26:9–10 belonging to both the frame and the declaration. The two sections, frame and declaration, each exhibit distinctive vocabulary and content and yet are related via the theme of land. As for the frame, the gifts of the land and its produce, the joyful receiving of these gifts with thanksgiving, and the generosity and inclusion that is a necessary reflex of thanksgiving are its theme. Regarding the declaration, the relation between Israel's ethical responsibility toward the *gēr* (26:11) and Israel's own prior sojourning, vulnerability, and redemption is a deliberate and central feature.

We begin with a brief discussion of the literary history of 26:1–11. Analysis of the structure and syntax of the text follows. Finally, the *gēr* in 26:1–11 is explored in detail.

### 5.3.1.1. Composition History

The composition history of 26:1–11 has been pivotal in discussion of the history of the Pentateuch. In 1938 Gerhard von Rad published his influential work *Das formgeschichtliche Problem des Hexateuch*,[102] arguing that 26:5–9 is an ancient creedal summary of salvation history that preceded the developed narrative of Israel's origins found in the final form of the Pentateuch.[103] Leonhard Rost offered an early critique of von Rad's thesis,

---

101. Peter C. Craigie suggests that the ritual is limited to the first generation in the land (*Deuteronomy*, NICOT [London: Hodder & Stoughton, 1976], 319). However, the phrase הכהן אשר יהיה בימים ההם (26:3) envisages future generations. Also, settled social structures are assumed by phrases such as והגר אשר בקרבך (26:11).

102. Translated as von Rad, "The Form-Critical Problem of the Hexateuch."

103. Wolfgang Richter argues that the historical summaries depend upon the prior formation of J and E and also other developments ("Beobachtungen zur theologischen Systembildung in der alttestamentlichen Literatur anhand des 'kleinen

demonstrating that phrases from 26:5b–9 depend upon the frame of Deuteronomy. Since Rost, numerous scholars have demonstrated the links between 26:1–11 and the frame of Deuteronomy, identifying 26:1–11 with Dtr.[104] Later scholars, including Calum Carmichael and Norbert Lohfink, have highlighted the creed's dependence upon non-Deuteronomic texts, noting in particular dependence upon P texts.[105] Also of relevance is the designation as Dtr of certain motifs in 26:1–11, such as "the fathers"[106] and the land-gift formula.[107] Consequently, Deut 26:1–11 appears to be of a later stratum than the other feasting texts—Dtr or post-Dtr.[108] Deuteronomy 26:1–11 displays the enhanced concern for displaced people that has been observed in Dtr and post-Dtr texts.[109]

Discerning an original text is fraught with difficulty. The double declaration is unusual (26:3–4, 5b–9), and the declaration before the priest

---

geschichtlichen Credo,'" in *Wahrheit und Verkündigung: Michael Schmaus zum 70. Geburtstag* [ed. Leo Scheffczyk, Werner Dettloff, and Richard Heinzmann; 2 vols.; Munich: Schöningh, 1967], 2:125–212).

104. Leonhard Rost, *Das kleine Credo und andere Studien zum Alten Testament* (Heidelberg: Quelle & Meyer, 1965). See more recently, Altmann, "Feast," 555–57.

105. E.g. Calum Carmichael, "A New View of the Origin of the Deuteronomic Credo," *VT* 19 (1969): 273–89; Norbert Lohfink, "The 'Small Credo' of Deuteronomy 26:5–9," in *Theology of the Pentateuch*, trans. L. M. Maloney (Minneapolis: Fortress, 1994), 265–289; trans. of "Zum 'kleinen geschichtlichen Credo' Dtn 26, 5–9," in vol. 1 of *Studien zum Deuteronomium und zur deuteronomistischen Literatur*, SBAB 8 (Stuttgart: Katholisches Bibelwerk, 1995), 263–90. See also Schmidt, *Old Testament*, 122; Altmann, "Feast," 556.

106. See, e.g., Thomas Römer, *Israels Väter: Untersuchungen zur Väterthematik im Deuteronomium und in der deuteronomistischen Tradition*, OBO 99 (Göttingen:Vandenhoeck & Ruprecht, 1990), 137; Römer, "Deuteronomy in Search of Origins," in *Reconsidering Israel and Judah: Recent Studies on the Deuteronomic History*, ed. Gary N. Knoppers and J. Gordon McConville, SBTS 8 (Winona Lake, IN: Eisenbrauns, 2000), 128. Römer, among others, argues that "the fathers" in Dtr refers to the generation of the exodus.

107. Lohfink, "Small Credo." For a preexilic date for the land-gift formula, see Crüsemann, *Torah*, 201–2, 208.

108. P material in Deuteronomy is generally thought to be post-Dtr. Achenbach states: "There is now in the research literature a discernible hesitation to accept a dependence on a donor Priestly text in a text supposedly Dtr" ("Eintritt," 251: "Es ist in der Forschungsliteratur nun ein Zögern erkennbar, in einem vermeintlich dtr Text eine Abhängigkeit von einem priesterschriftlichen Gebertext anzunehmen"). See also Römer, *Israels Väter*, 155–57.

109. See the exegesis of 5:12–15 (§3.7) and especially ch. 6.

(26:3–4) is considered by many to be a later redaction.[110] However, resumptive repetition of "set before Yahweh" (26:4b, 10b) may indicate that the credo is the later declaration (26:5b–9).

Rost found an ancient original in the first-person singular affirmations of 26:5b, 10a. These two texts juxtaposed read:

> A wandering Aramean was my father. And now behold I bring the first-fruits of the soil, which you have given me, Yahweh.

The majority of scholars accept this suggestion.[111] However, the following analysis casts doubt on Rost's construction, for 26:10a may not be considered in abstraction from its *form* as an expression of the land-gift formula. Deuteronomy 26:10a represents a predictable and highly contextualized use of a variety of the land-gift formula.[112]

Since von Rad's work, most studies of 26:1–11 have focused on the credo and have been concerned with historical-critical issues. Studies of 26:5b–9 have proceeded largely in abstraction from its literary context, 26:1–11,[113] and extended studies of the whole of 26:1–11 are few in number. Attention to the structure, syntax, and patterning of the whole

---

110. See Altmann, "Feast," 557.

111. For example, Mayes, *Deuteronomy*, 333; Nelson, *Deuteronomy*, 307; Lohfink, "Small Credo," 269–89.

112. If 26:10a is an ancient original, then it must be shown to *predate* other expressions of the land-gift formula. The land-gift formula in 26:10a uses אדמה as head word. To be sure, אדמה may be used interchangeably with ארץ, yet אדמה also has its own distinctive set of relations. Within the land-gift formula אדמה is the word of choice in relation to the fathers (7:13; 11:9, 21; 26:15; 28:11; 30:20). The word אדמה tends to be used in reference to the ground or soil as the location of agricultural blessing, and it often has this reference within the land-gift formula (7:13; 11:9; 26:2,10,15; 28:11). Usage in 26:10a is associated with these themes. Deuteronomy 26:10a then represents a predictable and highly contextualized use of a variety of the land-gift formula. As such, it seems unlikely that 26:10a contains the original core of the declaration or is an original and ancient expression of the land-gift formula.

113. E.g., J. Philip Hyatt, "Were There an Ancient Historical Credo in Israel and an Independent Sinai Tradition?" in *Translating and Understanding the Old Testament: Essays in Honor of Herbert Gordon May*, ed. Harry Thomas Frank and William L. Reed (Nashville: Abingdon, 1970), 152–70; John. A. Thompson, "The Cultic Credo and the Sinai Tradition," *RTR* 27 (1968): 53–64; Dwight R. Daniels, "The Creed of Deuteronomy XXVI Revisited," in *Studies in the Pentateuch*, ed. J. A. Emerton, VTSup 41 (Leiden: Brill, 1990), 231–42.

of 26:1–11 brings the motif of displacement to the fore and highlights an ethic of inclusion as a primary theme.

5.3.2. Structural Analysis of 26:1–11

Translation:[114]

[Frame]
1 <u>When you have</u> **come into** <u>the land, which Yahweh your God is giving to you for an inheritance and have taken possession of it and settled in it,</u> 2 **you shall take** some of every first fruit of the soil that you gather in from your land that Yahweh God is giving you, **put it** in a basket and journey to the place that Yahweh your God chooses to make his name dwell. 3 **Go** to the priest who is in office at that time and **say** to him:
　　"I declare this day before Yahweh your God that <u>I have come into the land that Yahweh solemnly swore to our forefathers to give to us.</u>"
4 And the priest **will take** the basket from your hand and **set** it before the altar of Yahweh your God. 5 And **you shall solemnly declare** before Yahweh your God:

　　[Declaration]
　　"A wandering Aramean was my father. And he **went down** to Egypt and he **dwelled** there as a stranger, few in number, and he **became** there a nation, great, mighty and populous. 6 The Egyptians **treated us harshly, oppressed us and imposed hard labor** on us. 7 And **we cried** to Yahweh the God of our forefathers and the Yahweh **heard** our voice and he **saw** our affliction, our toil and our oppression. 8 And Yahweh **brought us out** of Egypt, with a strong hand and an outstretched arm and with great terror and with signs and wonderful deeds. 9 He **brought us into** <u>this place and **gave** us this land, a land flowing with milk and honey.</u> 10 And now behold <u>I bring the firstfruits of the soil, which you have given me, O Yahweh.</u>"

[Frame]
**And you shall set it down** before Yahweh your God **and worship** before Yahweh your God 11 and **feast** on all the bounty that Yahweh your God has

---

114. Key to the translation (which is mine): underlining indicates six expressions of the land-gift formula; bold indicates the twelve *waw* + suffix-conjugation verbs (of the frame); bold italics indicates the twelve *waw* + prefix-conjugation verbs (of the declaration).

given you and your household—you and the Levite and the stranger who is in your midst.

## 5.3.2.1. The Land-Gift Formula and Word Patterning

Examining the land-gift formula in 26:1–11 shows how the text anchors an ethic of inclusivism for the *gēr* in a theology of land gift and a ritual of thanksgiving. The vocabulary of the passage's frame is small, with only four words conveying much of the content, נתן, יהוה, ארץ, and בוא, a pattern also observable in 11:1–32. This vocabulary is shaped by the theme of land gift and contrasts with the vocabulary associated with blessing that characterizes 14:22–29 and 16:1–17: ברך, כל, אכל, and נתן. The land-gift formula occurs six times in 26:1–11,[115] and the ritual of Firstfruits is described with small variations within this repeated theme sentence, which constitutes much of the frame (marked with underline in the above text). The simplest form of the land-gift formula occurs twelve times in Deuteronomy[116] and is configured הארץ אשר יהוה אלהיך נתן לך. Through the land-gift formula, the theme of the divine gift of land and its abundance is ubiquitous in Deuteronomy, occurring forty-three times in its full form, with ארץ as head word, the relative pronoun אשר, and נתן in the relative clause. In its full form with אדמה as head word, the land-gift formula occurs an additional twelve times,[117] totaling fifty-five. Analyzing the land-gift formula in its parts is instructive. The formula begins with a governing clause, for example, כי תבוא אל הארץ. Within 26:1–11, the governing clauses mostly describe movement, both into the land and to the place of worship, with the verb בוא (26:1, 2, 3c; cf. 26:10). Two other verbs are also used: נתן (26:9) and שמח (26:11). The head words for the

---

115. Underlined in the text above, 26:1, 2a, 3b, 9, 10a, 11. A seventh occurrence in 26:15 is likely related, forming a heptad and strengthening the literary and theological connection between 26:1–11 and 26:12–15. See Weinfeld's list of Deuteronomic formulas (*Deuteronomy and the Deuteronomic School*, 341).

116. Deuteronomy 1:25; 2:29; 5:16; 9:23; 15:7; 16:20; 26:2; 27:2, 3; 28:8, 52; 32:52. The altar law shares its syntactical form with the land-gift formula, e.g., המקום אשר יבחר יהוה אלהיך לשכן שמו שם (26:2). Juxtaposition between the two formulas has the affect of locating the altar law within the larger framework of the divine gift of land (e.g., 26:2a, 2b).

117. Deuteronomy 4:40; 5:16; 7:13; 11:9, 21; 21:1, 23; 25:15; 26:10, 15; 28:11; 30:20. Other forms of the formula may be added to these, with various head words or with alternatives to אשר, and נתן.

relative clauses are ארץ (26:1, 2a, 3b, 9), אדמה (ground/soil, 26:10a), and
הטוב (26:11). The land and its produce then is the syntactical focus of the
land-gift formula that makes up the frame. The land is the location, means,
and content of God's gifts. The relative pronoun אשר signals the relative
clause that modifies the head word (except 26:9). In 26:1–11, five relative
clauses reflect a form that is almost identical (e.g., אשר יהוה אלהיך נתן לך,
26:1, 2a, 3b, 10a, 11). The relative clause highlights Yahweh as the source of
the land and its abundance. The sixfold affirmation of Yahweh's gift of land
with its produce is the theological heart of 26:1–11.[118]

Repetitions of seven within 26:1–11 also highlight these central
themes.[119] Heptadic patterning is already present in the earliest festival
regulations via the seven days of Unleavened Bread (Exod 23:14–17 and
34:18–20; cf. Deut 16:8). In the Firstfruits regulations (26:1–11), the word
נתן occurs seven times, expressing the completeness of the gift. The word
יהוה, the giver, occurs fourteen times. Less certain is the combination of
ארץ, used five times, and אדמה, used twice, to equal seven.[120]

### 5.3.2.2. Verbal Patterning and the Ritual of Thanksgiving

Examining the verbal patterning of the frame (26:1–5a, 10–11) displays
how an ethic of inclusion is embedded in a theology of land gift. A ritual
pilgrimage is described within the frame of 26:1–11 through a string of
twelve *waw* + suffix-conjugation verbs (bold in the text above): "take," "put,"
"journey," "go," "say," "take," "set," "declare" (וענית ואמרת), "set," "worship,"
"feast" (so also SP and LXX). These verbs trace the progress of the wor-

---

118. The fifth and sixth occurrence of the land-gift formula (26:10a, 11) position
the predicate, לך, לי, before the nominative, יהוה, highlighting the worshiper as recipient. Josef Plöger has demonstrated that variations upon the land-gift formula tend to
prefer particular contexts and the present analysis develops his thesis; see *Literarkritische, formgeschichtliche und stilkritische Untersuchungen zum Deuteronomium*, BBB
26 (Bonn: Hanstein, 1967), 121–29.

119. On heptads, see Arvid S. Kapelrud, "The Number Seven in Ugaritic," *VT* 18
(1968): 494–99.

120. Whether this constitutes heptadic patterning or not does not diminish the
effect of word repetition. On broken heptads, compare the six plus one days of creation and the five loaves and two fishes of the gospels. A related text, 16:1–17, repeats
the number seven, seven times. On ארץ and אדמה, see J. Gordon McConville and J. G.
Millar, *Time and Place in Deuteronomy*, JSOTSup 179 (Sheffield: Sheffield Academic,
1997), 127–30.

shiper from the field where the first produce of the season is harvested, to placing the firstfruits in a basket, to the place where Yahweh chooses, and into Yahweh's presence for declaration, prostration, and inclusive feasting. The concatenation of twelve verbs may be taken cumulatively as representing a ritual response to the gift represented by the land-gift formula with its own distinctive vocabulary: נתן, יהוה, ארץ, and בוא. Indeed, the verbal syntax of the frame casts the whole ritual as a grateful response to the gift of land. The verb תבוא (26:1a) is the governing verb for the twelve *waw* + suffix-conjugation verbs listed above: והיה כי תבוא אל הארץ (26:1). The word כי has a contingent future sense: "*When* you come into the land." A three-part thematic movement infuses the frame (26:1–5a, 10–11), beginning with Yahweh's generosity, which in turn inspires thanksgiving, leading to generosity and inclusion, namely, for the *gēr* and Levite. This three-part movement may be laid out as follows: gift; thanksgiving; generosity and inclusion.

## 5.3.2.3. Verbal Patterning and the Declaration

A corresponding pattern of twelve verbs is present in the declaration (26:5b–10).[121] The declaration recites Yahweh's transforming deliverance that brings his people from displacement and oppression in Egypt to the land with its abundance. Twelve uninterrupted *waw* + prefix-conjugation verbs form a narrative sequence: "went down," "dwelled," "became a nation," "treated us harshly," "oppressed us," "imposed hard labor on us," "we cried," "Yahweh heard," "he saw," "brought us out," "brought us into," "gave" (so also SP and LXX).[122]

The twelve *waw* + prefix-conjugation verbs of the declaration correspond to the twelve *waw* + suffix-conjugation verbs that form the grammatical structure of the ritual of Firstfruits. The two verbal chains share a similar narrative contour. Both narrate a journey, and it is Israel who is journeying. On the one hand, the verbs of the frame describe a movement from the farm to the sanctuary for thanksgiving and celebration. On the other hand, the verbs of the declaration recite a movement in and out of

---

121. Regarding the significance of the number twelve, Deut 1:23, 25 refer to "twelve men ... one man from each tribe" who spied out the land, along with reference to פרי הארץ and also the land-gift formula. There may be a deliberate association between the two texts.

122. SP 26:6: וירעו takes the form ויריעו (cf. Sir 38:21).

Egypt, entailing a transformation of vulnerable wanderers into a nation that is landed and blessed. The correspondence between the verbs of the frame and of the declaration links Israel's formative story of deliverance with thanksgiving, and it links salvation history (26:5b–10) with themes of providence (26:1–5a, 10–11).[123] The ritual of the frame may be taken as the dramatic fulfillment of the narrative of the declaration, and Deut 26:10 transitions the latter into the former seamlessly, belonging to both narrative and frame.

The word נתן within the phrase ויתנו עלינו עבדה קשה (26:6) is the fourth and center of seven uses of נתן within 26:1–15, and it is the only occurrence of the seven that does not refer to land gift. Here נתן is an unlikely choice in an otherwise formulaic expression for slavery in Egypt (see also Isa 30:20). The juxtaposing of these two senses of נתן, of oppression and of divine gift, contrasts Yahweh's gift of land with the violence of oppressors, with implications for Israel's treatment of the vulnerable in its midst (cf. 26:11).

### 5.3.3. An Ethic of Inclusivism in 26:1–11

The significance of the preceding analysis is that 26:1–11 anchors its ethic of inclusivism in a theology of land gift and within a ritual of thanksgiving. In a sense, Deut 26:1–15 poses the question: How may the gift of land be received aright? The answer is given: the gift is to be shared (26:11). In what follows I will explore the ways in which the inclusion of the *gēr* within the festivity and life of the community is a prominent theme, not only of 26:11, where the *gēr* is specifically mentioned, but also of the whole of 26:1–11. The salvation-historical summary, 26:5b–10, is salient here. Alasdair MacIntyre's assertion that ethics only have meaning in the context of a narrative is true of the DC's vision for Israel's responsibility toward the *gēr*. MacIntyre claims: "I can only answer the question, 'What am I to do?' if I can answer the prior question, 'Of what story do I find myself a part?' "[124] Deuteronomy's ethics of inclusion for the *gēr* is embedded in the particu-

---

123. On the relation of salvation history to creation theology, see Rolf P. Knierim, *The Task of Old Testament Theology: Method and Cases* (Grand Rapids: Eerdmans, 1995), 171–224.

124. Alasdair MacIntyre, *After Virtue: A Study in Moral Theory* (Notre Dame: University of Notre Dame Press, 1985), 370.

lar narrative of Israel's own journey from displacement and oppression to being placed and blessed.

### 5.3.3.1. Feasting That Incorporates the Outsider

Deuteronomy 26:11 comprises a revision of the usual list of the vulnerable (cf. ללוי לגר ליתום ולאלמנה in 26:12, 13).

26:11

ושמחת בכל הטוב אשר נתן לך יהוה אלהיך ולביתך אתה והלוי והגר
אשר בקרבך

The appearance of the *gēr* and the Levite without the fatherless and the widow in 26:11 is not to be explained in terms of "aesthetic purposes," as Awabdy claims.[125] The *gēr* appears without the fatherless and the widow only here within Deuteronomy's feasting texts, suggesting that 26:1–11 has a particular interest in the *gēr*. McConville suggests that it is explained by the inability of the Levite and the *gēr* to inherit land and by the importance of the theme of land gift in 26:1–11.[126] I add three points. First, I will show that the whole of 26:1–11 is concerned with themes of displacement. Second, the social-historical context that 26:1–11 originally addressed was probably a part of the impetus for the Levite-*gēr* combination. As with other Dtr and post-Dtr texts, Deut 26:1–11 probably addressed a context of widespread displacement.[127] Third, the fatherless and the widow's inclusion in the festival is assumed, the reduced list aiming to highlight the inclusion of the landless rather than to limit the scope of inclusion.

Deuteronomy 26:11 is a call to an inclusive harvest feast. Deuteronomy 26:1 and 26:11 form an *inclusio* framing the whole of 26:1–11: the list of those who celebrate, אתה והלוי והגר, is structurally parallel to three verbs describing land gift in 26:1, בוא, ירש, and ישב, giving the sense that the appropriate result of the divine gift of land is the joy of familiar unity that is forged in feasting. The verb שמח is the final of the twelve *waw* + suffix-conjugation verbs that characterize the frame (26:11). The text of 26:1–11 moves persistently toward feasting through the narrative arc of

---

125. Awabdy, *Immigrants*, 119.
126. McConville, *Deuteronomy*, 380.
127. See further §§4.7.3, 6.4.3, and 6.4.5.1.

these verbs. The *gēr* and the Levite are to שמח with the household with which they are associated. Furthermore, the interconnectedness of the *waw* + suffix-conjugation verbal chain of the frame implicates the vulnerable in the whole sequence of the ritual that these verbs describe: harvest, pilgrimage, worship, and feasting. We have observed how cultural anthropology has explored the potential of sharing in food consumption to foster kinship. For the Maori, "Food can give a new nature since it can introduce a new kind of life into the eater.... The eater is not only bound to the givers, but they on the other hand recognize their own life in the guest who has eaten and respect this."[128] Similarly, the Malays studied by Janet Carsten acquire the same "blood" by living in the same house and eating from the same hearth. "Those who eat the same food together in one house also come to have blood in common, and this is one way in which foster children and affines become connected to those with whom they live.[129] In order to interpret dynamics of kinship in the Festival of Firstfruits, it is necessary to attend to the symbols and meanings that are native to the text itself. In 26:1–11, inclusivism is embedded within a shared narrative (26:5b–10) and a shared pilgrimage feast (26:1–5, 10–11), through which an "intersubjective solidarity" with the *gēr* is forged.[130]

Further, we see here a dialectic between cohesion and inclusivism. Feasts function as communal boundary markers,[131] and the festival calendar reconfirms the group identity of the people of Yahweh through seasonal cultic performances. However, these feasts are both cohesive and inclusive. Through regular seasonal pilgrimages, Israel is renewed as the people of Yahweh, a community whose edges always extend to the vulnerable.[132]

### 5.3.3.2. "The *Gēr* in Your Midst," 26:11

The prepositional use of the noun קרב is a part of Deuteronomy's semantics of integration (see also comments on בשעריך in §5.5.2 and on גרך in

---

128. Nancy Munn, *The Fame of Gawa: A Symbolic Study of Value Transformation in a Massim (Papua New Guinea) Society* (Cambridge: Cambridge University Press, 1954), 108.

129. Casten, *After Kinship*, 129.

130. Sahlins, *What Kinship Is*, 43.

131. Hendel, *Remembering Abraham*, 22.

132. See further, §6.10.2.

§3.3.5). The word קרב occurs with peculiar frequency in Deuteronomy, forty-one times, and Braulik notes that the term is especially related to laws concerning the *gēr*.[133] In texts concerning the *gēr*, קרב occurs as בקרבך (16:11, 23:16–17, 26:11, 28:43) and בקרב מחניך (29:10). Ebach refers to the image of the "center" of the community of Israel, and בקרבך evokes this image. "So the weak are received and cared for in the center; evil is carried away from this center."[134] The geography of בקרבך may concern the בית, the settlement, or the city. The word קרב is used in relation to the *gēr* in contexts of feasting together (16:11, 26:11), of including a flee-ing slave (23:16–17), and of participating with the household in "national" covenant ratification (29:10–11). Thus in relation to the *gēr* בקרבך is used in contexts that foster the inclusion of the stranger at the protective center of the community.

### 5.3.3.3. The Motif of Displacement in 26:1–11 and the *Gēr*

Ethics of inclusion for the *gēr* is associated with Israel's own narrative of displacement in 26:1–11. The theme of displacement is ubiquitous in this text; movement in the narrative is dizzying. Israel is wandering, sojourn-ing, enslaved, brought out, brought in, and finally journeying to the sanc-tuary. The text ends with the inclusion of the *gēr*, one characterized by dis-placement, within the community. As McConville notes: "The dominant contrast [is] between homelessness and 'home.'"[135] In the first declaration, כי באתי אל הארץ אשר נשבע יהוה לאבתינו לתת לנו (26:3b), the worshiper affirms that the land is no longer merely promised; it is now a possession. In other words, the days of wandering are past.

The second declaration opens with a statement of dislocation, ארמי אבד אבי (26:5), and it seems possible, especially in light of the uniqueness of this phrase, that here is a deliberate relation to the dislocation of the *gēr*. There are two likely senses for אבד: "wandering" and "perishing."[136] The

---

133. Braulik, "Deuteronomy and Human Rights," 249 n. 21.

134. Ebach, *Fremde*, 314: "So werden die Schwachen in der Mitte aufgenommen und versorgt, das Böse ist aus dieser Mitte wegzuschaffen."

135. McConville, *Deuteronomy*, 380.

136. See, e.g., *HALOT*, s.v. "אבד," 2. J. Gerald Janzen has argued with a minority of scholars that אבד should be construed "perishing," also plausibly narrowing the sense to "starving;" see "The Wandering Aramean Reconsidered," *VT* 44 (1994): 359–75. Yair Zakovitch's recent suggestion, "Edom served my father" is unlikely as this has

gloss "wandering" aligns with the motif of sojourn throughout 26:1–11, though Jan Christian Gertz has demonstrated that "perishing" is better supported lexically.[137] In addition, it should be noted that both ויגר and עלינו עבדה קשה are status signifiers,[138] suggesting that אבד likewise may signify status, perhaps alien status. Whatever the precise reference of אבד, Millard rightly states, "What is remembered about the fathers and mothers of Israel is that they wandered about—that is, they did not yet have a place and a land."[139] The long physical journey to Jerusalem for the Festival of Firstfruits (26:2, הלך) would recall the wandering lifestyle of the forebears in a context where Israel's responsibility to vulnerable, displaced, and possibly despised people is required. Both Altmann and MacDonald have highlighted the relation of land and food in the text. They trace a movement within the text that begins with the landlessness and food insecurity that was experienced by the patriarchs, advancing toward land gift along with an abundant harvest. "What may be striking here is that *wandering and perishing* (from hunger) can have significant overlap.... The festive meal of 26:11 emerges as the pinnacle of the contrast to the deprivation."[140]

Further, the significance of the self-identification as ארמי must not be passed over. Israel's provenance is one not only of displacement but also of an identifiable ethnic designation other than Israelite.[141] This opens the

---

little relation to the context of 26:1–11, which is a highly unified text; see "'My Father Was a Wandering Aramean' (Deuteronomy 26:5) or 'Edom Served My Father'?," in *Mishneh Todah: Studies in Deuteronomy and Its Cultural Environment in Honor of Jeffrey H. Tigay*, ed. Nili Sacher Fox, David A. Glatt-Gilad, and Michael James Williams (Winona Lake, IN: Eisenbrauns, 2009), 133–37.

137. Jan Christian Gertz, "Die Stellung des kleinen geschichtlichen Credos in der Redaktionsgeschichte von Deuteronomium und Pentateuch," in *Liebe und Gebot: Studien zum Deuteronomium*, ed. Reinhard G. Kratz and Hermann Spieckermann, FRLANT 190 (Göttingen: Vandenhoeck & Ruprecht, 2000), 36–37.

138. עלינו עבדה קשה refers to corvée labor of an unusually harsh and permanent kind (cf. 1 Kgs 12:4). While corvée does not generally entail a change of status (Dexter E. Callender Jr., "Servants of God(s) and Servants of Kings in Israel and the Ancient Near East," *Semeia* 83–84 [1998]: 77), that Israel did experience a change in status in Egypt is indicated by יצא (26:8), a technical expression for exiting slavery (see Daube, *Exodus*, 31; Braulik, "Deuteronomy and Human Rights," 135).

139. Patrick Miller, *Deuteronomy*, IBC (Louisville: Westminster John Knox, 1990), 181.

140. Altmann, "Feast," 561; MacDonald, *Not Bread Alone*, 77–78.

141. A common suggestion is that ארמי ("Aramean") designates a people group with a reputation for wandering (Janzen, "Wandering," 372–73; Abraham Malamat,

possibility that the designation "Israel" itself is a fluid one. It is explored in §§4.7.3 and 6.4.4 how the social-historical context of Persian Yehud was characterized by both displacement and a crisis of identity—the question of who was, and who was not, Israel was paramount. This assertion of Israel's provenance demonstrates an inclusive posture, especially toward vulnerable and displaced people. This is consistent with what is observed in other post-Dtr texts (see §§4.7.3, 6.4.4).

The emotional and social impact of the pilgrimage surrounding First-fruits must have been immense.[142] Sojourning to the place that Yahweh had chosen, together the household and the landless experienced *landlessness* (or a deeper sort of landedness) as they feasted from the best of the harvest. By sojourning, Israel was reminded of its landless past, forging, to use Sahlin's phrase, a "mutuality of being," an "intersubjective solidarity" with the *gēr*.[143] Dislocated from systems of land ownership, patronage, and division of labor, they shared the lesson that the land was a gift from God. This is a lesson that is, in a sense, learned best by the landless.[144] The altar law may be viewed in this light, for it seems that Deuteronomy considers local sanctuaries to have led the Hebrews to forget their own past as pilgrims and that establishing a sanctuary to which they must pilgrimage—along with the *gēr*—inevitably recalled this important part of their experience.

### 5.3.3.4. The Exodus and 26:5b–9: Liberative Ethics

Further evidence that an ethic of inclusion is a primary focus not only of 26:11 but also of the whole of 26:1–11 is the narrative of slavery in Egypt and the subsequent deliverance (26:6–8). Within the current form of the Pentateuch, law and narrative are inextricably intertwined. Law "is woven into the narrative throughout."[145] In the previous section, fol-

---

"The Aramaeans," in *Peoples of Old Testament Times*, ed. D. J. Wiseman [Oxford: Clarendon, 1973], 149). Alan R. Millard, however, has shown that this conclusion is doubtful ("A Wandering Aramean," *JNES* 39 [1980]: 153–55).

142. Turner describes practises of pilgrimage and feasting as "liminal" events (*Dramas*, 13–14).

143. Sahlins, *What Kinship Is*, 19–31, 43.

144. A danger of possessing land is satiation, leading to idolatry (e.g., Deut 8:11–18). On this theological theme, see Brueggemann, *Land*, 40.

145. Terrance E. Fretheim, *Exodus*. IBC (Louisville: Westminster John Knox, 1991), 201.

lowing David Daube, we observed that the exodus narrative as presented across the sources of the Pentateuch is narrated in terms of ancient Near Eastern laws and customs regarding the release of slaves, which were established previous to the composition of the exodus narrative itself.[146] This dynamic is also observed in the credo, 26:5b–9. The verb יצא (26:8) is the most common expression for deliverance from Egypt in Deuteronomy, occurring sixteen times as causative (הוֹצִיא) and ten times as qal. It is a legal term for release appropriated to the exodus narrative.[147] The verb ענה ("oppress," 26:6) appears in Exod 1:11, 12 and may predate the exodus narrative in two incidents in the patriarchal narratives.[148] It also appears in what is likely an ancient law preserved in the Covenant Code (Exod 22:21). The verb לחץ ("oppress," 26:7) appears in Exod 3:9 and in texts that clearly depend upon the exodus narrative (e.g., Judg 2:18, 6:9). It has an early association with social justice, appearing in two laws of the CC regarding the gēr that may predate the composition of the exodus narrative, Exod 22:20 and 23:9. The verb צעק ("cry," 26:7) is used in laws likely to be of ancient origin (Exod 22:22; Deut 22:24, 27).[149] The exodus narrative is using a common term for the cry of oppressed in the face of a violation of human rights.[150]

In thus using concepts and lexemes from slave culture that also convey a carved ethical dimension due to their being used in the exodus narrative, the declaration itself is deeply ethical in character. The declaration has a deliberate motivating function in relation to the inclusion of gēr and the Levite in 26:11. This observation is enhanced by Rodd's assertion of a peculiar connection between the exodus motif and ethics concerning the gēr (see §3.4.3).[151] Accordingly, including the gēr is an example of an imitatio Dei correspondence.

---

146. Daube, *Exodus*.

147. Daube, *Exodus*, 31; Braulik, "Deuteronomy and Human Rights," 135. The contexts for יצא include slave release (e.g., 15:16), divorce (e.g., 24:2), and property release (e.g., Lev 25:30–31). Cf. Akkadian *waṣu* (*CAD*, "aṣû," 1.2:356–85).

148. "And Sarai dealt harshly with Hagar, and she fled from her" (Gen 16:6 [my translation]; also Gen 31:50). See further Daube, *Exodus*, 26–27.

149. Daube, *Exodus*, 27.

150. José Porfirio Miranda, *Marx and the Bible: A Critique of the Philosophy of Oppression* (Maryknoll, NY: Orbis, 1974), 88–89.

151. Rodd, *Glimpses*, 182–83.

## 5.3.3.5. Israel as *Gēr* in Egypt 26:5b

The relation between Israel's ethical responsibility toward the *gēr* and Israel's own formative story is a deliberate and central feature of 26:1–11. Consider first the phrase ויגר שם ("he dwelled there as a stranger"), which is omitted in the other credo texts (26:5b). While within Deuteronomy's narrative and in motive clauses Israel's prior status as slave is a primary basis for an ethic of inclusion for the *gēr*, Israel's prior status as *gēr* in Egypt is also prominent. While a small number of studies have investigated the motif of Israel as *gēr* in Egypt, further analysis is necessary.[152] These references are describing Israel in Egypt before the period of enslavement, a time when Israel received hospitality from the Egyptians, though the hospitality was short-lived (see Exod 1:8).[153] The three occurrences in Deuteronomy of Israel referenced as *gēr* in Egypt are:

> Love the stranger, therefore, for you were strangers in the land of Egypt
> [כי גרים הייתם בארץ מצרים]. (10:19 ESV)

> You shall not abhor an Egyptian, because you were a stranger in his land
> [כי גר היית בארצו]. (23:8 [Eng. 23:7] ESV)

> A wandering Aramean was my father. And he went down into Egypt and sojourned there [וירד מצרימה ויגר שם], few in number. (26:5 ESV)

In each case, Israel's identity as *gēr* undergirds a posture of inclusivism. Both 10:19 and 26:5, 11 foster the inclusion of the *gēr*. In the CC, social law is framed by stipulations concerning the *gēr*, along with the *gēr*-in-

---

152. For Israel as *gēr* in Egypt see also Rodd, *Glimpses*, 26; Garrett Galvin, *Egypt as a Place of Refuge*, FAT 2/51 (Tübingen: Mohr Siebeck, 2011), 93–94; Kidd, *Alterity*, 78–80, 86–98; Awabdy's recent extensive discussion helpfully locates this motif within the narrative context of Gen 35–Exod 1:5 (*Immigrants*, 127–64). However, Awabdy's intertextual analysis is flawed.

153. MacDonald suggests that Deut 23:8 refers to Israel's time of enslavement. The text positions Egypt as hospitable slave masters (*Not Bread Alone*, 93). However, the relation of Deut 23:8 to Gen 15:13 supports my suggestion that all three *gēr*-in-Egypt references refer to Israel in Egypt before the period of enslavement. See further Awabdy, *Immigrants*, 127–36.

Egypt formula (22:20; 23:9). Similarly, the *gēr*-in-Egypt motif frames the DC (10:19, 26:5b).[154]

There is clear lexical and syntactic correspondence between Gen 15:13 and two of the three texts, Deut 10:19 and 23:7.

> Then Yahweh said to Abram, "Know for certain that your offspring will be sojourners in a land that is not theirs [כי גר יהיה זרעך בארץ לא להם] and will be slaves there, and they will be afflicted for four hundred years." (Gen 15:13 ESV modified)

Genesis 15:12 is a reference to Israel as *gēr* in Egypt with strong Deuteronomistic connections, thought by many to be late non-P material.[155] Otto assigns Deut 10:19 to the postexilic *Fortschreibung* of Deuteronomy.[156] Deuteronomy 23:8 is also regarded as post-Dtr.[157] So, Gen 15:12 is roughly contemporary with Deut 10:19 and 23:8, and the direction of dependence is not clear. Rhetorically, in Gen 15:13 Israel as *gēr* is a displaced people who are vulnerable to exploitation. The narrative of Gen 15:13 moves rapidly from Israel as *gēr* to Israel as exploited slave. This narrative demonstrates what must have been well appreciated in the ancient Near East, that only a thin line exists between one's status as *gēr* and a status as slave, as the economic vulnerability of the *gēr* and lack of kinship connection make the *gēr* vulnerable in every way. One historical context for Israel's sojourn in Egypt is Jacob's migration into Egypt during the famine. On the basis of the connection with Gen 15:13, I conclude that this is indeed the reference of Deut 10:19 and 23:8. "Joseph's ultimately positive experience

---

154. The larger sections that form the inner frame around the law corpus are 10:12–11:32 and 26:1–19.

155. Carr, *Reading*, 163–67; Anbar, "Genesis 15"; Jan Christian Gertz concludes that Gen 15:11, 13–16 are a later addition; see "Abraham, Mose und der Exodus: Beobachtungen zur Redaktionsgeschichte von Gen 15," in *Abschied vom Jahwisten: Die Komposition des Hexateuch in der jüngsten Diskussion*, ed. Christian Gertz, Konrad Schmidt, and Markus Witte, BZAW 315 (Berlin: de Gruyter, 2002), 66–69.

156. Eckart Otto, "The Books of Deuteronomy and Numbers in One Torah: The Book of Numbers Read in the Horizon of the Postexilic *Fortschreibung* in the Book of Deuteronomy; New Horizons in the Interpretation of the Pentateuch," in *Torah and the Book of Numbers*, ed. Christian Frevel, Thomas Pola, and Aaron Schart, FAT 2/62 (Tübingen: Mohr Siebeck, 2013), 391; Otto, *Deuteronomium*, 1003–72.

157. For a postexilic date for 23:7–8, see H. D. Preuss, *Deuteronomium*, EdF 164 (Darmstadt: Wissenschaftliche Buchgesellschaft, 1982), 150–52; Achenbach, "*gêr*," 35, and n. 20. For alternative dates, see Nelson, *Deuteronomy*, 277–78.

in Egypt allows him to save the people of Israel from famine. This experience lays the foundation for the biblical motif of Egypt as a place of refuge. Without Egypt, Israel could not have survived."[158] Deuteronomy 10:19 and 23:7 evoke the memory of Israel's past vulnerability in Egypt and of Egyptian hospitality in order to inform the new context of Israel's responsibility toward strangers in the postexilic period. Deuteronomy Deut 10:19 and 23:8 call Israel to extend to the *gēr* (10:19) and to the Egyptian (23:8) the hospitality that Israel must have desired to receive in Egypt.

On the other hand, Deut 26:5b's וירד מצרימה ויגר שם echoes a different passage, Gen 12:10, a reference to Abraham in Egypt: וירד אברם מצרימה לגור שם.[159] The significance of this should not be missed.[160] The clause ויגר שם, with its reference to *Abraham* (rather than Jacob) in Egypt, is highly surprising within the text's final form. Through it, the whole sweep of the Genesis narrative of Israel's forebears as displaced foreigners is evoked. In light of the close connection between Egypt and oppression in Deuteronomy, the phrase probably alludes to Abraham's and Sarah's vulnerability in Egypt. Genesis 12:10 is proto-Genesis material[161] and concerns the Abraham wife-sister narrative;[162] Deut 26:5a, as later material, in effect rereads Gen 12:10 in light of the Joseph narrative and of the exodus.

Deuteronomy 26:5b is assigned to Dtr[163] and is likely the original *gēr*-in-Egypt expression in legislative texts.[164] Deuteronomy 10:19b and Exod 22:21b, 23:9b have identical motive clauses, כי גרים הייתם בארץ מצרים (cf. Deut 29:15). This later post-Dtr *gēr*-in-Egypt formula is an adaptation

---

158. Galvin, *Egypt*, 62.

159. Tigay, with many others, mistakenly reads 26:5b as a reference to Jacob (*Deuteronomy*, 240). Within a final form reading, a different phrase, לגור בארץ (Gen 47:4), is used for *Jacob's* sojourn in Egypt, and we would expect this phrase to be used in Deut 26:5. The phrase refers to Isaac in Hebron in a later text (Gen 35:27).

160. The significance is missed in recent studies, e.g., Awabdy, *Immigrants*, 136–41.

161. "Proto-Genesis" designates the first "Genesis," which was, in part, a compilation of earlier traditions. See Carr, *Reading*, 177, 218.

162. Carr designates Gen 12:10 as "proto-Genesis" (*Reading*, 306, 339); cf. Schmid, *Old Testament*, 161. Other occurrences of גור in the Abraham material (20:1, 21:23, 21:34) are likely later (see Carr, *Reading*, 20–21; Carr, *Formation*, 485; Schmidt, *Old Testament*, 86–87).

163. The composition history of 26:1–11 is discussed in §5.3.1.1.

164. The priority of 26:5b is supported by the use the verb, גור, which corresponds to the proto-Genesis references to sojourn that also use the verb (Gen 12:10, 19:19, 26:3, 32:5).

of the Dtr slave-in-Egypt formula: כי עבד היית בארץ מצרים (5:15), and it
is perhaps composed also in light of Deut 26:5b // Gen 12:10.[165] It may
be that in Persian Yehud, Israel identified herself with the *gēr* in order to
foster a spirit of inclusivism in a period of fragmented identity and widespread land-alienation.[166]

### 5.3.3.5.1. Literary Development of the Israel-as-Gēr-in-Egypt Formula

The literary development of the Israel-as *gēr* formula may be traced in this
way:[167]

1. The early occurrences of the Israel-as-*gēr* motif in the book of Genesis are the source for the Israel-as-*gēr* cluster of texts. Two proto-Genesis,
Israel-as-*gēr* texts occur within the Jacob narrative: Gen 26:3 and 32:5.[168]
Two other proto-Genesis references are found in material connected with
the Abraham tradition: in the Abraham wife-sister narrative and in reference to Lot in the city of Sodom (Gen 12:10, 19:9).[169] (While Gen 15:13
relates to Deut 10:19 and 23:8, all three texts are much later.)

2. The Israel-as-*gēr* motif does not occur in Dtn or in the original CC.
Rather, legislation concerning the *gēr* associates with the Israel-as-slave-
in-Egypt motive clause. Further, while proto-Genesis material uses the
verb גור, legislative texts use the noun גר. Thus the earlier Dtn legislative
material concerning the *gēr* ignores the lexical and conceptual domain of
the proto-Genesis narrative.

3. Deuteronomy 26:5b is assigned to Dtr and is likely the original
*gēr*-in-Egypt expression in legislative texts; its source, Gen 12:10, is proto-

---

165. Critical scholarship is in agreement that Exod 22:21b and Exod 23:9b are
later additions (see, e.g., Na'aman, "Sojourners," 242). The contention that Exod 22:21b
and Exod 23:9b depend upon Deuteronomic development is clarified in that the slave-
in-Egypt formula is distinctively Deuteronomistic.

166. The *gēr* within Persian Yehud is discussed in §§4.7.3 and 6.4.6. Alternatively,
Kidd, suggests that the sixth century exilic experience in Egypt is a likely context for
the formula (*Alterity*, 96–98).

167. This analysis develops upon the discussion of the historical development of
the *gēr* motif in §4.9.

168. For Gen 26:3, see Carr, *Reading*, 177, 205, 257; Carr, *Formation*, 475; for 32:5,
see Carr, *Reading*, 258. Other references in the Jacob story are probably later: 35:27
is likely P; 47:4 is later than the Joseph material that surrounds it (see Carr, *Reading*,
106, 273).

169. Carr designates these as "proto-Genesis" (*Reading*, 306, 339).

Genesis. The three texts Deut 10:19b and Exod 22:21b, 23:9b have identical motive clauses: כי גרים הייתם בארץ מצרים. This is a post-Dtr adaptation of the Dtr slave-in-Egypt formula: כי עבד היית בארץ מצרים (5:15) and is composed in light of Deut 26:5b // Gen 12:10.

### 5.3.3.5.2. Theology and Ethics

Whether viewed through the lens of redaction strata or the final form, the *gēr*-in-Egypt motif is pregnant with theology and ethics. First, Israel's own shift from *gēr* in Egypt to slave nation illustrates the perilous circumstances in which the *gēr* lives: slavery is an ever-present danger. Second, it characterizes Israel's own cultural narrative as one of displacement and vulnerability, with Israel playing the role of guest, dependent upon another nation more powerful and wealthy than they are. Israel is invited to offer to the stranger the welcome that Israel initially received in Egypt and that Israel rightly ought to have received into perpetuity. This is a movement of solidarity. Third, with this motif Yahweh is asserted to be the God of displaced people, for the small credo specifies no prior election of the fathers; the fathers are simply displaced (26:5), and Yahweh hears their cry (26:8). As the God of displaced people, Yahweh also loves the *gēr* within Israel (10:19a), and Yahweh will defend the cause of the *gēr* (10:17b–18).

### 5.4. Third-Year Tithe (Deut 14:28–29, 26:12–15): The *Gēr* as Holy

McConville writes: "The special provision [of the third-year tithe] in verses 28–29 is remarkable—one of the best expressions of Deuteronomy's aim to create a society in which no one would be permanently disadvantaged, or consigned to a second-class status."[170] This section will examine the ways in which the third-year tithe provision may shift the status of the *gēr* by bringing him or her into association with the holy portion. Within the Hebrew Bible, the third-year tithe is present only in Deut 14:28–29 and in the corresponding text, 26:12–15. No tithe is mentioned in the CC (cf. Exod 22:28), and, as Altmann reflects, its presence in the DC demonstrates the capacity of the DC to extend beyond the CC in order to achieve its own goals.[171] The third-year tithe is an innovation of Dtn.[172] Deuter-

---

170. McConville, *Deuteronomy*, 254.
171. Altmann, *Festive*, 220.
172. Mayes, *Deuteronomy*, 244, 246. Mayes argues that 14:22 is an older law on

onomy 26:12–15 appears to be a Dtr development of 14:28–29.[173] The phrase כי תכלה לעשר (26:12aα) links 26:12–15 with 14:28–29. In 14:28–29, the third-year tithe was commanded, and in 26:12–15 the instructions are imagined in their fulfillment.

It appears that the third-year tithe was to be paid in the third and sixth years of a seven-year sabbatical cycle (assuming that there is no tithe in the seventh year). In the third year, produce was to be stored within the community for the ongoing sustenance of landless people. The tithe stipulations are characterized by a distinctive lexical field. Blessing upon agriculture, ברך, is the theological node around which the tithe is transformed (14:24, 29; 26:15).[174] The larger text block, 14:22–29, concerns both the annual tithe and the third-year tithe. The phrase יהוה אלהיך occurs seven times in 14:22–29, highlighting Yahweh as the source of blessing for his people.[175] The verb אכל figures three times, tracing a movement from agricultural blessing to provision for the vulnerable as a play on words: "you will eat" (14:23); "you will eat" (14:26); "they will eat and be satisfied" (14:29). [176]

## 5.4.1. The Tithe in the Ancient Near East

The Deuteronomic provision—for the tithe to be consumed by the household and its associated vulnerable people (14:22–27) and to be stored up for vulnerable people in the third year—is remarkable, given the traditional function of the tithe.[177] Consistent with its etymology, עשר signifies a tax

---

the basis that there is nothing in 24:22 that is distinctively Deuteronomic. Veijola also delineates the original text of the tithe and the third-year tithe to Dtn (*Das 5. Buch Mose*, 305).

173. See further, Mayes, *Deuteronomy*, 335. Altmann suggests that the household consumption of the tithe in the late pre-exilic period is a means of keeping it out of the hands of the Assyrian empire (*Festive*, 229–30).

174. See §5.2.6.3 for a discussion of ברך. Lohfink has observed that ברך is a *leitwort* in the instruction of the tithe, the *smittah* year, firstlings, and festivals, see *Das Hauptgebot: Eine Untersuchung literarischer Einleitungsfragen zu Dtn 5–11*, AB 20 (Rome: Pontifical Biblical Institute, 1963), 83.

175. For heptadic patterning in the DC feasting texts, see the exegesis of 16:1–17 and 26:1–11. Heptadic verbal patterning unifies 14:22–29, with fourteen verbs in governing clauses.

176. Similarly, כול occurs six times in 14:22–29, expressing both the blessing of abundance and abundant generosity and relating the two.

177. For a study of the tithe in ancient Mesopotamia, see Erikki Salonen, *Über*

of one tenth of production.[178] Most commonly in the ancient Near East, tithes were paid to the temple, including tithes of money, produce, animals, and manufactured goods.[179] Temples grew enormously wealthy as a result, in part, of the tithe. Mesopotamian temples were often massive economic establishments owning great estates and commanding thousands of laborers, skilled workers, and clergy. Robert McC. Adams states that the temple to Eanna in Uruk was "surely one of the largest landed economic establishments of the time."[180] A tithe for the poor is not to be found in extant ancient Near Eastern texts.[181] The DC appropriates the tithe, which was traditionally paid to the temple, for inclusive household feasting (14:22–27) and for provision for vulnerable people (14:28–29, 26:12–15).[182] Dandamajew observes that in Old Babylonian texts, not only yield but also social station determined the tithing level, noting in particular that the contribution of the king and his relatives is well below the customary 10 percent.[183] The Deuteronomic tithe texts resist the massive accumulation of wealth that the tithe traditionally secured for the temple elite.[184] As Altmann asserts,

---

*den Zehnten in alten Mesopotamien: Ein Beitrag zur Geschichte der Besteuerung*, StOr 43.4 (Helsinki: Societas Orientalis Fennica, 1972).

178. A. Dandamajew has noted that in Neo-Babylonian texts tithes approximated 10 percent of produce and that some variety of percentage around this mark seems to have been permissible; see "Der Tempelzehnte in Babylonien während des 6.–4. Jh. v.u.Z.," in vol. 1 of *Beiträge zur Alten Geschichte und deren Nachleben: Festschrift für Franz Altheim zum 6. 10. 1968*, 2 vols. (Berlin: de Gruyter, 1969), 82–90.

179. H. Jagersma, "The Tithes in the Old Testament," in *Remembering All the Way: A Collection of Old Testament Studies Published on the Occasion of the Fortieth Anniversary of the Oudtestamentisch Werkgezelschap in Nederland*, ed. B. Albrektson et al., OtSt 21 (Leiden: Brill, 1981), 123.

180. Robert McC. Adams, *Heartland of Cities: Surveys of Ancient Settlements and Land Use on the Central Floodplain of the Euphrates* (Chicago: University of Chicago Press, 1981), 190.

181. Jagersma, "Tithes," 119.

182. Salonen observes that a number of Late Babylonian texts refer to a tithe meal or sacrificial offering (*Zehnten*, 38). H. Jagersma observes an Ugaritic verb *'šr* in connection with eating and drinking, and this may be relevant to the use of עשר in the feasting texts of the DC ("Tithes," 118).

183. Dandamajew, "Tempelzehnte," 85–86.

184. Mayes reflects that the sanctuary in all likelihood always required a contribution for its maintenance (*Deuteronomy*, 224). Just the same, the DC's instructions concerning the tithe, insofar as they were practised, would have drastically reduced the portion of the tithe available for the sanctuary.

"The conception of the Israelites cast here is radically decentralized in this aspect."[185]

## 5.4.2. Divine Gift and the *Gēr*

In a manner of speaking, Deut 14:22–29 describes two meals: the annual tithe feast and the third-year tithe provided for the landless. Comparing the distinctive qualities of these two meals with the aid of anthropological categories is illuminating. Festal meals share with mundane meals the same culinary structure. Meals of different kinds are distinguished, for the most part, by intensity.[186] We might represent the distinctive qualities of the two meals in this way:

Table 5.1: The Annual Tithe and the Third Year Tithe as Meals

|  | Annual Tithe 14:22–27 | Third-Year Tithe 14:28–29 |
| --- | --- | --- |
| meal location | at the sanctuary | localized |
| participants | kinship group with landless | landless |
| kind of meal | ritual (marked) meal | mundane (unmarked) meals |
| quantity of food | intensified | ordinary |
| food types | meat, abundant alcohol | no meat, less alcohol |
| elements of communitas | a pilgrimage feast is shared between the household and their associated vulnerable | no pilgrimage feast; generosity is experienced in the context of a local community (thus the phrase בשעריך) |
| key vocabulary | אכל and שמח | אכל and שבע |

---

185. Altmann, *Festive*, 235 (italics original).

186. Mary Douglas, "Deciphering a Meal," in *Myth, Symbol, and Culture*, ed. Clifford Geertz (New York: Norton, 1971), 68.

The annual tithe (14:22–27) and the third-year tithe (14:28–29, 26:12–15) entail two different departures from general ancient Near Eastern practice: the annual tithe that was customarily paid to the clergy and the crown is transformed into fare for household feasting that includes landless people; and every three years the tithe is to be used exclusively as provision for the landless. While שמח signifies the cultic feasting of the annual tithe, שבע signifies sufficient food for the vulnerable or even their subsistence.

*Lamed*-noun phrases are a primary rhetorical motif in 26:1–15, marking the theological movement of divine gift to the provision for the vulnerable. In 26:1–15 heptadic repetition of the phrase יהוה אלהיך נתן לך foregrounds the divine gift of land and its bounty (see 26:1, 2a, 3b, 9, 10a, 11, 15). Eight *lamed*-noun phrases in 26:12, 13 have a corresponding rhetorical force: ללוי לגר ליתום ולאלמנה (repeated).[187] The resulting association between the divine gift (26:1–11) and the third-year provision (26:12–15) frames the third-year tithe as a response to the very personal and attentive generosity of Yahweh. In both texts concerning the third-year tithe, the landless will ואכלו ושבעו (14:29, 26:12). This reflects Wehmeier's comment that, "as long as the weakest member of the community does not also participate in the fullness of Yahweh's blessing, the promise remains unfulfilled."[188]

## 5.4.3. The Holy Stranger

The consumption of the tithe by all Israel (14:22–27), including the vulnerable, displays Deuteronomy's theology of corporate holiness. In Deuteronomy the priests and the laity alike are holy: עם קדוש אתה ליהוה אלהיך (14:2, 21; cf. 14:1, בנים אתם ליהוה אלהיכם). Corporate holiness is visible, for example, in the laws concerning נבלה. While in the HC only priests are forbidden from eating the נבלה (Lev 22:8), in the DC all Israel is forbidden (14:21). Indeed, "Deuteronomy … makes no distinction between priests

---

187. The lamed prefix is attached to each of the vulnerable groups in 26:12b, indicating that while the tithe is stored within the town, it is ultimately offered to provide for the landless (see also 26:13).

188. G. Wehmeier, "ברך," *TLOT* 1:278–79. שבע forms a couplet with אכל seven times in Deuteronomy, as an expression for being sustained upon the abundance of the land.

and laity in matters concerning holiness."[189] The consumption of the tithe by all Israel epitomizes this theology of corporate holiness. While in the ancient Near East the tithe could be a mere tax,[190] in the DC the tithe is the הקדש (26:13) and is eaten לפני יהוה אלהיך (14:26).[191] Truly, "In Deuteronomy, tithes are considered as a means of having fellowship with God."[192] Further, while in Num 18:21–25 and Lev 27:30–33 the tithe is consumed by the priests alone, in the DC the whole community feasts on the tithe, and in the third year the tithe is consumed by vulnerable people exclusively. The provision of the third-year tithe for the *gēr*, whose membership within the assembly may be in question by virtue of her or his displacement, is remarkable. By participation in the tithe, the stranger is marked as holy and shares in fellowship with Yahweh. Yu rightly reflects that "the fact that aliens are allowed to consume the sacred portion (14:29; 26:13) and participate in the national festivals (16:11, 14) at the single sanctuary is … explained on the ground that they are regarded as members of the covenant community."[193]

Deuteronomy 26:13a–15 is an affirmation of purity and obedience, which the worshiper declares during the offering of the third-year tithe. This affirmation ensures that the worshiper presents this offering for the landless with the reverence and faithfulness that befits a sacred offering, offering the tithe, as it were, to Yahweh himself. The affirmation has two concerns. First, the whole tithe must be provided, with "no skimping."[194] The word כל (26:12) suggests that the tithe is a fixed and recognizable proportion (see also 14:22, 28; cf. 14:29). Second, the worshiper affirms the cultic purity of the tithe. The declaration of 26:13–15 forms a chiasmus.[195] Parallel expressions of Israel's gift (26:13a) and Yahweh's gift (26:15) asso-

---

189. Weinfeld, *Deuteronomy and the Deuteronomic School*, 227. Suee Yan Yu reflects: "D's treatment of the people corresponds to P's treatment of the priests" ("Tithes and Firstlings in Deuteronomy" [PhD diss., Union Theological Seminary, 1997], 88).

190. See, e.g., "Land Grant Along with Tithe Obligations," tran. Michael Heltzer in *COS* 3.82:201.

191. Ian Wilson has established that the phrase לפני יהוה refers to Yahweh's presence (*Out of the Midst*, 197).

192. Yu, "Tithes," 68.

193. Yu, "Tithes," 91–92.

194. Nelson, *Deuteronomy*, 187.

195. See, e.g., Duane Christensen, *Deuteronomy 21:10–34:12*, WBC 6B (Grand Rapids: Zondervan, 2015), 641.

ciate with the theology of the larger section, 26:1–15. The center of the chi-asmus (26:14a) is highlighted structurally and contains three affirmations of the purity of the tithe:

לא אכלתי באני ממנו ולא בערתי ממנו בטמא ולא נתתי ממנו למת

Taken together, the three affirmations address the possibility of rendering the tithe unclean via contact with death. Mourning rituals that involve touching a corpse render a person unclean and are incompatible with the holy nature of the tithe (e.g., Num 19:22). The phrase ולא נתתי ממנו למת may refer to offering food to dead relatives[196] or perhaps a mourning ritual.[197]

This concern with cultic purity is unusual in Deuteronomy. None-theless, Mayes and others who suggest that a question of ritual purity is irrelevant to an offering for the poor are mistaken.[198] Rather, Deut 26:14a highlights the sacred character of the third-year tithe. Other indicators of the sacred nature of the third-year tithe are the formal marker ואמרת לפני יהוה אלהיך (26:13), the designation of the tithe as הקדש (26:13), and the verb בער (26:13).[199] The verb נוח (14:28), which here references present-ing the tithe at the town gates, is a specialized cultic expression for leaving an offering before Yahweh (see also Deut 26:4).[200] Thus, Deut 26:12–15 emphatically affirms that the third-year provision for the landless is "a religious duty like the tithe of the first and second years."[201] Providing for the stranger in this way is a cultic performance, the means of approaching the divine.

---

196. Thedore J. Lewis suggests that the offering may relate to a cult of the dead (*Cults of the Dead in Ancient Israel and Ugarit*, HSM 39 [Atlanta: Scholars Press, 1989], 103).

197. Nelson, *Deuteronomy*, 310. Taken together, the three prohibitions seem most likely to be describing mourning rituals.

198. Mayes, *Deuteronomy*, 336. Cf. Nelson, *Deuteronomy*, 311.

199. בער is used elsewhere for separation from evil (e.g., 13:6; 17:7, 12; 19:19; 21:21), and here it "is carefully chosen to express a rigorous separation" (McConville, *Deuteronomy*, 381).

200. E.g., Exod 16:33, 34; Jud 6:18, 20; 1 Sam 10:25; 1 Kgs 8:9; Ezek 40:42. See further, H. D. Pruess, "נוּחַ," *TDOT* 9:286. McConville helpfully suggests that the con-fession "substitutes for bringing the goods to the sanctuary" (*Deuteronomy*, 380).

201. Tigay, *Deuteronomy*, 242.

## 5.4.4. Solidarity with the Vulnerable through Fasting

> The satiated day is never the greatest.
> The best day is a day of thirst.[202]

A household may have had to fast in order to provide the third-year tithe. Hayden has observed that, in many feasting cultures, fasting is required in order to accumulate the necessary surplus for a feast.[203] Sutton notes that this requisite fasting contributes to a sense of anticipation of the feast.[204] Rosemary Radar categorizes fasts that precede feasting as "preliminary" or "preparatory."[205] Most Israelites must have had to fast in order to supply the third-year tithe, for most Israelites produced at a subsistence level.

The limited paleopathological data available to us indicate a general deficiency in food intake in Iron Age Israel.[206] MacDonald remarks, "Iron Age Israel was no different from earlier and later periods in exhibiting a high level of pathologies that relate to poor nutritional status and acute infection.... The health of the population was far from good."[207] In light of the limited resources of the community, it seems likely that this dynamic of fasting and feasting was present in Israel's harvest feasts. It warrants reflection, then, that the third-year tithe would likely have entailed fasting not in order to feast but in order to provide for the landless.

The question then arises: What is the significance of fasting that is engaged for the sustenance of others? It would seem that voluntary fasting that was not rewarded with feasting but rather with the opportunity to give to those in need must have been charged with symbolism. André Möller has highlighted the joy of fasting in certain cultures.[208] The themes of divine blessing (14:22–29) and of land gift (26:1–15) suggest that for the DC a season of fasting with the prospect of sharing the blessing could be

---

202. Karin Boye, *To a Friend*, trans. J. Nunn (Hull: Voice, 1985), cited in André Möller, *Ramadam in Java: The Joy and Jihad of Ritual Fasting* (Lund: Department of History and Anthropology of Religions Lund University, 2007), 5.

203. "People will essentially fast for weeks or months before a feast in order to have more food to distribute at the feast" (Brian Hayden, e-mail message to author, 6 June 2013).

204. Sutton, *Remembrance*, 29.

205. Rosemary Rader, "Fasting," *ER* 5:287.

206. See MacDonald, *Eat*, 57–60.

207. MacDonald, *Eat*, 85–86.

208. Möller, *Ramadam*, 380–81.

filled with joy. Van Gennep describes rituals that precede feasting as "pre-liminal," or "rites of separation."[209] For Israel, the experience of want that preceded the third-year tithe offering had the potential to produce a visceral and empathic connection with the landless that eroded status lines, forging solidarity. It also would have evoked memory of Israel's earlier status as *gēr* and slave (26:5b–10), reminding worshipers that "one does not live by bread alone but by everything that proceeds from the mouth of Yahweh" (8:3). This practice was repeated every three years, contributing to what Sutton calls the "sensory experience of calendar customs."[210]

## 5.5. Locations for Inclusion

With the above exegesis in mind, we turn to explore some social locations for the inclusion of the *gēr*, also exploring how such inclusion may have transformed the community itself, challenging settled relations and identities.

### 5.5.1. Social Archaeology and the *Gēr*: Rural or Urban?

The process of reconstructing the objectives of legislation in Deuteronomy is influenced by the imagined social setting for these laws, the question of rural and urban environments being one significant variable.[211] While scholarship often comments on the effect of urbanization upon the society that Deuteronomy addresses, the evidence from Deuteronomy's response to the *gēr* suggests a more moderated view. In the following description I rely in particular upon the conclusions of Avraham Faust, and alternative views will be referenced in the notes.

In the seventh century, Judah's rural countryside comprised many farms and a few villages. The large majority of rural habitations were of the four-room house variety, and these averaged around 130 square meters in size.[212] Based upon cross-cultural data, a dwelling of this size likely housed around thirteen people, and it is likely that these relatively large dwellings housed an extended family (as observed above).[213] Farms tended to con-

---

209. Arnold van Gennep, *The Rites of Passage* (London: Routledge & Kegan Paul, 1960), 21.

210. Möller, *Remembrance*, 30.

211. I am grateful for Avraham Faust's comments on an earlier draft of this section.

212. Faust, *Archaeology*, 160, 176, 206.

213. Naroll suggests an allowance of 10 square meters per person ("Floor," cited

tain one or a small number of four-room houses, and farms were probably generally inhabited by one extended family.[214] Faust analyses the tendency of villages to have large production facilities, such as oil production
installations, storage facilities, and terrace systems, concluding that the
number of such facilities in most villages "indicates organization beyond
the extended family." Village communities operated as "protective associations of families" and were united by a common genealogy that may have
been more or less fictitious.[215] Rural residents shared a higher standard
of living than urban residents, and this difference is displayed in the size
and the quality of dwellings. Faust, Stager, and others challenge much of
the scholarship that emphasizes the poverty of the rural sector in the late
Judahite monarchy.[216]

Archaeology of cities in Judah and in Israel during the eighth and
seventh centuries presents a strikingly different picture from that of rural
settlements. Housing density in the cities was congested. The houses of
the elite were larger and grander, and they likely housed extended families along with slaves. The majority of the houses in cities, however, were
between 40 and 70 square meters in size, of the three-room design, and
large enough for only four to seven people. Scholars generally agree that
these smaller dwellings would have housed one nuclear family. These
smaller houses were the dwellings of the laboring class that formed the
majority of urban populations. The urban economies were household
based, and poorer dwellings often had small production facilities within
them.[217] The significant wealth inequality in the cities suggests that the
state acquired the surplus production of the poorer households.

---

in Faust, *Archaeology*, 110). While there are other views regarding this density coeffi-
cient, I follow Naroll and Faust in this discussion. Divergence in the scholarship does
not make a substantial difference to my argument.

214. Faust, *Archaeology*, 175. Z. Safrai argues that one isolated habitation is more
likely to be occupied by an extended family than by a nuclear family; see "Ancient
Field Structures: The Village in Eretz Israel During the Roman Period," *Cathedra* 89
(1998): 38, cited in Faust, *Archaeology*, 175.

215. Gottwald, *Tribes*, 257; Faust, *Archaeology*, 165–66, 173.

216. Faust, *Archaeology*, 174; Bendor, *Social Structure*, 216–24. For the view that
kinship structures are retained in the late monarchy, see Faust, *Archaeology*, 162;
Schloen, *House*; Na'aman, "Sojourners," 276 n. 99. For an opposing view, see Halpern,
"Jerusalem and the Lineages," 71–89.

217. Faust, *Archaeology*, 42, 80, 109, 111–13.

Certainly some texts in Deuteronomy seem to be addressing an urban environment. The appointment of judges (1:16), for example, diminishes the priority of kinship structures in a way that more naturally applies to cities than the rural countryside.[218] Nonetheless, the feasting texts project a society where many of those designated *gēr* likely dwelled under the same roof as the nuclear family. However, this arrangement would have been difficult or impossible for most of the families that dwelled within the smaller urban dwellings described above.[219] Also, the surplus produce required for the feasting described in Deuteronomy—feasting that also included the vulnerable (14:22–27, 16:1–17, 26:1–11)—would likely have been more than a poor urban nuclear family could manage. Most urban households probably could not include the *gēr* in the way envisaged in Deuteronomy.[220] Moreover, in the aftermath of the invasion of Sennacharib in 701 BCE, few cities existed in Judah, apart from Jerusalem.[221] For these reasons, it seems likely that Deuteronomy's feasting texts, and other social law that envisages the *gēr* dwelling within a household, addresses a rural environment. At the risk of overgeneralizing, it is possible that cities had the capacity to supply charity for the *gēr*, whereas clan-based rural settlements had the capacity for their full familial inclusion within a household and within a settlement.

This analysis also allows us to revisit the meaning of the phrase "within your gates."

## 5.5.2. "Within Your Gates"

The phrase בשעריך in the social laws of Dtn refers to the protective circumference of a town, a city, and a local village. The *gēr* is said to be בשעריך

---

218. See ch. 4 for a full discussion of judicial law in Deuteronomy.

219. To be sure, elite household buildings in cities were large enough to house vulnerable people. However, Deuteronomy does not address the urban elite exclusively but the whole population of Israel, as McConville has demonstrated ("Singular Address"). Thus, it is better to see these laws as addressing the circumstances of rural settlements, in particular.

220. The urban elite certainly had the capacity to fulfil the demand for inclusivism within the household, and Deuteronomy extends this demand to them also.

221. Due to the invasion of 701 BCE, and in particular to the decimation of the Shaphelah, the population was concentrated within and around Jerusalem, and we may assume that the rural population would have been co-opted for massive rebuilding projects in urban centres such as Lachish and Ramat Rahel.

seven times in Deuteronomy (5:14; 14:21, 29; 16:14; 24:14; 26:12; 31:12). The gate is basic to pre-Dtn family law, and it is "one of the pillars" of Dtn.[222]

Jack R. Lundbom reflects a common assumption when he states, "'Gates' in the OT is a synecdoche for '(walled) cities.'"[223] This is at least partially inaccurate, however, as we have seen that many of the social laws address a rural context rather than an urban one (see §5.5.1). Indeed, there were many different kinds of walls in ancient Israel, including low walls around farms and settlements to contain animals, thin walls around villages to deter raiders (that often joined with the walls of dwellings),[224] and high and thick walls of large cities (the Jerusalem wall is over 7 meters thick at the western hill). As there were many kinds of walls, so there were many kinds of gates.[225] The word שער is used in Deuteronomy to refer to city gates (e.g., perhaps 14:29), the gates of provincial towns (e.g., probably 16:18), and the gates of villages and farms (e.g., perhaps 5:14, 16:14, 22:24, 24:14–15, 25:7–9, 31:12).[226]

It is well known that the gate was the civic center of Israelite *cities*. The city gate was the place of assembly, legal procedure, commerce, and worship. Otto notes that Akkadian *bābtu(m)* operates in a similar way to the Hebrew שער, referring to a local district within a city or the community of people within.[227] In Israel and in the ancient Near East, the city gate was the place where the poor gathered to receive charity, to find work, or to seek justice (Amos 5:12).[228] Similarly, in a village context the gate had a social and a symbolic function. In Deuteronomy, the elders judge disputes

---

222. Otto, "שער," 15:382. The phrase בשעריך is distinctive to Deuteronomy, occurring sixteen times here; the three other occurrences in the Hebrew Bible are almost certainly appropriated from Deuteronomy.

223. Lundbom, *Deuteronomy*, 286; see similarly Sneed, "Israelite," 501. Achenbach's contention that, "The gate is a symbol for the realm where Jewish jurisdiction is acknowledge by the Persians and where it is accepted as valid," does not fit with the variety of references for שער in Deuteronomy (Achenbach, "gêr," 36 n. 26); Albertz is unusual in his interpreting בשעריך rightly as referring to a settlement ("Aliens," 56).

224. Faust, *Archaeology*, 149, 167–68. Low walls were common around farms (149). There is explicit reference to the settlement of an extended family in Judg 18:16–17.

225. Sandra Richter made this point to me in a personal communication, 2014.

226. For scholarship that reflects the present analysis, see Faust, *Archaeology*, 168, and citations there.

227. Faust, *Archaeology*, 367–68.

228. See further, Faust, *Archaeology*, 100, 105–6; Otto, "שער," 15:395.

and deliver punishment at the village gate (25:7–9). The village gate is symbolic for shelter and succor for the vulnerable (16:14). The third-year tithe is stored בשעריך (perhaps primarily a reference to a larger township or city, 14:29), the fleeing slave may reside בשעריך (23:16–17), and the laboring *gēr* resides בשעריך (24:14).[229] These references demonstrate that the phrase בשעריך in Deuteronomy can operate by synecdoche as a reference to a whole village and to the protective shelter that the village offers for the vulnerable.[230] Therefore, the formula is not merely a reference of location but is a key motif in Deuteronomy's semantics of inclusion, an "integration formula,"[231] in Otto's words.

The phrase בשעריך also has a genealogical reference, as Otto explains:

> Like the suffixes in the list of members of the nuclear family and their slaves in 12:18; 16:11, 14, the suffix added to *ša'ar* in the integration formula shows clearly that this lexeme … has not only a local connotation but also a genealogical connotation, in the sense of "clan" or "extended family" (cf. Ruth 3:11; 4:10).[232]

This gentilic association of אשר בשעריך, indicated by the second-person suffix, hints at the inclusion of the *gēr* within the clan grouping. In this vein, Faust asserts that the gate is a "liminal space," a "transitional space," between a place outside the community and full participation in the community.[233] In Deuteronomy's social laws, then, the gate is not an exclusionary boundary but a demarcation of responsibility. The gate is the social perimeter within which the *gēr* finds economic support, social support, and social and religious identity.

---

229. In a settlement, the threshing floor may have played this role as a place of public assembly and of legal proceedings (Otto, "שַׁעַר," 15:396).

230. Similarly Otto, "שַׁעַר," 15:367–68. The protective sense of the phrase בשעריך explains the fact that the נכרי is never said to be בשעריך. This does not signify that the נכרי does not dwell within the community; rather the נכרי is not dependent upon the protection and generosity of the community.

231. Otto, "שַׁעַר," 15:378.

232. Faust, *Archaeology,* 380.

233. Faust, *Archaeology,* 107–8.

### 5.5.3. Being/Becoming Israel

Finally, we consider the implications of the inclusion of the *gēr* in cultic feasting for Deuteronomy's vision for Israel as the people of Yahweh. Otto articulates the basic need of the *gēr*: "The landless and their families needed to be integrated into the clans."[234] By virtue of being incorporated locally, within a household and a clan, the *gēr* is also incorporated into the nation, the people of Yahweh (which is also conceived of in terms of kinship), as the people appear לפני יהוה אלהיך. Indeed, this Deuteronomic requirement entails appearing alongside the stranger and other vulnerable people. Cultic worship has an explicitly inclusive and incorporative dimension, and attempts to worship Yahweh, the divine kinsperson, that do not also embrace the vulnerable "other" as kin are unacceptable.

However, as Israel reaches out to displaced people, it is not only the stranger who may be transformed in the encounter. Identity is never fixed; rather, it is created through culture and practice. Such inclusivism contests and defines what it means to be/become Israel: Israel always remains a redeemed community, a receiving community. Israel becomes cohesive as the family of Yahweh only as it accepts both the disruption and the opportunity that comes from embracing the other. Israel is not to see itself as a nation among nations but as a family of ex-slaves, an inclusive and celebrating community into which Yahweh can incorporate those whom Yahweh emancipates. Such a conclusion is dramatically in contrast with the reigning discursive binary that views the *gēr* as a foreigner who ought to receive Israel's charity and hospitality and Israel as the unchanging host nation.

One wonders how the author(s) first imagined such a response to displacement—for the vulnerable stranger to be included within the household, the clan, and the nation, as kin. Perhaps this innovation had twin roots, both in theological reflection and also in practical examples of inclusivism that the author(s) had observed. As for practical examples, a modern analogue would be the thousands of households in Lebanon who have offered a home to Syrian refugees during the Syrian civil war. Perhaps the author observed such hospitality in ancient times, and perhaps in light of such hospitality, and also on the basis of Israel's own adoption by

---

234. Otto, "שַׁעַר," 15:380.

Yahweh, their divine kinsperson, the author(s) revised the cultic calendar (cf. Exod 23:14–17) according to an ethic of inclusivism.

### 5.5.4. The Rights, Responsibilities, and Practices of Kinsfolk

If we allow that the goal of Deuteronomy regarding the *gēr* is for inclusion of the *gēr* as kinsfolk, then the experiences, benefits, and obligations that the authors of Deuteronomy ultimately envisage for the *gēr* are identical to the experiences, benefits, and obligations of kinsfolk. *Ultimately* is an important qualifier, as the *gēr* in Deuteronomy is a liminal figure, on the cusp of inclusion within the community. So, Deuteronomy is concerned more with practices that foster inclusion than with the full ramifications of inclusion. Nonetheless, in Deuteronomy the obligations due to the *gēr* are nothing less than familial rights and familial obligations. So, explicitly in the text, judicial justice is stipulated both for the "brother" and also for the *gēr* (1:16–17), and both the *gēr* and the "brother" shall be paid on the day of their work (24:14–15). Most important, the *gēr* is included within household cultic feasting. We may list other customary rights and duties of kinsfolk, some of which are not made explicit in Deuteronomy concerning the *gēr* but which nonetheless unfold the full implications of Deuteronomy's vision for the inclusion of the *gēr*:

1. Kinsfolk may be grafted into a genealogy, into the formative stories of a community (see exegesis of 29:10–12 in §5.3).[235]
2. Kinsfolk-in-blood share a connection to the land (the *gēr* is intertwined with Deuteronomy's land theology; see the exegesis of 24:19–22 in §2.4).
3. "Kinsfolk are expected to be loving, just and generous to one another and not to demand strictly equivalent return of one another" (compare the social law, discussed in ch. 3).[236]
4. Kinsfolk are subject to the paterfamilias and to the elders.
5. Kinsfolk share an obligation to provide mourning rites and burial or inhumation for the corpses of their dead.[237] (Saul M.

---

235. Cross, *Epic*, 7.

236. Meyer Fortes, *Kinship and the Social Order*, cited in Cross, *Epic*, 5.

237. See further Gabriel Barkay, "Burial Caves and Burial Practices in Judah in the Iron Age," in *Graves and Burial Practices in Israel in the Ancient Period* [Hebrew],

      Olyan gives examples from the Hebrew Bible of the obligation
to offer rites for the dead between fictive kindred.[238])

6.   Kinsfolk share an obligation to provide protection and military solidarity, both in defense and in offense.[239]

Fundamentally, kinship is experienced as a mutuality of being, as Sahlins
states: "Kinsmen are people who live each other's lives and die each other's
deaths. To the extent they lead common lives, they partake of each other's
sufferings and joys, sharing one another's experiences even as they take
responsibility for and feel the effects of each other's acts."[240]

## 5.6. Conclusion

In the ancient Near East, the *gēr*, fatherless, and widow commonly offered
cheap labor in order to survive. Despite reform efforts to the contrary,
the vulnerable would often be exploited and forced into semifree bonded
arrangements or into slavery. Deuteronomy's feasting texts intervene in
these potentially exploitative relationships, implicitly asking: What kind
of relationship ought the *gēr* share within the community, with the land,
and with Yahweh?

    The feasting texts answer this question in three ways. We observed
first that the festival calendar (16:1–17) transforms relationships between
the *gēr* and the landed in the direction of kinship. Second, in the Festival
of Firstfruits (26:1–11) an ethic of inclusion for the *gēr* is embedded in
Israel's own formative narrative of wandering and vulnerability. Third, the
provision of the third-year tithe for the *gēr* (14:28–29, 26:12–15) signifies
the holiness of the stranger, demonstrating that the *gēr* also belongs to the
people of Yahweh.

    The intention of Deuteronomy's feasts to effect social change may be
seen in the distinctive character of these feasting texts, vis-à-vis ancient

---

ed. Itamar. Singer (Jerusalem: Yad Izhak Ben Zvi/Israel Exploration Society, 1994),
96–164.

    238. Saul M. Olyan, "The Roles of Kin and Fictive Kin in Biblical Representations
of Death Ritual," in *Family and Household and Religion: Toward a Synthesis of Old Testament Studies, Archaeology, Epigraphy, and Cultural Studies*, ed. Rainer Albertz and
Rüdiger Schmitt (Winona Lake, IN: Eisenbrauns, 2012), 257–61.

    239. See further Cross, *Epic*, 4.

    240. Sahlins, *What Kinship Is*, 28.

Near Eastern feasting texts. While ancient Near Eastern texts describe the dining practices of the gods or their sponsored elite, the DC feasting texts center on the household, and the participation of vulnerable people is dominant. Also, Turner's research on communitas helps to clarify that in Deuteronomy's pilgrimage feasts kinship was to be experienced, through which the vulnerable were included within a kinship grouping as family. Deuteronomy's vision for the *gēr* is that she or he ultimately was to become grafted into the household, the clan, and the nation, as kinsfolk. Regarding this third social domain of the nation, the study now turns to investigate the *gēr* within Deuteronomy's framework (Deut 1–11, 27–34), where the grouping of all Israel is dominant.

# 6

# The *Gēr* in Deuteronomy's Framework
## (Deut 1–12, 27–34)

### 6.1. Introduction

This chapter investigates the *gēr* in the framing texts of Deuteronomy, chapters 1–11, 27–34. Chapters 3, 4, and 5 have examined the *gēr* within various subgroups of law in Deuteronomy, exploring the economic participation of the *gēr* in social law (ch. 4), protection in legal disputes via the law of judicial procedure (ch. 4), and the incorporation of the *gēr* into the households and the clans via cultic feasting (ch. 5). This chapter studies the *gēr* in Deuteronomy's framework, focusing especially on texts that position the *gēr* in relation to all Israel. In particular, we will be alert to the ways in which the *gēr* may be being incorporated within the kinship grouping of all Israel and of its divine kinsperson.

In an effort to be sensitive to the various subgroupings of law in Deuteronomy, I have already examined 1:16–17 and 10:17–19 as law of judicial procedure, and I have examined the Sabbath law (5:12–15) as social law. In this way I have attended to the distinctive contributions of each legal subgroup as well as to the intertextuality within each group. Deuteronomy 10:17–19 is explored a second time in this chapter in terms of covenant and kinship.

The theme of the inclusion of the *gēr* is intensified in the framing chapters of Deut 1–11, 27–34 vis-à-vis the law corpus. A call for just judicial procedure for the *gēr* is the foremost stipulation in the book (1:17–19). The Sabbath command stipulates rest for the *gēr* (5:12–15). The *gēr* also appears in two texts that frame the law corpus (10:17–19, 27:19), and the *gēr* is included within the covenant-renewal ceremony (29:9–14) and within the seventh-year reading of Torah ritual (31:9–13). In the frame of Deuteronomy, other vulnerable categories of people recede into the background, and the inclusion of the stranger becomes the prominent social issue.[1]

Deuteronomy's framework locates Israel as poised on the brink of the land. This geographical crisis point is also a point of decision: to be faithful or to not be faithful, to worship the one true God or to worship other gods and thereby abandon the life of justice and generosity that Yahweh has set out in his Torah.[2] The *gēr* plays a dual role in this drama, appearing both as one who is enfolded within the covenant with Yahweh (29:9–14) and as one to whom justice and inclusion are due as a matter of covenant faithfulness (27:19).

Lohfink points to a striking distinction between Deuteronomy and the Laws of Hammurabi in regard to their framing material. In Deuteronomy, both the frame and the law corpus envision a community without poverty. Within the Laws of Hammurabi, however, while the prologue and the epilogue praise the justice of the king, the law corpus itself contains little or no social law. "Suppose an 'oppressed man,' or an orphan or a widow, following Hammurabi's advice, went to Esagila and read the 282 paragraphs of the lawcode proper. They would not find even a single occurrence of the words 'poor' or 'oppressed.'"[3] Lohfink concludes that these references to justice in the Laws of Hammurabi are royal propaganda. However, "Deuteronomy, in opposition to the Mesopotamian laws, is not silent about the poor.... in harmony with the Exodus narrative, it sketches out a world where there are no longer any poor."[4]

### 6.1.1. Composition History

Scholars agree that Deut 1–11, 27–34 postdates the law corpus.[5] For one, the frame is not a revision of the CC, as is the DC. Rather, the frame is dependent upon the DC, as I will show. The framing texts of Deuteronomy have a distinct lexical and conceptual domain vis-à-vis the law corpus. Some key characteristics of Dtr texts are a relative absence of the central-

---

1. Though there is reference to slaves (5:12–15) and to the vulnerable triad (10:17–18, 27:19).

2. See further McConville and Millar, *Time and Place,* 44.

3. Lohfink, "Poverty," 43.

4. Lohfink, "Poverty," 46.

5. For an analytical demarcation between Dtn and Dtr, see Otto, *Das Deuteronomium: Politische Theologie,* 238–351.

ization formula, the pronominal suffix form for *gēr*, a focus on all Israel, the plural address,[6] and a narrowed social concern that focuses on displacement. Nonetheless, assigning texts to redactional layers is an uncertain task, not least because the reuse of earlier motifs is common.[7] I have argued that Dtr may possibly be assigned to the exile and post-Dtr to the postexilic period.[8] A sign of postexilic dating may be an association with other postexilic texts. A social profile of the exilic period was briefly outlined in §2.7.5; a social profile of Persian Yehud is offered in §§4.7.3 and 6.4.5.1.

## 6.1.2. The Content and Structure of This Chapter

This analysis of the *gēr* in Deuteronomy's frame will focus on five key themes. More specifically, this chapter will:

1. explore the ways in which *gēr* may be incorporated within the kinship grouping of all Israel and its divine kinsperson. We have seen that Dtn fosters the grafting of the *gēr* into the clan and into the household. Deuteronomy's framework concerns the kinship grouping of all Israel.[9]
2. interrogate the common assumption that the *gēr* should be identified according to a supposed dialectic between the native and the nonnative.
3. interrogate the consensus opinion that the frame texts demonstrate an unprecedented religious inclusivism for the *gēr* in Deuteronomy.
4. inquire into the social-historical context for the widespread displacement of Dtr and of post-Dtr.
5. investigate the possibility that at the heart of Deuteronomy is a movement toward being/becoming the family of Yahweh.

---

6. On the plural address as a characteristic of Dtr, see Mayes, *Deuteronomy*, 237; Veijola, *Das 5. Buch Mose*, 295.

7. E.g., the use of the Dtn formula of the vulnerable triad in 27:19.

8. See, on dating, §§1.3.3, 4.9, 6.1.1. Many scholars distinguish between an early exilic Horeb redaction (Deut 4:45; 5; 9–10; 27; 28) and a later exilic Moab redaction that emphasizes the imminence of return to the land (1–3, 29–30); e.g., Otto, *Deuteronomium*, 243–48. Alexander Rofé defends a pre-eight century date for the original text of much of the frame ("Covenant," 269–80).

9. Within the DC, the *gēr* is grafted into all Israel in the feasting texts, as described in §5.2.

These five themes will be investigated via a detailed exegesis of texts concerning the *gēr* in Deuteronomy's framework: 10:17–19, 29:9–14, and 31:9–13. The appearance of the *gēr* in the curse texts (27:19, 28:43–44) is treated more briefly. Following this exegesis, the chapter explores the dialectic of external and internal boundaries in Deuteronomy. Two texts from the frame of Deuteronomy that have been examined in previous chapters will not reappear here (1:16–17, 5:12–15).

## 6.2. Divine Kingship, Divine Kinship (Deut 10:12–11:1)

### 6.2.1. Introduction

The section 10:12–11:1 is a unit framed by the phrase "and now" (10:12a, 22b) and by the word אהב (10:12, 11:1).[10] The section begins with a rhetorical question that echoes Mic 6:8, "So, now, O Israel, what does Yahweh your God require of you?" (10:12a), introducing the social concern of the section. The formulaic "fear-love-serve" exhortation constitutes the outer frame of a chiasm. The specific covenant stipulations at the center of the passage concern the *gēr* in particular. On a sequential reading of Deuteronomy, the triad of the vulnerable appears for the first time here, though the formulaic sequence והגר והיתום והאלמנה is interrupted.[11] The larger section, 10:12–11:31, is a cohesive speech that operates as a transition text, both as an abstract of what has preceded and as an introduction to the law, preparing for life in the land. Motifs from ancient Near Eastern covenant treaties are found throughout this text, though the overall form of ancient Near Eastern treaty texts is not followed. I have demonstrated that 10:17b–18 characterizes Yahweh as the guarantor of just judicial processes for the most vulnerable (see §4.3). "Loving" the *gēr* must include the provision of a fair hearing and a fair judgment for the *gēr*. The present analysis will take as demonstrated the function of 10:17b–18 as judicial law[12] and will focus instead upon the *gēr* within the covenant.

---

10. With McConville, *Deuteronomy*, 197. Scholars dispute the limits of this section. Lohfink takes 10:12–11:17 as a unit, interpreting the section as a covenant formulary (*Hauptgebot*, 219).

11. Thomas Krapf, "Traditionsgeschichtliches zum deuteronomischen Fremdling-Waise-Witwe-Gebot," *VT* 34 (1984): 89.

12. See the analysis at §4.3.

Regarding composition history, Mayes suggests that 10:12–11:32 was likely authored as a unit, perhaps in connection with 4:1–40, dating most of the text to Dtr.[13] Similarly, Veijola assigns 10:12–11:32 to Dtr, taking 10:14–11:1 and 11:29–30 as secondary.[14] Otto, however, observes the many parallels between 10:12–11:30 and postexilic texts, including the close correlation between the command to love the *gēr* and a similar command in the HC at Lev 19:34, and he assigns most of the unit to the postexilic *Fortschreibung* of Deuteronomy (excepting 11:18–21a, 11:31–32).[15] My argument for the dependence of 10:19 (כי גרים הייתם בארץ מצרים) upon Gen 15:13, which is most commonly designated as late non-P material, supports Otto's conclusion.[16] Against Kidd, Lohfink, and others, Deut 10:19 is not an interpolation,[17] for there is no discrepancy in the textual sequence. Further, 10:19a reflects the peculiar focus upon the *gēr* of Dtr and post-Dtr vis-à-vis other vulnerable categories. If 10:19 were an addition, then 10:18 would be the only occurrence of *gēr* in all of Deuteronomy where the *responsibility* of the community is omitted. The following analysis will examine the use of אהב in relation to the *gēr*.

## 6.2.2. Love

Deuteronomy 10:12–11:1 is unified by five occurrences of the verb אהב. In the center, the word אהב appears three times in related assertions: Yahweh loves Israel, Yahweh loves the *gēr*, Israel is to love the *gēr*. These assertions are structurally central, determined by the chiastic structure of 10:12–11:1 and also by the plural address, which highlights the Moab generation (and, in the time of the narrator, the addressees) as covenant participants and as hearers of the law (10:15–19).[18] The three central occurrences are:

רק באבתיך חשק יהוה לאהבה אותם :10:15a

---

13. See further, Mayes, *Deuteronomy*, 208–9.

14. Otto, *Deuteronomium*, 244–45.

15. See Otto, "Deuteronomy and Numbers," 391; Otto, *Deuteronomium*, 1003–72.

16. See the discussion of Gen 15:13 in §5.3.3.5.

17. Kidd, *Alterity*, 78–81; also Mayes, *Deuteronomy*, 211; Lohfink, *Hauptgebot*, 223, and n. 14; Alfred Cholewiński, *Heiligkeitsgesetz und Deuteronomium: Eine vergleichende Studie*, AB 66 (Rome: Pontifical Biblical Institute, 1976), 275.

18. On this interpretation of the *Numeruswechsel* in Deut 4, see further Otto, *Deuteronomium*, 523–32.

10:18b: ואהב גר לתת לו לחם ושמלה

10:19:   ואהבתם את הגר כי גרים הייתם בארץ מצרים

Three related references of the verb אהב, when it is used in the context of a covenant, are attested in the scholarship. I will examine how all three senses operate in 10:17b–18 and contribute to Deuteronomy's vision for the inclusion of the *gēr*. The social institutions of kinship and politics are central and unifying: (1) אהב and the covenant; (2) אהב and kinship; (3) אהב and emotions.

### 6.2.2.1. אהב and the Covenant

William L. Moran demonstrated in a seminal article that אהב in Deuteronomy belongs to the ancient Near Eastern terminology of international relations.[19] A great king had the responsibility to love his vassal, and a vassal had the responsibility to love the suzerain as a loyal servant. Also, subjects must love their king.[20] This is "a love defined by and pledged in the covenant—a covenantal love."[21] This covenant love characterizes three relationships in 10:15–19. First, love in 10:12–11:1 is an obligation of the covenant between Yahweh and Israel (10:15, 21). Israel's obligation to keep the covenant is related to fearing Yahweh, serving him (a key term in ancient Near Eastern treaties), and walking in his ways (10:12, 20).[22]

Second, Yahweh loves the *gēr*. The clearest connection between Yahweh's love for Israel and his love for the *gēr* is their shared vulnerability (10:19b).[23] The assertion that Yahweh has made a covenant with the *gēr* may be the strongest expression of Yahweh's commitment to the stranger in the Hebrew Bible. Analogous to ancient Near Eastern treaties, this covenant commitment also entails Yahweh's opposition to all those who would

---

19. William L. Moran, "The Ancient Near Eastern Background for the Love of God in Deuteronomy," *CBQ* 25 (1963): 77–87. As Cross and others have demonstrated, the language of ancient Near Eastern covenants is taken from language of kinship (Cross, *Epic*, 6–7).

20. Moran, "Ancient Near Eastern Background," 80.

21. Moran, "Ancient Near Eastern Background," 78.

22. See further Bill T. Arnold, "The Love-Fear Antinomy in Deuteronomy 5–11," *VT* 61 (2011): 551–69.

23. See, too, Jacqueline E. Lapsley, "Feeling our Way: Love for God in Deuteronomy," *CBQ* 65 (2003): 362. Though, Yahweh's choice of Israel ultimately defies explanation (7:9, 10:14–15).

oppose a *gēr*, even as a suzerain typically would pledge military protection for his vassal.[24] Yahweh hears the cry of the *gēr*, Yahweh blesses those who bless the *gēr*, and Yahweh curses the *gēr*'s oppressors (24:13, 15).

Third, Israel is to love the *gēr*. Critically, the general admonitions to obedience that frame the text are made specific in the requirement to "love the *gēr*" in the center. This stipulation is also couched in terms of a covenant, for the syntax frames Israel's love for the *gēr* as a logical consequence of Yahweh's love for the *gēr*:

> For Yahweh is God of gods … the one who loves the stranger … so you are to love the stranger.

The *waqtl* form ואהבתם follows the participle ואהב, designating a logically consequent situation with volitional force.[25] Israel's love is consequent upon Yahweh's love, and presumably this is also the same *kind* of love. Some ancient Near Eastern treaties contain stipulations concerning the relationship between two vassals of a great king that evinces a triangular relationship:

> Whoever is My Majesty's friend should also be your friend; whoever is My Majesty's enemy should also be your enemy.[26]

Somewhat analogous to this, both Israel and the *gēr* are covenant partners with Yahweh, the great king, and Israel has a concomitant responsibility toward the *gēr*, Yahweh's "friend." The stipulation that Israel is to show covenant love to the *gēr* requires that attributes such as permanence, faithfulness, and loyalty characterize the relationship between a local household and settlement and the *gēr*.

---

24. See, e.g., "Treaty between Šuppiluliuma and Aziru," trans. Itamar Singer, *COS* 2.17A:94: "Or if someone oppresses Azira, either […] or anyone else, and you send to the king of Hatti (saying): '[Come] to my rescue!' then I, My Majesty, will [come to your] aid…."

25. The situation is indefinite, requiring the *waw* + suffix conjugation instead of *waw* + prefix conjugation following the participle. See further Waltke and O'Connor, *Syntax*, §32.2.5.

26. "Treaty between Šuppiluliuma and Aziru," *COS* 2.17A:94.

## 6.2.2.2. אהב and Kinship

Second, the word אהב references kinship. Following upon (and partly in reaction to) Moran's work, Dennis J. McCarthy suggested that the father-son relationship is a part of the conceptuality of covenant both in the Hebrew Bible and in ancient Near Eastern treaties.[27] Indeed, the deity is the divine kinsperson, visible in West Semitic theophorous names: *'abī-'Il*, "my father is 'El."[28] To enter a covenant is "to enter another bond of blood and also to take the partner into one's own."[29] Thus, international treaty texts often express the brother-sisterhood between the citizens of two nations (cf. Amos 1:9). Kings may refer to one another as "brothers."[30] Kinship terminology and "love" are interchangeable expressions for the relationship between rulers.[31]

Kinship is the plane across which the love statements are moving in 10:12–11:1. First, in Deuteronomy Yahweh loves Israel as the divine father (e.g., 1:31, 10:15).[32] Second, we may infer that Yahweh's אהב for the *gēr* includes his assuming the role of the paterfamilias, supplying the *gēr* with the kinship protection and the group identification that the *gēr* lacks (לתת לו לחם ושמלה, 10:18b).[33] Third, we may infer that the command for Israel to "love" the *gēr* is nothing less than an instruction to enfold the stranger as kin (10:19). Together Yahweh, Israel, and the *gēr* form a triangle of kinship relations, representing Israel's adoption of the *gēr* as kin as a most sacred affair, an affair upon which Israel's own sonship is predicated (e.g., 29:24).

---

27. "The very ancient Israelite concept of Israel as Yahweh's son is very close to or even identical with the Deuteronomic conception articulated in terms of the treaty or covenant and should not be separated entirely from it" (Dennis J. McCarthy, "Notes on the Love of God in Deuteronomy and the Father-Son Relationship between Yahweh and Israel," *CBQ* 27 [1965]: 145). See 1:31, 8:5, 14:1.

28. Cross, *Epic*, 6.

29. Gottfried Quell, "διαθήκη," *TDNT* 2:114.

30. See, e.g., "Treaty Between Šuppiluliuma and Aziru" (*COS* 2.17A).

31. See further Moran, "Love," 79. See, e.g., "The Treaty of Tudḫaliya IV with Kurunta of Tarḫuntašša on the Bronze Tablet Found in Ḫattuša," trans. Harry A. Hoffner Jr., *COS* 2.18:100–106, esp. §14.

32. The obedience required of Israel often appears within the rubric of Yahweh as Israel's father (10:12, 20); see McCarthy, "Notes," 146.

33. Hiebert observes regarding the widow that Yahweh plays the role of the (missing) male kin ("Whence Shall Help," 137).

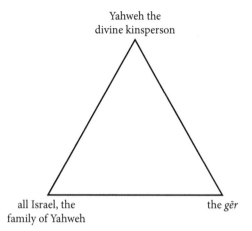

Figure 6.1. A Triangle of Kinship Connections between Yahweh, Israel, and the *Gēr*

Represented by the phrase ואהבתם את הגר, this adoptive kinship between the *gēr* and Israel is "a state of fellowship posited among blood brothers"[34] with mutual obligations. Quell reflects upon the strength of such connections in ancient cultures:

> The legal covenant … makes the participants brothers of one bone and one flesh, and thus creates the consequent legal situation. It is a totality, which can be no more broken or altered than the blood relationship itself.[35]

## 6.2.2.3. אהב and Emotions

Jacqueline E. Lapsley has critiqued the exclusive focus upon "dutiful action" in the scholarly discussion of love in the Hebrew Bible. "On this view one's emotional life is irrelevant for ethics."[36] An emotive dimension is clearly evident, for example, in the covenant between David and Jonathan (1 Samuel). An Ugaritic cognate, *ahbt*, translated "love" by Gregorio del Olmo Lete and Joaquín Sanmartín,[37] has an affective dimension, clarified by parallel clauses:

---

34. Quell, "διαθήκη," 2:114.
35. Quell, "διαθήκη," 2:114.
36. Lapsley, "Feeling," 350–69.
37. Gregorio del Olmo Lete and Joaquín Sanmartín, *A Dictionary of the Ugaritic*

Or does affection for El the king move you,
love of the bull [a metonym for El] rouse you?[38]

In the present text, there is an affective component in Yahweh's love for Israel (10:15a):

רק באבתיך חשק יהוה לאהבה אותם

The word קשח commonly refers to the affection between a man and a woman, and the affective dimension is also present in reference to love for God (Gen 34:8, Deut 21:11, Ps 91:14). The infinitive construct form לאהבה is likely explanatory or epexegetical and is best translated as "by loving" or "in love."[39] This is "an evidently emotional attachment for which no explanation of a prior cause is possible."[40] Yahweh's affection for Israel calls for a corresponding inner dimension in Israel's love for Yahweh (10:16).[41]

Lapsley rightly argues that the focus on the inner dimension of Yahweh's love for Israel and on Israel's love for Yahweh signals that Israel's love for the stranger also ought to have an emotional dimension.[42] Israel should feel affection for the vulnerable and displaced person in its midst. Indeed, the motive clause regarding Israel's own provenance as displaced persons in Egypt aims to elicit an emotional response of empathy and kindness toward the *gēr* (10:19).

---

*Language in the Alphabetic Tradition*, ed. and trans. Wilfred G. E. Watson, HdO 1/67, 2 vols. (Leiden: Brill, 2003), 1:31–32, s.v. "ahbt."

38. Jesús-Luis Cunchillios, Juan-Pablo Vita, and José-Ángel Zamora, eds., *Ugaritic Data Bank: The Texts with English Commentaries* (Madrid: Laboratorio de Hermeneumatica, 2003), 53, text 1.4, iv.38–39; translation from Gibson, *Canaanite*, 60.

39. See Waltke and O'Connor, *Syntax*, §36.2.3.e. The infinitive construct could also be a result clause; however, this seems less likely in light of the other occurrences of אהב in 10:12–11:1. "Fathers" is emphasized by its placement before the verb and the subject and by the corresponding pronoun at the end of the sentence.

40. Lapsley, "Feeling," 361.

41. Targums Onkelos and Pseudo-Jonathan read: "put away foolishness."

42. Lapsley, "Feeling," 362.

6.2.3. Conclusion

In sum, the *gēr* is adopted within the kinship grouping of Israel and of Israel's divine kinsperson. Israel is to love the *gēr* because Yahweh loves the *gēr*, even as Yahweh loves Israel. This complex of relations may be presented in tabular form.

Table 6.1: "Love" in Deut 10:12–11:1

|  | אהב as covenant | אהב kinship | אהב and emotion |
|---|---|---|---|
| Yahweh loves Israel, 10:15a | choice (10:15); historical narrative (10:21–22) | father-son relationship as covenant | רק באבתיך 10:15a חשק יהוה לאהבה אותם |
| Yahweh loves the *gēr*, 10:18b | Yahweh chooses the vulnerable | Yahweh as pater-familias | 10:18b; supply of food and clothing |
| Israel loves the *gēr*, 10:19a | a triangular relationship: Yahweh/Israel/*gēr* | *gēr* is included as family | emotional affection for the *gēr* as kin |

A final reflection is the universalism within 10:17–19 and also in the broader unit: Yahweh, the great emancipator of slaves, is God of gods and Lord of lords (10:17–19). Thus, inherent to Deuteronomy's theological and social vision is also a universal appeal: the vulnerable stranger is to be welcomed and enfolded as kindred at all times and in all places.

6.3. The *Gēr* in the Covenant-Renewal Ceremony (Deut 29:9–14)

6.3.1. Translation of 29:9–14

The following translation of Deut 29:9–14 is formatted to highlight its chiastic structure.[43]

---

43. The chiastic analysis follows Lundbom, *Deuteronomy*, 805.

A. 29:9–10 You stand here this day, all of you, before Yahweh your God: tribal chiefs,[44] elders, officers, all the men of Israel, your children, your wives, and[45] <u>your stranger in the midst of your camp, from the woodcutter to the water-drawer,</u>

> B. 29:11 <u>to enter into a covenant with its oath with Yahweh your God, which Yahweh your God is making with you this day;</u>
>
>> C. 29:12 <u>in order that he may establish you today as a people to himself. And he will be God to you as he promised you and as he swore to your fathers, to Abraham, Isaac, and Jacob.</u>
>
> B[1]. 29:13 It is not with you alone that I make this covenant and oath,

A[1]. 29:14 but with s/he who is standing here with us this day before Yahweh our God and with s/he who is not here with us this day.

## 6.3.2. Introduction

The *gēr* figures in the covenant ceremony at Moab (29:8–14). This figure is emphasized, for the phrase וגרך אשר בקרב מחניך מחטב עציך עד שאב מימיך is the most extended expression for the stranger in Deuteronomy. The stranger is referenced a second time for added emphasis: "It is not with you alone ... but with the one who is standing here with us this day before Yahweh our God" (29:13–14).

Parallel phrases (29:9, 14a) bracket the unit concerning the making of the Moab covenant. The unit centers on kinship and identity, and three key motifs reoccur:

1. An assembly to establish the Moab covenant (29:9–13)
2. Traditional kin groups and their patriarchal associations (29:9–10a, 12, 14b)
3. Those who are not affiliated within the traditional kin groups (29:10, 13)

---

44. ראשיכם שבטיכם (MT) is an irregularity. SP agrees with the MT. LXX and Syr emend *rā'šêkem* to *rā'šê*, "the chiefs of your tribes." Nelson translates שבטיכם as an old designation for leader (Nelson, *Deuteronomy*, 335). However, the emendation is preferable. See also Timothy A. Lenchak, "*Choose Life!*": *A Rhetorical-Critical Investigation of Deuteronomy 28,69–30,20*, AB 129 (Rome: Pontifical Biblical Institute, 1993), 94–95. McConville accepts the emendation (*Deuteronomy*, 412).

45. The underlined text (10aα–12) uses the second-person singular address. The remainder of the text uses the second-person plural.

Thus the unit is occupied with the themes of rootage, of consanguinity, and of the absence of affiliation. Given this focus, the figure of the stranger is crucial in the text. This special interest in incorporating displaced people is characteristic of Deuteronomy's framing texts, as I observe throughout this chapter.

### 6.3.2.1. Composition History

The assembly of Israel, the covenant, and the "national" focus of the participant list is characteristic of Dtr.[46] As a result, many scholars take Deut 1–3, 29–30 as part of a second exilic redaction.[47] Achenbach reflects the common view that the singular address (29:10aβ–12; underlined in the translation above) is a post-Dtr insertion, while the remainder of the text is Dtr.[48] However, nowhere is covenant making expressed only in the negative, the result of Achenbach's reconstruction (29:13a).[49] Still, the phrase וכאשר נשבע לאבתיך לאברהם ליצחק וליעקב (29:12b) may be a postexilic interpolation, as the sworn covenant with the patriarchs is characteristic of the final (Pentateuch) redaction and the doubling of כאשר is highly unusual (29:12a, b; cf. Gen 26:29).[50] The following analysis probes the interest to include displaced people within the covenant in 29:9–14.

---

46. See further, Dennis T. Olson, "How Does Deuteronomy Do Theology? Literary Juxtaposition and Paradox in the New Moab Covenant in Deuteronomy 29–32," in *A God So Near: Essays on Old Testament Theology in Honour of Patrick D. Miller*, ed. Brent A. Strawn and Nancy R. Bowen (Winona Lake, IN: Eisenbrauns, 2003), 201–2; Mayes, *Deuteronomy*, 65. Nonetheless, with Daniel Fleming ("Israelite," 30) and others I consider that the covenant was an early tradition in Israel.

47. For this section I am indebted to personal e-mail correspondence with Nathan MacDonald. Many scholars hold that the so-called Moab redaction locates the covenant participants at the boundary of the River Jordan; the historical address is the second-generation community in exilic Judah (e.g., Otto, "History of the Legal-Religious," 232; Otto, *Deuteronomium*, 239–48; Mayes, *Deuteronomy*, 43–44, 359).

48. Achenbach, "Eintritt," 249–51; Achenbach, "*gēr*," 35–36. Against this view, see Römer, *Israels Väter*, 153–59.

49. Though this occurs in Deut 5:3 within a historical recollection.

50. Römer observes that the double phrase with different addressees occurs only here (*Israels Väter*, 157). On the possible use of P in 29:9–11, see Römer, *Israels Väter*, 153–59. On the function of the patriarchs in the Pentateuch redaction, see Römer, *Israels Väter*, 136, 561–565; Römer, "Deuteronomy in Search of Origins," 130–31, 136–37.

### 6.3.3. The Stranger within Israel

#### 6.3.3.1. Covenant and Incorporation

Themes of kinship are paramount in the text. The participation of the whole community in the covenant is asserted emphatically in the frame of the chiasmus, as shown by כלכם (29:9a), ולא אתכם לבדכם (29:13a), and the extensive list of participants (29:9–10). The context clarifies that the phrase ולא אתכם לבדכם (29:13a) addresses the nation as a whole rather than the paterfamilias of the household, as in the DC (e.g., 16:11).[51] Who, then, are those referred to: כי את אשר ישנו פה עמנו עמד היום לפני יהוה אלהינו(29:14a)?[52] The singular collective form ישנו (29:14a) corresponds to the singular collective form וגרך (29:10a), relating the two, and both phrases are anomalous in the context of the plural address. So, the unaffiliated crowd must be those who are referred to as גרך. What is to be done with these congregating strangers? Deuteronomy 29:14a is parallel to 29:9a (and in chiastic relation to 29:11b), bracketing the unit and asserting the legality of the stranger's presence in the assembly. Both נצבים (29:9a) and עמד (29:14a) are stative participles with durative force. עמד is Dtr's word of choice for coming before Yahweh, and its use here regarding the stranger asserts the stranger's inclusion in the covenant community (cf. 4:10, 11; 10:8; in the DC, 19:17).[53]

Traditionally, lineage and patrimony are constitutive for inclusion within the assembly. Compare, for example, the importance of tracing lineage in Ezra-Nehemiah (Ezra 2; 8:3–14; Neh 7; 11:4–20).[54] People who are both vulnerable and displaced stand outside of traditional kinship groupings and therefore have no formal association within the gathering. I have observed above that widespread displacement and dissolved clan groups obtained in post–Iron Age Judah, and therefore the inclusion of dislocated individuals and families within traditional structures was of paramount

---

51. This is clarified by כלכם (29:9a) and by the list of participants (29:9–10). Also, compare the comprehensive reference of the plural address in 4:11–12.

52. On 29:14b, see Lenchak, *Choose Life,* 104; Rofé, "Covenant," 272.

53. נצב (*niphal*, 29:9a) is a common phrase for standing before the Lord, though only here in Deuteronomy (see Exod 33:8, 34:2, Num 16:27, 23:6).

54. See further, Williamson, "Family."

concern for the Deuteronomist. "Those who remained in Judah lost their extended families in the war and subsequent destructions."[55]

The secondary explanatory clause, וכאשר נשבע לאבתיך לאברהם ליצחק וליעקב (29:12b), operates as an implicit ancient covenantal basis for the integration of the stranger.[56] Achenbach notes:

> When Abraham was an alien in the promised land (Gen 23:4), it was promised that his descendants would have possession of the former country of his sojourn (Gen 17:7). This means, conversely, that with the conquest the alien status of the Israelites would be canceled, but the strangers who move with the Israelites into the land would be subject both to the promises and the obligations, which have been imposed upon Israel on the basis of covenant of Moab.[57]

The vision for Israel projected in the text may now be seen. On the one hand, the covenanting community identifies with the traditional kinship structures of Israel, ראשיכם שבטיכם זקניכם ושטריכם כל איש ישראל (29:9 [Eng. 29:10]), reclaiming the traditional origins of Israel for the new post-destruction context. In this vein, the narrative of the twin generations of the Deuteronomistic History, the Horeb generation and the Moab generation, is referenced (29:1–7), as well as the narrative of the patriarchs and the covenant that was sworn to them (29:11–12b). On the other hand, these structures are emphatically inclusive, as the disparate and dislocated Judahite population is incorporated again as a community with whom Yahweh has covenanted. Here, with unique clarity, "the resident alien is drawn into the salvation story of the people of God."[58] Hendel states, "A group can change its status from outsider to insider by assuming a new

---

55. Faust, *Judah*, 108.

56. The *gēr* and the patriarchs are linked by their positioning at the beginning and at the end of the *Numuruswechsel* (29:10aβ, 12b).

57. Achenbach, "Eintritt," 251: "Abraham als Fremdem im Verheißungland (vgl. Gen 23. 4) samt seinen Nachkommen der Besitz des ehemaligen Landes seiner Fremdlingschaft (ארץ מגריך) Gen 17:7 zugesagt worden war, so bedeutet dies im Umkehrschluss, dass mit der Landnahme der Fremdlingsstatus tür die Israeliten aufgehoben wird, die Fremdlinge aber. die mit den Israeliten in das land einziehen unterliegen den Verheißungen wie den Verpflichtungen."

58. Corcoran, "Alien," 230. Kennedy discerns a similar dynamic in the Sodom narrative of Gen 19, stating: "Ethnic establishment, the guarantee of a viable future for the ethnie, is shown to be dependent upon opening, rather than guarding, the boundaries against the Other" (*Seeking*, 171).

social identity and entering the genealogy. One's place in the genealogy is a sign of cultural self-definition more than it is a sign of biological descent."[59] Genealogical association is established here as the *gēr* is caught up in the salvation history of the people of Israel (29:1–9): "your fathers" (29:12) become the fathers of the *gēr*. As another way of putting it, the family metaphor is the vehicle for a process of "naturalization" whereby the national identity of a partially diffuse people group becomes cohesive through the metaphor of genetics and genealogy. Of course, these observations invalidate the assertion of Van Houten and others that "the exclusive relationship which the Israelites had with God meant that no way was open for aliens to become members of the Israelite community."[60]

It is clarifying to recount the identity crisis that the Judahite community faced in the wake of the Babylonian conquest. The Neo-Babylonian invasion destroyed the cities, and these were left largely uninhabited. Rural sites were largely destroyed or abandoned.[61] In the wake of the invasion and the famine and disease that followed, the population of Judah decreased to as low as 10 percent of preconquest levels, stabilizing at 20 percent, which was maintained until the beginning of the Persian era (around 30,000 inhabitants).[62] Seth Sanders demonstrates that the Hebrew language disappears from the epigraphic record from the close of the Iron Age until the Hellenistic period;[63] this disappearance is a mark of the cultural devastation of exilic Judah. Into this context of devastation, Dtr renews the community as Israel,[64] identifying the community once again with its lineage traditions and its salvation history. Want of kin, dislocation, and ethnicity are no longer barriers as the community is covenanted to Yahweh. As the old hymn says, "Whoever will may come."

---

59. Hendel, *Remembering Abraham*, 10. See the discussion of adoptive kinship in the §1.3.2.

60. Van Houten, *Alien*, 107.

61. Faust, *Judah*, 234. It was observed that Faust challenges the so called "continuity school" that argues for a high degree of social continuity between the late Iron Age and the Neo-Babylonian period in rural Judea and in the urban areas of Benjamin and the Northern Highlands.

62. Faust, *Judah*, 270.

63. Sanders, *Invention*, 162.

64. Römer rightly states: "The ideological crisis for the small kingdom of Judah signified by the exile of 597–587 can scarcely be overestimated" ("Deuteronomy in Search of Origins," 117).

The *Numeruswechsel* from the plural address to the singular at the center of the text supports this analysis (10aα–12). The singular address begins with the phrase וגרך, interrupting the participant list. The singular continues throughout the description of covenant making with the effect of enfolding within the covenant dislocated persons in particular. The singular *Numeruswechsel* connects with the singular address of the DC, associating this text with the social dimension of social law.[65]

### 6.3.3.2. The *Gēr* and the Land

In this text the *gēr* is also associated with the land. The phrase לעברך בברית (29:11a) occurs only here in relation to establishing a covenant.[66] All other occurrences of the form לעברך—except for one—refer to crossing over the Jordan into the land (4:21; 27:3, 4, 12; cf. 17:2). The phrase intentionally connects the Moab covenant to a new beginning in the land. One implication of this connection is that the stranger, as a co-participant in the covenant, is also a co-recipient of the gift of land. At risk of overreading, we might extrapolate that Dtr 29:9–14 entails the practical possibility that the *gēr* may, in time, own land. Such a connection between the *gēr* and land is of great significance for the exilic period, for the availability of unused land would have created opportunity for the *gēr* that was unimaginable during the monarchic period: the possibility of land holdings and subsistence.[67] This observation is significant, as most scholars assert that it is only in the later HC that the *gēr* may inherit land.[68] The conversation is confused, however, as the *gēr* in the CC and Dtn/Dtr is *by definition* dependent. As far is Deuteronomy is concerned, the *gēr* is not a priori

---

65. The *Numeruswechsel* may be an allusion to the Horeb generation (cf. 4:10). On this stylistic function of the *Numeruswechsel* in Deut 4, see Otto, *Deuteronomium*, 261–63. The *Numeruswechsel* has been interpreted as representing different literary layers; see, e.g., G. Minette de Tillesse, "Sections 'tu' et sections 'vous' dans le Deutéronome," *VT* 12 (1962): 29–87. The *Numeruswechsel*, however, is also used for stylistic and theological reasons (Otto, *Deuteronomium*, 261–63).

66. ברית and עבר are commonly paired in order to express transgressing the covenant (see, e.g., Deut 17:2 [same form]; Josh 7:11, 15; 23:16; Judg 2:20; 2 Kgs 8:12; Jer 34:18; Hos 6:7).

67. Faust, *Judah*, 237.

68. In the HC, the *gēr* is of some means; see the discussion of the *gēr* in the HC in §2.2.3.

prohibited from owning land; this is a question of definition: when such a person is no longer landless, then he or she is no longer a *gēr*!

### 6.3.3.3. "And Your Stranger in the Midst of Your Camp"

The phrase וגרך אשר בקרב מחניך is pregnant with intertextual connections. The word מחניך connects with descriptions of the wilderness period (Num 5:2; 10:2; Deut 2:14, 15), embedding the covenant within salvation history. The addition of מחניך adapts the integration formula (והגר אשר בקרבך) to the present setting of the Moab assembly (cf. Num 4:5, 15; 5:2; Deut 2:14, 15). The phrase הגר אשר בקרבך is interpolated from Dtn, echoing Dtn's requirement that the *gēr* be included within the life and kinship of an Israelite village (see 26:11). The pronominal suffix form וגרך belongs to Dtr and references the location of the *gēr* within a nuclear family (see §3.3.5). On account of the erosion of larger kinship structures in the exilic period, the nuclear family was the primary locus of inclusion for the *gēr*.[69] Thus, the *gēr* participates in the assembly by virtue of his or her relation to the household within which the *gēr* lived and worked. Evidently the unusual phrase וגרך אשר בקרב מחניך references, at least implicitly, three social spheres: the household, the settlement, and the nation, as laid out in the table.

Table 6.2. Social Locations for the Relative Construction
וגרך אשר בקרב מחניך

| Phrase | Social location |
| --- | --- |
| וגרך | Dtr; inclusion within the *household* |
| אשר בקרב | echoes of Dtn references to the *settlement*, *town*, or *city* |
| בקרב מחניך | the nation gathering at *Moab* |

Achenbach asserts that the *gēr* "stands outside of the federation of Israel,"[70] interpreting 29:9–14 as referring to an *independent* non-Israelite. [71] This

---

69. Williamson, "Family," 474–75. Often, in Ezra and Nehemiah, primary allegiances were determined by concerns other than blood kinship (Williamson, "Family," 475–76).

70. Achenbach, "Eintritt," 242: "die außerhalb des Verbandes Israels stehen."

71. "Warum mit Kaleb ein Nichtisraelit sogar Anteil an der *nahalāh* erhalten konnte (Jos 14.13)" ("so … has explained why Caleb, a non-Israelite, could receive

profile for the *gēr* would correspond to the profile for the *gēr* in the HC.[72] However, both the alleged independence of the *gēr* as well as the *gēr*'s alleged foreignness should be challenged. The pronominal suffix form וגרך identifies the *gēr* as a household dependent, and the *gēr* "stands" before Yahweh by virtue of his or her association within a household. Further, the "otherness" of the *gēr* is circumscribed at the household level: not "the stranger within Israel," but "your stranger" (וגרך), addressing the paterfamilias.[73] Displacement is identified at a household level rather than at a "national" level. Thus exegetically the phrase וגרך could be referring to internal displacement just as readily as to foreign immigration. Dtr is quite possibly addressing a context of postconquest societal collapse in which as many people were displaced as were not. If this social-historical reconstruction is correct, for Dtr it is the displaced and vulnerable Judahite in particular who must be enfolded within the covenant. The plea of Dtr is not to include a large number of non-Israelites as Israel is re-formed. Rather, the plea is: in this context of postconquest societal collapse, where many people are displaced both geographically and socially, as Israel is reconstituted, it is the stranger in particular who must be enfolded within the covenant.

### 6.3.3.4. "From Woodcutter to Water-Drawer" (29:10b)

This "stock phrase" is also observed in Arabic and Ugaritic.[74] The phrase is also used for the menial tasks that the Gibeonites were required to perform as "cutters of wood and drawers of water for all of the congregation" (Josh 9:21; cf. 9:23, 27).

John Gray's translation of the phrase in Ugaritic *KRT* 111–114 (I iii 7–10) interprets both tasks as performed by a female, on the basis that the first word *sᶜt* is the feminine plural participle of *sᶜ*, "to rush," a cognate of Hebrew *sāᶜâ* and Arabic *saᶜâ*.[75] Indeed, gathering water and wood was segregated as women's work in many pan-Mediterranean cultures, for exam-

---

a share of the *nahalāh* [Josh 14:13]") (Achenbach, "Eintritt," 251). In a similar vein, Crouch views the *gēr* in 29:9–14 and 31:9–13 as a proselyte (*Making*, 217).

72. See the discussion of the HC in §2.2.3.

73. See my discussion of the pronominal suffix form for *gēr* in §3.3.5.

74. D. J. A. Clines, "KRT 111–114 (I iii 7–10): Gatherers of Wood and Drawers of Water," *UF* 8 (1976): 25.

75. John Gray, *The Krt Text in the Literature of Ras Shamra: A Social Myth of Ancient Canaan*, 2nd ed. (Leiden: Brill, 1964).

ple, among the Aith Waryaghar of the Moroccan Rif.[76] Thus this phrase seems to refer to the *gēr* in the terms of women's work, yet it is difficult to see why it would do so. David Clines suggests that the phrase in Deut 29:10 and Josh 9:21, 23, 27 is "designedly humiliating."[77] This seems to fit the context in Joshua better than Deuteronomy, since humiliation is not consistent with the goal to incorporate the *gēr* within the community in 29:9–14. Two other options are that women were relatively dominant within displaced populations within the period of Dtr (this possibility was mentioned above, at §3.10) or that the phrase may reference the humble labor and the lowly status of the *gēr*, whom Yahweh here honors as a covenant partner.

### 6.4. The *Gēr* in the Seventh-Year Reading of Torah (Deut 31:9–13)

#### 6.4.1. Introduction

The *gēr* is included in the assembly of "all Israel" for the seventh-year reading of Torah (31:9–13), which assumes its importance as the acme of what is arguably the most important event in the Deuteronomic cultic calendar, the seventh-year שמטה of the Feast of Booths.

The broader section of 31:1–29 has three foci, each aimed to address the question: How shall the Moab covenant remain central in the life of the nation after Moses's death? Joshua's succeeding Moses provides a continuity of faithful leadership. The provision for the seventh-year reading of Torah in the assembly and the deposit of the law beside the ark of the covenant locates the law at the center of the Deuteronomic cultus. "The Song" is a "witness" for future generations to Israel's propensity to break the covenant.[78] Deuteronomy 31:9–13 is a textual unit that institutes the seventh-year reading of Torah, a "Torah beyond Moses."[79]

---

76. David Montgomery Hart, *The Aith Waryaghar of the Moroccan Rif: An Ethnography and History*, Viking Fund Publications in Anthropology 55 (Tucson: University of Arizona Press, 1976).

77. Clines, "KRT 111–114," 26.

78. McConville, *Deuteronomy*, 437; Dennis T. Olson, *Deuteronomy and the Death of Moses: A Theological Reading* (Minneapolis: Fortress, 1994), 133–38; Otto, *Das Deuteronomium im Pentateuch und Hexateuch: Studien zur Literaturgeschichte von Pentateuch und Hexateuch im Lichte des Deuteronomiumrahmens*, FAT 30 (Tübingen: Mohr Siebeck, 2000), 175–76.

79. J. P. Sonnet, *The Book within the Book: Writing in Deuteronomy*, BibInt 14 (Leiden: Brill, 1997).

### 6.4.1.1. Composition History

Deuteronomy 31:10–13, though not 31:9, reuses formulas and motifs from Dtn and Dtr with a frequency unique within the frame of Deuteronomy. Most significantly, Deut 31:10–12 is composed as analogous to the extended Dtn formula for cultic feasting (see below), and the *hear, learn, fear, do* Dtr formula is reused in no less than three motive clauses within 31:12b–13. These patterns and others relate the seventh-year reading of the law to the law corpus and to the Horeb covenant.[80] This reuse of motifs exhibits an explicit development of Dtn ethics of inclusion for the *gēr* for a later context.[81] As for 31:10–12, Otto dates this to the postexilic period on the basis of the combined role of the Levitical priesthood and the elders.[82] In addition, the reappearance of the chosen place (31:12) is consistent with the presentation of Jerusalem as a location of blessing instead of curse during this period.[83] However, the compositional development of the larger unit (31:1–29) is complex, and Nelson discerns four stages: Deuteronomic History (31:1–13), the song (31:16–22), JE related texts (31:14–15, 16–22), installing the book of law (31:24–29).[84] Ideologically, 31:9–13 is closest to Zech 1–8 within postexilic literature, as explained below.

### 6.4.2. The Relation of 31:9–13 to Deuteronomy's Feasting Texts

Deuteronomy 31:10–12 is composed on analogy to the Dtn cultic feasting texts. The structure of 31:10–12 follows the formulaic structure of these texts, with the elements appearing in order. Deuteronomy 31:10–12 relates not only to Booths (16:13–15) but also to the corpus of feasting texts, as illustrated in table 6.4.

---

80. Correspondences to Dtn are observed in the table below. Characteristic Dtr elements, in addition to the formula quoted above, are: צוה (10a), כל ישראל (11a), את העם (12a), כל דברי התורה (12b), האדמה אשר (13b), ירש (13b).

81. It is possible 31:10–13 preexisted 31:9. This possibility is strengthened by the relation of this text with 4:10, which is likely exilic (Veijola, *Das 5. Buch Mose*, 98).

82. Otto, *Pentateuch und Hexateuch*, 184. Achenbach argues that the Levitical Priesthood has been incorporated into Deuteronomy after the Dtr redaction ("Eintritt," 251). Nicholson asserts of Deut 31–34, "They are considered as belonging less to the book of Deuteronomy proper than to the Pentateuch as a whole" (*Tradition*, 22). Mayes dates 31:9–13 to Dtr (*Deuteronomy*, 374).

83. On Jerusalem in postexilic texts, see Carr, *Formation*, 213.

84. Nelson, *Deuteronomy*, 355–56.

Table 6.3. The Order of Elements in 31:10–13 and in the Feasting Texts

| Feasts (16:9–15; cf. 14:22–27) | Seventh-Year Reading |
|---|---|
| timing (sevens) | timing (seventh year) |
| ritual institution (ועשית חג) | ritual location (בחג הסכות) |
| "to the Lord your God" | "before the Lord your God" |
| injunctive (שמח) | injunctive (הקהל) |
| household list | clan list |
| place formula | place formula |

The *gēr* appears in both the source texts (14:28–29; 16:11, 14; 26:11) and in 31:12. The composition of 31:9–13 on analogy with Deuteronomy's feasting texts is of significance because it represents a developing thread of ethics and theology for the stranger that runs through the social and literary history of Israel, via the Deuteronomic feasting trope. While scholarship acknowledges the explicit connection of the seventh-year reading of Torah with the Feast of Booths, there is no recognition as far I am aware that 31:9–13 is composed on analogy to Deuteronomy's feasting texts more broadly.[85]

Table 6.4. Formulaic Elements of Dtn Feasting Texts in Order in 31:10–13

| Deut 31:10–12 | Source: feasting texts | Comments |
|---|---|---|
| מקץ שבע שנים במעד שנת השמטה (31:10bα) | מקץ שבע שנים תעשה שמטה (15:1; linked to feasting texts within the literary block 14:22–16:17) | a related phrase begins the Feast of Weeks, 16:9; cf. 16:15; heptadic patterning is present throughout 16:1–17. |
| בחג הסכות (31:10bβ) | חג הסכת (16:13; cf. 16:16)[86] | noun חג follows the timing of the feast (16:10, 13) |

85. Otto briefly acknowledges the relation of the order of elements in 31:10 to the feast of Booths (16:13–15) and the relation of 31:10 to the Šemitta legislation (15:1) see Otto, *Pentateuch und Hexateuch*, 185. However, the analogy is not only with the feast of Booths but also with the whole corpus of feasting texts.

86. Strictly, בחג הסכות follows 16:16, for in 16:13 the base is extended to form a plural through the *ōh* syllable, חג הסכת. Regarding this noun pattern, see Waltke and O'Connor, *Syntax*, §7.4b.

| | | |
|---|---|---|
| בבוא כל ישראל (31:11) | באספך מגרנך ומיקבך (16:13b) | Israel coming in (31:11) // gathering in the produce (compare 14:16; 16:10aβ; 26:2) |
| לראות את פני יהוה (31:11aα) | יראה כל זכורך את פני יהוה אלהיך (16:16a); cf ושמחת לפני יהוה אלהיך (16:11, 26:11, etc.) | cultic formula; לפני יהוה אלהיך is omitted in Booths (16:13–15). |
| במקום אשר יבחר (31:11aβ) | במקום אשר יבחר (16:16; cf. 12: 5–7; 14:23; 16:11, 15; 26:2) | place formula is relocated before the list in 31:11. |
| הקהל את העם האנשים והנשים והטף וגרך אשר בשעריך (31:12a) | אתה ובנך ובתך ועבדך ואמתך והלוי והגר והיתום והאלמנה אשר בשעריך (16:14) | only *gēr* appears both in 31:12a and in the source texts |
| למען ישמעו (31:12bα) ולמען ילמדו ויראו (31:12bβ) ולמדו ליראה (31:13, children) | למען תלמד ליראה את יהוה אלהיך כל הימים (14:23b, concerning the annual tithe) | 31:12b, 31:13a and 17:19b are appropriated from 14:23b. |

The table outlines the close correspondence of 31:10–12 to the formulaic structure of the Dtn feasting texts.[87] Perhaps most strikingly, Deut 31:11a repeats verbatim an excerpt from 16:16a, יראה כל זכורך את פני יהוה אלהיך במקום אשר יבחר (16:16a), interpolating בבוא and replacing כל זכורך with כל ישראל.[88] The extended feasting formula is reproduced in order to secure, within the traditional Deuteronomic cultic framework, the recurring promulgation of Torah for the new scenario of life in the land after Moses's death. The reuse of Dtn motifs both adapts the Feast of Booths and in a sense *authorizes* the regular public reading of Torah. Significantly, the feasting formula evokes "the joy of the feast,"[89] the forging of kinship through feasting for the seventh-year reading of Torah institution, along with the emphatic inclusion of the *gēr*. We have observed that, in the Dtn cultic feasting texts, the *gēr* was to be included in cultic feasting before Yahweh. These feast texts were ordered to nourish kinship between the *gēr* and the household and the clan. Now, in the seventh year of Torah, the *gēr*

---

87. Note also the prominence of the Levites (31:9, cf. especially, 12:12; 14:27; 26:11; see also, 16:11, 14; 26:12, 13).

88. A shift in ordering accommodates the addition of בבוא.

89. See further Braulik, "Joy," and the discussion in §5.2.2.

is being incorporated within the "nation" through feasting and in association with Torah.

Insights from cultural anthropology clarify the social implications of these textual associations. David Schneider argues that American kinship is experienced with a high degree of correspondence across a number of cultural domains: the family, the nation, religion, and also perhaps education. These domains are structured by the same terms. "All of the symbols of American kinship seem to 'say' one thing: they provide for relationships of diffuse, enduring solidarity."[90] A coherence of cultural domains is visible also in Deuteronomy. For example, there is the correspondence of the "gates" of a town or city in Deuteronomy to the chosen place, as Otto has observed: "The 'šeʿārîm' open on the central sanctuary the māqôm that God has chosen; from it they receive their beneficence and their power to sustain life."[91] Coherence of cultural domains is visible in the text at hand, for while in 16:13–15 the Feast of Booths fosters cohesion and inclusivism at the household and clan level, in the seventh-year reading of Torah text the same feast fosters cohesion and inclusivism at the level of all Israel. Through such fusing of cultural domains, Deuteronomy provides for "relationships of diffuse, enduring solidarity" not only between cultural domains but also between the landed and the landless within every cultural domain.

### 6.4.3. Incorporating the *Gēr*

Deuteronomy 31 establishes a relationship between the *gēr* and the book of law. The three motive clauses concerning hearing, learning, fearing, and obeying Torah apply to the stranger also (31:12–13). The phrase ולמען ילמדו ויראו (31:12b) and related texts (31:13a, 17:19b) are appropriated from 14:23b (concerning the tithe). Most translations render 31:12b, "learn to fear."[92] That translation, however, is an assimilation from the formulaic, למען תלמד ליראה (14:23a, 17:19b; 31:13a). Uniquely in the present text, the *lamed* prefix is omitted; the form ויראו is a *waw*-relative whereby the "fearing" is both future and relative to the "learning."[93] Here the stress is

---

90. Schneider, "Kinship, Nationality, and Religion," 67.

91. Otto, "שַׁעַר," 15:377.

92. E.g., ESV, NRSV, NIV. The majority of commentators, however, avoid this error.

93. See Waltke and O'Connor, *Syntax*, 519–20.

upon instruction. The *gēr*, as a member of Israel, will also hear and learn, and in so doing the *gēr* will fear and obey Yahweh. The book of law is "entrusted" to the Levites (31:9), and in the resumption of the narrative (31:24–28) the book of law is installed beside the ark. As a participant in the reading of Torah, then, the *gēr* is thereby also associated with the ark, a poignant symbol of the giving of the Torah to Israel at Horeb.[94] It is illuminating also to consider the stranger's relation to the song. By extension, the song of witness is the stranger's song, too, both for warning and for succor (31:19–22, 32:1–43).

Assuming an early postexilic context for 31:9–13, the inclusion of the *gēr* appears with a new dynamic in the Persian period, during which questions of identity were paramount. "In the Persian period, the question of what the people of Israel was and who belongs to it becomes more and more acute."[95] On a number of planes, social fragmentation characterized the period. Group distinctions are foregrounded in Ezra-Nehemiah, the most essential distinction being between the returnees (sons of the *golah*) and the people of the land.[96] A second division was between rich and poor (e.g., Neh 5:1–13, Mal 3:5).[97] After the Neo-Babylonian invasion, an upper class connected to the Babylonian elite rose quickly within Judah, and with this indebtedness, land alienation, and enslavement.[98] The return of the exiles produced conflict over patrimony and further land alienation. These social forces may have produced much of the displacement behind post-Dtr Deuteronomy's concern for the *gēr*. By virtue of their dislocation from kindred and patrimony, the *gēr's* standing in the assembly was in question.[99] The passage explicitly names the *gēr* as among those in assembly (*hiphil* קהל, 31:12) before the Lord, endowing those who were root-

---

94. "By being bound to the ark, the Torah 'book' is launched as the communicational device meant to pervade and shape Israel's existence in the land" (Sonnet, *Book*, 260).

95. Kessler, *Social History*, 130.

96. See Kessler, *Social History*; Charles E. Carter, *The Emergence of Yehud in the Persian Period: A Social and Deographic Study*, JSOTSup 294 (Sheffield: Sheffield Academic, 1999), 307–16; Erhard S. Gerstenberger, *Israel in the Persian Period: The Fifth and Fourth Centuries B.C.E*, trans. Siegfried S. Schatzmann (Atlanta: Society of Biblical Literature, 2011), 434.

97. See Kessler, *Social*, 134–36.

98. Smith, "Politics of Ezra," 92–93. See further Grabbe, *Yehud*, 172, 191–94.

99. Compare the importance of tracing lineage in Ezra-Nehemiah (Ezra 2; 8:3–14; Neh 7; 11:4–20; see my discussion above).

less with identity within the community and even identity within a shared communal history (31:1–8).

Social cohesion is a goal of 31:9–13. Yahweh's people are referred to as a unity; the threefold כל ישראל (31:9, 11a, b) seems to be an implicit polemic against group divisions. The term *Israel* here is a "literary and theological usage" that "emphasize[s] the identity of the inhabitants of Yehud, as well as the Jewish communities elsewhere, with Israel."[100] The inclusive stance of post-Dtr Deuteronomy is close to its contemporary Zech 1–8, which also "presents a highly *inclusivistic, nonpolemical, non-exclusionary* perspective."[101] It contrasts with Nehemiah-Ezra's concern to reinforce the boundaries of the community. In Deut 31:9–13, community-creating cultic feasting, which was traditionally ordered to enfold the vulnerable within a household/settlement (see §§5.2.3, 5.2.4), here unites and even re-creates "all Israel" in the presence of Yahweh, under Torah, with the stranger emphatically included. As a consequence of the redaction of 31:9–13, earlier feasting texts are, in a sense, "reread" with the knowledge that the *gēr* participates in the covenant of all Israel, via the seventh-year reading of Torah.

There is an implicit social ethic for the stranger in 31:10–13. This is manifested both in locating the seventh-year reading at the time of שמטה (31:10; cf. 15:1) and also by the literary association with the inclusive feasting of the Dtn cultic texts. We might reflect that in the seventh-year reading of Torah ritual, Yahweh reveals himself as a God of authentic community, of humankind as kin. The joy of the harvest is the occasion for thankful celebration before Yahweh in light of Yahweh's abundant supply. Yet it is not enough for the well-to-do to appear before Yahweh; Israel must appear before Yahweh in diversity, enfolding the fatherless, widow, and stranger (16:14). Nor is it sufficient for only those with patrimony to receive Yahweh's words, for Yahweh is especially the God of the displaced (cf. 10:18). In a sense, Yahweh's words may only be properly heard by those who come alongside with the stranger as kindred. Here at the feast, the community is *being/becoming* the people of Yahweh, a community that is centered upon Torah, and that also enfolds the displaced.

It is clarifying to state again at this point that the *gēr* in Deuteronomy is a liminal figure. These texts do not address the *gēr* as a member of the

---

100. Grabbe, *Yehud*, 170. By comparison, Jer 24:8, which is perhaps contemporary with Deut 31:9–13, is in support of the sons of the *golah*.

101. Kessler, "Diaspora," 165, emphasis original.

community, for absence of kinship is the very definition of the *gēr* (if the *gēr* were a member of the community, then there would be no problem to fix). Deuteronomy is concerned with practices that foster the incorporation of this liminal figure into the community.

## 6.4.4. The *Gēr* within the Community

The *gēr* is emphasized in 31:9–13 by the sheer allocation of space within the list of participants, וגרך אשר בשעריך, and also in that the *gēr* is the only participant referred to in both the cultic source texts (16:11, 14) and 31:12a. The pronominal suffix form גרך is characteristic of Dtr, and it locates the stranger within the בית אבותם. The בית אבותם appears to have been the primary social unit during the Persian period, which seems often to have been somewhat larger than in the monarchic period and in some cases to have been an adoptive grouping based on locality or vocation.[102]

The list of participants resembles the household lists of Dtn feasting texts (e.g., 16:11, 14) but with substantial differences.[103]

31:12a:   את העם האנשים והנשים והטף וגרך אשר בשעריך

16:11:   אתה ובנך ובתך ועבדך ואמתך והלוי אשר בשעריך והגר והיתום
          והאלמנה אשר בקרבך

Given the close correspondence of 31:10–13 with Dtn feasting texts, one can reasonably assume that the differences between the participant lists are significant. In 31:12a, the paterfamilias is not directly addressed, and the rather generic reference to "men, women, and children" (31:12a) may evince some separation of the בית אבותם from traditional lineage structures. The fading of the household in this list (in comparison to Dtn) may also evince a new or enhanced focus upon the קהל (31:12a). In a context of social fragmentation and land alienation, postexilic Deuteronomy is concerned to include and to protect the vulnerable stranger, enfolding him or her within the בית אבותם, within the "gates," and within העם.

The phrase "the stranger within your gates" is indigenous to the DC, a circumlocution for the protective circumference of a rural settlement.[104]

---

102. Smith, "Politics of Ezra," 82; Williamson, "Family," 477, 479.

103. The list of participants in the covenant ceremony (29:8–9) does not resemble the lists of Dtn.

104. On this phrase, see §5.5.2.

Within the frame of Deuteronomy, this phrase occurs only here and in the Sabbath command (5:14), and both of these texts reproduce the lexical field of the DC.[105]

Table 6.5. Social Locations for the
Relative Construction וגרך אשר בשעריך

| Phrase | Social location |
| --- | --- |
| העם | *gēr* is included in the assembly of all Israel |
| וגרך | originally Dtr; inclusion within the household |
| אשר בשעריך | echoes of Dtn references to the settlement, town, or city |

### 6.4.5. Questions in Scholarship

#### 6.4.5.1. Is the *Gēr* Native to the Land?

Again we must ask if the *gēr* is necessarily a foreigner in this text. The focus upon all Israel leads many scholars to identify the *gēr* within a dialectic of native/foreigner.[106] However, the identification of the *gēr* with a household (וגרך, 31:12a) and within a settlement/city (בשעריך, 31:12a) locates the insider/outsider distinction not only at the level of the "nation" but also at the level of the household and the settlement. In fact, these two gentilic phrases signal that the *gēr* appears in the assembly precisely by virtue of her or his association within a household and clan/town/city. We have observed the importance of tracing lineage in Ezra-Nehemiah for inclusion within the assembly (Ezra 2; 8:3–14; Neh 7; 11:4–20).[107] For readers who are enmeshed within the hyper-individualism of Western culture, it is difficult to imagine that an ancient person who was born within the boundaries of Israel did not thereby naturally belong within the assembly of Israel or under the rubric of כל ישראל. Western readers must recall that, in communal Mediterranean societies, an individual's identity was embedded in the group's identity, and an individual's honor was embedded in the honor of the paterfamilias. Individuals without kinship connection were

---

105. On clans and settlements in the postexilic period, see Williamson, "Family."
106. E.g., Achenbach, "Eintritt," 242.
107. See further Williamson, "Family."

nonpersons and customarily of no more value than a shrub or a boulder.[108] A displaced person, therefore, belonged within the larger kinship group-ing of כל ישראל only by virtue of his or her first belonging within a nuclear family and clan grouping. Even dwelling within a household, a displaced person was still dependent upon the paterfamilias's willingness to incor-porate him or her as "family," and such incorporation is exactly what Deu-teronomy is striving to foster.

Of course, this observation does not settle the question of the prov-enance of the displacement, whether external or internal: both are pos-sibilities. The provenance of the *gēr* can only be guessed at by means of social-historical reconstruction. The prominence of the figure of the *gēr* in 31:9–13 suggests a large number of displaced people in the society that the text addresses. The large contingent of scholars who maintain that the *gēr* is largely non-Israelite/non-Judahite must explain why a large number of immigrants would have infiltrated Persian Yehud.[109] Indeed, they must explain why these supposed immigrants desired what has been called the "harsh realities of life" in Persian Yehud, which included such widespread socioeconomic stratification and poverty that some scholars have con-cluded that Persian Judah was "undesirable as a location for immigration."[110] Indeed, the harshness of life in Yehud was the very thing that made many in the exilic community reluctant to return to Yehud![111] The prosperity of proximate locations, such as Phoenecia and Gaza, must have detracted further from Yehud's appeal.[112] In this light, the majority of scholars who hold that the *gēr* is non-Israelite/non-Judahite would do well to heed Grabbe's assertion that, "as far as we can tell from our sources, there seem to be few non-Jewish males wanting to become a part of the community at this time."[113] Strikingly, in light of the prominence of the *gēr* in 31:9–13, these scholars must demonstrate that foreign immigration was among *the* pressing social issues in early Persian Yehud. Instead, Naʾaman is correct to

---

108. Malina, *New Testament World*, 41, 42, 63.

109. Achenbach asserts both that post-Dtr addresses Persian Yehud and also that the *gēr* was a foreigner ("*gêr*," 35–37).

110. Kessler, "Diaspora," 165.

111. See further Kessler, "Diaspora."

112. On Phoenicia and Gaza in the Persian period, see Grabbe, *Yehud*, 159–62.

113. Grabbe, *Yehud*, 171. Grabbe continues, "The matter is different with females, however, since there are a number of examples of taking 'foreign wives' in our literary sources" (171).

describe the *gēr* as "a person whose membership of the religious community in the province of Yehud and in the exile was uncertain, as opposed to the citizen whose membership was unquestioned,"[114] though I would add that the element of vulnerability remains germane to the term *gēr* in these texts. Nonetheless, there is an ambivalence to the term *gēr* (see §4.8.3), and we should not suppose that any one explanation for the provenance of this figure has comprehensive explanatory power.

### 6.4.5.2. Joshua 8:30–35

The appearance of the *gēr* in Josh 8:30–35 may, at first glance, seem to force the conclusion that the *gēr* was a non-Israelite/non-Judahite. Joshua 8:30–35 narrates the ritual of the Shechem covenant (Deut 27:1–26) that follows Joshua's succession of Moses (34:9): "And all Israel, the *gēr* as well as native [וכל ישראל ... כגר כאזרח], with their elders, officers and judges" (Josh 8:33; cf. 8:35).[115] To be sure, the *gēr* and the native appear as binaries in this text. However, the reference to the *gēr* here is related to the HC and to the so-called Holiness redaction rather than to the DC, via the phrase כגר כאזרח.[116] Similarly, Josh 20:9 associates with the HC and with the Holiness redaction via the phrase ולגר הגר בתוכם.[117] In the HC and in the Holiness redaction, with the exception of a few texts reminiscent of the DC social law, the *gēr* assumes a distinctly different social profile from that of the *gēr* in Deuteronomy.[118] In these texts the *gēr* may be of some means and may even own Israelite slaves (25:35–38; cf. 17:8; 22:18).[119] There is a clear demarcation between the Israelite and the *gēr* in these texts.[120] It is significant in this light that the later Deuteronomy redactions avoid certain Priestly phrases altogether, such as אזרח and הגר אשר יגור בתוכם. Deu-

---

114. Naʼaman, "Sojourners," 257.

115. See further Otto, *Pentateuch und Hexateuch*, 230–31.

116. Cf. HC: Lev 17:5; 18:26; 19:33; 24:16, 22; in the Holiness redaction: Lev 16:29; Num 15:29, 30. On the Holiness redaction, see Christophe Nihan, *Priestly*, 569–72. Achenbach holds that Josh 8:33–35 is a part of the Hexateuch redaction of the Pentateuch ("Eintritt," 251).

117. In the HC: Lev 17:8, 10, 12, 13; 18:26; 19:33; 20:2; 25:35; in the holiness redaction: Lev 16:29; Num 9:14; 15:14, 15, 26, 29; in other priestly material: Num 19:10.

118. See my discussion of the HC in §2.2.3.

119. See Vieweger, "Vom 'Fremdling,'" 274–75.

120. See further Naʼaman, "Sojourners," 257.

teronomy seems to be carving out a specific and unique lexical domain for the *gēr* in order to consistently present the *gēr* as a liminal and vulnerable figure on the cusp of full inclusion within the community. Thus, Josh 8:30–35 does not challenge the thesis that many of those designated *gēr* that post-Dtr was addressing were internally displaced people.

### 6.4.5.3. An Evolving Trope

Achenbach, Awabdy, and Ebach represent the majority view that the framing texts of Deuteronomy evince a new level of religious inclusion that surpasses that of Dtn.[121] However, this view underestimates the religious significance of references to the *gēr* appearing in Dtn feasting texts פני יהוה אלהיך (e.g., 16:16). This point is sharpened when we note that the public reading of Torah is an addition to the already-established tradition of Booths within which the *gēr* was previously included; it is not the religious participation of the *gēr* that has changed but the additional institution of the public reading of Torah for the whole nation. The seventh-year reading of Torah in 31:9–13 is presented syntactically as an additional practice within an already-established cultic tradition. The phrase בבוא כל ישראל ("when all Israel comes") is an infinitive, offline clause that is subordinate to the verbs תקרא and הקהל (31:11–12). The seventh-year reading of Torah, then, is not a new and unprecedented religious inclusivism for the *gēr* in the postexilic period as much of the scholarship asserts but a new *practice* for the whole community in light of the religious and social crisis of the Persian period.

### 6.5. The *Gēr* in the Shechem Curse Ceremony, 27:19

The *gēr* appears in a curse formula within the Shechem covenant-renewal ceremony (27:1–26).[122]

ארור מטה משפט גר יתום ואלמנה ואמר כל העם אמן

---

121. Achenbach, "Eintritt," 251; Awabdy, *Immigrants*, 241–45; Ebach, *Fremde*, 200.

122. For this section I am indebted to personal correspondence with Gary Knoppers. Ralph K. Hawkins has produced the most authoritative discussion of the site that is thought to be Mount Ebal (Jebel Islamiya) to date. His work discusses the relation of Mount Ebal to Deut 27:1–26 and Josh 8:30–35; see *The Iron Age I Structure on Mt. Ebal: Excavation and Interpretation*, BBRSup 6 (Winona Lake, IN: Eisenbrauns, 2012).

Cursed be anyone who perverts the justice due to the *gēr*, father-less, or widow. And all the people shall say, "Amen." (Deut 27:19)

In §4.5 I observed the function of this text as law of judicial procedure. I will confine my comments at this point to the contribution of 27:19 to Deuteronomy's frame and to the significance of this text for Deuteronomy's concept of being/becoming the family of Yahweh.

Concerning composition history, Melissa Ramos has recently argued for a seventh-century date for Deut 27–28 on the basis of association with seventh-century inscriptions found within Judah and also with treaties and other curse texts.[123] However, numerous clear associations with material from the HC and the interweaving of Dtr and Priestly concerns signals that 27:15–26 postdates these texts. Thus many scholars designate 27:15–26 as a postexilic composition of the so-called Hexateuch redaction.[124] The northern motifs also suggest Persian Yehud as a likely context for 27:1–26, as explained below.

The unit 27:1–26 forms an *inclusio* with 11:26–32 around the law corpus. It consists of a call to obey the commands of Deuteronomy and a ceremony of blessing and curse. Deuteronomy 27:1–26 forms a further *inclusio* with 5:23–27, where the elders commission Moses for his task in declaring Yahweh's commands. Moses's task is now complete (27:1, 9), and the framing conjoins the assembly at Horeb with the assembly at Moab and at Shechem, foregrounding the commitment of the community to obey Yahweh's commands.[125] Stelae shall be erected that are inscribed with the "whole commandment" (27:1), a phrase that probably refers not only to the DC but also to what will follow.[126]

The ceremony at Shechem concerns being/becoming the family of Yahweh: "Today you have become the people of Yahweh your God" (27:9). As McConville asserts, "Today" in Deuteronomy "is not strictly confined to what happens in either Moab or Shechem. The 'today' of Deuteronomy

---

123. Albrecht Alt, *Essays on Old Testament History and Religion* (Oxford: Blackwell, 1966), 114–15; Melissa Ramos, "Spoken Word."

124. See Achenbach, "*gêr*," 35; Otto, *Pentateuch und Hexateuch*, 230–31; Mayes, *Deuteronomy*, 345. Other parallels: Deut 27:18 // Lev 19:14; Deut 27:23 // Lev 18:17, 20:14. For further associations to the HC, see Mayes, *Deuteronomy*, 346–47.

125. McConville, *Deuteronomy*, 387.

126. With Nelson, *Deuteronomy*, 317.

… is always present."[127] Yet what does it mean to become the people of Yahweh? At the forefront in 27:1–26 is the constitutive function of Yahweh's commands for the community. Also present in 27:1–26 is Israel's identity as an inclusive community, which appears on at least two levels. First, the northern location of the text suggests that 27:1–26 is, in part, concerned to provide a bridge between northern and Judahite communities.[128] During the Persian period, a contingent of the population within the Persian province of Samaria looked to the Jerusalem temple as their spiritual home. The location of the ceremony on the sacrosanct Mount Ebal (27:4, 13) may suggest that there "was an interest among the Jewish settlers that people from Samaria and strangers or sojourners could be integrated into the *Qahal* of the Judean/Jerusalemite Jews."[129] Second, in this curse text the full participation of the *gēr* within Israel is secured by the *gēr*'s access to just judicial procedure at the gate. There is dialectic here between cohesiveness and incorporation. On the one hand, the assembly on Mounts Ebal and Gerezim symbolizes cohesion. On the other hand, the northern location and the participation of the *gēr* are incorporative dimensions. In its context of Persian Yehud, this inclusivist ethic contrasts to the strong external boundaries of Ezra-Nehemiah, and it echoes the inclusivism of Zech 1–8.

### 6.6. The *Gēr* Who Rises Higher (Deut 28:43–44)

43 The stranger in your midst will rise above you, higher and higher, and you will descend lower and lower. 44 The stranger will lend to you, and you will not lend to him or her; the stranger will be the head, and you will be the tail. (Deut 28:43–44)

The curse of 28:43–44 envisions a social inversion in which the *gēr* rises to be head over the kinsfolk. The consequence of disobedience is "an upside down world in which the high will be made low, and vice versa."[130] Syntactically redundant repetition and personal pronouns highlight the transfer

---

127. McConville, *Deuteronomy*, 395.

128. See further Gary N. Knoppers, *Jews and Samaritans: The Origins and History of Their Early Relations* (Oxford: Oxford University Press 2013), in particular chapters 4 and 6; see also Cynthia Edenburg and Reinhard Müller, "A Northern Provenance for Deuteronomy? A Critical Review," *HBAI* 4 (2015): 148–61.

129. Achenbach, "*gêr*," 35.

130. Na'aman, "Sojourners," 253.

of fortune from the kinsperson to the (formerly) impoverished stranger. A displaced person was likely to borrow in order to eat or to plant a crop. Now the kinsperson's indebtedness signifies his or her impoverishment and vulnerability. Dtn's ethics of generosity and inclusion for the stranger are not in mind here. According to Dtn, the *gēr* would be treated generously (14:28–29), perhaps given a loan without interest (23:20), and incorporated within the settlement and household (16:11, 14). In contrast, the "curse" of poverty is in the forefront in 28:43–44. The *gēr*'s "headship" signifies that the displaced person is now the ruler, in consequence of Israel's rebellion.[131]

### 6.6.1. Blessings and Curses

Deuteronomy 28:43–44 is embedded within a list of covenant curses (28:15–68). Tigay interprets ארר as "destined for divinely imposed misfortune."[132] The curse of 28:43–44 follows upon a string of five futility curses (28:38–42), a formula that Melissa Ramos describes as "maximum effort, minimal result."[133] For example, "You shall carry much seed into the field and shall gather in little, for the locust shall consume it" (28:38). The curse at hand is a climactic conclusion to the futility curses, now in the social sphere. This theme of futility is significant for clarifying the identity of the *gēr* in 28:43–44, which I will now explore in detail.

### 6.6.2. Identity of the *Gēr*

The appearance of the *gēr* in 28:43–44 is highly unusual. Two key questions regarding the *gēr* in Deuteronomy should be addressed: In this text,

---

131. The Babylonians became the "head" over Judah (Lam 1:5, cf. Judg 11:11; Jer 13:21); see further Lundbom, *Deuteronomy*, 786.

132. Tigay, *Deuteronomy*, 254. The blessings and curses of Deut 28 reflect, and at times correspond very closely to, the curses of ancient Near Eastern treaties. The dominance of curses over blessings also reflects the ancient Near Eastern pattern. See further Bernard M. Levinson, "Esarhaddon's Succession Treaty as the Source for the Canon Formula in Deuteronomy 13:1," *JAOS* 130 (2010): 337–47.

133. Melissa Ramos attributes this phrase to Mario Fales, "Massimo sforzo, minima resa: Maledizioni divine da Tell Fekheriye all Antico Testamento," *ACF* 21 (1982): 1–12. Ramos discusses this work in her paper, "Malediction and Oath: The Curses of the Sefire Treaties and Deuteronomy 28" (paper presented at the Annual Meeting of the Society of Biblical Literature, Baltimore, 23 November 2013).

is the *gēr* a dependent or of independent means? Is the *gēr* in this text a foreigner? Regarding the former question, Kidd is incorrect to assert that the *gēr* in this text may be wealthy.[134] The association of the present text with the futility curses (28:38–42) confirms that the movement within 28:43–44 is a reversal of the usual state of affairs. Thus the former poverty of the *gēr* is in view.

Second, that the addressee is all Israel, referred to in the second-person singular, argues strongly that the *gēr* here is a foreigner, one who is not subject to the covenant stipulations and whose fate relative to Israel brings into stark relief what Israel receives from the divine hand. Indeed, this is the consensus opinion on this text in the scholarship.[135] Throughout this study I have argued that the term *gēr* in Deuteronomy refers to displaced people without reference to their provenance and that this category of people likely included both internally displaced people and foreigners. However, as with 14:29 discussed above, it would seem likely that this text has foreigners in mind. This is the contextual meaning of *gēr* here.[136]

Nonetheless, there are good reasons to think that ancient readers would also have read this text as referring to *any gēr* in their midst, no matter where the *gēr* came from. Deuteronomy 28:43–44 reverses the blessing of 28:12b–13a, so that *gēr* is parallel to nations: "You shall lend to many nations, but you shall not borrow." This association supports the notion that *gēr* refers to a displaced foreigner. However, the parallel is incomplete. First, Deut 28:7–14 is likely a Dtr addition.[137] Second, the subject of 28:7–14 is *all Israel*, a characteristic focus of Dtr, with attention to the defeat of enemies: "Yahweh will cause your enemies who rise before you to be defeated before you" (28:7a). In distinction, the arena of 28:38–44 is localized agricultural work: "You shall carry much seed into the field and shall gather in little, for the locust shall consume it" (28:38).[138] Further, the phrase הגר אשר בקרבך (28:43) associates the *gēr* with the settlement and the household (cf. 16:11, 26:11). In 28:43–44, then, the focus

---

134. Kidd, *Alterity*, 34.

135. E.g., Awabdy, *Immigrants*, 94–96; Tigay, *Deuteronomy*, 254. Naʾaman, however, also identifies the *gēr* as a displaced Judahite in this text ("Sojourner," 252–53).

136. See §3.9 regarding the contextual meaning of *gēr*.

137. See further Mayes, *Deuteronomy*, 350.

138. On the multivalence of the second-person singular address in referring both to the individual and also to the whole community and also in identifying the two with one another, see McConville, "Singular Address."

is not international warfare, as with 28:7–14, but rather the futility of one's endeavors, specifically in the local arena. The purview of 28:38–44 is not international relations, as with 28:7–14, and ancient readers may well have understood the text as referencing any and every *gēr* who dwelled in their midst. If it should be doubted that a locally displaced person could be spoken of in such a way ("The stranger in your midst will rise above you, higher and higher..."), we must recall Hendel's assertion that "being cast out of the household and clan is a kind of social death; one is 'cut off' from kin and culture, and the promise of descendants is annulled."[139]

### 6.6.2.1. The Context of the Reader/Hearer

The immediate context of a reader/hearer of Deuteronomy will strongly influence precisely what the term *gēr* identifies. It has been shown that the provenance of this figure, whether native or otherwise, is not germane to the lexical meaning of the term *gēr*. So, while I have argued earlier that the *gēr* in 16:1–17 is simply one who is displaced at the level of a household and clan, readers in the context of the late Iron Age who encountered massive immigration in the wake of Sennacherib's invasion of Samaria may, while reading 16:1–17, have thought of the impoverished northerner in their midst as the *gēr*. Similarly, while 28:43–44 may have originally conceived of the *gēr* as a foreigner, a hearer within Persian Yehud faced with the internal displacement that was the result of economic stratification may nonetheless have interpreedt *gēr* in this text as referring to a locally displaced person. Notwithstanding these caveats, the contextual meaning for *gēr* in this text is certainly a non-Judahite/non-Israelite.

### 6.6.2.2. A Minority Group?

A third question surrounding this text concerns whether the "*gēr* who rises higher" denotes a minority group. Awabdy reflects the reigning confusion over the identity of the *gēr* in his recent monograph, where he asserts regarding 28:43–44: "This text envisions the majority subservient to the minority."[140] In the same context Awabdy refers to the "majority population." While the concept of a minority group may apply to designations

---

139. Hendel, *Remembering Abraham*, 34.

140. Awabdy, *Immigrants*, 95. This distinction between a majority population and a minority population is not a major aspect of Awabdy's work.

such as עֲמוֹנִי and מוֹאָבִי (23:4), the term *gēr* does not reference a segment of the community as such. There is no evidence of this whatsoever. Rather, a person or a family is a *gēr* in relation to a social unit upon whom the *gēr* was dependent. The vulnerability of the *gēr* was located precisely in her or his lack of a "group" to belong to.

## 6.6.3. Composition History

The unusual rhetoric of 28:43–44 concerning the *gēr* raises the question of composition history. Attempts to determine the composition history of Deut 28 have produced a large variety of suggestions in scholarship.[141] Deuteronomy 28:43–44 seems to post-date Dtn, as there is a shift in focus between Dtn's ethic of inclusion for the *gēr* and the flourishing of that same figure represented as a curse upon Israel. Here the social ethic of Dtn is omitted; the *gēr* is simply the "other" who lives within the community. Further, the text appears to precede Dtr, for *gēr* here lacks the pronominal suffix that characterizes Dtr and the localized setting for the *gēr*, as opposed to a national context, which may distinguish 28:43–44 from the later constitutional texts (29:9–14, 31:9–13). The present exegesis endorses the theory that 28:43–44 is a part of the original block of curses and is late preexilic, though certainty eludes us.[142]

## 6.7. An Alleged New Religious Inclusivism in the Framing Texts?

In light of the foregoing exegesis, the remainder of this chapter takes another look at some broader questions arising in scholarship on the *gēr*. In his recent monograph, Awabdy asserts that, while the DC provides for the social integration of the *gēr*, the prologue and epilogue of Deuteronomy integrate the *gēr* both socially and religiously.[143] With more nuance, Achenbach acknowledges that the Dtn feasting texts "offer the possibility

---

141. See Mayes, *Deuteronomy*, 348–51; Josef Plöger, *Literarkritische*, 130–36.

142. With Achenbach, *"gēr,"* 32–33. Otto notes: "In Deut. 28:2–13 the deuteronomistic authors of the Horeb-redaction expanded the curses of the pre-exilic Deuteronomy in Deut. 28:20–44 by blessings and in so doing introduced a western scheme of treaties this way to the book of Deuteronomy" (Otto, "History of the Legal-Religious," 230–31).

143. Awabdy, *Immigrants*, 241–45.

of *religious integration*" for the *gēr*,[144] while in another place he posits that the most significant integration of the *gēr* into the religious beliefs and practices of Israel occurs in Dtr and post-Dtr texts.[145] Ebach asserts that the *gēr* is a nonactive recipient of the Israelite citizen's support in Dtn, while in Dtr and post-Dtr the *gēr* is an active member of the people of Yahweh.[146] The near unanimity with which this contrast is assumed in the scholarship warrants revisiting the question, as I conclude this study.

I have observed that the view that the frame initiates a new religious inclusivism underestimates the religious significance of the *gēr* appearing in earlier Dtn feasting texts פני יהוה אלהיך (16:16, etc.). The *cultic formula* is Dtn's expression for worship at the chosen place—there is no other. Thus, if the *gēr* is not included in the religious life of the nation in Dtn via the cultic formula, it is difficult to see how Dtn includes anyone in the religious life of the nation. Similarly, I have observed that in the third-year tithe (14:28–29, Dtn; 26:12–15, Dtr) the *gēr* is to consume the holy portion. Yu states: "The fact that aliens are allowed to consume the sacred portion (14:29; 26:13) and participate in the national festivals (16:11, 14) at the single sanctuary is … explained on the ground that they are regarded as members of the covenant community."[147] I also observed that the inclusion of the *gēr* within the public reading of Torah ritual is an addition to the already-established tradition of Booths within which the *gēr* was previously included. It is not the religious participation of the *gēr* that changed with 31:9–13 but the additional institution of the public reading of Torah. Thus the frame does not institute an unprecedented religious inclusivism; rather, it institutes a new set of cultic practices in which the *gēr* is included. Aside from all of this, the separation of social and religious inclusion in the scholarship cited above entails a false dichotomy as far as Deuteronomy is concerned.[148]

Nonetheless, there is indeed a shift in Deuteronomy's framework vis-à-vis the DC. The frame distinctively emphasizes the renewal of all Israel, incorporating the *gēr* into the covenant life of the nation. The *gēr* is grafted into the kinship grouping, not only of the household and clan as with Dtn,

---

144. Achenbach, "*gêr*," 32.

145. Achenbach, "Eintritt," 251.

146. Ebach, *Fremde*, 200, 312.

147. Ebach, *Fremde*, 91–92.

148. By comparison, חרם texts stipulate both religious and social separation (e.g., 7:1–16).

but also of the nation. Indeed, the *gēr* is grafted into the genealogy of all Israel. Furthermore, by virtue of his or her inclusion within the covenant, the *gēr* becomes more clearly the addressee in these texts (see especially 31:9–13).

## 6.8. The *Gēr*'s Kinship within the Nation

The grouping of all Israel is conceived in terms of kinship. Clan-based ties are inadequate to structure the social realities that a growing lineage group encounters. Mendenhall asserts that, as a group's size increases, kinship ties become less "real": "As social units become larger, kinship ties become increasingly dysfunctional as the basis for the larger group; but kinship terminology seems to become more and more used to express the new bond that ties the larger group together."[149] Recent insights into national kinship from cultural anthropology clarify the strength and capacity of the kinship metaphor at this level: "Metaphors of [national] kinship have the ability to take on meanings that are more literal than metaphorical."[150]

Kinship at a national level is especially observable in the covenant texts of the frame of Deuteronomy. The phrase the "people of Yahweh" is an intimate expression for the relation between Israel and its divine kinsperson: למען הקים אתך היום לו לעם (29:12aα).[151] Through participation in the covenant (29:10–11), through sharing in Israel's formative historical story (29:1–8), and through sharing in the lineage connection with the forefathers (29:12), the stranger was being grafted into the all-Israel group. Nonetheless, we should be wary of assuming that the primary identification of the common people was as Israel. On the contrary, family-based kinship is also visible in the frame of Deuteronomy, and in these texts the *gēr* is still identified in relation to the family or clan (see §§6.3.3.1 and 6.4.5.1).[152]

---

149. George E. Mendenhall, *The Tenth Generation: The Origins of the Biblical Tradition* (Baltimore: Johns Hopkins University Press, 1973), 176, cited in Braulik, "Rights," 7.

150. Carsten, *Kinship*, 158.

151. Cross uses the phrase "divine kinsman" (*Epic*, 6).

152. See §6.3.3.

Deuteronomy fosters the inclusion of the *gēr* in diffuse and related cultural domains in a variety of related ways. At the risk of oversimplifying, we have observed:

1. The feasting formula, which consists of the command שמח ("feast!"), followed by the household list (e.g., 16:11, 14), fosters inclusion within a household.[153]
2. The phrase בשעריך, which refers to the protective circumference of a local settlement, town, or city, fosters inclusion within a clan or town.[154]
3. The *gēr*'s participation within a covenant-renewal ceremony fosters inclusion within all Israel (e.g., 29:9–14).

We have seen that diffuse social domains can appear within the same texts. This overlapping of domains at the level of semantics reflects a deeper association of societal domains in Deuteronomy (see §5.2.3.1). Indeed, cross-culturally, "houses (which might be thought of as quintessentially domestic spaces) have myriad links to the polities of which they are part."[155]

The incorporation of the *gēr* within all Israel again raises the question of the provenance of the *gēr*, and our conclusions are summarized here.

### 6.9. Summary of the Evidence that *Gēr* is a Vulnerable Person from outside the Core Family

Here I gather into one place the evidence put forward throughout this study that the *gēr* is simply a vulnerable person from outside the core family. This is especially important given that there is a near consensus in most recent scholarship that the *gēr* is a foreigner, a non-Judahite/non-Israelite. The footnotes link each point to the location where the point is explained more fully.

#### 6.9.1. Ethnicity and Kinship

♦ Some scholarship on the *gēr* incorrectly considers ethnicity in exclusively "national" categories, whereby "Israel" is a clearly

---

153. See §5.2.2.
154. See §5.5.2.
155. Carsten, *Kinship*, 60.

defined group in the eyes of all actors and whereby the primary identification of the members of the community before the text is as "Israel," yielding a simple binary distinction: Israel/not-Israel. Rather, the primary identity of an "Israelite" was within the clan and the household. Correspondingly, an *outsider* may simply be a person from another clan.[156]

◆ In some Mesopotamian and Egyptian texts, a "stranger" is a person from a different household or clan grouping.[157]

### 6.9.2. Displacement in Deuteronomy

◆ Deuteronomy most often refers to the *gēr* in relation to the household (observe the household list, for example, in 16:11, 14) and the clan (בשעריך). Otherness is located at this local level.[158]

◆ Foreignness is not germane to the lexical meaning of *gr* in Northwest Semitic cognates.[159]

◆ Certainly in Deuteronomy's frame all Israel is a dominant group identity.[160] However, when the *gēr* appears in the context of all Israel, the *gēr* is nonetheless identified in relation to the household and to the clan (29:10, 31:12). The *gēr* is an "outsider" at a local level. The concern to include the *gēr* within the covenant rituals (e.g., 29:9–14) is not necessary due to the *gēr*'s foreignness. Rather, severance from kinship and from land may bring into question the displaced person's standing in the assembly.[161]

◆ The *gēr* is not considered a religious threat. Ebach, who considers that the *gēr* is a foreigner, makes this point strikingly: "Even in the postexilic period there is no warning that the *gēr* could seduce you to join a strange cult. This is remarkable, as it is precisely contact with the nearby stranger that is considered a dangerous source of apostasy."[162]

---

156. See further §§5.2.3, 5.2.4, and 6.10.1.
157. See §§2.1, 4.2.3.
158. See further §§5.2.3, 5.2.4, and 5.5.2.
159. See further §2.1.
160. See further §6.10.
161. See further §6.4.5.1.
162. Ebach, *Fremde*, 199: "Auch in nachexilischer Zeit erfolgt keine Warnung, dass der ger zu einem fremden Kult verführen könnte. Dies ist insofern bemerkenswert,

### 6.9.3. Displacement in Judah's Social History

- ♦ The periods in which redactional strata in Deuteronomy were likely produced were contexts of massive internal displacement in Judah:
    - ♦ In seventh-century Judah, two likely causes of massive internal displacement were Sennacharib's invasion (701 BCE) and a cycle of deepening indebtedness and land alienation.[163] Dtn respond to this context of displacement.
    - ♦ As a result of the Neo-Babylonian conquest and its aftermath, post–Iron Age Judah was a postcollapse society with a widespread and unprecedented level of displacement. As Deuteronomy reconstitutes Israel in this context of devastation, it is the one who has been severed from land and from genealogy in particular who must be enfolded in the covenant (so Dtr).
    - ♦ In Persian Yehud, socioeconomic stratification produced indebtedness and land alienation. The return of the exiles produced further conflict over patrimony and further land alienation.[164] Post-Dtr responds to this displacement.
- ♦ Scholars who both ascribe much of the frame to the exilic period and regard the *gēr* as exclusively a foreigner (e.g., Achenbach, Veijola) must explain how the primary social dilemma of exilic Judah and Persian Yehud was the inclusion of foreigners. This contention pays insufficient attention to the social realities of Judah during the sixth century and beyond.

### 6.10. External and Internal Boundary Markers

At least on the surface of the text, the ethic of inclusion for the *gēr* in Deuteronomy that has been observed in this study stands in tension with "national," exclusivist, and violent texts in this book. So we now turn to probe boundary markers in Deuteronomy.

---

als ja gerade der Kontakt zu den nahen Fremden als Gefahrenquelle der Apostasie gewertet wird."

163. See further §3.7.5.

164. See further §§4.7.3, 6.4.3, and 6.4.5.1.

## 6.10.1. Terms for Otherness in Deuteronomy: Is the Term *Gēr* a Boundary Marker?

On an axis of liminality, the term *gēr* differs from alternative terms for otherness in Deuteronomy, namely, נכרי and זר. All three terms distinguish the "other" from the community, whether at the level of the whole community of Israel or at the level of a local settlement. The נכרי is a foreigner who is of independent means and who is not assimilated into the community.[165] The five uses of the term נכרי in Deuteronomy appear in contexts that highlight the distinction between the נכרי and the native Israelite (14:21, 15:3, 17:15, 23:21, 29:21). For example, the נכרי may be charged interest, while the Israelite may not (23:21). "This clarifies that נכרי means a foreigner who in addition stands by Israel in a reserved, nonintegrated position."[166] The term נכרי operates at a "national" level: the נכרי is a non-Israelite. The term זר is used in Deuteronomy only once, in the context of remarriage. A widow who remarries may not marry a זר (25:5). Patrick Miller incorrectly identifies the זר here as a foreigner.[167] Rather, here זר is opposed to אח, in a law where אח clearly references a local kinship group (as opposed to national identity), and זר here simply refers to a man who is from outside of the group. In the HC, the word זר is used in the context of cultic distinctions (e.g., Num 17:5). In its essence, then, זר designates "a person who is not part of a social unit."[168] It is evident that, unlike the *gēr*, the נכרי and the זר are not liminal figures. These terms designate otherness without any anticipation of further inclusion. Archaeology may provide insight into these terms. Avraham Faust observes the presence in large villages of individual dwellings with agricultural facilities. Faust postulates

---

165. Sparks makes a similar distinction between the נכרי and the *gēr* (*Ethnicity*, 242). However, Sparks's additional category of a nonassimilating *gēr* in Deuteronomy is of his own invention (*Ethnicity*, 241–42), for it is unlikely that an impoverished, unconnected, and landless person would seek independence. See also Ebach, *Fremde*, 62–69; and see §5.2.5.1.

166. Zehnder, *Umgang*, 373: "Diese Präzisierung macht deutlich, dass es sich beim per נכרי definitionem um einen Fremdstämmigen handelt, der zudem zu Israel in einer distanzierten, nichtintegrierten Stellung steht." It may be that in some cases the נכרי is identified as much by mercantile vocation as by ethnicity (15:3).

167. Patrick D. Miller, "Israel as Host to Strangers," in *Israelite Religion and Biblical Theology*, ed. Patrick D. Miller, JSOTSup 267 (Sheffield: Sheffield Academic, 2000), 550.

168. Achenbach, "gêr," 45.

that the residents of these dwellings did not belong to the kinship group of the village, as they were not sharing in the communal means of production.[169] These residents may be of the kind referenced in Deuteronomy as נכרי or as זר.

The reference of these various terms is expressed here in tabular form, though allowing for a certain ambivalence and multivalence, not least as various social domains are correlated in Deuteronomy.

Table 6.6. Insider/Outsider Terms and Social Domains

|  | National Level | Clan/Town/City Level | Household Level |
|---|---|---|---|
| kinsperson | אח or רע | אח or רע | אח |
| other: vulnerable and dependent | gēr | gēr | gēr |
| other: independent | נכרי | זר (from another clan) | — |

At this point the common claim that the term *gēr* is a boundary marker may be tested.[170] In the Hebrew Bible, certain terms function as external boundary markers that distinguish between native and foreign members of the community, such as עמוני (23:4), מואבי (23:4), אדמי (23:8), and מצרי (23:8); compare with ארמי (26:5). The contexts in which these terms are used reassert limits upon the admission of these groups into the community. These references illustrate that the "world behind the text" of Deuteronomy has a high level of ethnic consciousness. They exemplify the observations of anthropologists that, "as a general rule, ethnic folk taxonomies are at their most detailed closest to the actor"[171] and that the memory of past interaction between ethnic groups (whether historical or mythical) may be evoked in order to authorize present behavior (23:5–6, 8; 26:18). However, the term *gēr* has quite a different function.[172] This is a legal term that facilitates not only the sustenance of a certain category of displaced

---

169. Faust, *Archaeology*, 175.

170. E.g., Kidd, *Alterity*, 46. Van Houten uses the insider/outsider distinction to compare the *gēr* with the native (*Aliens*, 107).

171. Erikson, *Ethnicity*, 27.

172. Contrary to Kidd, *Alterity*, 46.

and vulnerable people but also their inclusion. The critical point is that, while the term *gēr* does indeed *reference* the otherness of its subject, it does not *produce* the otherness, as do the gentilics listed above. The only ethnic memory associated with the term *gēr* is that of Israel's own displacement, which in turn fosters a compassionate response to the *gēr*. Altmann's description of the *gēr* as the "special insider" is apt.[173] The *gēr* is a liminal figure, and Deuteronomy is fostering the *gēr*'s full participation in the household as kindred.

### 6.10.2. External Boundary Markers

In Deuteronomy a primary social category is national Israel, often referred to in binaries: Israel/non-Israel. "Tribal distinctions are hinted at only *sotto voce*."[174] "Just as the land is unified rather than reflecting tribal divisions, so it is with the people."[175] Indeed, Deuteronomy can be seen as a constitution for an Israelite polity, as McBride has observed.[176] The paramount external boundary marker of the community is devotion to Yahweh, expressed in the covenant (10:12–21, 29:9–13), in the centralization command, and in the cultic formula.[177] Indeed, as a number of studies have concluded, the boundaries surrounding Deuteronomic identity are primarily religious boundaries rather than ethnic ones.[178] Ethical distinctiveness for the sake of the poor and the displaced is another prominent external marker (e.g., 4:5–8), as well as identification within Israel's corporate history, with the "fathers," with the patriarchs, and through the practice of rituals.[179] Deuteronomy aims to shape Israel as a contrastive community in relation to

---

173. Altmann, *Festive*, 109 n. 234.

174. McConville, *God and Earthly*, 92.

175. McConville, *God and Earthly*, 92.

176. McBride, "Polity."

177. See further Robert R. Wilson, "Deuteronomy, Ethnicity, and Reform," in *Constituting the Community: Studies on the Polity of Ancient Israel in Honour of S. Dean McBride Jr.*, ed. John T. Strong and Steven S. Tuell (Winona Lake, IN: Eisenbrauns, 1995), 114–17; Nestor, *Cognitive*, 195–96.

178. "Deuteronomic identity" is Sparks's phrase, *Ethnicity*, 272; see also 264; E. Theodore Mullen, *Narrative History and Ethnic Boundaries: The Deuteronomic Historian and the Creation of Israelite National Identity*, SemeiaSt 35 (Atlanta: Scholars Press, 1993); Nestor, *Cognitive*, 195–96.

179. See further Hendel, *Remembering Abraham*, 7–8, 21–22, 34; Sparks, *Ethnicity*, 225–36.

the nations, in light of Yahweh's gracious rule (4:5–8). In the framing texts, all Israel becomes a dominant trope.

However, there is also a surprising fluidity, or inclusivism, in Yahweh's covenant with Israel. As Deuteronomy renews Israel in light of the gracious rule of Yahweh,[180] the *gēr* is swept up in the divine invitation. Contrary to some scholarship, joining the family of Yahweh does not require a "conversion" or a "confession of faith." Rather, as I observed in chapter 5, the *gēr* is to be caught up in the joy, the ritual, the community, and the abundance of the family of Yahweh.[181]

### 6.10.3. Internal Boundary Markers

"The varying internal boundaries in Israelite religion and culture suggest a real cultural pluralism."[182] Internal boundary markers in Deuteronomy largely have been ignored in scholarly discussions of the *gēr*, yet internal boundaries are not only evident in Deuteronomy; they are prominent. There are, for example, "latent internal fissures, as between the northern and southern tribes, which the appeal to a common lineage could not help spinning apart."[183] Joshua Berman correctly discerns a fading of tribal identities in Deuteronomy. [184] However, Berman overstates the case when he writes, "In presenting its federated bureaucratic structure, Deuteronomy seems to know of two units only: the nation and the city."[185] Instead, uniquely prominent in Deuteronomy is the household, referenced in the household list (e.g., 5:14; 16:11, 14, 26:11), and the settlement or clan, referenced in the phrase בשעריך (e.g., 5:14; 14:21, 29; 16:14).[186] Indeed, the household and the clan are charged with the primary responsibility to ful-

---

180. See below on "becoming Israel." See also Sanders, *Invention*, 169.

181. See §5.2.5.1.

182. Hendel, *Remembering Abraham*, 19. Avraham Faust has defended the early existence of a shared identity between Judah and Israel; see *Israel's Ethnogenesis: Settlement, Interaction, Expansion and Resistance* (London: Equinox, 2006); for a more recent account, see Faust, "Between Israel and Judah." Against this view, see Norman K. Gottwald, *The Politics of Ancient Israel*, LAI (Louisville: Westminster John Knox, 2000), 21; Finkelstein, "State." I use the notion of group identity cognizant of the nature of ethnicity as process (see further, Nestor, *Cognitive*, 193–94).

183. Hendel, *Remembering Abraham*, 37. See also the analysis at §6.5.

184. Berman, "Constitution," 527–28.

185. Berman, "Constitution," 542.

186. See the discussion of gates in §5.5.2.

fill the social program of the DC (see §§5.2.3, 5.2.4). The evidence both from Deuteronomy and from the ancient Near East suggests that the primary identification of common people was within a household and a clan. As Altmann states, Deuteronomy presents the "participation of all Israel as a conglomeration of household units" (e.g., 16:11, 14).[187] Nonetheless, Hendel's assertion holds true for Deuteronomy: "The individual is a point of intersection among many genealogical relationships, both to living relatives and dead ancestors…. An individual is the child X, of the clan of Y, of the tribe of Z, of the people of Israel."[188]

The nature of the category *outsider* is determined in relation to the boundaries of who is considered as an *insider*. So, if an insider is a clansperson, an outsider may simply be a person from outside of the clan. In Deuteronomy, the term *gēr* simply identifies a vulnerable person who is from outside of the core family. This person may indeed be from another nation, but foreign identity is not germane to the word *gēr*.

The all-Israel focus of the framework does not require that *outsiderism* be identified at a national level. Rather, in the framework *gēr* is consistently referenced at the level of the settlement via phrases such as וגרך אשר בשעריך (31:12) and at the level of the household via the pronominal suffix on וגרך (29:10, 31:12). The *otherness* of the *gēr* clusters at the local level. Indeed, the central social dynamic related to the *gēr* is not a dialectic between the native and the nonnative but a defining of the people of Yahweh: what being/becoming Israel entails, and this in the distinctive setting of a postcollapse society.[189] For Deuteronomy's framework, given the widespread displacement that followed the Neo-Babylonian conquest, as Israel was reconstituted the displaced person in particular needed to be enfolded within the covenant.

The *gēr* is mentioned specifically in these texts, since traditionally lineage and patrimony were constitutive for inclusion within the assembly. Compare, for example, the importance of tracing lineage in Ezra-Nehemiah (Ezra 2; 8:3–14; Neh 7; 11:4–20).[190] Displaced and vulnerable people stood outside of the traditional kinship groupings, and therefore their association within the gathering was in question.

---

187. Altmann, "Festive," 3.
188. Hendel, *Remembering Abraham*, 34.
189. On the phrase "postcollapse society," see Faust, *Judah*, 167–80.
190. See further Williamson, "Family," 469–85.

Being cast out of the household and clan is a kind of social death; one is "cut off" from kin and culture, and the promise of descendants is annulled. In this respect, the collective past, as encoded in the genealogy, is a regulative presence in daily life, a constitutive charter of rights, obligations, and identity.[191]

To repeat, the point of the *gēr* texts throughout Deuteronomy is not to include lots of non-Israelites as Israel is renewed. Rather the question is: In this context of social upheaval, where as many people are displaced as are not, how may those who have been displaced from kindred and from patrimony, whether native or foreign, be enfolded within the covenant? The question may be posed differently: With what kind of community is Yahweh covenanting? Deuteronomy answers that Yahweh is covenanting not merely with those of means, of land, and of lineage but also with the displaced—these people also may identify with the history of exodus, wilderness wanderings, and even the patriarchs.

6.10.4. Inclusion and Exclusion: Antithesis or Contextualization?

Deuteronomy's exclusivist texts, of which the חרם commands (see especially 20:16–18) and the laws of admission (23:2–9) are the most famous examples, exhibit an *insiderism* that is disparaged in some of the scholarship.[192] In Deuteronomy, חרם signifies the complete loyalty to Yahweh and to Yahweh's design for community that Yahweh himself demands and that deep human flourishing requires. Other societies were shaped by a different kind of rule and were therefore in many ways an aberration of Yahweh's intention for a society. Israel is meant to reject utterly the false worship of these kingdoms.[193] Clarifying is the observation of Smith that, for communities that are marginal and oppressed, social boundaries are established as mechanisms for religious and social survival.[194] Also clarifying is the above observation that Deuteronomic identity hinges primar-

---

191. Hendel, *Remembering Abraham,* 34. See further Jacob Milgrom, *Leviticus 1–16,* AB 3 (New York: Doubleday, 1991), 457–60.

192. E.g., Regina M. Schwartz, *The Curse of Cain: the Violent Legacy of Monotheism* (Chicago: University of Chicago Press, 1997); Keith W. Whitelam, *The Invention of Ancient Israel: The Silencing of Palestinian History* (London: Routledge, 1996), 3.

193. See further McConville, *Deuteronomy,* 90, 161.

194. Smith, "Politics of Ezra," 97.

ily upon religious boundaries rather than ethnic boundaries, so that ethnic boundaries are surprisingly permeable.

Deuteronomy's relentless ethic of inclusion for the *gēr* is, as Albertz reflects, all the more "amazing" in light of the exclusion of others.[195] This apparent tension begs for discussion. Gerstenberger explains these differing postures by the existence of "varied theological groupings" within the community that was devoted to Yahweh.[196] However, in certain texts insider themes coexist with themes of inclusivism in the same redactional layer, challenging this assertion (e.g., 23:1–7; see also 23:8, 29:9–14; cf. 29:10aβ). Gerstenberger's solution runs the risk of obscuring deeper theological aims within Deuteronomy. It is preferable to understand this complex of responses as an authentic attempt, on the one hand, to preserve the religious and social identity of Judah as a marginalized community and, on the other hand, to express an inclusivism *that is central to this very identity*. By this logic, the *gēr* is, by definition, vulnerable and isolated, so the *gēr* is unlikely to threaten the faithfulness of the community. However, consolidated groups who do not worship Yahweh may pose a real threat. As Sparks says,

> The supposed theological diversity that one observes in the sources with respect to ethnic boundaries actually reflects, in a certain sense, a kind of theological coherence. It supports the theological legitimacy of efforts to adjust the character and intensity of community boundaries in response to both the threats and the opportunities that are presented to the community of faith. But such efforts must necessarily be circumscribed … by an unyielding allegiance to Yahweh and by a community life that reflects a commitment to his revealed word.[197]

### 6.11. Being/Becoming the Family of Yahweh

At the heart of Deuteronomy is the movement of *being/becoming the community of Yahweh*.[198] Deuteronomy is shaping Israel as a contrastive community, living in the sight of the nations, transformed by the word of

---

195. Albertz, "Aliens," 55.

196. Gerstenberger, *Israel in the Persian*, 441.

197. Sparks, *Ethnicity*, 331.

198. For this section I am indebted to verbal and e-mail communication with Peter Altmann. See also Altmann, *Festive*, 2–3.

Yahweh.[199] This book is not ultimately shaping a nation-state or an ethnic group but a people who are responsive to his word. Seth Sanders notes,

> The Deuteronomistic covenant is not intended to constitute a state (let alone a democratic republic) but to imagine a people, constituted by their attention and response to a set of texts (both spoken and written); to the extent that the texts share a goal it is to elicit this attention and response: for addressees to imagine themselves as part of this people. The ideal reader it presupposes is not a member of an already constituted kingdom or polity, but a constituting member.[200]

While Sanders overstates the case, he rightly discerns Deuteronomy's purpose in reconstituting the family of Yahweh and in shaping this people by Yahweh's word. This reconstitution, as Sanders observes, is invitational. Indeed, it sweeps up the displaced within the divine invitation. There is an inherent vulnerability in such an open-ended invitation: "Racial categories themselves are formed, transformed, destroyed and reformed."[201] The *gēr* herself or himself contests and defines what it means to be/become Israel, and this challenge to Israel's identity is relentless, as inclusivism is at the heart of Israel's identity. It is a constitutive part of Israel's *ethics* (5:14), *history* (5:15), *religion* (16:14), and *mandate* (10:17–19).

It appears that Deuteronomy is occupied with the questions of identity that arose through a series of fractures. These fractures may have included the destruction of Judah by Sennacherib in the seventh century, the decimation of the Neo-Babylonian conquest that created a "generational problem" whereby traditional faith was in danger of fading,[202] and, as Kessler states, "in the Persian period, the question of what the people of Israel is and who belongs to it becomes more and more acute."[203] Into these contexts of fracture, Deuteronomy held out a vision for being/becoming the family of Yahweh. Three characteristics of a movement toward being/

---

199. See further Mark Glanville, "A Missional Reading of Deuteronomy: Communities of Gratitude, Celebration, and Justice," in *Reading the Bible Missionally*, ed. Michael Goheen (Grand Rapids: Eerdmans, 2016), 124–50.

200. Sanders, *Invention*, 170.

201. Omi and Winant, *Racial*, 61. Nestor has applied theory of racial formation to biblical studies (*Cognitive*, 192–215).

202. Gerhard von Rad, *Old Testament Theology*, 2 vols. (New York: Harper & Row, 1962), 2:225.

203. Kessler, *Social*, 130.

becoming the family of Yahweh are salient. First, in earlier times Deuteronomy achieved this vision through festal ritual and through law, and in later times Deuteronomy achieved this through covenant assemblies and through the public reading of Torah.

Second, Torah defines the character of the covenant family. The stone tablets of the covenant at Horeb (5:22) and the book of law of the covenant at Moab (31:26) contain Yahweh's laws that shape a most remarkably egalitarian community.[204] These laws foster the incorporation of the displaced in a way that is unique among extant ancient Near Eastern law corpora. Indeed, as a participant in the covenant, the *gēr*, too, is to hear and to learn the Torah and so to fear and to obey Yahweh.

Third, identity is inseparable from origins. Deuteronomy addresses the community as contemporaries of Moses on the brink of the Jordan and as the generation through whom the covenant with the patriarchs may be realized. In this way, Deuteronomy holds out the hope that a new beginning is possible.[205] The *gēr* is most emphatically caught up in the genealogy of Israel and grafted into the community as kin-in-blood (29:1–14, 31:10–12). The origin narrative that looms largest over the DC is the exodus event, which introduces Yahweh as the just king and the emancipator of slaves and which casts Israel as both stranger and as slave, radically destabilizing any pretense to grandiose conceit and challenging self-interest.

At the heart of Deuteronomy, then, is being/becoming the community of Yahweh. The inclusion of displaced people is primary in this process, and their participation in the community shapes this process.

## 6.12. Conclusion

While in the DC there is a particular focus upon the clan and the household, in the framing texts (Deut 1–11, 27–34) the *gēr* is incorporated within the kinship grouping of all Israel and of Israel's divine kinsperson. This chapter has examined some key texts in Deuteronomy's frame relating to the *gēr*. In 10:12–11:1, a matrix of kin and covenant relations is established: Israel is to love the *gēr* because Yahweh loves the *gēr*, even as Yahweh loves Israel. In the covenant-renewal text (29:9–14), the covenant creates relations of adoptive kinship between the *gēr* and the kinsperson.

---

204. "The picture that emerges is one of collective power par excellence" (Berman, "Constitution," 534). Berman is speaking in particular of 1:9–18.

205. Römer, "Deuteronomy in Search of Origins," 118.

Here the *gēr* is also enfolded within the foundational stories of the nation. In 31:9–31 the *gēr* is included in the public reading of Torah during the Feast of Booths every seven years at the time of the שמטה (31:9–13). The *gēr* is to hear and to learn the Torah and so to fear and to obey Yahweh. Deuteronomy 31:9–13 appropriates the feasting trope from Dtn, forging, via a kin-making cultic ritual, a covenant community that is centered on Torah. Deuteronomy 27:19 protects via a curse ceremony the judicial rights of the *gēr*. The curse of 28:43–44 envisions a social inversion, the consequence of disobedience, in which the *gēr* rises to be head over the kinsfolk. In this text, Dtn's ethics of generosity and inclusion for the stranger are not in mind.

Six key theses were established throughout the exegesis of the *gēr* in Deuteronomy's frame:

First, while in Dtn the *gēr* was grafted into the clan and into the household—local kinship groupings—in Deuteronomy's framework the *gēr* is incorporated into the kinship grouping of all Israel and of its divine kinsperson.[206]

Second, the all-Israel focus of the frame does not require that outsiderism is therefore to be identified at a national level. The *gēr* is simply a vulnerable person who is from outside the core family.

Third, the frame does not demonstrate an unprecedented religious inclusivism for the *gēr*, as the majority of scholars suggest. Rather, the frame prescribes a further set of cultic practices in which the *gēr* is included, this time with an all-Israel focus. Nonetheless, displacement becomes the central social concern of the framework, and the prominence of other categories of vulnerability is diminished.

Fourth, I offered a tentative sociohistorical reconstruction. The Neo-Babylonian conquest and its aftermath decimated the population, culture, and society of Judah. Within this context of massive displacement, Dtr renewed the community as Israel,[207] identifying the community once again with its lineage and with its salvation history. The *gēr* was formally incorporated within Israel as kin via the covenant with Yahweh (29:9–14). In Persian Yehud, pervasive displacement due to socioeconomic stratifi-

---

206. Nonetheless, in Dtn the *gēr* is incorporated into the people of Yahweh conceived as an entity in Dtn through the centralization formula and through cultic feasting.

207. See again Römer's comment in n. 64.

cation and the return of the *golah* prompted new expressions of Deuteronomy's ethic and theology of inclusivism.

Fifth, at the heart of Deuteronomy's program is being/becoming the community of Yahweh. The *gēr* is swept up in the divine invitation, and with this movement the *gēr* contests and defines what it means to be/become Israel.

Sixth, the apparent tension in Deuteronomy between the inclusion of the *gēr* and the exclusion of others was addressed. It is preferable to understand this complex of responses as an authentic attempt, on the one hand, to preserve the religious and social identity of Judah as a marginalized community and, on the other hand, to express the inclusivism that is central to this identity.

# 7
# Conclusion

This study has examined an ethic of inclusivism for the *gēr* as found in the book of Deuteronomy. The study has adopted an integrative methodology, bringing together social-historical, comparative, legal, sociological, literary, theological, and literary-historical approaches. These approaches have informed an exegesis of all of the texts in Deuteronomy concerning the *gēr*. A key methodological lens has been the concept of adoptive kinship articulated by cultural anthropologists. The creativity that communities may invest in enfolding displaced and vulnerable people as kindred, explored by Janet Carsten, for example, has been of particular interest.[1] The conclusions and broader implications of the study may be comprehended under five headings, as follows.

### 7.1. Implications for Understanding the *Gēr* in Deuteronomy

### 7.1.1. Deuteronomy Fosters the Inclusion of the *Gēr* as Kindred

A primary social need within the communities that Deuteronomy addressed was that displaced people be integrated into the clans. Deuteronomy responded to this basic need, for the central transformative impulse of Deuteronomy's ethic for the *gēr*, expressed in a multiplicity of ways, was to foster the inclusion of the *gēr* as kindred. In ancient societies (as in any and every society), individuals and families could be adopted into a kinship group.

In Deuteronomy this is observable, for example, in social law. The persistent expectation that the household and the clan care for the well-being of the *gēr* is a signal to us that Deuteronomy is nourishing the *gēr*'s inclu-

---

1. Carsten, *After Kinship*, 9.

sion as kindred. In Mediterranean communal cultures, nothing is owed to outsiders, but kindred share in mutual protection and subsistence. Deuteronomy's household pilgrimage feasts also foster this inclusion. Anthropology of feasting shows that in pilgrimage feasting social structures may be rearranged and kinship may be forged. Through feasting before Yahweh, the *gēr* was to be incorporated into the household and into the clan as kindred. While the law corpus focuses upon the clan and upon the household, in Deuteronomy's frame the *gēr* is included within the kinship grouping of all Israel and of its divine kinsman. For example, in 29:9–13 the *gēr* is grafted into the genealogy of Israel.

Nonetheless, the *gēr* remains a liminal figure. The *gēr* is never explicitly designated a brother in Deuteronomy, as the absence of affiliation is definitional for the term *gēr*. Deuteronomy does not address the *gēr* as a member of the community; rather, it is concerned with practices that foster the incorporation of this liminal figure.

The conclusion that Deuteronomy is fostering the inclusion of the *gēr* as kindred is dramatically contrastive to the reigning discursive binary that views the *gēr* as a foreigner who ought to receive Israel's charity and hospitality and views Israel as the unchanging host nation. In addition, this study challenges the consensus view that the frame of Deuteronomy evinces a new level of religious inclusion that surpasses that of Dtn. This view underestimates the religious significance of the *gēr* appearing פני יהוה אלהיך in Dtn feasting texts (e.g., 16:16), as well as the significance of the *gēr* consuming the tithe (14:22–27, 28–29). This conclusion invites further exploration of the ways in which other aspects of biblical law may be operating in the realm of kinship.

### 7.1.2. Each Category of Law Has a Distinct Function in Relation to the *Gēr*

Uniquely, this study has observed that each category of law has a distinct function in relation to the *gēr*. A system of protection and inclusion for the *gēr* is established within and between the interplay between these subgroups of laws. Chapter 3 examined social law, which aimed to protect vulnerable people against exploitation. This law restrained a creditor's power to accumulate indentured workers and slaves. These laws provide that the *gēr* is a co-participant in the community and a co-recipient of the gift of land and its abundance. Chapter 4 demonstrated that judicial law was the most important legal category for the protection and inclusion of the stranger within the community. Indeed, the very first stipulation in

Deuteronomy concerns just judicial processes for the *gēr* (1:16–17). These laws require that the *gēr* receive a hearing and receive judgment without regard to his or her landlessness and lack of kinship connection. The core judicial texts (16:18–20, 17:2–13, 19:15–21) are concerned with judicial probity. However, there is a later Dtr social redaction of judicial law that is especially concerned to protect the *gēr*. Chapter 5 demonstrated how Deuteronomy's feasting texts seek to transform the relationship of *gēr* to the community, to the land, and to Yahweh. Through pilgrimage feasting, the *gēr* is knit into the household and the clan grouping as kindred. In the Festival of the Firstfruits (26:1–11), ethics of inclusion for the *gēr* are embedded in Israel's own formative narrative of wandering and vulnerability, forging "intersubjective solidarity"[2] and "mutuality of being."[3] The reappropriation of the sacred tithe for the *gēr* signifies the holiness of the stranger, demonstrating that the *gēr*, too, belongs to the people of Yahweh (14:22–27).

These findings demonstrate both the specificity of distinct categories of law as well as the complexity of the interrelation of these categories within the biblical law corpora. Further investigation of these categories and their interrelation will help to clarify the social vision of the law corpora and of the Pentateuch.

7.1.3. The *Gēr* Is a Vulnerable Person Who Is from outside of the Core Family

Against a growing consensus in the most recent scholarship that the *gēr* is a foreigner, I have argued that the term *gēr* in Deuteronomy simply designates a vulnerable person who is from outside of the core family. *Gēr* is a legal term that refers to people who have been displaced from their former kinship group and patrimony and from the protection that kinship and land affords and who seek sustenance in a new context. The *gēr* often appears in Deuteronomy as an outsider in relation to a household and to a clan, within which the *gēr* is seeking protection and sustenance. Many of those designated *gēr* were internally displaced Judahites, some were non-Judahites/non-Israelites, and some may have been northerners who had fled Assyrian invasion.

---

2. Carsten, *After Kinship*, 43.
3. Sahlins, *What Kinship Is*, 19–31.

Whereas much scholarship of the Hebrew Bible proceeds on the assumption that ethnicity obtains in exclusively national categories whereby Israel is a clearly defined group in the eyes of all actors and the primary identification of the members of the community is as Israel, this study suggests that social identity is far more complex. First, a person identifies within various social domains: the nuclear family, the household, the clan, the tribe, and the nation. Thus a displaced person may be an outsider in relation to any of these levels. Second, ethnicity and culture themselves are "defined and contested throughout society,"[4] and any act of inclusivism necessarily unsettles shared conceptions of identity. Thus, Deuteronomy's vision for the *gēr* also addresses the question, what does it mean to be/become Israel?

### 7.1.4. An Ethic of Inclusivism Is Embedded in Yahweh's Actions and Character and in Israel's Own Narrative

Deuteronomy's ethic of inclusion for the *gēr* is embedded theologically within Yahweh's own actions and character and also within Israel's own formative narrative. For example, the exodus motif in the law corpus is especially related to stipulations concerning the *gēr* and the slave. In the exodus Israel was "brought out," יצא, from under the rule of Pharaoh and "brought into," בוא, a new allegiance to Yahweh its deliverer in Yahweh's land (e.g., 26:8–9). Israel's own vulnerability as *gēr* in Egypt identifies Israel with the *gēr*, inviting Israel to offer the kind of hospitality that Israel would have liked to receive in Egypt (e.g., 26:1–11). The theme of Yahweh's judgment extends from the exodus event into judicial law, where Yahweh is characterized as the guarantor of just judicial processes for the most vulnerable. Yahweh's role as the divine king who establishes justice is also a part of Deuteronomy's conception of appearing פני יהוה אלהיך (e.g., 16:1–17).

In the framework of Deuteronomy (Deut 1–11, 27–34), different theological themes emerge (see ch. 6). Here the *gēr* is adopted within the kinship grouping of all Israel and of Israel's divine kinsman. Israel is to love the *gēr* because Yahweh loves the *gēr*, even as Yahweh loves Israel (10:17–19). Further, as an *imago Dei* correspondence, Israel's love for the *gēr* is to be conceived of in terms of a permanent covenant commitment, of kinship,

---

4. Omi and Winant, *Racial*, 61.

and even of emotional connection (10:17–19).[5] There is a surprising fluidity, or inclusivism, in Yahweh's covenant with Israel. Deuteronomy seeks the renewal of Israel in light of the gracious rule of Yahweh, and the *gēr* is swept up in the divine invitation (29:9–14). The *gēr*'s joining the family of Yahweh does not require a "religious conversion" or a "confession of faith." Rather, the *gēr* is caught up in the joy, the community, and the abundance of the family of Yahweh (see §5.2.5.1). To be sure, there is a complex of responses to the "other" in Deuteronomy's framework. However, we may understand these as an attempt, on the one hand, to preserve the religious and social identity of Judah as a marginalized community and, on the other hand, to express inclusivism that is central to this very identity. We observed in these covenant texts that being/becoming the community of Yahweh is at heart of Deuteronomy and that inclusivism is at the heart of Israel's becoming, for inclusivism is a constitutive part of Israel's ethics (5:14), history (5:15), religion (16:14), and mandate (10:17–19).

### 7.1.5. Deuteronomy Addressed Yahweh's People over Connected Periods of Massive Displacement

Dtn projects a society before the text that is confronted with widespread displacement. The widespread displacement seems to be intensified in Dtr, for the *gēr* is the dominant social issue of Deuteronomy's framing texts, almost to exclusivity (e.g., 1:16–18; 29:9–14). Displacement remains a pressing social issue in texts that seem to be authored later again, referred to as post-Dtr (e.g., 10:17–19; 31:9–13). I have suggested that Deuteronomy was authored over connected episodes of deep and persistent but differentiated internal displacement. The following settings have been proposed:

1. Sennacherib's invasion of Judah (701 BC) is a possible starting point for Deuteronomy's developing response to displacement. A cycle of deepening indebtedness and land alienation also contributed to displacement during the late monarchy.
2. Dtr may respond to the widespread destruction of the Neo-Babylonian conquest and its aftermath. During this period Judah, as a postcollapse society, experienced widespread and

---

5. See §6.2.

unprecedented displacement. This explains Dtr's heightened ethic for the *gēr* vis-à-vis Dtn. In this context of devastation, whereby as many people were displaced as were not, as Israel is reconstituted it is the displaced person in particular who must be enfolded within the covenant, the one who has been severed from land and from genealogy (see on 29:9–13, at §5.3).

3.  Post-Dtr may respond to displacement created by socio-economic stratification and by land conflict created by the return of the *golah* in Persian Yehud.

The close study of Deuteronomy's framework in chapters 4 and 6 demonstrated three points that are of great significance for the *gēr* in Deuteronomy and that have not been observed in the scholarship: (1) displacement was *the* pressing social issue within the community before the text (Dtr and post-Dtr); (2) as Israel was reconstituted, the inclusion of those who had been separated from patrimony and from kindred was a primary goal of Deuteronomy's framing texts; (3) judicial law was the most important legal category for the protection and inclusion of the stranger within the community.

## 7.2. Contemporary Implications: Family for the Displaced

At the time of my writing, sixty-five million displaced people globally are fleeing conflicts and seeking a home. The human suffering that this displacement entails as well as the challenges that arise for potential host nation-states means that inquiry into displacement and inclusion in the Hebrew Bible is particularly pressing at the present time. Chapter 6 has explored an apparent tension in Deuteronomy between, on the one hand, expressions of election and exclusivism and, on the other hand, an ethic of incorporating the stranger, in an attempt to find theological coherence between these twin poles. This dialectic may be related to tensions in contemporary Western discourse between, on the one hand, national identity and security and, on the other hand, granting admission to outsiders. We have observed this dialectic in Deuteronomy as an authentic attempt to preserve the religious and social identity of ancient Israel, a community under threat of extinction at certain phases, while also fostering an inclusivism that is central to Israelite identity. Deuteronomy projects a social vision for the contemporary scenario that acknowledges the risks that can accompany permeable national borders while also embracing the opportunity to pursue the mutual transformation that occurs when nation-states welcome vulnerable outsiders. Using Benedict Anderson's notion of the nation as an "imagined community" (Deuteronomy, too, projects an imagined community), we may contend that nations have both an opportunity and a responsibility to "reimagine" themselves and their disposition toward displaced strangers today in light of Deuteronomy's call to include the stranger as kindred.[6]

---

6. Benedict Anderson, *Imagined Communities: Reflections on the Origin and Spread of Nationalism*, rev. ed. (London: Verso, 1991).

# Bibliography

Achenbach, Reinhard. "Der Eintritt der Schutzbürger in den Bund (Dtn 29, 10–12): Distinktion und Integration von Fremden im Deuteronomium." Pages 240–55 in *"Gerechtigkeit und Recht zu üben" (Gen 18,19): Studien zur altorientalischen und biblischen Rechtsgeschichte, zur Religionsgeschichte Israels und zur Religionssoziologie; Festschrift für Eckart Otto zum 65. Geburtstag.* Edited by Reinhard Achenbach and Martin Arneth. BZABR 13. Wiesbaden: Harrassowitz, 2009.

———. "*Gêr – nåkhrî – tôshav – zâr*: Legal and Sacral Distinctions regarding Foreigners in the Pentateuch." Pages 29–52 in *The Foreigner and the Law: Perspectives from the Hebrew Bible and the Ancient Near East.* Edited by Reinhard Achenbach, Rainer Albertz, and Jakob Wöhrle. BZABR 16. Wiesbaden: Harrassowitz, 2011.

Achenbach, Reinhard, Rainer Albertz, and Jakob Wöhrle, eds. *The Foreigner and the Law: Perspectives from the Hebrew Bible and the Ancient Near East.* BZABR 16. Wiesbaden: Harrassowitz, 2011.

Adams, Robert, McC. *The Evolution of Urban Society: Early Mesopotamia and Prehispanic Mexico.* New Brunswick: Aldine Transaction, 1966.

———. *Heartland of Cities: Surveys of Ancient Settlements and Land Use on the Central Floodplain of the Euphrates.* Chicago: University of Chicago Press, 1981.

Aḥituv, Shmuel. *Echoes from the Past: Hebrew and Cognate Inscriptions from the Biblical Period.* Jerusalem: Carta, 2008.

Albertz, Rainer. "From Aliens to Proselytes: Non-Priestly and Priestly Legislation Concerning Strangers." Pages 53–70 in *The Foreigner and the Law: Perspectives from the Hebrew Bible and the Ancient Near East.* Edited by Reinhard Achenbach, Rainer Albertz, and Jakob Wöhrle. BZABR 16. Wiesbaden: Harrassowitz, 2011.

———. *Israel in Exile: The History and Literature of the Sixth Century B.C.E.* Translated by David Green. StBibLit 3. Atlanta: Society of Biblial Literature, 2003.

Alt, Albrecht. *Essays on Old Testament History and Religion*. Oxford: Blackwell, 1966.

Altmann, Peter. "Feast, Famine, and History: The Festival Meal *Topos* and Deuteronomy." *ZAW* 124 (2012): 555–67.

———. *Festive Meals in Ancient Israel: Deuteronomy's Identity Politics in Their Ancient Near Eastern Context*. BZAW 424. Berlin: de Gruyter, 2011.

Anbar, Moshe. "Genesis 15: A Conflation of Two Deuteronomic Narratives." *JBL* 101 (1982): 39–55.

Anderson, Benedict. *Imagined Communities: Reflections on the Origin and Spread of Nationalism*. Rev. ed. London: Verso, 1991.

Anderson, Gary A. *A Time to Mourn, a Time to Dance: The Expression of Grief and Joy in Israelite Religion*. University Park, PA: Pennsylvania State University Press, 1991.

Arnold, Bill T. "The Love-Fear Antinomy in Deuteronomy 5–11." *VT* 61 (2011): 551–69.

Awabdy, Mark A. *Immigrants and Innovative Law: Deuteronomy's Theological and Social Vision for the* גר. FAT 2/67. Tübingen: Mohr Siebeck, 2014.

Barbiero, Gianni. "Der Fremde im Bundesbuch und im Heiligkeitsgesetz: Zwischen Absonderung und Annahme." Pages 220–54 in *Studien zu alttestamentlichen Texten*. Edited by Gianni Barbiero. SBAB 34. Stuttgart: Verlag Katholisches Bibelwerk, 2002.

Barkay, Gabriel. "Burial Caves and Burial Practices in Judah in the Iron Age." Pages 96–164 in *Graves and Burial Practices in Israel in the Ancient Period* [Hebrew]. Edited by Itamar Singer. Jerusalem: Yad Izhak Ben Zvi/Israel Exploration Society, 1994.

Barr, James. *The Semantics of Biblical Language*. Oxford: Oxford University Press, 1961.

Becker, Anne E. *Body, Self, and Society: The View from Fiji*. Philadelphia: University of Philadelphia Press, 1995.

Beckman, Gary. "Foreigners in the Ancient Near East." *JAOS* 133 (2013): 203–25.

Bendor, Shunya. *The Social Structure of Ancient Israel: The Institution of the Family* (beit'ab) *from the Settlement to the End of the Monarchy*. Jerusalem: Simor, 1996.

Benjamin, Don C. *The Social World of Deuteronomy: A New Feminist Commentary*. Eugene, OR: Cascade, 2015.

Bennett, Harold V. "Constitution, Class, and the Book of Deuteronomy." *HPS* 1 (2006): 523–48.

———. *Injustice Made Legal: Deuteronomic Law and the Plight of Widows, Strangers, and Orphans in Ancient Israel.* Grand Rapids: Eerdmans, 2002.

Bertholet, Alfred. *Die Stellung der Israeliten und der Juden zu den Fremden.* Freiburg; Leipzig: Mohr, 1896.

Bickerman, Elias, J. *From Ezra to the Last of the Maccabees: Foundations of Post-Biblical Judaism.* New York: Schocken Books, 1962.

Blenkinsopp, Joseph. "Yahweh and Other Deities: Conflict and Accommodation in the Religion of Israel." *Int* 40 (1986): 354–66.

Blum, Erhard. "The Decalogue and the Composition History of the Pentateuch." Pages 289–301 in *The Pentateuch: International Perspectives on Current Research.* Edited by T. B. Dozeman. FAT 78. Tübingen: Mohr Siebeck, 2011.

———. *Die Komposition der Vätergeschichte.* WMANT 57. Neukirchen-Vluyn: Neukirchener, 1984.

Boecker, Hans Jochen. *Law and the Administration of Justice in the Old Testament and Ancient Near East.* Minneapolis: Augsburg, 1980.

Boissevain, Jeremy, et al. "Towards a Social Anthropology of the Mediterranean [and Comments and Reply]." *Cultural Anthropology* 20 (1979): 81–93.

Boye, Karin. *To a Friend.* Translated by J. Nunn. Hull: Voice, 1985.

———. "Notes Phéniciennes." *BMB* 13 (1956): 87–95.

Braulik, Georg. "Die Abfolge der Gesetze in Deuteronium 12–26 und der Dekalog." Pages 252–72 in *Das Deuteronomium: Entstehung, Gestalt, und Botschaft.* Edited by N. Lohfink. BETL 68. Leuven: Leuven University Press, 1985.

———. "Deuteronomy and Human Rights." Pages 131–50 in *Theology of Deuteronomy: Collected Essays of Georg Braulik, O.S.B.* Translated by U. Lindblad. N. Richland Hills, TX: Bibal, 1994. Translation of "Das Deuteronomium und die Menschenrechte." *TQ* 166 (1986): 8–24.

———. "The Joy of the Feast." Pages 27–66 in *Theology of Deuteronomy: Collected Essays of Georg Braulik, O.S.B.* Translated by U. Lindblad. Richland Hills, TX: Bibal, 1994.

Brueggemann, Walter. *Deuteronomy.* Abingdon Old Testament Commentaries. Nashville: Abingdon, 2001.

———. *The Land: Place as Gift, Promise and Challenge in Biblical Faith.* OBT. Philadelphia: Fortress, 1977.

———. "Pharoah as Vassal." *CBQ* 57 (1995): 27–51.

———. *Theology of the Old Testament.* Minneapolis: Fortress, 1997.

Bultmann, Christoph. *Der Fremde im antiken Juda: Eine Untersuchung zum sozialen Typenbegriff "ger" und seinem Bedeutungswandel in der alttestamentlichen Gesetzgebung.* FRLANT 153. Göttingen: Vandenhoeck & Ruprecht, 1992.

Callender, Dexter E., Jr. "Servants of God(s) and Servants of Kings in Israel and the Ancient Near East." *Semeia* 83–84 (1998): 67–82.

Carmichael, Calum. "A New View of the Origin of the Deuteronomic Credo." *VT* 19 (1969): 273–89.

Carr, David M. *The Formation of the Hebrew Bible.* New York: Oxford University Press, 2011.

———. *Reading the Fractures of Genesis: Historical and Literary Approaches.* Louisville: Westminster John Knox, 1996.

Carroll R., M. Daniel. "Welcoming the Stranger: Toward a Theology of Immigration in Deuteronomy." Pages 441–62 in *For Our Good Always: Studies on the Message and Influence of Deteronomy in Honor of Daniel I. Block.* Edited by Jason S. DeRouchie, Jason Gile, and Kenneth J. Turner. Winona Lake, IN: Eisenbrauns, 2013.

Carsten, Janet. *After Kinship.* Cambridge: Cambridge University Press, 2004.

Carter, Charles E. *The Emergence of Yehud in the Persian Period: A Social and Demographic Study.* JSOTSup 294. Sheffield: Sheffield Academic, 1999.

Chiera, Edward. *Texts of Varied Contents.* Harvard Semitic Series 5. Cambridge: Harvard University Press, 1929.

Chirichigno, Gregory C. *Debt-Slavery in Israel and the Ancient Near East.* JSOTSup 141. Sheffield: JSOT, 1993.

Cholewiński, Alfred. *Heiligkeitsgesetz und Deuteronomium: Eine vergleichende Studie.* AB 66. Rome: Pontifical Biblical Institute, 1976.

Clines, D. J. A. "KRT 111–114 (I iii 7–10): Gatherers of Wood and Drawers of Water." *UF* 8 (1976): 23–26.

Cooke, G. A. *A Textbook of North-Semitic Inscriptions: Moabite, Hebrew, Phoenician, Aramaic, Nabataean, Palmyrene, Jewish.* Oxford: Clarendon, 1903.

Corcoran, Jenny. "The Alien in Deuteronomy 29 and Today." Pages 229–39 in *Interpreting Deuteronomy: Issues and Approaches.* Edited by David G. Firth and Philip S. Johnston. Downers Grove, IL: InterVarsity Press, 2012.

Craigie, Peter C. *Deuteronomy.* NICOT. London: Hodder & Stoughton, 1976.

Cross, Frank Moore. *From Epic to Canon: History and Literature in Ancient Israel.* Baltimore; London: John Hopkins University Press, 1998.

Crouch, Carly. *The Making of Israel: Cultural Diversity in the Southern Levant and the Formation of Ethnic Identity in Deuteronomy.* New York: Brill, 2014.

Crüsemann, Frank. *The Torah: Theology and Social History of Old Testament Law.* Translated by Allan. W. Mahnke. Minneapolis: Fortress, 1996.

Cunchillos, Jesús-Luis, Juan-Pablo Vita, José-Ángel Zamora, and Raquel Cervigón, eds. *Ugaritic Data Bank: The Texts with English Commentaries.* Madrid: Laboratorio de Hermeneumática, 2003.

Dandamajew, A. "Der Tempelzehnte in Babylonien während des 6.–4. Jh. v.u.Z." Pages 82–90 in vol. 1 of *Beiträge zur Alten Geschichte und deren Nachleben: Festschrift Franz Altheim zum 6. 10. 1968.* 2 vols. Berlin: de Gruyter, 1969.

Daniels, Dwight R. "The Creed of Deuteronomy XXVI Revisited." Pages 231–42 in *Studies in the Pentateuch.* Edited by J. A. Emerton, VTSup 41. Leiden: Brill, 1990.

Daube, David. *The Exodus Pattern in the Bible.* London: Faber & Faber, 1963.

Davies, Eryl W. *Prophecy and Ethics: Isaiah and the Ethical Tradition of Israel.* JSOTSup 16. Sheffield: JSOT, 1981.

Davis, Ellen F. *Scripture, Culture, and Agriculture: An Agrarian Reading of the Bible.* Cambridge: Cambridge University Press, 2009.

Dearman, Andrew. "Historical Reconstruction and the Mesha Inscription." Pages 155–210 in *Studies in the Mesha Inscription and Moab.* Edited by Andrew Dearman. Atlanta: Scholars Press, 1989.

Dietler, Michael. "Theorizing the Feast: Rituals of Consumption, Commensal Politics, and Power in African Contexts." Pages 65–114 in *Feasts: Archaeological and Ethnographic Perspectives on Food, Politics, and Power.* Edited by Michael Dietler and Brian Hayden. Washington, DC: Smithsonian Institution, 2001.

Dietrich, Manfield, O. Loretz, and Joaquín Sanmartin, eds. *Die keilalphabetischen Texte aus Ugarit.* Münster: Ugarit-Verlag, 2013. 3rd enl. ed. of *KTU: The Cuneiform Alphabetic Texts from Ugarit, Ras Ibn Hani and Other Places.* Edited by Manfield Dietrich, O. Loretz, and Joaquín Sanmartin. Münster: Ugarit-Verlag, 1995.

Dion, P. E. "Israël et l'Étranger dans le Deutéronome." Pages 221–33 in *L'Altérité: Vivre ensemble différents; Approches Pluridisciplinaires; Actes du Colloque pluridisciplinaire tenu à l'occasion du 75e anniversaire du Collège dominicain de philosophie et de théologie, Ottawa, 4, 5, 6 octobre 1984.* Edited by M. Gourgues and G. D. Mailhiot. Recherches n.s. 7. Montreal: Bellarmin, 1986.

Donner, Herbert, and Wolfgang Röllig. *Kanaanäische und aramäische Inschriften.* 3 vols. Harrassowitz: Wiesbaden, 2002.

Douglas, Mary. "Deciphering a Meal." Pages 61–82 in *Myth, Symbol, and Culture.* Edited by Clifford Geertz. New York: Norton, 1971.

Driver, S. R. *A Critical and Exegetical Commentary on Deuteronomy.* ICC. Edinburgh: T&T Clark, 1896.

Ebach, Ruth. *Das Fremde und das Eigene: Die Fremdendarstellungen des Deuteronomiums im Kontext israelitischer Identitätskonstruktionen.* BZAW 471. Berlin: de Gruyter, 2014.

Edenburg, Cynthia, and Reinhard Müller. "A Northern Provenance for Deuteronomy? A Critical Review." *HBAI* 4 (2015): 148–61.

Erikson, Thomas Hylland. *Ethnicity and Nationalism: Anthropological Perspectives.* 2nd ed. Sterling, VA: Pluto Books, 2002.

Fales, Mario. "Massimo sforzo, minima resa: Maledizioni divine da Tell Fekheriye all Antico Testamento." *ACF* 21 (1982): 1–12.

Falk, Zeʾev W. *Hebrew Law in Biblical Times.* Utah: Brigham Young University Press, 2001.

Faust, Avraham. *The Archaeology of Israelite Society in Iron Age II.* Winona Lake, IN: Eisenbrauns, 2012.

———. "Between Israel and Judah: Politics, Economy and Identity." Paper presented at the Annual Meeting of the Society of Biblical Literature. San Diego, 25 November 2014.

———. *Israel's Ethnogenesis: Settlement, Interaction, Expansion and Resistance.* London: Equinox, 2006.

———. *Judah in the Neo-Babylonian Period: The Archaeology of Desolation.* ABS 18. Atlanta: Society of Biblical Literature, 2012.

Fensham, F. Charles. "Widow, Orphan, and the Poor in Ancient Near Eastern Legal and Wisdom Literature." *JNES* 21 (1962): 129–39.

Finkelstein, Israel. "Migration of Israelites into Judah after 720 BCE: An Answer and an Update." *ZAW* 127 (2015): 188–206.

———. "State Formation in Israel and Judah: A Contrast in Context, A Contrast in Trajectory." *NEA* 62 (1999): 35–52.

Finkelstein, Jacob J. "Ammiṣaduqa's Edict and the Babylonian 'Law Codes.'" *JCS* 15 (1961): 91–104.

———. *The Ox That Gored*. TAPS 17/2. Philadelphia: American Philosophical Society, 1981.

Finsterbusch, Karin. "The Decalogue Orientation of Deuteronomic Law: A New Approach." Pages 123–46 in *Deuteronomium: Tora für eine neue Generation*. Edited by Georg Fischer, Dominik Markl, and Simone Paganini. BZABR 17. Wiesbaden: Harrassowitz, 2011.

Fleming, Daniel E. "The Israelite Festival Calendar." *RB* 106 (1999): 8–34.

Fortes, Meyer. *Kinship and the Social Order: The Legacy of Lewis Henry Morgan*. Chicago: Aldine, 1969.

Fretheim, Terrance E. *Exodus*. IBC. Louisville: Westminster John Knox, 1991.

———. "Law in the Service of Life: A Dynamic Understanding of Law in Deuteronomy." Pages 183–200 in *A God So Near: Essays on Old Testament Theology in Honour of Patrick D. Miller*. Edited by Brent A. Strawn and Nancy R. Bowen. Winona Lake, IN: Eisenbrauns, 2003.

Galvin, Garrett. *Egypt as a Place of Refuge*. FAT 2/51. Tübingen: Mohr Siebeck, 2011.

Garroway, Kristine Henriksen. *Children in the Ancient Near Eastern Household*. Winona Lake, IN: Eisenbrauns, 2014.

Gelb, Ignace J. "From Freedom to Slavery." Pages 81–92 in *Gesellschaftsklassen im Alten Zweistromland und in den angrenzenden Gebieten: XVIII; Rencontre assyriologique internationale, München, 29. Juni bis 3. Juli 1970*. Edited by D. O. Edzard. ABAW 75. München: Verlag der Bayerischen Akademie der Wissenschaften, 1972.

———. "Household and Family in Early Mesopotamia." Pages 1–98 in *State and Temple Economy In the Ancient Near East: Proceedings of the International Conference Organized by the Katholieke Universiteit Leuven from the 10th to the 14th of April 1978*. Edited by E. Lipiński. OLA 5. Leuven: Department Oriëntalistiek, 1979.

———, et al. *The Assyrian Dictionary of the Oriental Institute of the University of Chicago*. Chicago: University of Chicago Press, 1965.

Gemser, Berend. "The Importance of the Motive Clause in Old Testament Law." Pages 50–66 in *Congress Volume: Copenhagen, 1953*. Edited by G. W. Anderson. VTSup 1. Leiden: Brill, 1953. Repr. as pages 96–115 in *Adhuc Loquitur: Collected Essays by B. Gemser*. Edited by A. van Selms and A. S. van der Woude. POS 7. Leiden: Brill, 1968.

Gennep, Arnold van. *The Rites of Passage*. London: Routledge & Kegan Paul, 1960.

Gerstenberger, Erhard S. *Israel in the Persian Period: The Fifth and Fourth Centuries B.C.E.* Translated by Siegfried S. Schatzmann. Atlanta: Society of Biblical Literature, 2011.

———. *Wesen und Herkunft des »apodiktischen Rechts«*. WMANT 20. Neukirchen-Vluyn: Neukirchener, 1965.

Gertz, Jan Christian. "Abraham, Mose und der Exodus: Beobachtungen zur Redaktionsgeschichte von Gen 15." Pages 66–69 in *Abschied vom Jahwisten: Die Komposition des Hexateuch in der jüngsten Diskussion*. Edited by Jan Christian Gertz, Konrad Schmidt, and Markus Witte. BZAW 315. Berlin: de Gruyter, 2002.

———. "Die Stellung des kleinen geschichtlichen Credos in der Redaktionsgeschichte von Deuteronomium und Pentateuch." Pages 30–45 in *Liebe und Gebot: Studien zum Deuteronomium*. Edited by Reinhard G. Kratz and Hermann Spieckermann. FRLANT 190. Göttingen: Vandenhoeck & Ruprecht, 2000.

Gibson, John C. L. *Canaanite Myths and Legends*. 2nd ed. London: T&T Clark, 2004.

———. *Textbook of Syrian Semitic Inscriptions*. 3 vols. London: Oxford University Press, 1971.

Gilmore, David D. "Anthropology of the Mediterranean Area." *ARA* 11 (1982): 175–205.

Gilroy, Paul. *The Black Atlantic: Modernity and Double Consciousness*. Cambridge, MA: Harvard University Press, 1993.

Glanville, Luke. "Christianity and the Responsibility to Protect." *SCE* 25 (2012): 312–26.

Glanville, Mark. "A Missional Reading of Deuteronomy: Communities of Gratitude, Celebration, and Justice." Pages 124–50 in *Reading the Bible Missionally*. Edited by Michael Goheen. Grand Rapids: Eerdmans, 2016.

Gordon, Cyrus. *Ugaritic Textbook*. AnOr 38. Rome: Pontifical Biblical Institute, 1965.

Gottwald, Norman K. *The Politics of Ancient Israel*. LAI. Louisville: Westminster John Knox, 2000.

———. *The Tribes of Yahweh: A Sociology of the Religion of Liberated Israel, 1250–1050 BCE*. BibSem 66. Sheffield: Sheffield Academic, 1999.

Gowan, Donald E. "Wealth and Poverty in the Old Testament: The Case of the Widow, the Orphan, and the Sojourner." *Int* 41 (1987): 341–53.

Grabbe, Lester L. *Ancient Israel: What Do We Know and How Do We Know It?* London: T&T Clark, 2007.

———. *Yehud: A History of the Persian Province of Judah*. Vol. 1 of *A History of the Jews and Judaism in the Second Temple Period*. LSTS 47. London: T&T Clark, 2004.

Gray, John. *The Krt Text in the Literature of Ras Shamra: A Social Myth of Ancient Canaan*. 2nd ed. Leiden: Brill, 1964.

Greengus, Samuel. *Laws in the Bible and in Early Rabbinic Collections: The Legal Legacy of the Ancient Near East*. Eugene, OR: Cascade, 2012.

Groden, Michael, Martin Kreiswirth, and Imre Szeman, eds. *The Johns Hopkins Guide to Literary Theory and Criticism*. 2nd ed. Baltimore: John Hopkins University Press, 2005.

Haag, E. "שָׁבַת." *TDOT* 14:387–97.

Haas, V. "Die Dämonisierung des Fremden und des Feindes im Alten Orient." *RO* 41(1980): 37–44.

Halbe, Jörn von. "Erwägungen zu Ursprung und Wesen des Massotfestes." *ZAW* 87 (1975): 324–46.

Hallo, W. W. "New Moons and Sabbath: A Case Study in the Contrastive Approach." *HUCA* 48 (1977): 1–18.

Halpern, Baruch. "Jerusalem and the Lineages in the Seventh Century B.C.E.: Kinship and the Rise of Individual Liability." Pages 11–107 in *Law and Ideology in Monarchic Israel*. Edited by Baruch Halpern and Deborah W. Hobson. JSOTSup 124. Sheffield: JSOT Press, 1991.

Hart, David Montgomery. *The Aith Waryaghar of the Moroccan Rif: An Ethnography and History*. Viking Fund Publications in Anthropology 55. Tucson: University of Arizona Press, 1976.

Hawkins, Ralph K. *The Iron Age I Structure on Mt. Ebal: Excavation and Interpretation*. BBRSup 6. Winona Lake, IN: Eisenbrauns, 2012.

Hayden, Brian. "Fabulous Feasts: A Prolegomenon to the Importance of Feasting." Pages 23–64 in *Feasts: Archaeological and Ethnographic Perspectives on Food, Politics, and Power*. Edited by Michael Dietler and Brian Hayden. Washington, DC: Smithsonian Institution, 2001.

———. "Feasting Research." https://tinyurl.com/SBL2638a.

Hendel, Ronald S. *Remembering Abraham: Culture, Memory, and History in the Hebrew Bible*. Oxford: Oxford University Press, 2005.

Hiebert, Paula S. "'Whence Shall Help Come to Me?': The Biblical Widow." Pages 125–41 in *Gender and Difference in Ancient Israel*. Edited by Peggy L. Day. Minneapolis: Fortress, 1989.

Hoffmeier, James K. *The Immigration Crisis: Immigrants, Aliens and the Bible.* Wheaton, IL: Crossway Books, 2009.

Hoftijzer, Jacob. *The Function and Use of the Imperfect Forms with Nun Paragogicum in Classical Hebrew.* SSN 21. Assen: Van Gorcum, 1985.

Hoftijzer, Jacob, and Karen Jongeling. *Dictionary of North-West Semitic Inscriptions.* HOS 21. Leiden: Brill, 1995.

Hossfeld, F. L. *Der Dekalog: Seine späten Fassungen, die originale Komposition und seine Vorstufen.* OBO 45. Freiburg: Göttingen, 1982.

Houston, Walter. *Contending for Justice: Ideologies and Theologies of Social Justice in the Old Testament.* London: T&T Clark, 2006.

Hyatt, J. Philip. "Were There an Ancient Historical Credo in Israel and an Independent Sinai Tradition?" Pages 152–70 in *Translating and Understanding the Old Testament: Essays in Honor of Herbert Gordon May.* Edited by Harry Thomas Frank and William L. Reed. Nashville: Abingdon Press, 1970.

Jackson, Bernard. *Wisdom-Laws: A Study of the Mishpatim of Exodus 21:1–22:16.* Oxford: Oxford University Press, 2006.

Jagersma, H. "The Tithes in the Old Testament." Pages 116–28 in *Remembering All the Way: A Collection of Old Testament Studies Published on the Occasion of the Fortieth Anniversary of the Oudtestamentisch Werkgezelschap in Nederland.* Edited by B. Albrektson et al. OtSt 21. Leiden: Brill, 1981.

Janzen, J. Gerald. "The Wandering Aramean Reconsidered." *VT* 44 (1994): 359–75.

Jones, Lindsay, ed. *Encyclopaedia of Religion.* 2nd ed. 15 vols. Detroit: Macmillan Reference USA, 2005.

Joosten, Jan. *People and the Land in the Holiness Code: An Exegetical Study of the Ideational Framework of the Law in Leviticus 17–26.* VTSup 67. Leiden: Brill, 1996.

Kapelrud, Arvid S. "The Number Seven in Ugaritic." *VT* 18 (1968): 494–99.

Kaufman, Stephen A. "The Structure of the Deuteronomic Law." *Maarav* 1–2 (1978–1979): 105–58.

Kellerman, D. "גּוּר." *TDOT* 2:439–49.

Kelm, George L., and Amihai Mazar. *Timnah: A Biblical City in the Sorek Valley.* Winona Lake, IN: Eisenbrauns, 1995.

Kennedy, Elizabeth Robertson. *Seeking a Homeland: Sojourn and Ethnic Identity in the Ancestral Narratives of Genesis.* BibInt 106. Leiden: Brill, 2010.

Kessler, John. "Diaspora and Homeland in the Early Achaemenid Period: Community, Geography and Demography in Zechariah 1–8." Pages 137–66 in *Approaching Yehud: New Approaches to the Study of the Persian Period.* Edited by Jon L. Berquist. SemeiaSt 50. Atlanta: Society of Biblical Literature, 2007.

Kessler, Rainer. *The Social History of Ancient Israel: An Introduction.* Minneapolis: Fortress, 2008.

Kidd, José E. Ramírez. *Alterity and Identity in Israel.* BZAW 283. Berlin: de Gruyter, 1999.

King, Philip J., and Lawrence E. Stager. *Life in Biblical Israel.* LAI. Louisville: Westminster John Knox, 2001.

Knauf, Ernst Axel. "Observations on Judah's Social and Economic History and the Dating of the Laws in Deuteronomy." *JHS* 9 (2009): 2–8.

Knierim, Rolf P. *The Task of Old Testament Theology: Method and Cases.* Grand Rapids: Eerdmans, 1995.

Knoppers, Gary N. *Jews and Samaritans: The Origins and History of Their Early Relations.* Oxford: Oxford University Press, 2013.

Koehler, Ludwig, and Walter Baumgartner, eds. *Hebrew and Aramaic Lexicon of the Old Testament.* 5 vols. Leiden: Brill, 1999.

Kramer, Samuel Noah. *The Sumerians: Their History, Culture and Character.* Chicago: University of Chicago Press, 1963.

Krapf, Thomas. "Traditionsgeschichtliches zum deuteronomischen Fremdling-Waise-Witwe-Gebot." *VT* 34 (1984): 87–91.

Kratz, Reinhard D. *The Composition of the Narrative Books of the Old Testament.* Translated by J. Bowden. London: T&T Clark, 2005. Translation of *Die Komposition der erzählenden Bücher des Alten Testaments.* Göttingen: Vandenhoeck & Ruprecht, 2000.

———. "Der Dekalog im Exodusbuch." *VT* 44 (1994): 205–38.

Lapsley, Jacqueline E. "Feeling our Way: Love for God in Deuteronomy." *CBQ* 65 (2003): 350–69.

Lavie, Smadar, and Ted Swedenburg. "Introduction: Displacement, Diaspora, and Geographies of Identity." Pages 1–25 in *Displacement, Diaspora, and Geographies of Identity.* Edited by Smadar Lavie and Ted Swedenburg. Durham: Duke University Press, 1996.

Lerberghe, Karel van, and Antoon Schoors, eds. *Immigration and Emigration within the Ancient Near East: Festschrift E. Lipiński.* Leuven: Peters, 1995.

Lenchak, Timothy A. *"Choose Life!": A Rhetorical-Critical Investigation of Deuteronomy 28,69–30,20*. AB 129. Rome: Pontifical Biblical Institute, 1993.

Leslau, Wolf. *Comparative Dictionary of Ge'ez (Classical Ethiopic)*. Wiesbaden: Harrossowitz, 1991.

Levenson, Jon D. "Exodus and Liberation." *HBT* 13 (1991): 134–74.

Levin, Christoph. "Rereading Deuteronomy in the Persian and Hellenistic Periods: The Ethics of Brotherhood and the Care of the Poor." Pages 49–72 in *Deuteronomy–Kings as Emerging Authoritative Books: A Conversation*. Edited by Diana V. Edelman. ANEM 6. Atlanta: Society of Biblical Literature, 2014.

———. *Die Verheissung des neuen Bundes: In ihrem theologiegeschichtlichen Zusammenhang ausgelegt*. FRLANT 137. Göttingen: Vandenhoeck & Ruprecht, 1985.

Levinson, Bernard M. *Deuteronomy and the Hermeneutics of Legal Innovation*. New York: Oxford University Press, 1997.

———. "Deuteronomy's Conception of Law as an 'Ideal Type': A Missing Chapter in the History of Constitutional Law." Pages 52–88 in *'The Right Chorale': Studies in Biblical Law and Interpretation*. Edited by Bernard M. Levinson. Tübingen: Mohr Siebeck, 2008.

———. "Esarhaddon's Succession Treaty as the Source for the Canon Formula in Deuteronomy 13:1." *JAOS* 130 (2010): 337–47.

Lewis, Theodore J. *Cults of the Dead in Ancient Israel and Ugarit*. HSM 39. Atlanta: Scholars Press, 1989.

Lichtenstein, Murray. "The Banquet Motifs in Keret and in Proverbs 9." *JANESCU* 1 (1968): 19–31.

Lichtheim, Miriam. *The New Kingdom*. Vol. 2 of *Ancient Egyptian Literature: A Book of Readings*. Berkeley: University of California Press, 1973.

Lipschits, Oded. "Demographic Changes in Judah between the Seventh and Fifth Centuries B.C.E." Pages 323–76 in *Judah and the Judeans in the Neo-Babylonian Period*. Edited by Oded Lipschits and Joseph Blenkinsopp. Winona Lake, IN: Eisenbrauns, 2003.

———. *The Fall and Rise of Jerusalem: Judah under Babylonian Rule*. Winona Lake, IN: Eisenbrauns, 2005.

Lohfink, Norbert. "Distribution of the Functions of Power: The Laws Concerning Public Offices in Deuteronomy 16:18–18:22." Pages 336–52 in *A Song of Power and the Power of Song: Essays on the Book of Deuteronomy*. Edited by Duane L. Christensen. Winona Lake, IN: Eisenbrauns,

1993. Repr. of "Die Sicherung der Wirksamkeit des Gotteswortes durch das Prinzip der Schriftlichkeit der Tora und durch das Prinzip der Gewaltenteilung nach den Ämtergesetzen des Buches Deuteronomium (Dt 16,18–18,22)." Pages 55–75 in *Great Themes from the Old Testament.* Translated by Ronald Walls. Chicago: Franciscan Herald, 1981.

———. "Gottesvolk: Alttestamentliches zu einem Zentralbegriff im konziliaren Wortfeuerwerk." Pages 111–26 in *Unsere großen Wörter: Das Alte Testament zu Themen dieser Jahre.* Freiburg: Herder, 1977.

———. *Das Hauptgebot: Eine Untersuchung literarischer Einleitungsfragen zu Dtn 5–11.* AB 20. Rome: Pontifical Biblical Institute, 1963.

———. "Poverty in the Laws of the Ancient Near East and of the Bible." *TS* 52 (1991): 34–50.

———. "The 'Small Credo' of Deuteronomy 26:5–9." Pages 265–89 *Theology of the Pentateuch.* Translated by L. M. Maloney. Minneapolis: Fortress, 1994. Translation of "Zum 'kleinen geschichtlichen Credo' Dtn 26, 5–9." Pages 263–90 in vol. 1 of *Studien zum Deuteronomium und zur deuteronomistischen Literatur.* SBAB 8. Stuttgart: Katholisches Bibelwerk, 1995.

———. *Theology of the Pentateuch: Themes of the Priestly Narrative and Deuteronomy.* Minneapolis: Fortress, 1994.

Lohr, Joel N. *Chosen and Unchosen: Conceptions of Election in the Pentateuch and Jewish-Christian Interpretation.* Siphrut 2. Winona Lake, IN: Eisenbrauns, 2009.

Louw, P. "How Do Words Mean—If They Do?" *EFN* 4 (1991): 125–42.

Lundbom, Jack R. *Deuteronomy.* Grand Rapids: Eerdmans, 2013.

MacDonald, Nathan. "Issues in Dating Deuteronomy: A Response to Juha Pakkala." *ZAW* 122 (2010): 431–35.

———. *Not Bread Alone: The Uses of Food in the Old Testament.* Oxford: Oxford University Press, 2008.

———. *What Did the Ancient Israelites Eat? Diet in Biblical Times.* Grand Rapids: Eerdmans 2008.

MacIntyre, Alasdair. *After Virtue: A Study in Moral Theory.* Notre Dame: University of Notre Dame Press, 1985.

Malamat, Abraham. "The Aramaeans." Pages 134–55 in *Peoples of Old Testament Times.* Edited by D. J. Wiseman. Oxford: Clarendon, 1973.

Malina, Bruce, J. *The New Testament World: Insights from Cultural Anthropology.* 3rd ed. Louisville: Westminster John Knox, 2001.

———. *The Social Gospel of Jesus: The Kingdom of God in Mediterranean Perspective*. Minneapolis: Fortress, 2001.

Margalit, Baruch. "Lexiographical Notes on the AQHT Epic (Part II: KTU 1.10)." *UF* 16 (1984): 119–79.

———. "The Ten Words Revealed and Revised: The Origins of Law and Legal Hermeneutics in the Pentateuch." Pages 13–27 in *The Decalogue and Its Cultural Influence*. Edited by Dominik Markl. HBM 58. Sheffield: Sheffield Phoenix, 2013.

Marshall, Mac. "The Nature of Nurture." *AmE* 4 (1977): 643–62.

Mayes, A. D. H. *Deuteronomy*. NCB. Grand Rapids: Eerdmans, 1979.

McBride, S. Dean, Jr. "Polity of the Covenant People: The Book of Deuteronomy." *Int* 41 (1987): 229–44. Repr. as pages 62–77 in *A Song of Power and the Power of Song: Essays on the Book of Deuteronomy*. Edited by Duane L. Christensen. Winona Lake, IN: Eisenbrauns, 1993.

McCarthy, Dennis J. "Notes on the Love of God in Deuteronomy and the Father-Son Relationship between Yahweh and Israel." *CBQ* 27 (1965): 144–147.

McConville, J. Gordon. *Deuteronomy*. ApOTC 5. Leicester: Inter-Varsity Press, 2002.

———. *God and Earthly Power: An Old Testament Political Theology*. LHBOTS 454. London: T&T Clark, 2006.

———. "Singular Address in the Deuteronomic Law and the Politics of Legal Administration." *JSOT* 97 (2002): 19–36.

McConville, J. Gordon, and J. G. Millar. *Time and Place in Deuteronomy*. JSOTSup 179. Sheffield: Sheffield Academic, 1997.

Meek, T. J. "The Translation of *Ger* in the Hexateuch and Its Bearing on the Documentary Hypothesis." *JBL* 49 (1930): 172–80.

Mendenhall, George E. *The Tenth Generation: The Origins of the Biblical Tradition*. Baltimore: Johns Hopkins University Press, 1973.

Merendino, Rosario Pius. *Das deuteronomische Gesetz: Eine literarkritische, gattungs- und überlieferungsgeschichtliche Untersuchung zu Dt 12–26*. BBB 31. Bonn: Hanstein, 1969.

Merlan, Francesca, and Alan Rumsey. *Ku Waru: Language and Segmentary Politics in the Western Nebilyer Valley, Papua New Guinea*. Cambridge: Cambridge University Press, 1991.

Meyers, Carol L. "The Function of Feasts: An Anthropological Perspective on Israelite Religious Festivals." Pages 141–68 in *Social Theory and the Study of Israelite Religion: Essays in Retrospect and Prospect*. Edited by Saul M. Olyan. RBS 71. Atlanta: Society of Biblical Literature, 2012.

Mezlekia, Nega. *Notes from the Hyena's Belly.* New York: Picador, 2000.

Milgrom, Jacob M. *Leviticus 1–16.* AB 3. New York: Doubleday, 1991.

Millard, Alan R. "A Wandering Aramean." *JNES* 39 (1980): 153–55.

Miller, Patrick D. *Deuteronomy.* IBC. Louisville: Westminster John Knox, 1990.

———. "Israel as Host to Strangers." Pages 548–71 in *Israelite Religion and Biblical Theology.* Edited by Patrick D. Miller. JSOTSup 267. Sheffield: Sheffield Academic, 2000.

Miranda, Jose P. *Marx and the Bible: A Critique of the Philosophy of Oppression.* Maryknoll, NY: Orbis, 1974.

Möller, André. *Ramadam in Java: The Joy and Jihad of Ritual Fasting.* Lund: Department of History and Anthropology of Religions Lund University, 2007.

Moor, Johannes C. de, and Paul Sanders. "An Ugaritic Expiation Ritual and Its Old Testament Parallels." *UF* 23 (1991): 283–300.

Moran, William L. "The Ancient Near Eastern Background for the Love of God in Deuteronomy." *CBQ* 25 (1963): 77–87.

Mullin, E. Theodore. *Narrative History and Ethnic Boundaries: The Deuteronomic Historian and the Creation of Israelite National Identity.* SemeiaSt. Atlanta: Scholars Press, 1993.

Munn, Nancy. *The Fame of Gawa: A Symbolic Study of Value Transformation in a Massim (Papua New Guinea) Society.* Cambridge: Cambridge University Press, 1954.

Na'aman, Nadav. "Population Changes in Palestine Following Assyrian Deportation." Pages 200–19 in vol. 1 of *Ancient Israel and Its Neighbors: Interaction and Counteraction; Collected Essays.* Winona Lake, IN: Eisenbrauns, 2005.

———. "Sojourners and Levites in the Kingdom of Judah in the Seventh Century BCE." *ZABR* 14 (2008): 237–79.

Naroll, R. "Floor Area and Settlement Population." *AAnt* 27 (1962): 587–89.

Nash, Dustin. "The Representation of Inter-Group 'Brotherhood' in the Hebrew Bible and the Mari Archives: The Akkadian Evidence and Its Biblical Implications." Paper presented at the Annual Meeting of the Society of Biblical Literature. Baltimore, 24 November 2013.

Nelson, Richard D. *Deuteronomy.* OTL. Louisville: Westminster John Knox, 2002.

Nestor, Dermot Anthony. *Cognitive Perspectives on Israelite Identity.* LBS. New York: T&T Clark, 2010.

Nicholson, E. W. *Deuteronomy and Tradition*. Philadelphia: Fortress, 1967.

Niehr, Herbert. *Rechtsprechung in Israel: Untersuchungen zur Geschichte der Gerichtsorganisation im Alten Testament*. SBS 130. Stuttgart: Katholisches Bibelwerk, 1987.

Nihan, Christophe. *From Priestly Torah to Pentateuch: A Study in the Composition of the Book of Leviticus*. FAT 2/25. Tübingen: Mohr Siebeck, 2007.

———. "Resident Aliens and Natives in the Holiness Legislation." Pages 111–34 in *The Foreigner and the Law: Perspectives from the Hebrew Bible and the Ancient Near East*. Edited by Reinhard Achenbach, Rainer Albertz, and Jakob Wöhrle. BZABR 16. Wiesbaden: Harrassowitz, 2011.

Olmo Lete, Gregorio del, and Joaquín Sanmartín. *A Dictionary of the Ugaritic Language in the Alphabetic Tradition*. 2 vols. HdO 1/67. Leiden: Brill, 2003.

Olson, Dennis T. *Deuteronomy and the Death of Moses: A Theological Reading*. Minneapolis: Fortress, 1994.

———. "How Does Deuteronomy Do Theology? Literary Juxtaposition and Paradox in the New Moab Covenant in Deuteronomy 29–32." Pages 201–13 in *A God So Near: Essays on Old Testament Theology in Honour of Patrick D. Miller*. Edited by Brent A. Strawn and Nancy R. Bowen. Winona Lake, IN: Eisenbrauns, 2003.

Olyan, Saul M. "The Roles of Kin and Fictive Kin in Biblical Representations of Death Ritual." Pages 251–64 in *Family and Household and Religion: Toward a Synthesis of Old Testament Studies, Archaeology, Epigraphy, and Cultural Studies*. Edited by Rainer Albertz and Rüdiger Schmitt. Winona Lake, IN: Eisenbrauns, 2012.

Omi, Michael, and Howard Winant. *Racial Formation in the United States: From the 1960s to the 1980s*. New York: Routledge & Kegan Paul, 1986.

Otto, Eckart. "Aspects of Legal Reforms and Reformulations in Ancient Cuneiform and Israelite Law." Pages 160–96 in *Theory and Method in Biblical and Cuneiform Law: Revision, Interpolation and Development*. Edited by Bernard M. Levinson. JSOTSup 181. Sheffield: Sheffield Academic, 1994.

———. "The Book of Deuteronomy and Its Answer to the Persian State Ideology: The Legal Implications." Pages 112–22 in *Loi et Justice dans la Littérature du Proche-Orient ancien*. Edited by Olivier Artus. BZABR 20. Wiesbaden: Harrassowitz, 2013.

———. "The Books of Deuteronomy and Numbers in One Torah: The Book of Numbers Read in the Horizon of the Postexilic *Fortschreibung* in the Book of Deuteronomy; New Horizons in the Interpretation of the Pentateuch." Pages 383–98 in *Torah and the Book of Numbers*. Edited by Christian Frevel, Thomas Pola, and Aaron Schart. FAT 2/62. Tübingen: Mohr Siebeck, 2013.

———. *Das Deuteronomium: Politische Theologie und Rechtsreform in Juda und Assyrien*. Berlin: de Gruyter, 1999.

———. *Deuteronomium 1–11*. 2 vols. HThKAT. Freiburg: Herder, 2012.

———. *Das Deuteronomium im Pentateuch und Hexateuch: Studien zur Literaturgeschichte von Pentateuch und Hexateuch im Lichte des Deuteronomiumrahmens*. FAT 30. Tübingen: Mohr Siebeck, 2000.

———. "The History of the Legal-Religious Hermeneutics of the Book of Deuteronomy from the Assyrian to the Hellenistic Period." Pages 211–50 in *Law and Religion in the Eastern Mediterranean*. Edited by Anselm C. Hagedorn and Reinhard G. Kratz. Oxford: Oxford University Press, 2013.

———. "שָׁבַע." *TDOT* 14:336–67.

———. "שַׁעַר." *TDOT* 15:359–405.

———. "The Study of Law and Ethics in the Hebrew Bible/Old Testament." Pages 549–621 in *The Twentieth Century: From Modernism to Postmodernism*. Part 2 of *Modern Interpretation of the Hebrew Bible/Old Testament: The Nineteenth and Twentieth Centuries*. Vol. 3 of *Hebrew Bible/Old Testament: The History of Its Interpretation*. Edited by Magne Saebø. Göttingen: Vandenhoeck & Ruprecht, 2003.

———. *Theologische Ethik des Alten Testaments*. TW 3.2. Stuttgart: Kohlhammer, 1994.

———. *Wandel der Rechtsbegründungen in der Gesellschaftsgeschichte des antiken Israel: Eine Rechtsgeschichte des "Bundesbuches" Ex XX 22–XXIII 13*. StudBib 3. Leiden: Brill, 1988.

Pakkala, Juha. "The Date of the Oldest Edition of Deuteronomy." *ZAW* 121 (2009): 388–401.

———. "The Dating of Deuteronomy: A Response to Nathan MacDonald." *ZAW* 123 (2011): 431–36.

Pardee, Dennis. "Judicial Plea from Meṣad Ḥashavyahu (Yavneh-Yam): A New Philological Study." *Maarav* 1 (1978): 33–66.

———. *Ritual and Cult at Ugarit*. WAW 10. Atlanta: Society of Biblical Literature, 2002.

———. "The Structure of RS 1.002." Pages 1181–95 in vol 2. of *Semetic Studies in Honor of Wolf Leslau*. Edited by A. S. Kayne. 2 vols. Wiesbaden: Harrassowitz, 1991.

Patrick, Dale. "Casuistic Law Governing Primary Rights and Duties." *JBL* 92 (1973): 180–84.

Pearce, Laurie, and Cornelia Wunsch. *Documents of Judean Exiles and West Semites in Babylonia in the Collection of David Sofer*. Ithaca, NY: Cornell University Press, 2014.

Perlitt, Lothar. "Ein einzig Volk von Brüdern." Pages 50–73 in *Deuteronomium-Studien*. FAT 8. Tübingen: Mohr Siebeck, 1994.

———. "Priesterschrift im Deuteronomium?" *ZAW* 100 Supp 1 (1988): 65–88 Repr. as pages 123–43 of *Deuteronomium-Studien*. FAT 8. Tübingen: Mohr Siebeck, 1994.

Pfeiffer, Robert H., and E. A. Speiser. "One Hundred New Selected Nuzi Texts." *AASOR* 16 (1936): 1–168.

Pitt-Rivers, Julian. "The Kith and the Kin." Pages 89–105 in *The Character of Kinship*. Edited by Jack Goody. Cambridge: Cambridge University Press, 1973.

Plöger, Josef. *Literarkritische, formgeschichtliche und stilkritische Untersuchungen zum Deuteronomium*. BBB 26. Bonn: Hanstein, 1967.

Postgate, J. Nicholas. *The Land of Assur and the Yoke of Assur: Studies on Assyria 1971–2005*. Oxford: Oxbow, 2007.

Pruess, H. D. *Deuteronomium*. EdF 164. Darmstadt: Wissenschaftliche Buchgesellschaft, 1982.

———. "נוּחַ." *TDOT* 9:277–86.

Quell, Gottfried. "διαθήκη." *TDNT* 2:106–24.

Rad, Gerhard von. *Deuteronomy*. OTL. Philadelphia: Westminster John Knox, 1966.

———. "The Form-Critical Problem of the Hexateuch." Pages 1–78 in *The Problem of the Hexateuch and Other Essays*. Translated by E. W. Trueman Dicken. New York: McGraw-Hill, 1966. Translation of *Das formgeschichtliche Problem des Hexateuchs*. BWANT 26. Stuttgart: Kohlhammer, 1938.

———. *Old Testament Theology*. 2 vols. New York: Harper & Row, 1962.

Rader, Rosemary. "Fasting." *ER* 5:286–90.

Radner, Karen. "Hired Labor in the Neo-Assyrian Empire." Pages 329–43 in vol. 5 of *Labor in the Ancient World*. Edited by Piotr Steinkeller and Michael Hudson. Dresden: ISLET, 2015.

Ramos, Melissa. "Malediction and Oath: The Curses of the Sefire Treaties and Deuteronomy 28." Paper presented at the Annual Meeting of the Society of Biblical Literature, Baltimore, 23 November 2013.

——. "Spoken Word and Ritual Performance: The Oath and the Curse in Deuteronomy 27–28." PhD diss., University of California Los Angeles, 2015.

Rendtorff, Rolf. "The Ger in the Priestly Laws of the Pentateuch." Pages 77–87 in *Ethnicity and the Bible*. Edited by Mark G. Brett. BibInt. New York: Brill, 1996.

Richter, Wolfgang. "Beobachtungen zur theologischen Systembildung in der alttestamentlichen Literatur anhand des 'kleinen geschichtlichen Credo.'" Pages 125–212 in vol. 2 of *Wahrheit und Verkündigung: Michael Schmaus zum 70. Geburtstag*. Edited by Leo Scheffczyk, Werner Dettloff, and Richard Heinzmann. 2 vols. Munich: Schöningh, 1967.

Rodd, Cyril. *Glimpses of a Strange Land: Studies in Old Testament Ethics.* Edinburgh: T&T Clark, 2001.

Rodriguez, Ralph E. "Race and Ethnicity." Pages 788–93 in *The Johns Hopkins Guide to Literary Theory and Criticism*. Edited by Michael Groden, Martin Kreiswirth, and Imre Szeman. 2nd ed. Baltimore: John Hopkins University Press, 2005.

Rofé, Alexander. "The Covenant in the Land of Moab (Deuteronomy 28:69–30:20): Historico-Literary, Comparative and Formcritical Considerations." Pages 310–20 in *Das Deuteronomium: Entstehung, Gestalt und Botschaft*. Edited by Norbert Lohfink. BETL 68. Leuven: Leuven University Press, 1985. Repr. as pages 269–80 in *A Song of Power and the Power of Song: Essays on the Book of Deuteronomy*. Edited by Duane L. Christensen. Winona Lake, IN: Eisenbrauns, 1993.

Römer, Thomas. "Deuteronomy in Search of Origins." Pages 112–38 in *Reconsidering Israel and Judah: Recent Studies on the Deuteronomic History*. Edited by Gary N. Knoppers and J. Gordon McConville. SBTS 8. Winona Lake, IN: Eisenbrauns, 2000.

——. *Israels Väter: Untersuchungen zur Väterthematik im Deuteronomium und in der deuteronomistischen Tradition*. OBO 99. Göttingen:Vandenhoeck & Ruprecht, 1990.

Rost, Leonhard. *Das kleine Credo und andere Studien zum Alten Testament*. Heidelberg: Quelle & Meyer, 1965.

Roth, Martha T. *Law Collections from Mesopotamia and Asia Minor*. WAW 6. Atlanta: Society of Biblical Literature, 1995.

Safrai, Z. "Ancient Field Structures: The Village in Eretz Israel during the Roman Period." *Cathedra* 89 (1998): 7–40.

Sahlins, Marshall. *What Kinship Is—and Is Not.* Chicago: University of Chicago Press, 2013.

Salonen, Erikki. *Über den Zehnten in alten Mesopotamien: Ein Beitrag zur Geschichte der Besteuerung.* StOr 43.4. Helsinki: Societas Orientalis Fennica, 1972.

Sanders, Seth L. *The Invention of Hebrew.* Urbana: University of Illinois Press, 2009.

Sasson, Jack M. "The King's Table: Food and Fealty in Old Babylonian Mari." Pages 179–215 in *Food and Identity in the Ancient World.* Edited by Cristiano Grottanelli and Lucio Milano. Padova: S.A.R.G.O.N. editrice e libreria, 2004.

Schloen, David. *The House of the Father as Fact and Symbol: Patrimonialism in Ugarit and the Ancient Near East.* SAHL 2. Winona Lake, IN: Eisenbrauns, 2001.

Schmid, Konrad. *The Old Testament: A Literary History.* Translated by Linda M. Maloney. Minneapolis: Fortress, 2012. Translation of *Literaturgeschichte des Altes Testaments.* Darmstadt: Wissenshaftliche Buchgesellschaft, 2008.

Schneider, David M. "Kinship, Nationality, and Religion in American Culture: Towards a Definition of Kinship." Pages 63–71 in *Symbolic Anthropology: A Reader in the Study of Symbols and Meanings.* Edited by Janet L. Dolgin and David M. Schneider. New York: Columbia University Press, 1977.

———. "What Is Kinship All About?" Pages 257–74 in *Kinship and Family: An Anthropological Reader.* Edited by Robert Parkin and Linda Stone. Mulden, MA: Blackwell, 2004.

Schniedewind, William M. *How the Bible Became a Book: The Texualization of Ancient Israel.* Cambridge: Cambridge University Press, 2004.

Schorch, Stefan. "The Samaritan Version of Deuteronomy and the Origin of Deuteronomy." Pages 23–37 in *Samaria, Samarians, Samaritans: Studies on Bible, History and Linguistics; Papers Presented at the Sixth International Conference of the Société d'Études Samaritaines Held at Pápa, Hungary in July 17–25, 2008.* Edited by József Zsengellér. Berlin: de Gruyter, 2011.

Schwartz, Regina M. *The Curse of Cain: The Violent Legacy of Monotheism.* Chicago: University of Chicago Press, 1997.

Schwienhorst-Schönberger, L. *Das Bundesbuch (Ex 20, 22—23, 33): Studien zu seiner Enstehung und Theologie*. BZAW 188. Berlin: de Gruyter, 1990.

Seitz, Gottfried. *Redaktionsgeschichtliche Studien zum Deuteronomium*. BWANT 93. Stuttgart: Kohlhammer, 1971.

Smith, Daniel L. "The Politics of Ezra: Sociological Indicators of Postexilic Judean Society." Pages 73–97 in *Second Temple Studies 1: Persian Period*. Edited by Philip R. Davies. JSOTSup 117. Sheffield: JSOT, 1991.

Smith, Mark S. *The Pilgrimage Pattern in Exodus*. JSOTSup 239. Sheffield: Sheffield Academic, 1997.

Sneed, Mark. "Israelite Concern for the Alien, Orphan and Widow: Altruism or Ideology?" *ZAW* 111 (1999): 498–507.

Sonnet, J. P. *The Book within the Book: Writing in Deuteronomy*. BibInt 14. Leiden: Brill, 1997.

Sonsino, Rifat. *Motive Clauses in Hebrew Law*. Chico, CA: Scholars Press, 1980.

Sparks, Kenton. "A Comparative Study of the Biblical נבלה Laws." *ZAW* 110 (1998): 594–600.

———. *Ethnicity and Identity in Ancient Israel: Prolegomena to the Study of Ethnic Sentiments and Their Expression in the Hebrew Bible*. Winona Lake, IN: Eisenbrauns, 1998.

Spencer, John R. "Soujourner." *ABD* 6:103–5.

Speiser, E. A. "New Kirkuk Documents Relating to Family Laws." *AASOR* 10 (1928–1929): 1–70.

Spina, Frank Anthony. "Israelites as *Gērîm*: 'Sojourners,' in Social and Historical Context." Pages 321–36 in *The Word of the Lord Shall Go Forth: Essays in Honor of David Noel Freedman in Celebration of His Sixtieth Birthday*. Edited by Carol L. Meyers and M. O'Connor. Philadelphia: American Schools of Oriental Research, 1983.

Stackert, Jeffery. *Rewriting the Torah: Literary Revision in Deuteronomy and the Holiness Legislation*. FAT 52. Tübingen: Mohr Siebeck, 2007.

Stager, Lawrence E. "The Archaeology of the Family in Ancient Israel." *BASOR* 260 (1985): 1–35.

Stolz, F. "נוח." *TLOT* 2:722.

Stone, Linda. "Has the World Turned? Kinship and Family in the Contemporary American Soap Opera." Pages 395–407 in *Kinship and Family: An Anthropological Reader*. Edited by Robert Parkin and Linda Stone. Mulden, MA: Blackwell, 2004.

Strathern, Marilyn. *The Gender of the Gift: Problems with Women and Problems with Society in Melanesia*. Berkeley, CA: University of California Press, 1988.

Sutton, David. *Remembrance of Repasts: An Anthropology of Food and Memory*. Berg: Oxford, 2001.

Thompson, John A. "The Cultic Credo and the Sinai Tradition." *RTR* 27 (1968): 53–64.

Tigay, Jeffrey H. *Deuteronomy*. JPSTC. Philadelphia: The Jewish Publication Society, 1996.

———. *The Evolution of the Gilgamesh Epic*. Philadelphia: University of Pennsylvania Press, 1982.

Tillesse, G. Minette de. "Sections 'tu' et sections 'vous' dans le Deutéronome." *VT* 12 (1962): 29–87.

Toorn, Karel van der. "The Babylonian New Year Festival: New Insights from the Cuneiform Texts and Their Bearing on Old Testament Study." Pages 331–44 in *Congress Volume: Leuven, 1989*. Edited by J. A. Emerton. Leiden: Brill, 1989.

———. *Scribal Culture and the Making of the Hebrew Bible*. Cambridge: Harvard University Press, 2007.

Tsai, Daisy Yulin. *Human Rights in Deuteronomy with Special Focus on Slave Laws*. BZAW 464. Berlin: de Gruyter, 2014.

Turner, Victor. *Dramas, Fields, and Metaphors: Symbolic Action in Human Society*. Ithaca, NY: Cornell University Press, 1974.

Van Houten, Christiana. *The Alien in Israelite Law: A Study of the Changing Legal Status of Strangers in Ancient Israel*. JSOTSup 107. Sheffield: Sheffield University Press, 1991.

Vanderhooft, David. "The Israelite *Mishpaha* in the Priestly Writings, and Changing Valences in Israel's Kinship Terminology." Pages 485–96 in *Exploring the Long Duree: Essays in Honor of Lawrence E. Stager*. Edited by D. Schloen. Winona Lake, IN: Eisenbrauns, 2009.

Vanstiphout, Herman L. J. "The Banquet Scene in the Mesopotamian Debate Poems." Pages 37–63 in *Banquets d'Orient*. Edited by R. Gyselen. Res Orientales 4. Bures Saint-Yves: Group pour l'Etude de la Civilisation du Moyen-Orient, 1992.

Vaux, Roland de. *Ancient Israel: Its Life and Institutions*. London: Darton, Longman & Todd, 1961.

Veijola, Timo. *Das 5. Buch Mose Deuteronomium: Kapitel 1, 1–16, 17*. DATD 8/1. Göttingen: Vandenhoeck and Ruprecht, 2004.

Vieweger, D. "Vom 'Fremdling' zum 'Proselyt': Zur sakralrechtlichen Definition des גר im späten 5. Jahrhundert v. Chr." Pages 271–84 in *Von Gott reden: Beiträge zur Theologie und Exegese des Alten Testaments; Festschrift für Siegfried Wagner zum 65. Geburtstag.* Edited by D. Vieweger and E. J. Waschke. Neukirchen-Vluyn: Neukirchener, 1995.

Waltke, Bruce K., and Michael Patrick O'Connor. *An Introduction to Biblical Hebrew Syntax.* Winona Lake, IN: Eisenbrauns, 1990.

Watts, James W. *Reading Law: The Rhetorical Shape of the Pentateuch.* Sheffield: Sheffield Academic, 1999.

Wazana, Nili. *All the Boundaries of the Land: The Promised Land in Biblical Thought in Light of the Ancient Near East.* Winona Lake, IN: Eisenbrauns, 2013.

Wehmeier, G. "ברך." *TLOT* 1:278–79.

Wenham, Gordon J. *Psalms as Torah: Reading Biblical Song Ethically.* Grand Rapids: Baker Academic, 2012.

Weinfeld, Moshe. "The Covenant of Grant in the Old Testament and in the Ancient Near East." *JAOS* 90 (1970): 184–203.

———. *Deuteronomy and the Deuteronomic School.* Oxford: Clarendon, 1972.

———. *Deuteronomy 1–11.* AB 5. New Haven: Yale University Press, 1991.

———. "Judge and Officer in Ancient Israel and in the Ancient Near East." *IOS* 7 (1977): 65–88.

———. *Social Justice in Ancient Israel and in the Ancient Near East.* Minneapolis: Fortress, 1995.

Weismantel, Mary. "Making Kin: Kinship Theory and Zumabagua Adoptions." *AmE* 22 (1995): 685–704.

Wellhausen, Julius. *Prolegomena to the History of Israel: With a Reprint of the Article* Israel *From the Encyclopedia Britannica.* New York: Meridian, 1957.

Westbrook, Raymond. "Biblical and Cuneiform Law Codes." *RB* 92 (1985): 247–64.

———. "The Old Babylonian Term, '*naptārum*.'" *JCS* 46 (1994): 41–46.

———. "Slave and Master in Ancient Near Eastern Law." Pages 161–216 in *Law from the Tigris to the Tiber: The Writings of Raymond Westbrook.* Edited by Bruce Wells and Rachel Magdalene. 2 vols. Winona Lake, IN: Eisenbrauns, 2009. Repr. of "Slave and Master in Ancient Near Eastern Law." *CKLR* 70 (1995): 1631–76.

Westbrook, Raymond, and Bruce Wells. *Everyday Law in Biblical Israel.* Louisville: Westminster John Knox, 2009.

Whitelam, Keith W. *The Invention of Ancient Israel: The Silencing of Palestinian History*. London: Routledge, 1996.

———. *The Just King: Monarchical Judicial Authority in Ancient Israel*. Sheffield: JSOT, 1979.

Williamson, Hugh. "The Family in Persian Period Judah: Some Textual Reflections." Pages 469–85 in *Symbiosis, Symbolism and the Power of the Past: Ancient Israel and Its Neighbors from the Late Bronze Age through Roman Palestine*. Edited by William G. Dever and Seymour Gitin. Winona Lake, IN: Eisenbrauns, 2003.

Wilson, Ian. *Out of the Midst of the Fire: Divine Presence in Deuteronomy*. SBLDS 151. Atlanta: Scholars Press, 1995.

Wilson, Monica. "Nyukyusa Kinship." Pages 111–39 in *African Systems of Kinship and Marriage*. Edited by A. R. Radcliffe Brown and Cyril Daryll Forde. London: Oxford University Press, 1950.

Wilson, Robert R. "Deuteronomy, Ethnicity, and Reform." Pages 107–23 in *Constituting the Community: Studies on the Polity of Ancient Israel in Honour of S. Dean McBride Jr.* Edited by John T. Strong and Steven S. Tuell. Winona Lake, IN: Eisenbrauns, 1995.

———. "Israel's Judiciary in the Pre-exilic Period." *JQR* 74 (1983): 229–48.

Winter, Irene. "The King and the Cup: Iconography of the Royal Presentation Scene on the Ur III Seals." Pages 253–68 in *Insight through Images: Studies in Honour of Edith Porada*. Edited by M. Kelly-Buccelati, P. Matthiae, and M. Van Loon. BMes 21. Malibu, CA: Undena, 1986.

Wunsch, Cornelia. "Glimpses on the Lives of Deportees in Rural Babylonia." Pages 247–60 in *Arameans, Chaldeans, and Arabs in Babylonia and Palestine in the First Millennium B.C.* Edited by Angelika Berlejung and Michael P. Streck. Wiesbaden: Harrassowitz, 2013.

Yadin, Yigael, Joseph Naveh, and Ya'acov Meshorer. *Masada: The Yigael Yadin Excavations 1963–1965; Final Reports*. 8 vols. Jerusalem: Israel Exploration Society, 1991.

Yu, Suee Yan. "Tithes and Firstlings in Deuteronomy." PhD diss., Union Theological Seminary, 1997.

Zaccagnini, Carlo. "Nuzi." Pages 565–618 in vol. 2 of *A History of Ancient Near Eastern Law*. Edited by Raymond Westbrook. 2 vols. Leiden: Brill, 2003.

Zakovitch, Yair. "'My Father Was a Wandering Aramean' (Deuteronomy 26:5) or 'Edom Served My Father'?" Pages 133–37 in *Mishneh Todah: Studies in Deuteronomy and Its Cultural Environment in Honor of Jef-

*frey H. Tigay.* Edited by Nili Sacher Fox, David A. Glatt-Gilad, and Michael James Williams. Winona Lake, IN: Eisenbrauns, 2009.

Zehnder, Markus. *Umgang mit Fremden in Israel und Assyrien: Ein Beitrag zur Anthropologie des Fremden im Licht antiker Quellen.* BWANT 168. Stuttgart: Kohlhammer, 2005.

# Scripture Index

# Modern Authors Index

CPSIA information can be obtained
at www.ICGtesting.com
Printed in the USA
FFHW02n1432161018
48825650-52998FF